A Navy SEAL's Bug-In Guide

How to Turn Your House into the Safest Place on Earth

Joel Lambert

Disclaimer Page

This book is designed only to provide information about bugging-in.

A NAVY SEAL'S BUG-IN GUIDE: HOW TO TURN YOUR HOUSE INTO THE SAFEST PLACE ON EARTH is sold with the knowledge that the publisher, editor, and author do not offer any legal or other professional advice regarding this or any other subject.

In the case of a need for any such expertise, you should always consult the appropriate professional, whether that is an electrician, plumber, or other.

This book does not contain all the information available on the subject of bugging-in. It has not been created to be specific to any individual's or organization's situation or needs.

While the author, editor, and publisher have made every effort to make the knowledge inside this book as accurate as possible there may still exist typographical and/or content errors that have made it through. Therefore, this book should serve only as a general guide and not as the ultimate source of information on the subject of bugging-in.

The foods described in this book do not comply with FDA, USDA, or FSIS regulations or local health codes. Dehydrating meat products does not reduce the health risks associated with meat contaminated with Salmonella and/or E. coli O157H7.

The author, editor, and publisher cannot and will not guarantee the shelf-life of any of the food products described in this book. Eating the foods will be done at your own risk and it will be your responsibility to test them for microbes, bacteria, viruses, or germs before consuming them.

The author, editor, and publisher shall have no liability or responsibility to any person or entity regarding any losses or damage incurred, or alleged to have incurred, directly or indirectly, by the information contained in this book. The instructions provided have not been reviewed, tested, or approved by any official testing body or government agency; you agree that by using them you waive any right of litigation.

The author and editor of this book make no warranty of any kind, expressed or implied, regarding the safety of the final products or of the methods used. Building and operating any of the projects described in this book will be done at your own risk. This includes but is certainly not limited to any physical injury which may occur to yourself or others by incorrectly or unsafely using the knowledge inside this book.

By reading past this point you hereby agree to be bound by this disclaimer, or you may return this book within the guarantee time period for a full refund.

Introduction

Hi. My name's Joel Lambert. I spent ten years in the United States Navy SEAL Teams, where, among many other things, I was first exposed to escape and evasion by attending several schools in SERE—Survival, Evasion, Resistance, and Escape. This is the specific skill set needed by military personnel—aircrew mostly—when they find themselves downed in a combat zone or behind enemy lines. In a situation like that, a serviceman or -woman relatively untrained on the ground will find themselves needing to survive, evade enemy forces, navigate to a pickup spot for extraction by friendlies, and, if captured, resist divulging sensitive information either voluntarily or by clever trickery and, if at all possible, make an escape.

I was fairly enamored with all the complex, various skills that being good at this required, so I attended basic, winter, advanced, and desert SERE schools over the course of my career.

After the Navy, I was recruited by Discovery Channel to star in Manhunt/Lone Target, a global television series on escape and evasion, where I would infiltrate different secured areas of various countries and then their special operations force, specialty tracking unit, or special police tracking team would then track me and attempt to outsmart, find, and take me down before I reached my extract point usually several days away. I would use counter- and anti-tracking techniques (passive and active), deception trails, and booby traps to attempt to evade them and get away clean (all while surviving a hostile environment). They would use all the tools at their disposal to try to take me down.

Around this time, on social media and in the public awareness, "bug-out bags" became fashionable in the overlap of tactical/military techniques and what the public finds cool—"bugging out" being the concept of grabbing your bug-out bag full of essential items and leaving your house, car, or office and getting away from what is threatening you with the items necessary to get by. Since I was on a global television show doing pretty much exactly that at the time, I would be asked often about my thoughts on the matter, what was in MY bug out bag, and if I would like to endorse or create a mass-marketed bug-out bag, etc.

I never, to my knowledge, ever addressed that question publicly (bug-out bags being different than a military escape and evasion kit), and here's why: Escape and evasion (the military version of bugging out) is a last resort, and except in very unique and rare circumstances, it is not the best strategic decision. It is the final option once everything that can go wrong has. The first option? Bugging IN—that is, setting up your place of residence for extremes and making sure that you and your family's' needs in a setting of partial or complete societal breakdown are provided for.

The reason this is a better strategic decision is that in a "bugging out" scenario, some of your first concerns will be addressing shelter, water, food, communication, and connection with friendlies, all things that one can set up without too much effort to be self-sufficient even in a complete social collapse AT YOUR PLACE OF RESIDENCE. Why would I ever want to leave my warm, weatherproof, secure house—with stores of food, clean water, and all my tools and weapons—only to go someplace else and spend massive resources of money, time, and energy to try to acquire the things I just abandoned? It makes much more strategic sense to set up your place of residence to be secure, stocked, defensible, and prepared for adversity as well as building community with friends and neighbors who have different skills and resources for meeting each other's needs and supporting one another through difficult circumstances, ranging from lockdowns to war/invasion, power/communication grid failure, and natural disasters to EMP attacks, martial law, or riots and civil unrest.

Joel Lambert

May, 2024

Table of Contents

FOOD

39 Foods to Stockpile

Food storage is the key to bugging in. When you have food, you can stay put. When you can prepare a delicious meal, it feels good to stay put. The moment you are out of food, the bug in comes to an end. You cannot sit around without food.

The types of foods you store, the way you store them, and the amount of food you need to sustain yourself and your family for 3 months are all going to be laid out in this chapter.

The first thing we need to discuss is what kinds of foods you should buy and store in your home. We have a comprehensive list of 39 foods to stockpile. With these foods you can create a number of tasty meals right out of the pantry.

It is this list of foods that we will build our entire bug in meal plan from later in this chapter. That meal plan will not only make mealtime easier on you, but it will give you confidence in the fact that you are buying and storing the right foods to make sure that you and your family can bug in during a disaster.

1. White Rice

Description

White rice is at the top of the list when it comes to food storage because it is an ideal food to store for the long term.

It is an affordable source of calories and one that is neutral in flavor, so it can act as a base for things like soups, stews, proteins, eggs, beans, and whatever else you can dream of.

White rice is a starch that gives you the calories of carbohydrates and the energy that they provide.

Unless you have some kind of allergy, you should have a large portion of your food storage made up of simple and affordable white rice

White rice is a starch that gives you the calories of carbohydrates and the energy that they provide.

Unless you have some kind of allergy, you should have a large portion of your food storage made up of simple and affordable white rice.

Storage Containers

Storing white rice is simple. In fact, it will outlast the plastic bags that it comes in at the supermarket. This food is best stored for the long term in some kind of fortified container or bag.

Rice will last very long in a nice thick Ziploc bag. The absolute best method of storage for rice is in Mylar bags with oxygen absorbers, nestled into a five-gallon bucket.

This setup will prevent pest growth in the rice and protection from larger pests that might be lurking outside.

Calories per Serving	200 (1 cup)
Calories per 5-Gallon Bucket	29,520

Sizes

In most supermarkets you can find white rice in 1 lb. to 10 lb. packages. Sometimes you can even find 25 lb. bags on the lowest shelves. In warehouse club stores you will find 50 lb. bags of rice.

Price	$6.08 / 5 lb. bag (Food Lion)

Tip

The most important thing to remember with white rice is that you cook it using a simple ratio of 2 parts water to 1 part rice. So, use ½ a cup of rice and 1 cup of water in a small pot. Boil this until the rice looks like oatmeal and then cover and steam until the rice is tender.

2. Black Beans

Description

Dry beans in general are an incredibly versatile food to store. Black beans are a bug in essential for your prepper's pantry and long-term food storage because they go so well with white rice. Billions of people eat some form of rice and beans or peas.

This combo is designed to sustain us. It only makes sense that you would store some of these beans. Black beans are also very inexpensive, so it makes them easy to stockpile week to week.

Storage Containers

The plastic bags they come in will hold them for a year or two, at most. The beans inside will outlast the plastic bags. 1 lb. bags or 5 lb. bags can be stored directly in a 5-gallon bucket. Mylar bags are a great option for dried beans, too.

Calories per Serving	227 (1 cup)
Calories per 5-Gallon Bucket	47,670

Sizes

Pintos can be bought at regular supermarkets in 1 lb. bags up to 5 lb. bags. In warehouse club stores you can find pinto beans in 25-50 lb. bags.

Price	$5.54 / 2 1-lb. bags (Publix)

Tip

When you are cooking dry beans you must not add salt to the cooking liquid until the beans are tender. The salt will make the beans overly tough and they will be horrible to eat.

Black beans are delicious as they are, but they also make a delicious puree that can be eaten with crackers or corn chips.

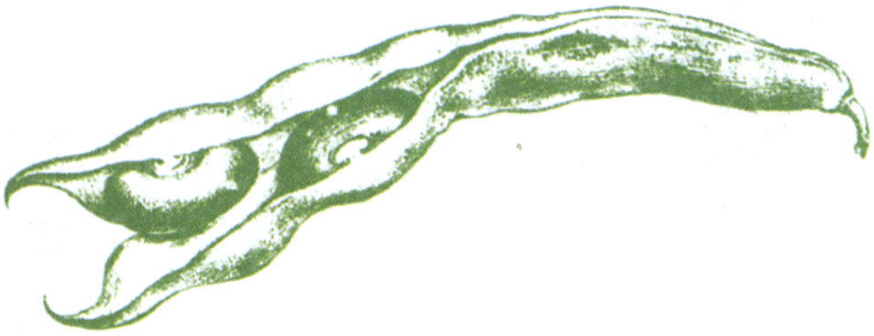

3. Pinto Beans

Description

Storing pinto beans is a terrific way to break up the monotony of eating only black beans as an accompaniment to rice or as a source of plant protein.

Pinto beans are incredibly affordable because they are the most popular bean crop in the southwestern United States and Northern Mexico.

Pinto means "speckled" in Spanish and that makes it very easy to recognize these beans. They are a great bean to include in soups, burritos, or even in rice (like you would with black beans).

Storage Containers

See BLACK BEANS

Calories per Serving	206 (1 cup)
Calories per 5-Gallon Bucket	47,736

Sizes

See BLACK BEANS

Price	$5.54 / 2 1-lb. bags (Publix)

Tip

Smoked pork is one of the very best things you can add to a pot of pinto beans. The flavor goes really well with the pinto beans and you can even shred the meat from the bone and let it mix in with your pinto beans.

4. Flour

Description

Flour is going to be the most diverse ingredient in your bug in food storage pantry. With flour you will be able to do so many different things.

Not only is it a key ingredient in making bread dough, but you will use it as a base for many desserts.

It is also the main ingredient in roux, which is a powerful thickener of soups and sauces.

Being able to make bread each day will take a massive burden off your caloric needs.

If you have flour or wheat to grind, then you have the base ingredient for making bread and that baked bread can account for a large portion of the family's daily calories during a bug in.

If possible, it's best to stockpile whole wheat flour rather than all-purpose flour because of the fiber content. Your diet will be more nutrient-rich if consuming whole wheat flour.

Storage Containers

Flour needs to be protected if you are going to store it for the long term. The truth is the paper bag that protects flour is not enough to protect it from pests like the Indian Meal Moth.

These moths will eat right through that paper bag whether it is a 5 lb. bag of flour or a 50 lb. bag.

You need to store your flour in Mylar bags but the added protection of 5-gallon buckets is the best option.

Calories per Serving	250 (1 cup)
Calories per 5-Gallon Bucket	39,402

Sizes

The most common sizes of flour at the supermarket are 1 lb. and 5 lb. bags. In warehouse club stores you can buy flour in 25 lbs. bags.

Price	$7.04 / 2 5-lb. bags (Walmart)

Tip

Take a portion of your flour and premix it with baking soda, baking powder, and salt to create a simple but effective quick baking mix.

To this mixture you can add eggs and milk to create things like quick pancakes or muffins.

5. Sugar

Description

Simple white sugar is an incredible sweetener. It is affordable but can absolutely wreak havoc on your overall health if you are not careful.

All that said, I would highly recommend keeping plenty of plain white sugar on hand.

White sugar is a key ingredient in sweet baking and it is also a tremendous help when making yeast-risen dough.

However, white sugar plays a serious role as a preservative in many foods and it is also essential to curing certain kinds of meat.

Storage Containers

Although sugar is protected by the same meager paper wrap that our flour is, it rarely takes the kind of damage that flour can over time. That is due in large part to the fact that sugar is just not as desirable to so many insects.

Still, I would not recommend keeping your sugar in the original packaging. If you must then nestle your sugar down into 5-gallon buckets so they are protected from things like moisture.

If sugar gets wet, it can basically turn into a brick. Repackaging completely into Mylar bags is your best option.

Calories per Serving	774 (1 cup)
Calories per 5-Gallon Bucket	64,639

Sizes

The most common sizes of sugar at the supermarket are 1 lb. and 5 lbs. bags. In warehouse club stores you can buy sugar in 25 lbs. bags.

Price	$2.84 / 4 lb. bag (Walmart)

Tip

A terrific way to sweeten drinks is by creating something called "simple syrup", with your stored sugar. The ratio for this rich and simple syrup is 2 parts sugar to 1 part water.

This can be slowly heated on the stove and then poured into a mason jar to store. Add this to your coffee, tea, or other drinks to add sweetness.

6. Salt

Description

Salt is one of the most overlooked and neglected foods to stockpile. We do not realize how much salt we use in a week. Salt is also one of the hardest things to reproduce on this list.

Most of our salt comes from mines deep down in the earth. Of course, sea salt comes from the sea but that is a complex process, too. Salt is essential to life.

It is not just something that we put on our food to make it taste good. Salt is made up of sodium, which is a vital electrolyte. It helps balance the amount of water you keep in your body.

Salt is also a key element in salting and drying meats, which is one of the best and easiest ways to store meat for the long term if you no longer have refrigeration.

Storage Containers

The important thing about salt is that you do not need to worry about pests. The enemy of salt is moisture, so you have to plan for that. As long as your container can keep out moisture, then you will be good to go.

Mylar is great, Ziploc and even piling all the salt into 5-gallon buckets will work.

Calories per Serving	N/A
Calories per 5-Gallon Bucket	N/A

Sizes

Salt can be bought in small table shakers and 1 lb. boxes.

Price	$6.24 / box 12 4-lb. boxes (Publix)

Tip

You could store smaller bags of salt, in sturdy Ziploc bags, which can be given out, bartered with, or even sold as others realize they have not stored enough salt.

7. Baking Soda

Description

Sodium Bicarbonate or common baking soda has so many uses! While it is often used in food as a leavening agent or a way to make pancakes and waffles rise, baking soda is also key in a variety of baking recipes.

Baking soda loses its effect over time and needs to be stored properly to avoid oxidation.

Best to also store some baking powder.

Storage Containers

The better you can protect your baking soda from the air, the longer it will be effective.

The compound of chemicals that makes up baking soda will virtually never spoil but it may not rise as it used to when you first bought it.

Mylar bags with oxygen absorbers are great containers for storing baking soda.

Calories per Serving	N/A
Calories per 5-Gallon Bucket	N/A

Sizes

Baking soda can be bought in 1 lb. cardboard boxes. It can also be bought in 5 lbs. plastic bags.

Price	$1.06 / 1lb. box (Food Lion)

Tip

While we consider it a food item and essential ingredient for creating some delicious foods, sodium bicarbonate is also great for cleaning tasks all around the home.

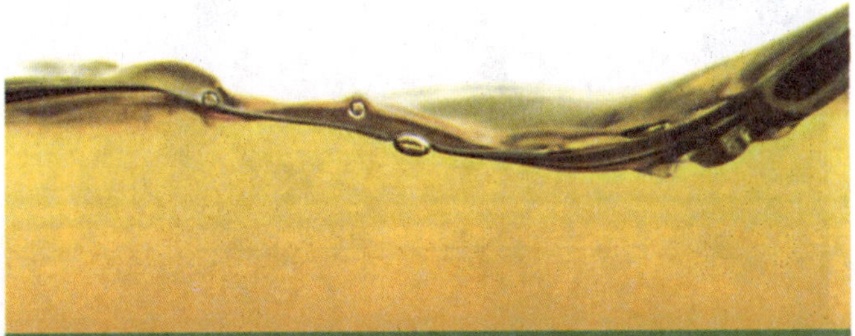

8. Cooking Oil

Description

Cooking oil is another seriously overlooked ingredient to stockpile. It is something you use every day, but most people are just not ready to bug in with a stockpile of cooking oil. Buy larger containers of oil and keep them in a cool dark place.

There are various kinds of cooking oils on the market. Things like vegetable and canola oil are cheap, while olive oil is on the more expensive side.

During an emergency, there is a good chance that you will not care what kind of cooking oil you have access to. However, if you have a preference, now is the time to stockpile that type.

Storage Containers

Storing cooking oil requires a sturdy container. Though most packages for cooking oil are clear so you can see the oil inside, the ideal container for storing oils is something that protects it from sunlight.

Dark glass jars or bottles, 5-gallon buckets with Mylar lining, and hard plastic opaque storage containers are great for storing oil.

Calories per Serving	120 (1 tbsp)
Calories per 5-Gallon Bucket	152,640

Sizes

Cooking oils come in a variety of sizes. At the supermarket you can buy olive oil in 3L cans. That is one of your largest options for long-term storage.

Most types of cooking oil can be found in 40 oz. containers. Warehouse clubs sell 1-gallon containers of cooking oil. The opaque containers are best.

Price	$24.92 / 4 16-oz. bottles

Tip

Oil can go rancid over time. The smell of the oil will change. You do not want to cook with rancid oil. Be sure to store oil in a cool dark place to preserve it for as long as possible.

Cooking Oil for the Meal Plan

If you plan to follow our meal plan, we will use olive oil in many of our recipes. Olive oil in the metal cans stores really well in a temperature-controlled environment.

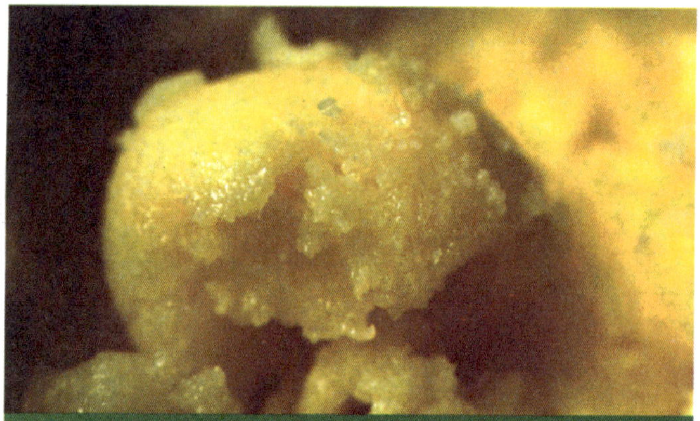

9. Ghee

Description

Ghee is also known as clarified butter. This cooking fat is made when you melt butter in a pot over low heat until it separates.

The butter will separate into 3 things: milk fat solids, clarified butter or ghee, and impurities. The impurities will float on top and can be removed with a ladle. The milk fat solids will sink to the bottom and you can pour the golden ghee out into a mason jar with a lid, for storage.

Treat it much like cooking oil and ghee will last for years at room temperatures.

This is a great fat for cooking and stockpiling, though it is a more expensive option than regular cooking oil.

Storage Containers

This is another food stockpile that requires some storage containers with a little backbone. I have always found that mason jars are great for storing ghee. Quality Tupperware can do an excellent job at storing the ghee, too.

Calories per Serving	112 (1 tbsp)
Calories per 5-Gallon Bucket	129,600

Sizes

Ghee can be bought in 5 oz. containers at most supermarkets.

Price	$8.98 / 13 oz. jar (Publix)

Tip

Ghee can also be made at home using regular butter. It is a pretty simple process of heating and separating the butter.

39. Powdered Chicken Bouillon

Description

Bouillon is a powdered broth base that can be reconstituted in water. The resulting broth can be used to make soups, gravy, or as the base for other types of meals.

This bouillon can sit on the shelf for years and because it lacks moisture, it will be safe to eat.

Storage Containers

You can buy bouillon in packets, cardboard container, or plastic jars. I prefer the plastic jars with the air seal. These are the best and can be bought at your regular grocery store.

Calories per Serving	6

Sizes

You can buy this broth base in .14-ounce packets or larger jars that make 113 cups of broth from each container.

Price	$3.98 / 1 15.9-oz. jar (Walmart)

Tip

If you happen to make too much broth, you can pour it into ice cube trays and freeze it for future use.

11. Pasta

Description

There are many varieties of pasta to stockpile. Pasta is a high carbohydrate food that will provide you with lots of energy-producing calories.

Pasta is also a food that small children and fussy eaters tend to really enjoy. It is a very affordable food to stockpile. These cheap carbohydrates are perfect for keeping your family fed during the bug in.

Of course, one of the absolute best aspects of pasta is that it can be a base for many different kinds of sauces: tomato sauce, alfredo sauce, butter sauce, carbonara, cheese sauce, olive oil and garlic, bolognaise sauce.

Storage Containers

The cardboard containers that most pasta comes in are not sufficient to protect your food long-term. These containers will protect your pasta for a year but after that, the pasta itself will start to deteriorate from oxidation and other things.

To best store spaghetti, you need a fortified container that will protect the spaghetti from moisture and oxygen that will break your pasta down over time.

Calories per Serving	157 (1/4 cup)
Calories per 5-Gallon Bucket	39,991

Sizes

Pasta can be purchased in 1 lb., 2 lbs., and 5 lbs. packages.

Price	$12 / 12 1-lb. boxes (Food Lion)

Tip

The most efficient type of pasta to store is elbow macaroni. This kind of pasta is small and can be piled into Mylar bags easier than most other types of pasta. It is also substantial enough to create a number of meals out of.

12. Oats

Description

Rolled oats are an incredibly affordable food that stores really well. It is a great bug in food to stockpile. When rolled oats are stored properly, they can last up to 20 years.

Oats stand out because, unlike most long-term food storage carbohydrate staples, they are a complex carb. Simple carbs like sugar, flour, and pasta digest quickly and hit your body with a flood of energy all at once. This often leads to a crash.

Complex carbs like oats take longer to digest and slowly power your body as the slower digestive process happens. This is a much healthier fuel for the body without the crash of simple carbs.

Storage Containers

Oats store really well in a variety of containers. They can attract pests and the cardboard containers will be eaten through. So, you should upgrade the containers at least to airtight containers. 1-gallon or 5-gallon Mylar bags with oxygen absorbers, packed in 5-gallon buckets is the best means of storing oats.

Calories per Serving	306 (1 cup, cooked)
Calories per 5-Gallon Bucket	15,000

Sizes

You can buy oatmeal at supermarkets from 18 oz. to 10 lbs. in bulk packages.

Price	$4.96 / 2 1-lb. 2-oz. containers (Publix)

Tip

Oats can be used in every meal. They are much more than just a breakfast food for you to add brown sugar to. Granola can be made using oats. Oats can be used in desserts. You can use oats as a filler or as a base for a delicious bread. Oats can even be used as a filler to extend meat and meat stuffing.

13. Corn Meal

Description

Cornmeal is made from ground dried corn that is the base for things like cornbread. Cornmeal can also be used in making bread. When ground coarser, this meal can be used to make things like grits or polenta.

Cornmeal is very versatile and is a great ingredient to store as part of your bug-in stockpile. It is also a high-calorie carbohydrate that will provide you with the energy you need.

Storage Containers

Corn meal is always sold in the same kind of paper bags that flour and sugar are sold in. You should treat this grain just the same way you treat sugar and flour.

Calories per Serving	441 (1 cup)
Calories per 5-Gallon Bucket	49,553

Sizes

The most common sizes are 1,2, and 5 lbs. bags.

Price	$2.52 / 2 lb. bag (Publix)

Tip

Cornmeal is great to lay on the bottom of a sheet pan or a pizza stone when baking pizza or bread. It adds flavor and crunch to the outside of whatever you are baking.

14. Ramen

Description

Ramen is a simple noodle bowl that is mostly carbohydrates and sodium. These packets of ramen are incredibly affordable and go a very long way in building a stockpile quickly with a limited budget.

You can also add vegetables and meats to the base of ramen to create a more substantial meal. In lean times you can eat the ramen as it is. Ramen is also an extremely easy soup to prepare and in the worst case, you can eat it raw for a quick calorie boost. There are many flavors available and I am certain you can find one you like, if you don't have a favorite already.

Storage Containers

Tossing packs of ramen into a 5-gallon bucket and sealing that bucket with oxygen absorbers inside is one of the best ways to store it. The worst thing that can happen is the noodles get stale.

Calories per Serving	290 (packet)

Sizes

Ramen always comes in the same small single package.

You can buy one package at a time or cases of 48.

Price	$3.28 / 1 12-pack (Walmart)

Tip

Think of ramen as a vehicle for other flavors and foods.

Sometimes you don't even need the flavor packet because you can make it whatever you like.

15. Popcorn

Description

Popcorn is a nutritious and healthy snack. It is a lot easier to prepare than you might think. Do not buy the popcorn that is in microwaveable packs with fake butter on them.

Instead, buy containers with unpopped popcorn in them that you can use in a popcorn popper or even a simple pot, with a little oil in the bottom.

Storage Containers

Popcorn stores in plastic containers for years at a time. You could transfer them to Mylar bags if you wanted even a longer shelf life for your popcorn.

Calories per Serving	30 (1 cup)
Calories per 5-Gallon Bucket	10,533

Sizes

1 lb. and 5 lbs. containers of popcorn are the most common.

Price	$7,52 / 2 1-lb. 14-oz. containers

Tip

Popcorn can be flavored with more than butter. Flavored oils are a great way to change the flavor of popcorn. Different seasonings, too. Get creative!

16. Crushed Tomato Can

Description

Crushed tomatoes are one of the most versatile ingredients on supermarket shelves. Cans of crushed tomatoes should have a place in your bug in stockpile.

These tomatoes can be used to make spaghetti sauce, chili, flavor soups, make pizza sauce, and many other things.

Growing tomatoes and crushing them yourself will take a lot of effort. Canned crushed tomatoes are cheap and easy to store.

Storage Containers

The can is the perfect storage container.

Calories per Serving	38

Sizes

Buy crushed tomatoes in 14.5 oz. cans and 28 oz. cans.

Price	$23.76 / 12 28-oz. cans (Walmart)

Tip

Crushed tomatoes flavored with basil are the very best to put up if you are going to make spaghetti sauce from scratch or use them for other Italian dishes.

Though you should keep some that are not flavored, as they can be used for everything else.

17. Canned Soup

Description

Canned soup is one of the most important items in a prepper's pantry. It is a canned, ready-to-eat meal that can contain meat, vegetables, and nutritious broth. These soups often have lots of calories.

One of your greatest struggles will be to store enough meat in your prepper pantry or even a standard freezer. For most preppers, the bug in will have limitations on the amount of protein and meat, unless you are intentional about what you store.

Soups give you the option of storing a variety of meats that are flavorful, seasoned, and ready to eat.

Storage Containers

The can is the perfect storage container for soups.

Calories per Serving	Varies based on soup
Price	$26.16 / 12 1-lb. 30-oz cans (Walmart)

Tip

Soups can be poured over starches that are already part of your food storage, like rice, mashed potatoes, and even barley or oats.

18. Canned Fish

Description

Fish is an incredibly healthy meal that contains healthy fats and high protein. Canned fish can be pretty tasty, too if you know which ones to buy.

Fish like salmon, mackerel, and tuna are all great fish to keep on hand. Sardines are cheap and if you can stomach them, they are another great protein source that lasts for years in your prepper pantry.

Buy as much of your canned fish stored in olive oil as possible. The other thing to consider is wild and line-caught fish.

Storage Containers

The can is the perfect storage container.

Calories per Serving	Varies
Sizes	

Canned fish come in many different sizes. Most are 2-4 oz. tins. Salmon can be purchased in larger cans.

Price	$13.08 / 6 4-oz. cans (Walmart)

Tip

Canned fish stored in oil has a tremendous shelf life. You can keep this fish on hand 5 years beyond the best buy date on the can, which is already a considerable amount of time.

19. Canned Meats

Description

Meat and palate fatigue will be two serious challenges when it comes to bugging in.

Most preppers only have so much space for frozen meat and you might find that goes quicker than you thought.

Canned meats give you access to meats. Canned meat is also ready to eat, which saves you cooking fuel if the power is out.

Canned roast beef, canned diced chicken, SPAM, and potted meat are some of the most common types of canned meats. Nearly every part of the animal can be found canned.

Buy the meats that you like.

Storage Containers

The can is the perfect storage container.

Calories per Serving	Varies

Sizes

12 oz. – 28 oz. cans

Price	$22 / 6 12-oz. cans (Walmart)

Tip

Cold salads are one of the best ways to eat canned meats. Cold salads like chicken and beef are very popular and these can be made quickly in a bowl and put on bread or crackers.

20. Canned Vegetables

Description

If nothing is growing in the garden, then the canned vegetables in the pantry will be all you have. Buy a variety but don't forget the golden rule of food storage: STORE WHAT YOU EAT. I always keep in my pantry the following: canned corn, canned peas, and canned peas and carrots.

Storage Containers

The cans these vegetables come in are perfect for storage.

Calories per Serving	Varies

Sizes

12 oz. – 28 oz. cans

Price	$7.44 / 6 12 oz. cans (Food Lion)

Tip

Non acidic canned vegetables will be fine to eat for at least 5 years after the Best By date.

21. Drink Mixes

Description

Depending on the types of drink mixes that you purchase and store, you can do things like increase your calorie intake or even improve your health.

If you drink things like sports drinks, then you can replace precious electrolytes.

Drink mixes are sealed and powdered. I suggest storing a variety of these mixes so that you can take plain water and turn it into a drink that your family can enjoy while also increasing calorie intake.

Storage Containers

Some of these juice powders come in plastic containers that are great storage containers.

Mylar bags are a great protection for drink mixes, if you are looking to repackage smaller amounts into larger containers like 5-gallon buckets.

Calories per Serving	~150
Calories per 5-Gallon Bucket	40,000 – 50,000

Sizes

These drink mixes come in 18 oz. -72 oz. packets.

Price	$6.36 / 2 1-lb. 3-oz. cannisters (Food Lion)

Tip

These drink mixes are not only great for breaking the monotony of water, but they are also great for bartering. You will not be the only person who gets tired of drinking plain water during a long bug in.

22. Coffee

Description

Coffee still runs the world. If you are a coffee drinker, then that hot cup of coffee will mean the world to you when you wake up while bugging in from some sort of catastrophe.

If you are not a coffee drinker, then know that you are surrounded by people who are addicted to this beverage.

There is a lot of influence and power to be had in the storage of coffee. You could sell hot coffee from your home; you could barter with coffee beans. So, as long as you have a good relationship with your neighbors, coffee will get you extremely far.

You should also consider adding tea to your stockpile too. Some people will come looking for that caffeine fix, but they might want it from tea leaves rather than coffee beans.

Storage Containers

Coffee tins and bags are designed for coffee storage. They could be thrown into 5-gallon buckets as protection.

Calories per Serving	0

Sizes

12 oz. – 37 oz. containers

Price	$14.25 / 3 1-lb. tins

Tip

Green coffee beans can be stored in Mylar bags with oxygen absorbers in 5-gallon buckets for the long term. They will have to be roasted in an oven or over a fire, but you can store green coffee for over 10 years and only roast it when you want a fresh batch.

Disastercoffee.com is one of the rare places where you can buy green coffee beans 5 lbs. at a time.

23. Parmalat

Description

If you really enjoy drinking or using milk in recipes, then you should consider Parmalat as a solution for your bug in prepper's pantry.

Parmalat is a UHT shelf stable liquid milk. This milk is tasty and lasts around 6 months.

If you keep it in rotation, then you will always have shelf-stable milk for up to 6 months.

The taste is superior to powdered milk and it is ready to drink when you pop the lid. If milk is important to you, then you should consider this product.

If you are looking for a long-term food storage milk option, then powdered milk might be better than Parmalat as it has a much longer shelf life. I store both.

Storage Containers

This product must be kept in its original container.

Calories per Serving	90 (1 cup)
Calories per 5-Gallon Bucket	N/A
Sizes	32 oz.
Price	$6.34 / 2 boxes 32 fl. oz. (Food Lion)

Tip

Whole milk can be separated using lemon juice or vinegar and the solids gathered in cheesecloth; this way you can make your own homemade cheese.

24. Potato Flakes

Description

Potato flakes are a dirt-cheap food that lasts forever!

I purchase the Idahoan packets. These can be had in regular potato, butter, garlic, and a bunch of other flavors. These potato flakes are the perfect base to dump a can of beef stew over top and create a nice filling meal.

These potato flakes are made by simply adding hot water and stirring. They are ready in minutes and are a food that everyone should stockpile for their bug in.

Storage Containers

The potato flakes that you buy in Mylar or foil bags are already in the most optimal storage. If you buy them in the box, then you might want to repackage them into larger Mylar bags.

Calories per Serving	150 (1/4 cup, cooked)
Calories per 5-Gallon Bucket	97,500

Sizes

4 oz. individual packet to 3.25 lbs. cartons.

Price	$7.25 / 6 2-oz. packs (Food Lion)

Tip

You can fold all kinds of flavorings and things into warm mashed potatoes. Bacon and cheese are great. Chives and buttermilk are great. You can even add flour and an egg to mashed potatoes to create a patty that fries up in a pan. These potato pancakes are delicious.

25. Dried Fruits

Description

Dried fruits are an incredible food to stockpile because they are high in sugar and fiber. There are some nutrients packed in them too, but most dried fruits are all energy.

That is an exceptionally good thing because these high-calorie foods are what you are after during your bug in. This is particularly true if you cannot leave the home and get to the supermarket.

Take the time to figure out which types of dried fruits you enjoy the most. These are the ones that you should store.

Storage Containers

Dried fruits mostly come in bags or cans. These are great for storing dried fruits for the long term. The moisture in the air is the worst enemy of anything dried. So, you want to make sure you store your dried fruits in a cool dry area.

Calories per Serving	Varies
Calories per 5-Gallon Bucket	N/A

Sizes

2 oz. packages to #10 cans

Price	$11.94 / 3 5-oz. packages (Walmart)

Tip

Dried fruits are great ingredients to add to your oats to make granola. You also need some dried fruits to make pemmican. Both of these are great survival foods.

26. Jellies and Preserves

Description

Jellies and jams are another high-sugar, high-calorie food that is great on your homemade bread or other baked goods. Jellies and jams come in a variety of flavors and they are pretty easy to make at home too.

Most food storage companies do not sell large quantities of jellies and jams, but they have a massive section of jams and jellies at the supermarket. They are cheap too!

Storage Containers

Jellies and jams come exclusively in glass jars. These canned preserves have an incredible shelf life.

Calories per Serving	55 (1 tbsp)

Sizes

2 oz. jars to 30 oz. jars

Price	$2.28 / 12-oz. jar (Walmart)

Tip

Buy the equipment and plant the fruits you need to make and can your own jellies and preserves. Blackberries and raspberries can go out of control with fruit in just a few years. Jellies can even be canned in a hot water bath and do not require a pressure canner. This makes them a great DIY.

27. Honey

Description

Honey is an incredible food. It is by far the most nutritious and effective sweetener in our world today. You can make your own honey if you're willing to keep bees.

Honey is an incredible food to stockpile because it basically lasts forever!

It is also an incredible topical medicinal treatment. There are lots of healing qualities in honey. Eating local honey can even help with allergies! This is something you must stockpile!

You could also store maple syrup for that same natural sweetness. It is a great food that lasts forever, can be made by tapping sugar maple trees, and can be used in our meal plan.

Storage Containers

The containers that honey comes in are always the best place to leave the honey. It lasts forever.

Calories per Serving	64 (1 tbsp)
Calories per 5-Gallon Bucket	N/A

Sizes

12 oz. jars to 10 lbs. buckets

Price	$4.22 / 6.oz container (Walmart)

Tip

Honey can be warmed and flavored with fresh herbs and spices. It works really well as a base for dips both sweet and savory.

28. Dried Herbs and Spices

Description

This is another ingredient that will really help you out with the palate fatigue of the long-term bug in menu. Herbs and spices can be added to meals to replicate all kinds of cuisine from around the world. My favorite ones are:

Indian – Curry, Coriander, Fennel Seeds

Italian – Ground Garlic, Basil, Oregano, Red Chili Flakes

Asian – Chinese 5 Spice, Ground Ginger, Chilis

Jamaican – Jerk Seasoning

South American – Chili Powders, Cumin, Canela.

Make sure to stockpile the herbs, spices, and flavorings you like. Here are some ideas: dried red pepper flake, cinnamon, garlic powder, onion powder, chili powder, paprika powder, red chili flakes, dried oregano, cumin, vanilla extract. You can also store things like pre-made spice rubs, seasoned salts, and other outlandish herbs and spices to play with. These will all allow you to take an ingredient like rice and eat it several times a week without complaint.

Storage Containers

There is no need to repackage your herbs and spices. The glass jars and plastic containers are very effective and the goal should be to rotate these as they lose flavor over time.

Calories per Serving	<10
Calories per 5-Gallon Bucket	N/A

Sizes

2 oz. to 18 oz. containers are the most popular sizes. Buying sizes larger than this might take too long to use and the spices could lose their flavor.

Price	$7.20 / 18 oz. container (Food Lion)

Tip

Stop buying small bottles of herbs and spices. Instead, buy your favorites in the larger-sized 18 oz. container. These purchases will save you money and will also keep you from running out when you bug in.

Refer to meal plan for necessary spices.

29. Apple Cider Vinegar

Description

Apple cider vinegar is another one of those incredible ingredients that can flavor foods but can also do tons of other things! Apple cider vinegar can be the acidic portion of your salad dressings, it can be an incredible marinade to break down tough meats, or just flavor other types of meats in general.

Raw unfiltered apple cider vinegar is going to give you the most flavor and the most benefits.

Along with eating this stuff you can also use it to take care of cleaning tasks around the home. Combined with your stored baking soda, you can create a very powerful foaming cleaning product!

Storage Containers

Leave your raw unfiltered apple cider vinegar in its glass container.

Calories per Serving	0
Calories per 5-Gallon Bucket	N/A

Sizes

16 oz., 32 oz., 1-gallon containers

Price	$2.12 / 33.8 fl. oz. bottle (Food Lion)

Tip

Start your day with a tall glass of water and a cap full of raw unfiltered apple cider vinegar. You can also add a pinch of sea salt to this. This elixir provides you with electrolytes and the vinegar kickstarts your metabolism.

30. Dry Yeast

Description

If you plan to store flour for your bug in, then you should definitely store dry yeast. While you can capture yeast out of the air to make your bread rise, it is much easier to use dry yeast.

In 2020 the world went crazy over making sourdough bread during the lockdown. It was a very interesting phenomenon. If you have dry yeast, you can create a simple sourdough starter of your own.

Dry yeast can be used in all kinds of bread recipes and is cheap and easy to stockpile for your own bug in.

Storage Containers

The packets that dry yeast comes in are perfect for your dry yeast. Most packets are foil and will even protect the yeast from moisture.

Calories per Serving	0
Calories per 5-Gallon Bucket	N/A

Sizes

75 oz. – 2 lbs. packages

Price	$2.40 / 2 4-oz. packs (Food Lion)

Tip

Yeast can also be used to rise sweet dough. Don't forget about delicious risen desserts like beignets.

31. Pemmican

Description

Pemmican is largely considered the ultimate survival food and was widely consumed on the American frontier. It is a paste made out of dried meat, animal fat, and ingredients like dried fruit or nuts. The fat acts as a major preservative and keeps this food for a very long time even without refrigeration.

This food can be purchased at a pretty high price, but it is also easy enough to make on your own and store as an important piece of your food storage.

Storage Containers

Pemmican can be pressed into mason jars and stored. If stored in a root cellar or refrigerator, then you will have a food that lasts a decade! In your climate-controlled pantry, you can get 1-5 years out of properly made pemmican.

Calories per Serving	290 (2 oz.)
Calories per 5-Gallon Bucket	N/A

Sizes

Pemmican is hard to find online, so make your own! Make as large a batch as you can. I found one brand called Lakeside that sold 6 oz. pemmican blocks.

Price	$39.99 / (See recipe)

Tip

Do yourself a favor and learn to make this.

32. Jerky

Description

Jerky is a food that is similar to pemmican, but more well known. This snack of dehydrated meat, which is often smoked and salted, is very popular and can be found at any convenience store or supermarket. It is a great food to stockpile.

Storage Containers

The bags that beef jerky comes packed in are a great storage container. Once you begin accruing a lot of them, you might want to start packing them away in a 5-gallon bucket to protect the plastic packaging.

Calories per Serving	82
Calories per 5-Gallon Bucket	N/A

Sizes

Jerky comes in a variety of sizes, both in packaging and in the size of the pieces. The best value will be had when you buy larger packages.

Price	$15-$20 / 8 oz. bag

Tip

All jerky is packed with an oxygen absorber. It's a huge benefit. Just protect your packaging and jerky will last a very long time.

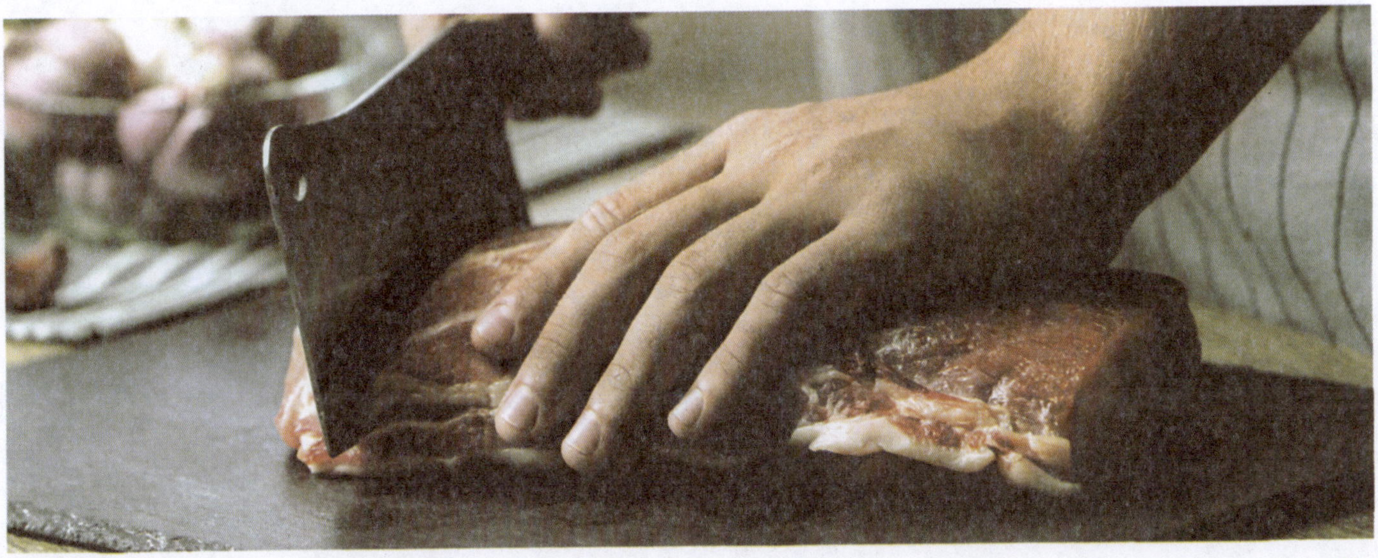

33. Nuts

Description

Nuts come in a large variety. Most are very nutritious. The good thing about nuts is that most people like at least one type.

They have healthy fats in them, but these fats also affect the overall shelf life of nuts.

Storage Containers

Nuts tend to come in bags or tins. If you buy nuts in bulk, they might be worth repacking in Mylar bags, but leaving them in tins is usually a very good storage container.

Calories per Serving	~170 (1/4 cup, mixed)
Calories per 5-Gallon Bucket	N/A

Sizes

I find that the larger tins are the best means of storing nuts for the long term. You can buy nuts in 1 oz. packages or multiple-pound bags.

Price	$5-$8 / 10 oz. tin

Tip

Just like all food storage, only store the foods that you are going to eat. Only store the types of nuts that you like to eat.

34. Peanut Butter

Description

Peanut butter is one of those foods that almost everyone likes! It is a great source of protein that is high in calories and fats. All of these things are exactly what you are after in an optimal food to stockpile.

Storage Containers

Keep peanut butter in the containers that it comes in.

Calories per Serving	180 (2 Tbsp.)
Calories per 5-Gallon Bucket	N/A

Sizes

There are a few different sizes of peanut butter jars. You can also buy peanut butter in bulk in 5 lbs. tubs.

Price	$8.28 / 3 1-lb 2-oz. jar (Publix)

Tip

Learn to use peanut butter both in sweet preparations and in savory ones. Pad Thai is a great example of how you can add peanut butter to an entrée.

35. Powdered Eggs

Description

Powdered eggs are a product that is freeze-dried. These eggs are reconstituted in water to eat as scrambled eggs or to use as a baking ingredient.

Powdered eggs are an essential ingredient to stockpile because of the high protein content and use in other recipes.

Storage Containers

Leave powdered eggs in the provided containers unless you freeze dry them yourself; then you can use Mylar bags.

Calories per Serving	80 (2 1/2 Tbsp.)
Calories per 5-Gallon Bucket	N/A

Sizes

Buy the large #10 cans which hold just over 2 lbs. of powdered eggs. These stack and store really well.

Price	$67.95 / 10 2-lb. cans (online stores)

Tip

Two tablespoons of powdered eggs are the equivalent of 1 whole egg. Use this for recipe purposes.

36. Freeze-Dried Shredded Cheese

Description

Cheese making is a skill I would recommend learning. Until then you should get yourself a #10 can of freeze-dried shredded cheese for your food stockpile.

This freeze-dried option will give you the ability to make recipes like our delicious frittata and cheesy scrambled eggs.

You can turn your pasta and milk into mac and cheese with some freeze-dried mac and cheese. I like the cheddar cheese shreds.

Storage Containers

#10 can

Calories per Serving	180

Sizes

#10 can

Price	$50 / 10 2-lb cans (online stores)

Tip

Stockpiling freeze-dried cheese is great for the short term. Your long-term solution for cheese should be to learn cheese making. It might sound intimidating but making cheese is actually pretty easy.

37. Cornstarch

Description

Cornstarch is a great thickening agent. It is also used in DIY personal hygiene recipes for things like deodorant. This is a great food item to store as it can turn simply chicken bouillon into a thick and delicious gravy. You can thicken soups and even milk to create a base for mac and cheese.

Storage Containers

Cornstarch should be repackaged in mylar bags with oxygen absorbers for long term storage.

Calories per Serving	30 (1 Tbsp.)

Sizes

Cornstarch comes in a variety of sizes; from 1 lb. boxes and jars to 25 lbs. bags.

Price	$1.54 / 1 box (Walmart)

Tip

A little cornstarch goes a long way, so make sure you reseal the mylar between uses.

38. Soy Sauce

Description

This traditional Chinese condiment is made from fermented soy beans and grains. It is popular all over the world now and is a shelf stable condiment that you can use to flavor everything from soups to entrée dishes. It can even be used in salad dressings.

Storage Containers

Buy your soy sauce in 64 fluid ounce plastic or metal containers.

Calories per Serving	8 (1 Tbsp.)

Sizes

You can buy a small condiment-sized container but I recommend you buy the largest you can find.

Price	$3.28 / 5 fl. oz. bottle (Walmart)

Tip

Ask for soy sauce from your local Chinese Restaurant and they will put 30 of those things in your bag. Save them. Free soy sauce!

How to Gradually Build Your 3-Month Stockpile

There was one prepping task that really put me at ease when I was still making my way. It wasn't putting up guns and ammo. It was putting up food in the pantry.

Over time I gradually built a stockpile in my pantry and then added larger 5-gallon buckets of grains like rice and flour. As the calories mounted, I came to realize that my family would eat.

If a crisis occurred tomorrow, my family would be fed. We would not need to stand in some long and dangerous line to get aid. We would not have to beg.

It took time to get here. This is a process that we all have to accomplish over time. There are many reasons to gradually build up your stockpile:

1. It enables you to do more with less money.
2. You learn the process of managing a growing stockpile.
3. You can buy a little each week and have a HUGE impact over time.
4. Menus and meals can easily be tweaked when you gradually build up.
5. New storage locations can be created gradually as needed.

If someone dropped a pallet on your front porch that had 3 months' worth of food on it, you would be scrambling. We do not want to be scrambling. To effectively manage a stockpile of food, you have to know exactly what is in that stockpile and rotate that food on a regular basis.

Building a Stockpile on a Budget

The rising cost of feeding your family has probably already been at the forefront of your mind. In fact, it is getting increasingly more expensive to not only buy the food you need at the grocery store, but also more expensive to gas up your vehicle to get there!

Given the shifting paradigm in the world, right now you can only expect these prices to continue to rise. While we are facing our own unique set of challenges here at home, there is a storm brewing abroad. It took the world some time to figure out how big of an issue the wheat exports from Ukraine were going to be. Just as we were understanding that, we were also hit with realization that fertilizer would also be affected!

At the end of the day, it means that the cost of food is going to continue to rise in America. For now, we need to focus on building our own stockpile.

There are two things that get in the way of the average person building a food stockpile for bugging in: money and storage space.

We will cover storage methods and inventory management later in this chapter. For now, let's focus on maximizing your budget.

$5 or $10 a Week

It might seem hard to believe, but you can actually have a serious impact on your food storage using just $5 per week! I bet you never imagined that getting prepared and stockpiling food could be achieved by using just $5 for the week.

That is just the cost of one fancy coffee each week. How much money do you think you spend on things like coffee and lunch? The average American spends around $1000 a year or $20 a week on coffee, and as much as $2000 a year or $37 a week on eating out for lunch.

We are asking a very small portion of that budget to go into the food that will feed you and your family in a crisis. Chances are you are spending an extra $5-$15 each week; that can be pushed into food storage rather than coffee and lunch.

For more expensive food items, you may have to put a couple weeks of budget together. If you are a good saver, then you may even squirrel that money away and do a separate shopping trip altogether.

The most effective way to, however, is to just build your stockpiling into those weekly trips to the supermarket.

In time you will not even realize you are buying extra food. It will become second nature to pick up that extra box of pasta and can of tomatoes. Before long you will have that 3-month stockpile and you will be wondering if it is time to go to 6 months.

Growing a Food Storage Budget

If you have no budget or if you would like to grow your budget so that you can buy even more food each week, I can help you with that. I am talking about the topic of money management.

The first and most important step is to be honest about what you spend your money on.

SLASH SUBSCRIPTIONS

How much money do you spend a month on subscriptions like Netflix and monthly subscription boxes? Do you even know? Most of us are spending way more than we should be on these kinds of subscriptions.

Eliminating a few of these can free up $10 - $20 to your budget a month.

STOP EATING OUT

The cost of food is going up. The price of eating out is affected by that, too. Eating out a couple of times a week can cost a family of 4 more than $100 dollars! What could you do with $200 a month in your stockpile budget?

FREEZE NON-ESSENTIAL SPENDING FOR A YEAR

After 2020 there were many preppers who decided they would freeze non-essential spending, not take a vacation, and focus that money on prepping. It is a radical move and it makes for a very tough year.

You will increase your budget for prepping overall and you will notice a serious impact in a matter of months.

SIDE HUSTLES

The world of side hustles and diverse streams of income is just exploding. There are many ways to make money outside of your regular income. You can do active work or use passive ways of making money with a side hustle.

These things take a little bit of learning and maybe even some work up front. It can be as complex as creating a sales funnel and selling digital products to something as simple as cutting grass in the neighborhood.

YARD SALES

Most of us have clutter. We have way too much stuff in our homes! You probably have at least a few hundred dollars sitting around doing nothing. Selling your unused or unwanted things can bring you lots of money to add to that stockpiling budget.

I have put together a list for you, grouped on categories, so you can start building your food stockpile. You can print the list below or take a picture of it, so you can always have it on hand.

Weekly Shopping List to Build Your Stockpile

Below you will find a list that you can print and keep on hand, ready to grab whenever you go grocery shopping.

Rice, Beans, and Seasonings	Grains and Pasta
Rice	Pasta
Black Beans	Oats
Pinto Beans	Cornmeal
Cinnamon	Popcorn
Garlic Powder	Ramen
Onion Powder	**Baking**
Chilli Powder	Flour
Paprika Powder	Salt
Red Chili Flakes	Sugar
Dried Oregano	Yeast
Cumin	Baking soda
Vanilla Extract	Cornstarch
Chiken Bouillon	**Canned Foods**
Potatoes, Eggs, Cheese	Canned Crushed Tomato
Potato Flakes	Canned Soup
Powdered Eggs	Canned Fish
Freeze-Dried Shredded Cheese	Canned Corn
Drinks	Canned Peas
Drink Mixes	Canned Diced Carrots
Parmalat	Canned Meats
Coffee	

Fats, Vinegar, and Condiments	
Cooking Oil	Apple Cider Vinegar
Ghee	Soy Sauce
Snacks	
Jerky	Honey
Nuts	Peanut Butter
Dried Fruit	Pemmican
Jelly	

What Item You Should Remove from Your Pantry Immediately

Crisco is a fat that can be used to cook hot food, make baked goods, or even grease pans.

This product is made from soybean oil and other hydrogenated oils. It is a chemistry experiment cooking fat that is not something you would want to eat each day if you had a choice.

In fact, I'm going to go one step further: Crisco—and all seed oils—is literal POISON. They destroy us hormonally, and I will never knowingly consume these substances again—and you shouldn't either. Plus, lard and tallow are easy to come by, are good for so many uses, store just as well, and, in fact, are easy to render yourself—and they are incredibly healthy. In a SHTF scenario, I would consume seed oils in very limited quantities, but know you are literally poisoning yourself and weigh the cost accordingly. The situation should ALWAYS dictate your choices. Since we're preparing, set yourself up with some tallow. I render my own with leaf fat from a family ranch near my house and use it for cooking, first aid, skin care, and candles.

Or you can stick a few wicks in the container and make a candle or use it to grease door hinges. Best use of Crisco, in my opinion.

Stockpiling Hardware

As you begin to accumulate food, you are going to run into our second big problem when it comes to stockpiling: storage. With the appropriate stockpiling hardware, you can clean up the overflowing pantry shelves and start packaging these foods for the long term.

It's going to take things like Mylar bags, oxygen absorbers, and food safe 5-gallon buckets with fitting lids. These components can be used to store food in a number of different ways. The Mylar bags are great for long term storage of dried fruits. Combine them with the 5-gallon buckets and you pack up rice and beans for decades!

So, where do you get the best price on this food stockpiling hardware?

5-GALLON BUCKETS

The cost of 5-gallon buckets can get a little crazy. The best deal on 5-gallon buckets is at Lowes. These blue buckets and lids are sold on the end caps of many aisles.

You can buy sturdier buckets with better lids online, but these are going to cost you. Quality buckets with sealing lids can cost as much as $30 each.

You could also ask your local supermarket if they have any spare buckets. If there is a bakery in the supermarket, they will have 5-gallon buckets of things like icing and margarin. Just make sure you have the lids, too.

These 5-gallon buckets are great for all kinds of preps. You can never have too many of them. If you start getting them free, then stack them inside one another and set them next to a stack of the lids.

You can make water filters, store first aid preps, and even grow food in them!

MYLAR BAGS AND OXYGEN ABSORBERS

I have found the best deals to be had on oxygen absorbers and Mylar bags are on Amazon and you can get 20 – 100 of these bags in a combo pack that will give you plenty of options for repackaging and storing your stockpile in protective, stackable 5-gallon buckets.

If you're going to stock up on these, then you should turn them into a big purchase item once a month. With $30 you can get 75 of these bags and oxygen absorbers to go inside of them.

Mylar Bags with Oxygen Absorbers: https://www.amazon.com/75pcs-Mylar-Storage-Oxygen-Absorbers/dp/B0B3XRH2H6?th=1

Shopping for the Best Deals

A $5 to $10 budget each week is more than adequate to build a stockpile. Using our lists will keep you on target. That being said, you can stretch that stockpile budget even further if you put in just a little more effort. Or you can build that budget up using the methods we've discussed.

Every week your supermarket has close dated items, items with damaged packaging, items they want to feature, and items they want out of the store. These kinds of foods most often find their way into some kind of discount.

These things happen each and every week at the supermarket you visit. The question is whether or not you are taking the time to notice. There are things you can do each week that will put you in a better position to save money and build that stockpile faster. Do you know where the clearance and sale shelves are at in your local grocery store?

Clearance racks can be set up near restrooms, pharmacies, or even endcaps in grocery stores.

Let's look at a few ways you can find the very best shopping deals and stretch that bug in stockpile budget to the max.

COUPONS

Coupons are still a great way to save money on food purchases at the supermarket. While most people don't receive the circulars that have coupons for clipping, there are still some incredible deals to be had.

Coupons are now a digital opportunity, but any major supermarket has digital coupons you can find on their website or on their phone app.

Of course, the struggle with coupons is that you cannot know when they will run coupons for the types of foods that are on your shopping lists. Even if the coupons aren't specifically for the foods that you have on your lists, they could help you save money elsewhere, which could be diverted into that new budget.

LOYALTY CARDS

If you aren't into searching for weekly coupons, then you should at least sign up for your local supermarket's loyalty cards. These cards can save you money each week and are often the key to some big discounts.

CLEARANCE

Every supermarket has a clearance section. They can be well hidden and you may have never even noticed the section before. Next time you are in the supermarket, seek out the clearance section. While these sections can be home to some obscure items, you might find great deals there.

I find that things like coffee, cooking oil, and canned foods are good bets for the clearance section.

SHOPPING AROUND

Depending on the kind of effort you want to put into your stockpile, you might consider visiting multiple shopping markets and retailers to find the best deals.

Different supermarkets and retailers are going to offer different price points.

Aldi is the cheapest supermarket in many categories. Walmart is a close second and one worth your time, too. Supermarkets like Kroger might offer some great deals, but when it comes to overall savings you won't do your budget any favors shopping at places like Kroger, Harris Teeter, Acme, or Fresh Market. Shop with overall savings in mind.

MONEY SAVING APPS

Money saving apps like Upside, Ibotta, and Dosh are more modern tools for saving money while shopping. These can be your ticket to great sales or even cash back that can go towards that stockpiling budget.

These apps are easy to use and since they are on your phone, they travel with you no matter where you decide to shop.

LOCAL FARMERS/RANCHERS/HERBALISTS

I have also found that where I live, in Middle Tennessee, there are plenty of local ranchers and farmers where I can get the absolute BEST quality produce, raw milk, eggs, beef, pork, chicken, and turkeys at WAY less than supermarket prices. I have a freezer stocked with cuts of beef and pork, fat to render into tallow and lard, bones for broth and soups, and several organic, pasture-raised turkeys, one of which will feed my family for days on end as well as make the most nutritious, flavorful, and filling soups. One turkey carcass, some veggies, spices, and rice or pasta and you will have countless easily made, delicious meals to eat right away or freeze or pressure can for long-term storage. This will take a little more effort than going to Walmart, but you will be rewarded with MUCH higher-quality products at economical prices, and just as importantly, you are building COMMUNITY, which is incredibly important in any kind of SHTF scenario. People want to help people they know and like, and I can always trade some honey from my beehives or eggs from my chickens to friends I've made for things I need that they provide. I also have made friends with some local herbalists so I can get medicinal plants for my stockpile or when SHTF.

Explore your community! You will be pleasantly surprised. Even if you live in the city, supporting someone's small business in the good times means you have a grateful friend when times are hard. Having eaten military rations for months on end at places where I've deployed, I can't tell you how much eating a real meal with fresh ingredients will mean to you when you're bugging in. Morale is incredibly important.

Weekly BUG-IN Meal Plan

Using the list of foods to stockpile I have compiled an incredible meal plan for you. This meal plan is going to use all of the items from your stockpile to prepare breakfast, lunch, dinner, and a snack each day.

The diversity of the meals and ingredients was designed with balance in mind.

We are after flavor, calorie content, but also nutrients. Getting the right amount of nutrients is what keeps our engines pumping. I also wanted to focus on foods that could provide us with essential vitamins and minerals.

I have put together 7 options for each category to help fight palette fatigue. You do not want to be stuck eating rice and beans and spaghetti with sauce 7 nights a week.

If you put yourself in that kind of position, then I can promise you that missing meals will become more and more frequent. Malnutrition will follow. When I was deployed to Afghanistan very early on, before we began to source local food and before the U.S. began flying in fresh food, I stopped eating more than the bare minimum just out of fatigue from eating highly preserved, bland military rations. I lost 25 pounds over several months. Variety and using as many fresh ingredients as possible will cure that.

Some of these recipes will be very simple and others may require you to follow a larger recipe. You might be asked to do a bit of baking with things like cornbread, or the recipes might be focused on the proper cooking of grains like rice.

Every meal in this list can be made better with the inclusion of fresh foods. Anything that you might grow in a garden or raise on your property could be added to these recipes.

Things like herbs and fresh fruits would go a long way in making these meals even more tasty. The more food we can produce on our own, the better the bug in will be.

However, even if you are completely locked down in your home, you will be able to produce all of these recipes with just the items you have stockpiled. Not to mention the average cost to feed each person in your home is $3.50.

That is around $14 a day for a family of four!

With the prices rising at the supermarket and in restaurants today, that is a figure that is, frankly, unheard of!

You will be consuming around 2000 calories per day if you eat all three meals and choose a snack item. Some combinations are going to be more calorie dense then others. If you are low on calories for the day, simply add another snack.

If you are going to follow this meal plan long term, make sure that each recipe you choose features a solid source of protein or some kind of fruit or vegetables. Frozen and canned produce is better than none at all.

As far as protein, I know it can be expensive, but I would look into the price of canned tuna, canned mackerel, sardines, Greek yogurt, cottage cheese, and lentils.

Animal protein is especially important to prevent deficiencies in iron or B12, which is poorly absorbed from grain, flour and fruits and vegetables.

Breakfast

Pancakes and Honey

Approx. Total Calorie Count	Approx. Cost per Person	Servings
1,620	$ 0.50	Makes 15-20 pancakes

Ingredients	Steps
• 1½ cups flour (preferably whole wheat flour, for nutrients) • 3½ teaspoons baking powder • ¼ teaspoon salt, or more to taste • 1 tablespoon white sugar • 1¼ cups milk • 2 tablespoons of egg powder • 3 tablespoons ghee, melted • Honey	1. Mix together all your dry ingredients in a bowl. Stir them well. 2. Create a well in the center of the bowl and pour in your milk and ghee. Mix thoroughly. 3. They key to cooking great pancakes is a batter with fat (like butter or ghee) in it and then heating a skillet to just the right temperature. Pancakes actually prefer a pretty hot skillet; this can be around medium high. On most electric stoves I cook on about a 6. The first pancake is almost always a mess up. Add a little cooking oil or ghee to the pan and then start turning them out. Just a minute or less on each side and they should be golden brown and delicious. Drizzle them with some of that incredible honey and you are in for a great breakfast.

Oatmeal

Approx. Total Calorie Count	Approx. Cost per Person	Servings
1,600	$ 0.05	Makes 4 servings

Oatmeal is another great example of a food that can be a great vehicle for other flavors and ingredients. I am giving you a base recipe but add fruits and spices to keep it new and different.

Ingredients	Steps
• 1 cup of oats • 1 cup of milk (Vitamin D milk or whole milk would be best) • 1 cup of water	1. Bring the milk and water mixture to a simmer. 2. Add your oats. 3. Cook until they are tender (quick oats take just a minute or two) 4. Add any flavorings or fruits that you would like and serve.

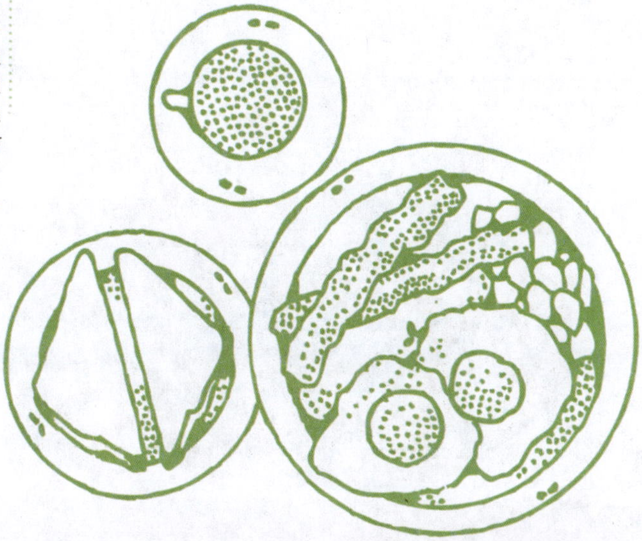

Breakfast

Eggs and Spam

Approx. Total Calorie Count	Approx. Cost per Person	Servings
2,250	$ 1.00	Serves 4-5 people

Ingredients	Steps
• 1 cup of powdered eggs • 1 can of Spam	1. Dice your spam into cubes about a ½ inch by ½ inch. 2. Sauté them in a skillet large enough to hold your eggs and Spam. 3. Start the Spam with a little bit of oil or ghee. 4. Reconstitute your eggs as per the instruction on your container. 5. Once the Spam has browned a little, mix in the reconstituted eggs and serve.

Honey Peanut Butter Granola

Approx. Total Calorie Count	Approx. Cost per Person	Servings
1,400	$ 0.40	Makes 8-10 servings

Oatmeal is another great example of a food that can be a great vehicle for other flavors and ingredients. I am giving you a base recipe but add fruits and spices to keep it new and different.

Ingredients	Steps
• 3 cups quick cooking oats • ½ cup chopped nuts, your choice • ⅓ cup honey • ⅓ cup sugar • ¼ cup vegetable oil • 2 tablespoons warm water • ½ teaspoon salt • 1 teaspoon vanilla extract	1. In a saucepot add your honey, oil, peanut butter, sugar, water, and vanilla extract. 2. Bring this mix to a simmer and stir. 3. In a large bowl add your oats and nuts. 4. Pour over the warm mixture and stir. 5. Spread the mix out on a baking sheet. 6. Bake in a 350°F oven for 15 minutes.

Breakfast

Scrambled Eggs on Biscuits

Approx. Total Calorie Count	Approx. Cost per Person	Servings
1,200	$ 0.65	Makes 4-6 servings

If you can get at preparing a basic biscuit recipe, then you have a vehicle for all kinds of things. In this recipe we are using them for eggs, but you could easily add spam to the eggs or even some fresh herbs from your garden.

To make this meal more nutritious, you can also add some frozen broccoli florets, steamed. Many frozen veggies like broccoli are super cheap if you buy store brand.

Ingredients

- 2 cups flour (preferably whole wheat flour, for nutrients)
- 1 tablespoon baking powder
- 1 teaspoon salt
- 1 tablespoon white sugar
- ⅓ cup ghee
- 1 cup cold milk
- 1 cup of powdered eggs

Steps

1. Preheat the oven to 425°F.
2. Stir together the dry ingredients in a large bowl.
3. Cut in the ghee until your mixture looks coarse.
4. Finally add the cold milk and mix the dough until dough pulls from the edges of the bowl.
5. Knead this mixture no more than 20 times.
6. Roll out onto a floured board and cut out your biscuits.
7. Bake for 13-15 minutes.
8. Rehydrate and scramble your powdered eggs with some butter.
9. Divide the eggs between your biscuits and you are eating!

Corn Muffins

Approx. Total Calorie Count	Approx. Cost per Person	Servings
800	$ 0.11	Makes 12 muffins

This is a very basic corn muffin mix that you can add all kinds of flavorings to. Everything from honey to country ham or even bacon!

Ingredients

- 1 cup cornmeal
- 1 cup flour
- ⅓ cup white sugar
- 2 teaspoons baking powder
- ½ teaspoon salt
- 1 egg, beaten or 2 tablespoons of powdered eggs
- ¼ cup canola oil
- 1 cup milk

Steps

1. Mix all of your dry ingredients in a large bowl.
2. Create a well at the center of the dry ingredients.
3. Add your wet ingredients and whisk until the mixture is smooth.
4. Pour some batter into each of the muffin tins, use paper cups if you have them.
5. Bake the corn muffins for 15-20 minutes or until a toothpick stuck into the center of one of the muffins comes out clean.

Breakfast

Frittata

Approx. Total Calorie Count	Approx. Cost per Person	Servings
2,100	$ 0.95	Makes 8 servings

A frittata is a baked egg dish. It is a lot like a quiche without the crust. It can be flavored with cheese and any mixture of ingredients that you like.

I like to bake my frittata in a small cast iron skillet, but a small pie pan can work, and even smaller muffin tins can be used to make mini frittatas to feed a group.

Ingredients

- cooking spray
- 1 tablespoon canola oil
- 1 cup chopped Spam or other meat
- 2 tablespoons chopped onion
- ¾ cup of powdered eggs
- 1 cup milk
- ¼ teaspoon salt
- ⅛ teaspoon ground black pepper
- 1 cup shredded cheese

Steps

1. Preheat your oven to 350°F.
2. Start by cooking your onion and Spam together until the onion is soft and the Spam is browned.
3. Mix together your milk and powdered eggs.
4. Combine the rest of the ingredients with the eggs, milk, onions, and Spam. Mix everything together thoroughly.
5. Place this mixture into the pan of your choosing and bake for 10-20 minutes depending on the size of your pan. Smaller portions will cook faster.
6. Check that the center of your frittata is firm at the end of cooking.

Lunch

Nut and Oat Bread

Approx. Total Calorie Count	Approx. Cost per Person	Servings
1,700	$ 0.60	Makes 10-15 servings

Being able to make homemade bread is a very important skill. This bread dough is studded with nutrition from the nuts and the oats.

Ingredients

- 1 cup oatmeal
- 1 cup warm milk
- ¼ cup honey
- 1 egg
- ½ cup chopped walnuts
- 1 teaspoon cinnamon
- 4 cups flour (preferably whole wheat flour, for nutrients)
- 2 packets of dry yeast
- ½ teaspoon salt

Steps

1. Preheat the oven to 400°F.
2. Mix your dry ingredients in a bowl.
3. Create a well in your dry ingredients. Add your warm milk, yeast, and honey.
4. Stir this mixture and let it sit for a few minutes until it starts to bubble and smell yeasty.
5. Add your egg to the mix.
6. Slowly start to incorporate the flour into the wet ingredients until you start to get a dough that is starting to come together and getting less stick.
7. Dump the dough out onto a floured table and begin to knead and add flour as needed to bring your dough together. I need for around 8 minutes to get a nice smooth bread dough.
8. Cover your dough with a warm damp towel and allow it to rise for 10 minutes.
9. Beat down the dough and shape it into loafs that will fit in a bread pan.
10. Allow the loaf or loaves to rise for another 10 minutes before putting them into the oven.
11. Bake for 20 minutes or until the bread is knocked on and sounds hollow.
12. Allow the bread to cool before cutting into it.

I'm a big fan of sourdough.

It's generally just starter, flour, water, and salt (but you can add pretty much anything you like, such as fresh jalapenos and cheddar cheese, cocoa powder, or chocolate chips), so it's extremely healthy and SIMPLE. I have an active sourdough starter that I use to bake artisan sourdough bread generally twice weekly. It's a bit of an art as well as a science, so it would pay off to develop your starter and learn to do this beforehand.

Sourdough is fantastic because it is much healthier than even homemade bread using commercial yeast—and, of course, WAY healthier than anything store bought. Sourdough is full of beneficial enzymes, so even people who have issues with gluten can usually eat it. And eating sourdough with your meal can actually lower the glycemic index of the entire meal!

Sourdough starter can be left alone in the back of your refrigerator for several months, and it will not lose any viability. You do NOT need to feed it often unless you are actively using it. Personally, while I have an active sourdough starter I use every week, I also have dehydrated a jar full of my sourdough starter, so if something were to happen to my active jar of starter, such as contamination or somebody throws it out accidentally, I can start again very easily. I can also give flakes of my dehydrated sourdough starter to friends or family so they can bake their own bread!

I have used my sourdough starter for cookies, brownies, bread, English muffins, bagels, crackers, a delicious Cinnamon Toast Crunch cereal, and an amazing strawberry cake. You can make pizza crusts, sandwich bread, artisan bread, rolls, and any bread or cracker-like product, really, using sourdough. I highly recommend getting some dehydrated starter for a few dollars from someone online or from a friend or family member and developing an active starter then learning to bake with it. It's easier than you think, but there is a learning curve. And in a bugging-in scenario, you should have an active sourdough starter and some starter you have dehydrated. To do this, I just feed my starter, and when it's active and bubbly, I spread some out on parchment paper and let it air dry for about 24 hours then break it up and put it into an airtight glass jar for storage. If you want to explore sourdough, there are many videos on YouTube and Facebook groups where you can learn all you need to.

Lunch

Peanut Butter and Jelly

Approx. Total Calorie Count	Approx. Cost per Person	Servings
1,750	$ 0.60	Makes 4 servings

This is a pretty standard recipe, right? To take it to the next level, you should try peanut butter and jelly on your own homemade bread. Use the bread recipe from our Oat and Nut Bread.

While slathering some white bread with PB&J is fine, making your own bread and eating it is much more rewarding and it will serve you much better in the bug in.

Soup and Rolls

Approx. Total Calorie Count	Approx. Cost per Person	Servings
750	$ 2.00	Makes 4-6 servings

Rolls are just a matter of baking a small piece of bread dough. If you can make a loaf of bread, then you can make rolls. How you shape them is up to you.

You could even make it really simple and just roll them into breadsticks like you would Play-Doh as a kid. Keep it simple.

Warm up some soup from your prepper's pantry and you have lunch taken care of.

Lunch

Black Beans and Rice

Approx. Total Calorie Count	Approx. Cost per Person	Servings
1620	$ 0.35	Makes 6-8 servings

Learning to cook rice properly is essential to cooking out of a prepper's pantry and bugging in. Remember that long grain rice requires a 2:1 ration of water to rice. This makes it very easy to cook any quantity of rice.

I like finely diced onion and cilantro on top of this.

Ingredients

- 2 cups of white rice
- 4 cups of black beans, washed, and soaked overnight
- Ghee
- Chili Powder
- Garlic Powder
- Salt

Steps

1. Prepare your black beans first by taking the presoaked beans and draining them.
2. Put some ghee into the pot you will be cooking the beans in and then over a low heat warm it up.
3. Add a tablespoon each of chili powder and garlic powder.
4. Cook the spices over low heat until they start to become very fragrant, then add your beans.
5. Cover with water.
6. Simmer for about 45-50 minutes or until the beans are soft.
7. While the beans are cooking you can also take your 2 cups of rice and place it into a medium sized pot.
8. Rinse the rise a couple of times and carefully drain the water from the pot without losing any rice.
9. Then add 4 cups of water to the 2 cups of rice.
10. Add a tablespoon of ghee and a few pinches of salt to the rice and stir.
11. Simmer until it looks stodgy like porridge or finished oatmeal.
12. Turn the dial to the lowest setting and cover the rice.
13. Steam until the rice is tender.
14. Season your beans with salt when they are tender.
15. You can mix the two together or serve them in separate containers.

Canned Chili with Sweet Cornbread

Approx. Total Calorie Count	Approx. Cost per Person	Servings
1,000	$ 2.25	Makes 6-8 servings

Ingredients

- 2 cans of chili with beans
- Sweet Cornbread (use our cornmeal muffin recipe but stir in ¼ cup of honey)

Steps

1. Preheat the oven to 375°F.
2. Heat your chili up in a saucepot.
3. Pour your batter into a pie tin.
4. Bake for 30 minutes.
5. Serve a slice of cornbread with each bowl of chili.

Lunch

Pemmican on Homemade Crackers

Approx. Total Calorie Count	Approx. Cost per Person	Servings
4,100	$ 2.20	Makes 8 servings

Pemican contains about 4,000 calories per pound and in this recipe, you are going to use a ¼ lb. of pemmican per serving.

This is such an easy lunch that it doesn't really warrant a recipe. Though you can try your hand at baking your own crackers. This recipe is very similar to the process of making biscuit dough in that you are going to cut the fat into the dry ingredients to create that coarse meal.

Use our provided pemmican recipe to create one of the greatest survival foods in all of history.

Ingredients

- 1 1/4 cups flour whole wheat, fresh ground, or all-purpose
- 1/4 teaspoon onion powder
- 1/4 teaspoon garlic powder
- 1/4 teaspoon chili powder
- 1/4 teaspoon smoked paprika (regular paprika works fine, too)
- 4 tablespoons ghee
- 1/4 cup water
- Sea salt to sprinkle on top

Steps

1. Preheat the oven to 375°F.
2. Add all of your dry ingredients into a large bowl.
3. Add the ghee.
4. Finally add the water and mix just until the dough starts to pull away from the sides of the bowl.
5. Dump out onto a floured table and roll out about ¼ inch.
6. Cut into your desired shape and bake for 10 minutes or until crunchy.

Spam and Cheese Quiche

Approx. Total Calorie Count	Approx. Cost per Person	Servings
3,200	$ 1.05	Makes 8 servings

Ingredients

- 1 homemade pie crust (recipe below)
- ¾ of a cup of dried eggs (rehydrated)
- ¾ cup milk
- ¾ teaspoon salt
- ¼ teaspoon black pepper
- 1 cup cooked spam chopped
- 1 cup shredded cheese
- 3 tablespoons green onions (optional)

Steps

1. Preheat the oven to 375°F.
2. Put your rehydrated eggs into a large bowl and then mix every other ingredient into the bowl.
3. Roll out your pie crust and form it into a pie pan.
4. Using a fork, poke holes in the bottom of your pie crust to keep it from rising and affecting the quiche.
5. Fill the pie pan with your quiche mix.
6. Bake for 35 minutes and serve.

Lunch

Pie Crust Recipe

A basic pie crust recipe can go a very long way. It can hold deserts, lunches like this, or even savory dinner meals like pot pie.

Ingredients

- 2 ½ cups flour
- ½ tablespoon sugar
- ½ teaspoon salt
- ½ pound of ghee
- 6 tablespoons of iced water

Steps

1. Start with all of your dry ingredients in a large bowl.
2. Add the ghee into the mix.
3. Keep this up until the mixture in the bowl looks granular or like very coarse sand.
4. Next, add your ice water and begin to mix everything together until the dough starts to come off the sides of the bowl.
5. Dump the dough out onto a table and knead 20-30 times max. Add just a little flour to keep it from sticking to your hands.
6. Place the dough in the fridge, wrapped in plastic, for 20 minutes to chill.
7. Roll it out and use as you see fit!

Dinner

Spaghetti and Homemade Sauce

Approx. Total Calorie Count	Approx. Cost per Person	Servings
1,720	$0.80	Makes 6-8 servings

You should add a tomato sauce recipe to your arsenal. It can go a long way. If you have meat to add to the sauce that can add flavor, too. Ground beef, turkey, canned TVP or other freeze-dried meats are great for food storage meat options, too.

Ingredients

- 1 can of crushed tomatoes
- 1 can of diced tomatoes Italian Style
- 1 tablespoon of onion powder
- 1 tablespoon of garlic powder
- ¼ cup of olive oil
- 2 tablespoons of Italian seasoning, dry basil, or dry oregano
- 1 tablespoon of sugar or honey
- 1 teaspoon of red chili flakes
- 1 lb. box of Spaghetti
- Meat (optional)

Steps

1. Cook or rehydrate your meat, if you are using it.
2. Place everything but the pasta into a large pot and bring it up to a simmer.
3. Let this sauce simmer for at least 30 minutes, uncovered.
4. Boil your pasta until it it's soft.
5. Serve!

Red Beans and Rice

Approx. Total Calorie Count	Approx. Cost per Person	Servings
2,000	$0.20	Makes 4-6 servings

Ingredients

- 2 cups water
- 1 cup uncooked rice
- 1 lb. of andouille sausage or smoked Spam
- 1 onion, chopped
- 1 green bell pepper, chopped
- 2 (15 oz.) cans of canned pinto beans
- ¼ cup of crushed tomatoes
- ½ teaspoon dried oregano
- ½ teaspoon pepper
- salt to taste

Steps

1. Rinse and prepare your rice as we mentioned above.
2. In a large sauce pot cook your onion and pepper in a little oil or ghee.
3. Add your meat and cook until it is warmed through.
4. Add the rest of the ingredients and simmer for 10 minutes.
5. When the rice is done steaming, spoon your beans and meat mixture over the rice and serve.

Dinner

Beef Stew over Mashed Potatoes

Approx. Total Calorie Count	Approx. Cost per Person	Servings
2,600	$ 3.75	Makes 4-6 servings

One of the simplest entrees on our list!

You are really only using your potatoes flakes and your canned beef stew. Follow the package instructions with the potato flakes and make a nice dense mashed potato. This is just a matter of heating water and stirring in the flakes.

Heat up your canned beef stew and serve each person with a healthy helping of potatoes and a ladle of beef stew over top. A meal in minutes.

Ultimate Ramen

Approx. Total Calorie Count	Approx. Cost per Person	Servings
2,500	$ 1.00	Makes 8-10 servings

While we know Ramen as a dried noodle in a soup packet, in its true form it actually comes with meats, vegetables, and highly nutritious broth. We are going to take the humble ramen packet and turn it into something much better.

Ingredients

- 4 packs of ramen
- 1 can of corn
- 1 can of peas
- 1 can of diced chicken or sliced spam
- 1 cup of cooked beans
- Fresh leafy vegetables from the garden, kale, chard, spinach (Optional)
- 4 Hardboiled eggs from your chickens (optional)

Steps

1. Prepare the Ramen per the package ingredients.
2. Add your corn, peas, and beans to the pot and heat the mixture over medium heat. Allow it to simmer for about 5 minutes to heat through.
3. Add the leafy vegetables.
4. Ladle your soup into 4 bowls.
5. Add sliced meat and 1 egg to each bowl before serving.

Dinner

Spam Chili

Approx. Total Calorie Count	Approx. Cost per Person	Servings
1,600	$0.70	Makes 4-6 servings

Ingredients

- 1 can of Spam diced
- 1 cup of crushed tomatoes
- ½ cup of black or pinto beans, fully cooked
- 2 tablespoons of chili powder
- 2 teaspoons of cumin
- 1 tablespoon of paprika
- 1 teaspoon of garlic powder
- 1 teaspoon of onion powder

Steps

1. Cook your diced spam in some oil or ghee until it starts to brown.
2. Add all of your spices and stir them until they become fragrant.
3. Then add your tomatoes and allow to simmer for 30 minutes.
4. Finally, add your beans and simmer for another 5 minutes before serving.

Chicken and Dumplings

Approx. Total Calorie Count	Approx. Cost per Person	Servings
1,100	$1.50	Makes 4 servings

Ingredients

- 1 can of diced carrots and peas
- 3 cans (14-1/2 ounces each) reduced-sodium chicken broth
- 3 cups canned diced chicken
- 1/2 teaspoon poultry seasoning
- 1/8 teaspoon pepper
- 1-2/3 cups biscuit mix
- 2/3 cup milk

Steps

1. Simmer your chicken broth with the poultry seasoning.
2. Thicken the broth by mixing a few tablespoons of flour with water into a cup. Stir this mix until it becomes milk and free of lumps. Take the pot off the heat and slowly stir in this thickener. Whisk the broth as the thickener goes in.
3. Bring the mixture to a simmer and see how thick it is. It should easily coat a wooden spoon.
4. Add the peas, carrots, and chicken.
5. Now mix together your biscuit mix and milk.
6. Using your hands or a spoon add balls of dough to the top of your simmering mixture.
7. Cover and cook on medium low for 15 minutes or until a toothpick inserted into your dumpling comes out clean.

Dinner

Spaghetti Aglio Olio with Focaccia

Approx. Total Calorie Count	Approx. Cost per Person	Servings
2,000	$ 0.35	Makes 4-6 servings

This simple dish only works if you are storing a good quality olive oil. You should. There are numerous health benefits to consuming and even applying olive oil to your skin and hair.

Aglio Olio translates to garlic oil in Italian.

Ingredients

- 1 lb. of spaghetti or angel hair
- 6 cloves of fresh garlic or 2 tablespoons of garlic powder
- 1 bottle of olive oil
- Parmesan cheese (optional)
- Flat leaf parsley (optional)

Steps

1. Start your pasta water boiling.
2. Cook the pasta until it is tender.
3. In another large pot heat your olive oil over a low heat.
4. Add the garlic or garlic powder to the olive oil and heat just until you start to see the garlic cook and smell or you get the fragrance of the garlic powder.
5. Add your finished pasta to the pot.
6. Toss the pasta with the garlic and olive oil. I usually add more olive oil at this point.
7. Stir in the parsley and parmesan cheese if you are using it.
8. Serve family style, in the pot with some tongs.

Focaccia

Servings	
Servings	Makes 4-6 servings

This is another opportunity to make bread from scratch. This is a simpler recipe then our oat and nut bread.

NOTES: If you have fresh herbs like thyme, rosemary, or even some sliced onions you can lay them all on top before packing. Focaccia is great with some toppings baked in. Quality Olives are good on top, too!

Ingredients

- 6 cups of flour
- 1 cup of water
- 2 packets of dry yeast
- One teaspoon of sugar
- One Tablespoon of salt
- ¼ cup of olive oil

Steps

1. Preheat the oven to 400°F.
2. Place your flour in a large bowl and create a well.
3. Add the water, yeast, and sugar into the well. Stir and wait till this mix begins to bubble.
4. Then add the rest of your ingredients and begin to slowly incorporate the flour into the well.
5. Before long you will get a dough that can be placed on a floured table.
6. Knead this dough and add flour for about 8-10 minutes.
7. Cover with a warm damp towel and allow to double in size.
8. Now press the dough into a sheet pan with sides that are at least ¼ inch high.
9. Press the dough out from the center and try to spread it out all over the pan.
10. Dimple the dough and brush it with olive oil.
11. Bake in a 400°F oven until the focaccia is brown and crisp on the outside.

Snack Ideas

Nuts and Dried Fruit

Approx. Total Calorie Count	Approx. Cost per Person	Servings
700	$ 0.50	Makes 4 servings

Alone they are a delicious snack but together on the tray they can make something very special.

Any foraged foods, garden fresh vegetables, or even homemade cheese turns this snack into a borderline lunch.

Use a variety of nuts and a variety of types of dried fruit.

Biscuits and Jelly

Approx. Total Calorie Count	Approx. Cost per Person	Servings
1,200	$ 0.25	Makes 10 servings

Using your biscuit mix or our biscuit recipe above you are going to bake some nice warm biscuits and put them out on a plate with jelly, jam, preserve or whatever else you would like to slather n them!

Canned Meat and Crackers

Approx. Total Calorie Count	Approx. Cost per Person	Servings
600	$ 0.55	Makes 10 servings

One of the best canned meats for this is deviled ham. This is a smooth potted style meat product that is great on crackers. Though sliced Spam can be great for this, too.

Sardines, mackerel in olive oil, and even canned tuna can be great on crackers, too.

They are cheap, go great with crackers, and contain the essential nutrient omega-3s that we should be having at least twice a week.

If you aren't storing crackers, then use our simple cracker recipe in the lunch section.

Focaccia

Approx. Total Calorie Count	Approx. Cost per Person	Servings
1,135	$ 0.10	Makes 10-12 servings

Focaccia is another great bread to have around as a snack. You can use it in several ways. It can be sliced and dipped in things like olive oil or tomato sauce.

You can also slice it in half and toast it to be used as a delicious sandwich bread.

It can even be diced to make great croutons for salad!

Snack Ideas

Black Bean Puree and Crackers

Approx. Total Calorie Count	Approx. Cost per Person	Servings
400	$0.25	Makes 4 servings

This is a great way to use up some of those extra black beans from your rice and beans. A simple black bean puree is actually delicious with some tasty crackers or even oven baked tortillas.

Throw some leftover black beans into a Cuisinart or food processor of some kind, drizzle in some olive oil or ghee while they blend. You can even add some cumin or chili powder if you like.

Jerky

Approx. Total Calorie Count	Approx. Cost per Person	Servings
320	$3.00	Makes 4 servings

Keep it simple. Eat some jerky.

Scones

Approx. Total Calorie Count	Approx. Cost per Person	Servings
3,600	$0.15	Makes 8 scones

A good basic scone recipe can be customized anyway you see fit. You can add nuts, oatmeal, dried fruits, citrus zest and really whatever you want to them! This base recipe will give you the ability to change things up while still making the same snack.

Ingredients

- 3 cups flour (preferably whole wheat flour, for nutrients)
- ½ cup white sugar
- 5 teaspoons baking powder
- ½ teaspoon salt
- ¾ cup butter
- 1 egg, beaten
- 1 cup milk

Steps

1. Preheat the oven to 400°F.
2. Add your dry ingredients into a bowl.
3. Cut in the butter to the mixture till it gets coarse.
4. Add your eggs and milk mixing till the dough comes together.
5. At this point add your nuts, fruits, chocolate or anything else.
6. Turn the dough out onto a floured surface and knead about 10-15 times
7. At this point you can rest the dough or roll it out to ½ an inch thickness.
8. Cut into 3-4-inch-wide strips and then cut those strips into wedges.
9. Bake the wedges at 400°F for 15 minutes in the oven.

Snack Ideas

Popped Corn

Approx. Total Calorie Count	Approx. Cost per Person	Servings
120	$0.05	Makes 4 servings

Popping corn is a cheap and easy food to store. It is also a very nutritious compared to many other types of snacks.

If you have a corn popper that is a great tool for this. However, you can also use a simple pot with a lid over medium low heat to pop the corn.

Take ¼ cup of popping corn and 1 tablespoon of cooking oil and put them into a large pot with a lid. Begin to heat the pot over a medium low heat.

After about 3 minutes begin to move the pot back and forth consistently. You will keep this up until the popping ends.

Keep moving the pot and after about 10 minutes you should see the popcorn starting to pop. Keep it covered while the corn is popping.

Once the popping stops you can remove the pot from the heat and uncover the pot.

Pour some melted ghee over the corn and salt. You can also get fancy and make some flavored oils to toss your popcorn in.

Hardtack Biscuits

Approx. Total Calorie Count	Approx. Cost per Person	Servings
3,000 /oz.	$0.05	Makes 4 servings

This is a civil war era survival food that was given to soldiers. It is cheap, simple, and lasts for years.

Ingredients	Steps
• 1 lb. flour • 1/2-pint water • 1/2 tablespoon sea salt	1. Preheat the oven to 350°F. Add the flour and salt into a mixing bowl, and then pour the water. Mix all ingredients together. 2. Use extra flour if necessary to make sure the dough is no longer sticky. However, be careful not to make the dough too dry. If you add too much flour, add slightly more water. 3. Knead the dough until it is easy to work with. 4. Use the rolling pin to roll the dough into a rectangular shape. Hardtack was around a half inch thick, so don't worry about making the dough thin. 5. Bake the dough for 30 minutes. 6. Take the dough out of the oven and cut it into large squares (around 3 inches by 3 inches). 7. Then poke four rows of four holes in the cracker using a stick (or a fork). 8. Flip the squares and return to the oven for 30 more minutes (even an hour just to make sure it gets completely dehydrated). 9. Allow the hardtack to completely cool inside the oven.

Snack Ideas

Pemmican

Approx. Total Calorie Count	Approx. Cost per Person	Servings
8,000	$4.00	Makes 40 200 calorie servings

Ingredients

- 8 cups lean meat or 2 pounds (deer, beef, caribou, or moose)
- 6 cups blueberries (or other dried fruits)
- 4 cups rendered fat (or 1/2 pounds)
- Optional – about 1 shot of honey

1. Get about a pound and a half of lean, grass-fed shoulder roast and let it firm up in the freezer so you can slice it thin.
2. Add salt and pepper. Set the oven to the lowest possible temperature (around 150°F) and put the strips of meat directly onto the rack. Crack the oven door to prevent moisture buildup.
3. At this point, you can also put a handful of frozen wild blueberries on a small oven pan to dry out with the meat.
4. Let the meat dry out for about fifteen hours, or until it is crispy. Toss it in the food processor until it becomes a powder. Do the same with the blueberries.

In the old days they'd pound it with a rock to turn it into a "powder".

5. For the fat portion of pemmican, you can use tallow (rendered beef or mutton fat) or lard (rendered pork fat). Cut up your fat in small pieces and place the fat into the crockpot. Set the crock pot on low heat and remove it only after it becomes completely liquid.

Use a strainer to avoid all the crispy bits; you just want the pure, liquid fat.

6. Mix the meat and berry powder together, then slowly add the hot liquid fat. Pour just enough so that the fat soaks into the powder – slowly.
7. Let it firm up, then cut it into squares or roll it into a ball.
8. If done and stored correctly it can last for decades.

Mix the powdered meat with tahe chopped berries

Add the fat to the bowl

Place into a dish and let it firm up before portioning

How to Safely Store

Your BUG-IN Food Stockpile

The beautiful thing about storing your long-term bug in food stockpile is that you do not have to figure anything new out! The storage of lots of food is handled by massive warehouses each and every day all over America and all over the world.

What's even better news for you is that I have spent some time managing these kinds of warehouses as a food safety manager. I taught other people how to store a large inventory of food safely! We do not have to rack our brains about the best and safest ways to store a food stockpile. We only need to look to best practices and procedures of people who do it each and every day.

The first step is to understand the importance of food safety. We are not just talking about things like contamination that can spoil your food, but also conditions that hasten the spoilage of food. There are practices that assure you are using your stockpile in a timely manner and getting rid of the oldest foods first.

Key Terms for Safe Food Storage

FIFO

This is an acronym for first in; first out. This is the concept of assuring the oldest foods get out the door first before they go bad. In a large distribution warehouse this is accomplished by loading the newest foods behind older ones or rotating them.

In your own food stockpile, you will replicate this process by moving the oldest foods to the front of racks, while adding the newest foods behind those ones. Having something like a can rack that is designed for FIFO can make this process much easier.

No matter if you have buckets of long-term food storage or 5 cans of beans, you want the oldest in the front and the newest foods behind them. This way when you reach for them, you get the oldest first.

Cross Contamination

Cross contamination is an important concept that involves using container, utensils, prep areas, and storage spaces for different kinds of foods without washing them before changing the food item.

For things like raw protein this can spread bacteria and get people sick. For people with allergies, this can also be deadly.

Let's say you use the same scoop to pour almond flour into Mylar bags and then you use that same scoop to fill Mylar bags with rice. If someone has a tree nut allergy, they could die from anaphylactic shock just by eating the rice that has that almond flour dust in it.

FAT TOM

This popular acronym is used in food safety training to explain the many conditions that cause food to spoil and spoil quickly.

If you can manage these 6 things, then you will be able to assure the maximum shelf life of your bug in food stockpile.

- Food
- Acidity
- Time
- Temperature
- Oxygen
- Moisture

Each one of these conditions has an effect on the growth of bacteria. Depending on how you manage them, you can either stifle the growth of bacteria or greatly increase it.

The better you understand FAT TOM, the safer your food stockpile will be.

Food

The type of food that you store will have a tremendous effect on the shelf life of your stockpile. This is why I recommend that you invest in dry food storage. Shelf stable foods naturally have the longest shelf life.

While frozen foods have a long shelf life too, if the power goes out then those foods will be at risk in a matter of days.

Starting with the right type of food is very important.

Acidity

Bacteria are a lot like us. They thrive in an environment with balanced ph. If the environment is too acidic, it can kill bacteria. That is why we can simply water bath can highly acidic foods. The acidity in the canned food takes care of the bacteria.

The more balanced the ph., the greater the chance there is of bacterial growth.

Time

Sometimes food heats up or cools down to temperatures that are unsafe. This is most common with fresh food, but it can happen with dried food, too. This is why we must store our food stockpile in a temperature-controlled environment.

In other words, we cannot store buckets of food out in your shed, where the temperatures fluctuate from freezing to 100°F in the hottest months. That is because the larger the amount of time a food stays in these fluctuating temperatures, the faster it will spoil.

Temperature

What do you have your thermostat set at? That is the temperature that you thrive in! Bacteria have a temperature range that they thrive in, too!

When you are dealing with fresh foods and foods that have been cooked already, you want to make sure you are not keeping those foods in the temperature danger zone. This is the range where bacteria grow rapidly.

You also have to worry about fluctuations of temperature. As we mentioned in our discussion about time, this can seriously affect the quality and lifespan of your stockpiled food.

Oxygen

Most bacteria require oxygen to survive. Remember, they are a lot like us! When you add those oxygen absorbers to your food storage then you are starving bacteria of oxygen. This is why dried foods stored this way can last so long.

If you start canning food than you do need to concern yourself with clostridium botulinum, which is a type of bacteria that can grow without oxygen. This bacterium can cause botulism, which is deadly if left untreated.

Moisture

Moisture is always going to invite spoilage. If dry food gets damp, then it is as good as gone! This is why we like to pack certain dry foods in mylar bags; because they are virtually waterproof when they are sealed.

Preventing Spoilage

You could say that preventing spoilage is all about managing FAT TOM. However, some of those conditions just do not apply to shelf stable foods.

So, we will focus on the aspects that will affect your food stockpile.

Storage Options

There are a number of ways you can store a stockpile of food. It is likely that you will use a number of these methods.

STORE-BOUGHT PACKAGING

Boxed dry goods are a great example of foods that can mostly stay in their store-bought packaging. Pasta packed in carboard is a great example of this. As long as you can keep these packages away from moisture, they will do great.

Of course, all of our canned goods are better off in their store-bought packaging. Things like nuts in tins, jerky, jelly, and peanut butter are also great to keep in their own packaging.

Some of the worst options to keep in store-bought packaging are things like beans, rice, sugar, and flour. The papery packaging for flour and sugar is just not enough. The rice and beans packaging is pretty thin and shreds over time. Then your food is exposed to whatever might be around.

5-GALLON BUCKETS

I know plenty of preppers who buy bags of rice and beans each week from the supermarket and throw them right into a 5-gallon bucket when they get home from the supermarket.

You can designate buckets for 1 lb. bags of white rice and other buckets for beans.

You can even do this with flour and sugar, if you wanted to. I would suggest stacking them upright if you go this route.

The 5-gallon bucket is useful because it protects your food from moisture and pests with its thick walls and lid. Once you have filled a bucket, you can toss an oxygen absorber into the bucket and seal it up.

MYLAR BAGS

Mylar foil bags are another great way to store food. These bags are stronger than the average supermarket packaging, so even things like dried fruits can be repacked into mylar bags. They also heat seal. You can add oxygen absorbers to them, too!

If you like the idea of storing in Mylar, then you should buy them in several sizes. 5-gallon will fill an entire bucket, 1-gallon bags are great for making buckets with multiple foods in them. Anything smaller and they can be great resealable containers for snacks and dehydrated foods.

5-GALLON BUCKETS AND MYLAR

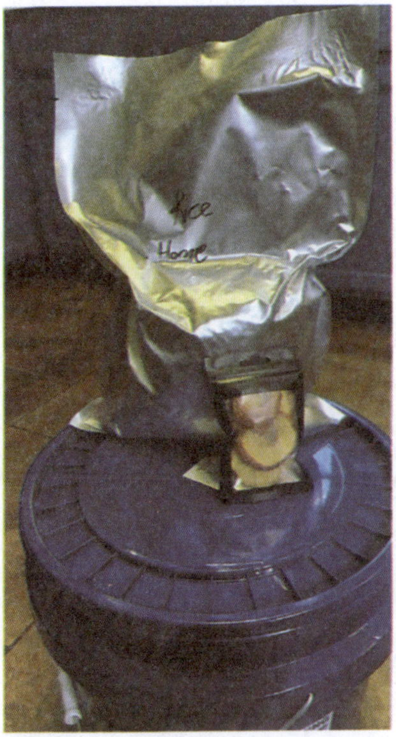

The best combination is the Mylar bags nestled down into 5-gallon buckets. If you put an oxygen absorber into those mylar bags, then you have basically created your own long term food storage.

This kind of food storage is meant to last for 20+ years. You will pay a lot of money if you buy a 5-gallon bucket of things like oats or rice from a big-name survival food company.

However, you can make your own using this method and a 50 lb. bag of rice, which would run you around $20.

Now that is how you assure that you and your family will eat when there is chaos and you have to bug in to survive it.

Diatomaceous Earth

This substance, which is rich in silica and made up mostly of fossilized algae, just happens to be an incredible ally in the preservation of dry foods!

BE SURE YOU USE 100% FOOD SAFE DIATOMACEOUS EARTH!

Though it feels soft to our touch, it is actually very sharp and can puncture soft bodied pests, eggs, and especially larvae.

It is a massive pest deterrent and also reduces moisture. This stuff has been used since the ancient times to store grain.

This method of storing long term food does not require anything but a 5-gallon bucket and the aforementioned diatomaceous earth.

1. Start by adding a thin layer of diatomaceous earth to the bottom of the bucket.
2. Then add about 3-4 inches of your dried food or grain.
3. Add another thin layer of DE to cover.
4. Add another 3-4 inches of food.
5. Continue this process until the container is full.
6. Then put the lid on your bucket and give it a few rocks back and forth to disperse the DE.

7. DONE!
8. Date and Label.

As you can see, this method is incredibly simple and does not require many materials or resources.

Storage Locations

When building a food stockpile, it doesn't take long for you to realize that you are going to need more room. You are going to need more places to store food. Chances are your current pantry is just not equipped to deal with the kind of storage constraints that you are going to put on it with a large bug in food stockpile.

So, where else can you store food?

The good news is, you are only limited by your imagination. Food storage can be stuffed into any crevice you like around the home. Just make sure you keep that food in a climate-controlled area. Remember what you learned about time and temperature.

Once you outgrow your pantry and cabinets, you are going to start looking at the whole home as a storage place for food. Here are some great locations in your home to store your food stockpile.

Remember, it doesn't have to be altogether but keeping similar items together does make getting to the food you need much easier.

Here are some great locations in your home to store food:

- Cabinets
- Under Sinks
- Bedroom and Utility Closets
- Rubbermaid Containers under the Bed
- Laundry and Washrooms
- Finished Basements.

COVERT STORAGE

Along with those closets and cabinets, you might also like the idea of having some covert storage. We are all different and some people are ok with 5-gallon buckets stacked up in the washroom.

Some people are really against that kind of clutter and that look. Well, with covert storage you can solve that.

Covert storage is all about storing your bug in food stockpile in places that people cannot see or do not recognize as food storage. I know a prepper who fills hollow doors with dry beans and rice. How many internal hollow doors do you have? How much food could you store in your doors?

During a bug in situation things can get bad. Your home could be broken into. If people break into your home, it means they are after what you have. This includes your bug in food stockpile.

If all of your food is sitting in the pantry, then you are going to have all of your food taken! All of the work we have done until now will be for nothing.

However, if your food storage is spread out and some is even stored covertly, well, then you are going to have some food leftover even if you get raided.

For most people though, covert storage is about keeping a nice tidy home that looks great but also is outfitted to keep your family safe in a disaster.

Now, the more you study your home, the more covert storage you will start to uncover.

- Space between Cabinets
- Space under Stairs
- Space under Cabinets
- Behind Books on Shelves
- Spaces in Couches and Furniture
- False Walls

At the end of the day your covert food storage can be as creative as you like. There are really no limits. I have seen people build false raised floors to a pillow filled reading nook and under that floor were preps and canned goods.

You can cut 12-to-18-inch diameter circles of plywood, drill them into the top of a 5-gallon bucket lid, use that lid to top a full bucket of food storage. Then cover the whole thing with a tablecloth and you have a covert side table food stockpile. This thing can sit in your living room with a lamp on it and none would be the wiser!

What can you come up with?

CACHING

Did you know that just 10 feet below the ground the insulation from the earth will maintain a temperature of around 40°F through all seasons? If you understand that, then you now understand that every inch of earth under your feet has the potential to store your food stockpile.

Some people dig root cellars in the same way that our ancestors had. However, you can use a simple cache in order to get your food storage down below the surface of the insulating earth. A survival cache is simply a watertight container large enough to store some food inside.

These can be Pelican cases that cost hundreds of dollars, or they can be large lengths of PVC pipes with caps on each end. These will cost you a fraction of what a large Pelican case will run you. No matter what airtight vessel you decide, caches are worth considering.

It is best to store foods in their original packaging or in a Mylar bag, if you are storing them in caches. This will better protect the food and will also make it easier to remove when you dig up the cache and begin using the food inside.

The best candidates for long term food storage in survival caches are going to be the grains like rice, wheat, oatmeal, and things like dry beans.

You will be surprised at how much food you can store in a 3-foot length of 3 inch PVC pipe with 2 caps glued on each end.

If you make these types of caches, do not fill them to bursting. Leave a little room to one side so that when you use a saw to cut one end off, you are not cutting open the precious food. You can even mark the side you wish to saw later with a marker.

Your cache locations should be marked, too. Maybe by a tree or some other natural feature that will likely be there even after a disaster or emergency. Some people use GPS to mark their caches, but of course that means other people might one day be able to find them, too!

You can use hand drawn maps or even codes that use cardinal directions. In other words, the biggest tree in the yard, two paces north of it. This way these caches remain your secret. Whichever method you use, the information should be shared with your family only.

Remember, these locations should be buried underground. This way you can both take advantage of the concealment and the consistent temperature. That is how caching food works.

You can cache other survival items in various places, but for food we have to worry about time and temperature.

Keep your survival food storage caches close to home. You will be bugging in, so traveling far would not be a good strategy.

Food Safety Is Everything

Look, it doesn't matter how much food you buy and store. If you don't rotate that food and store it safely, then you will lose it all! Don't make that mistake with your bug out food stockpile.

With a little focus, maintenance and maybe storage improvements, you can be ready to bug in at a moment's notice and feed you and your family.

If you decide to go to alternate locations or cache away food, just remember that rotation and food safety principles apply to those foods as well.

Of course, there is one more threat to your food and it lives and breathes all around you. I am talking about pests. You have got to be able to manage pests and keep them from your food supply.

Protecting Your BUG-IN Food Stockpile Against Pests

Now that you understand many of the challenges storing a food stockpile can present, it is time we face one of the greatest risks of all. I am talking about pests and pest infestation. Do not make the mistake of underestimating pests and their ability to completely destroy a bug in food stockpile.

If food is stored improperly and pests make their way into your home, then they will find your food. Creatures like mice can be utterly ravenous and they don't mind taking your uncooked rice and beans. However, creatures much smaller can pose serious problems, too.

There is a little pest called the Indian Meal moth, you will get to know them later in the chapter. They can infest bulk stored grains like flour and rice. Then they reproduce rapidly, and these small flying bugs can contaminate your entire pantry.

Knowing how to deal with these pests is not only essential for your bug in food stockpile but for your entire bug in plan. A home infested with pests will not only affect your food storage but also your overall health!

1. Pest Triangle

Do you know the fire triangle? I hope so. Each side makes up the necessary elements of creating fire. Fuel, heat, oxygen, without these three you cannot have fire. Well, there is a pest triangle, too!

Pests require different things than a fire, but should you remove one of these requirements it can drastically affect the pets that are pestering you.

- Food
- Water
- Harborage

Understanding the pest triangle is one of the very best ways for you to prevent pests from getting into or even living around, your home. Of course, it all starts with understanding where to look for food, water, and harborage.

Harborage

This is a pest's home. It can be an established home or a sign that a home is being made. Outside of your own home you might find things like burrows or nests. However, harborage is not just about finding completely built homes. It is also about inspecting for things that can be used to build nests and harborage.

Things like shredded paper, fabric, memory foam, stuffing, and anything soft and insulative can be used to create harborage for pests. Even the insulation in your home can be used as harborage for pests.

When you see chewing or holes in the walls or even these signs outdoors, then you should be cautious.

If pests can live in it or make a home of it then it is harborage.

Food

Given what this chapter is all about then we know you have food around. You have lots of shelf stable food and it might not all be in cans and 5-gallon buckets. This means if pests do determine your home to be a suitable place of harborage, then they are going to go after any of the food they can find.

Having lots of food makes it much harder to know when a pest's infestation has started. They can be eating a 2lb bag of flour and you might not know until you reach back there and grab it or rotate that flour.

Water

Pests love standing water. If that standing water is outside of your home, then it will bring pests onto your property. Some pests are happy to stay outside. They will drink from that standing water and go about their business.

Other types of pests, like deer mice, will want to get inside where there is warmth and more food. If they can find a way in, then they will get inside.

Managing the 3 sides of the pest triangle will assure that your home and property stays free of pests. If you take away any one of these things, then pest populations will decline dramatically.

If you can take all three away, then you give pests no reason to stick around. Without food, water, and harborage pests will simply find another place to live.

2. Common Types of Food Storage Pests

Mice

Description: There are a variety of mice that get into homes. If it is a mouse of any kind, then you need to take action as these creatures breed quickly and can eat and poop all over your food supply.

They are brown furred mammals that with white undersides. They can be heard crawling around the walls and home at night.

You will know them by the droppings and shredded food packaging they leave behind. This packaging they often use as harborage.

Habitat: Mice are warm blooded so they love to be in your home in a nice cozy nest they often build whatever they can find close by.

Removal: Killing traps can be effective but if you have many mice then you should employ rodenticide traps as they can kill mice more effectively.

Ants

Description: There are worse problems to have then simple ants in the house. Be careful of carpenter ants as they can pose another set of challenges.

Habitat: Ants make their way into your home for food, but they always head back out. They do not want to live indoors with you. They want to return to the nest

Removal: Ant sprays can be effective but if you can use poison to carry them back

German Cockroaches

Description: German cockroaches are smaller than American cockroaches, but they infest quickly and can become a nightmare.

German cockroaches prefer to live indoors.

They are about 1 to 1 ½ inches long and have a two stripe (racing stripe) set of bands on their head.

The stripes are black, and their bodies are brown.

Take extreme action quickly if you see these in your home. Call pest control if you can and if not deploy roach motels and roach bait stations immediately in affected areas like kitchens and bathrooms.

Habitat: They like your home and the like if you do not clean often. Leave food out and water, they will proliferate.

Removal: Act fast and employ roach motels and bait stations if a pest control professional is unavailable. Also do a thorough cleaning of your entire home focusing on bathrooms and kitchens.

Indian Meal Moth

Description: These moths have tan and maroon wings when looked at up closely. They are small in stature but can infest a bag of rice or flour in a hurry. They reproduce fast and can decimate shelf stable grains if they are not stored effectively.

Habitat: They like your home but prefer your pantry. They want a nice dry environment with plenty of food. Dog treats and food can bring them on, too.

Removal: Pheromone stick traps lure them in and they get stuck. This also effects reproduction and the population will decrease rapidly. Store these.

Flour Beetles

Description: If you have ever held onto flour too long then you have seen these little beetles before.

Their eggs are already in your flour. They just need some time to mature.

These beetles are black with two segmented bodies and black antennas.

Habitat: Your flour.

Removal: Repacking your flour with oxygen absorbers in Mylar is going to give you your best chance at keeping these beetles at bay.

What My 3-Month Food Stockpile Looks Like

Here we have a picture of each of the foods from our stockpile. These are the same foods from our shopping list.

We thought adding a picture of each would give you an idea of what you need to buy and examples of the kinds of brands that we purchased.

Shopping List

Protein

Great Value
Pinto Beans

2lb | $1.98 | x 2

Great Value
Small Red Kidney Beans

1lb | $1.42 | x 2

Great Value
Black Beans

2lb | $2.74 | x 2

Great Value
Chunk Light Tuna in Water
(4-pack)

5oz | $3.52 | x 2

Great Value
Lentils

1lb | $1.34 | x 3

Great Value
Black Eyed Peas

1lb | $1.66 | x 2

Great Value
Navy Beans

1lb | $1.36 | x 2

Great Value
Chunk Style Pink Salmon

5oz | $1.80 | x 14

Protein

Beach Cliff
Sardines

3.75oz | $0.98 | x 8

Great Value
No-stir Creamy Natural Peanut Butter Spread

16oz | $1.84 | x 2

Great Value
Instant Nonfat Dry Milk

25.6oz | $8.43 | x 1

Great Value
Chunk Chicken Breast
(4-pack)

12.5oz | $9.36 | x 1

Eggylicious
Whole Egg Powder

16oz | $29.99 | x 1

Carbs

Great Value
All-purpose Flour

5lb | $2.34 | x 1

Quaker
Quick Grits White Hominy

24oz | $2.18 | x 2

Great Value
Long Grain Enriched Rice, White

5lb | $3.34 | x 2

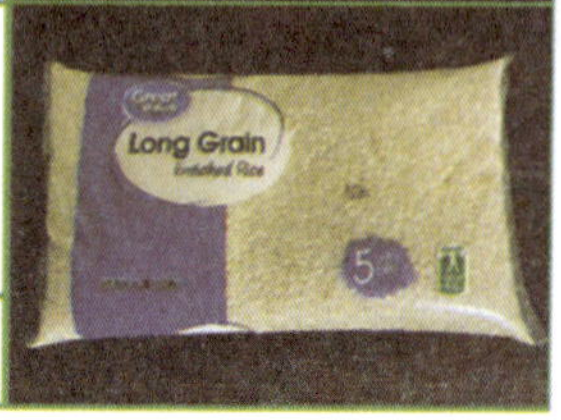

Great Value
Yellow Popping Corn

32oz | $2.28 | x 1

Martha White
Yellow Cornmeal Mix

32oz | $2.28 | x 1

Maruchan
Ramen

6-pack | $2.58 | x 2

Carbs

Great Value
Instant Mashed Potatoes

26.7oz · $3.62 · x 2

Great Value
Spaghetti

16oz · $0.98 · x 2

Great Value
Old Fashioned Oats

42oz · $3.98 · x 2

Fruits and Veggies

Great Value
Sun-Dried Raisins

20oz · $4.28 · x 2

Great Value
Canned Gren Peas
(6-pack)

15oz · $3.96 · x 12

Great Value
Canned Carrots
(6-pack)

14.5oz · $5.26 · x 12

Great Value
Green Beans
(6-pack)

14.5oz · $3.84 · x 8

Great Value
Sweetened Dried Blueberries

3.5oz · $3.28 · x 2

Great Value
Canned Petite Diced Tomatoes

14.5oz · $0.96 · x 6

Great Value
Fruit Cocktail

15oz · $1.48 · x 5

Condiments / Spices

Wyler's
Instant Bouillon Cubes

3.25oz | $2.37 | x 1

Great Value
Taco Seasoning

1.25oz | $0.52 | x 10

Great Value
Ranch Salad Dressing & Recipe Mix

1oz | $0.50 | x 1

Wyler's
Baking Soda

16oz | $0.92 | x 1

Clabber Girl
Baking Powder

8.1oz | $2.63 | x 1

Great Value
Ground Black Pepper

3oz | $3.82 | x 1

Great Value
Baking Cocoa

8oz | $2.48 | x 1

Morton
Iodized Salt

26oz | $1.46 | x 1

Morton
Ground Cinnamon

2.5oz | $1.28 | x 1

Great Value
Pure Cane Granulated Sugar

20oz | $2.12 | x 1

Great Value
Less Sodium Soy Sauce

15oz | $1.58 | x 1

Condiments / Spices

Great Value
White Vinegar

32oz | $1.38 | x 1

Folgers
Classic Roast Coffee Single Serve Packets

7-pack | $1.00 | x 2

Watkins
Vanilla Extract

1oz | $2.13 | x 1

Great Value
Raw Honey

12oz | $3.94 | x 1

LouAna
Coconut Oil

14oz | $4.94 | x 1

90-Days Meal Plan

1st MONTH

Week 1	Breakfast	Lunch	Dinner	Snack
DAY 1	• 2 **Biscuits** • 2 tbsp. peanut butter • 1 tbsp. honey	• 1 **Flatbread** • 1 svg. **Black Beans** • ½ pk. taco seasoning	• 1 svg. **Black Beans** • 1 pk. taco seasoning • 1 svg. **Rice** • 1 slice **Cornbread**	• 1 slice **Brownie**
	Calories 650	**Calories** 345	**Calories** 479	**Calories** 270.25
	Carbs 69 g	**Carbs** 58.5 g	**Carbs** 86 g	**Carbs** 40.5 g
	Fat 59 g	**Fat** 8.1 g	**Fat** 10.5 g	**Fat** 10 g
	Protein 13.1 g	**Protein** 12 g	**Protein** 14.2 g	**Protein** 5.6 g
DAY 2	• 1 svg. **Oatmeal** • 2 tbsp. peanut butter • 1 tsp. cocoa	• 1 can tuna • 1 **Flatbread** • ½ can peas	• 1 can tuna • 1 svg. **Potatoes** • ½ can peas	• 1 serv. **Popcorn**
	Calories 360	**Calories** 370	**Calories** 312.5	**Calories** 110
	Carbs 37 g	**Carbs** 34.5 g	**Carbs** 17.5 g	**Carbs** 25 g
	Fat 18.5 g	**Fat** 10.6 g	**Fat** 2 g	**Fat** 1 g
	Protein 13 g	**Protein** 36 g	**Protein** 25 g	**Protein** 4 g
DAY 3	• 2 **Biscuits** • 1 **Egg** • 1 oz pecans	• 1 **Flatbread** • 2 tbsp. peanut butter • 1 tbsp. honey	• 1 svg. **Lentils** • 1 svg. **Potatoes** • 2 slices **Cornbread**	• 1 serv. **Popcorn** • ½ cup raisins
	Calories 630.5	**Calories** 439	**Calories** 409	**Calories** 350
	Carbs 26.2 g	**Carbs** 49.5 g	**Carbs** 68 g	**Carbs** 89 g
	Fat 64.1 g	**Fat** 21.6 g	**Fat** 10 g	**Fat** 1 g
	Protein 12.6 g	**Protein** 11.1 g	**Protein** 14.2 g	**Protein** 6 g
DAY 4	• 1 svg. **Grits** • 2 **Flatbread** • 1 **Egg**	• 1 svg. **Lentils** • 1 svg. **Rice**	• 1 svg. **Pinto beans** • 1 svg. **Rice** • 1 slice **Cornbread**	• 1 svg. **Cornbread Delight** • 1 oz pecans
	Calories 544.5	**Calories** 270	**Calories** 479	**Calories** 553
	Carbs 78.1 g	**Carbs** 58 g	**Carbs** 86 g	**Carbs** 61 g
	Fat 19 g	**Fat** 0 g	**Fat** 10 g	**Fat** 30 g
	Protein 14.7 g	**Protein** 12 g	**Protein** 14.2 g	**Protein** 14 g

Biscuits, with peanut butter and honey

Flatbread, with Black Beans and taco seasoning

Rice, with Black Beans and taco seasoning, and Cornbread

One slice of Brownie

1st MONTH

Week 1	Breakfast		Lunch		Dinner		Snack	
DAY 5	• 1 svg. **Oatmeal** • 1 svg. milk powder • ¼ cup raisins		• 1 **Flatbread** • 1 svg. **Pinto beans** • 1 svg. **Small red beans** • 1 svg. **Rice**		• 1 svg. **Pinto beans** • 1 svg. **Small red beans** • ¼ pk. taco seasoning • 1 svg. **Rice** • 2 slices **Cornbread**		• 1 slice **Brownie** • 1 svg. **Cornbread Delight**	
	Calories	370	**Calories**	525	**Calories**	808	**Calories**	633.25
	Carbs	72 g	**Carbs**	103.5 g	**Carbs**	141 g	**Carbs**	65.5 g
	Fat	2.5 g	**Fat**	8.1 g	**Fat**	20.5 g	**Fat**	11 g
	Protein	11.5 g	**Protein**	23 g	**Protein**	24.5 g	**Protein**	9.6 g
DAY 6	• 2 **Biscuits** • 2 tbsp. peanut butter • 1 tbsp. honey		• 1 svg. **Lentils** • 1 svg. **Rice**		• 1 svg. **Pinto beans** • 1 svg. **Rice** • 1 slice **Cornbread**		• 1 serv. **Popcorn** • 1 oz pecans	
	Calories	650	**Calories**	270	**Calories**	479	**Calories**	300
	Carbs	69 g	**Carbs**	58 g	**Carbs**	86 g	**Carbs**	29 g
	Fat	59 g	**Fat**	0 g	**Fat**	10 g	**Fat**	21 g
	Protein	13.1 g	**Protein**	12 g	**Protein**	14.2 g	**Protein**	7 g
DAY 7	• 1 svg. **Grits** • 2 **Flatbread** • 1 **Egg**		• 1 can salmon • 1 svg. **Potatoes** • 1 tbsp. coconut oil • ½ can green beans • ½ can carrots		• 1 pk. ramen • ½ can peas • ½ can carrots • 1 can salmon		• 1 slice **Brownie** • 1 oz pecans	
	Calories	544.5	**Calories**	479	**Calories**	663	**Calories**	460.25
	Carbs	78.1 g	**Carbs**	36 g	**Carbs**	70 g	**Carbs**	44.5 g
	Fat	19 g	**Fat**	20 g	**Fat**	20.6 g	**Fat**	30 g
	Protein	14.7 g	**Protein**	36 g	**Protein**	44 g	**Protein**	8.6 g

Oatmeal, with peanut butter and cocoa

Potatoes, with tuna and peas

One serving of Popcorn

Egg, with Biscuits

Lentils, with Potatoes and Cornbread

One serving of raisins

Grits, with Egg and Flatbread

Cornbread Delight

1st MONTH				
Week 2	**Breakfast**	**Lunch**	**Dinner**	**Snack**
DAY 1	• 1 svg. **Cornbread delight**	• 1 **Flatbread** • 1 svg. **Pinto beans** • 1 svg. **Small red beans** • 1 svg. **Rice**	• 1 svg. **Pinto beans** • 1 svg. **Small red beans** • ¼ pk. taco seasoning • 1 svg. **Rice** • 2 slices **Cornbread**	• 1 serv. **Popcorn**
	Calories 363	**Calories** 525	**Calories** 808	**Calories** 110
	Carbs 57 g	**Carbs** 103.5 g	**Carbs** 141 g	**Carbs** 25 g
	Fat 10 g	**Fat** 8.1 g	**Fat** 20.5 g	**Fat** 1 g
	Protein 11 g	**Protein** 23 g	**Protein** 24.5 g	**Protein** 4 g
DAY 2	• 1 svg. **Oatmeal** • 2 tbsp. peanut butter • 1 tsp. cocoa • 1 oz pecans	• 1 can sardines • 2 **Flatbreads** • ½ can green beans	• 1 can sardines • 1 svg. **Potatoes** • ½ can green beans	• 1 slice **Brownie**
	Calories 550	**Calories** 565	**Calories** 275	**Calories** 270.25
	Carbs 41 g	**Carbs** 56 g	**Carbs** 25 g	**Carbs** 40.5 g
	Fat 38.5 g	**Fat** 27.2 g	**Fat** 12 g	**Fat** 10 g
	Protein 16 g	**Protein** 26.1 g	**Protein** 20 g	**Protein** 5.6 g
DAY 3	• 2 **Biscuits** • 1 **Egg**	• 1 **Flatbread** • 2 tbsp. peanut butter • 1 tbsp. honey	• 1 svg. **Lentils** • 1 svg. **Potatoes** • 2 slices **Cornbread**	• ½ cup raisins
	Calories 440.5	**Calories** 439	**Calories** 409	**Calories** 240
	Carbs 44.1 g	**Carbs** 49.5 g	**Carbs** 68 g	**Carbs** 64 g
	Fat 47.3 g	**Fat** 21.6 g	**Fat** 10 g	**Fat** 0 g
	Protein 9.6 g	**Protein** 11.1 g	**Protein** 14.2 g	**Protein** 2 g
DAY 4	• 1 svg. **Creamy grits** • 1 svg. milk • 2 tbsp. coconut oil	• 1 **Flatbread** • 1 svg. **Lentils** • 1 svg. **Rice**	• 1 svg. **Pinto beans** • 1 svg. **Rice** • 1 slice **Cornbread**	• 1 svg. **Cornbread Delight** • 1 oz pecans
	Calories 530	**Calories** 455	**Calories** 479	**Calories** 553
	Carbs 53 g	**Carbs** 82.5 g	**Carbs** 86 g	**Carbs** 61 g
	Fat 28.5 g	**Fat** 7.6 g	**Fat** 10 g	**Fat** 30 g
	Protein 19 g	**Protein** 16 g	**Protein** 14.2 g	**Protein** 14 g

Pinto Beans and Small Red Beans, with Rice and Flatbread

2 Bean Chili (Pinto Beans, Small Red Beans, Rice and Cornbread)

Pinto Beans, with Rice and Cornbread

Creamy Grits

1st MONTH

Week 2	Breakfast		Lunch		Dinner		Snack	
DAY 5	• 1 svg. **Oatmeal** • 1 svg. milk • ¼ cup raisins		• 1 svg. **Creamy grits** • ½ can chicken		• 1 svg. **Spaghetti** • ½ can chicken • ½ can tomatoes • ½ can peas • ½ can carrots		• 2 serv. **Popcorn**	
	Calories	300	**Calories**	350	**Calories**	540	**Calories**	220
	Carbs	71 g	**Carbs**	41 g	**Carbs**	80 g	**Carbs**	50 g
	Fat	2.5 g	**Fat**	3.7 g	**Fat**	4 g	**Fat**	2 g
	Protein	14 g	**Protein**	39 g	**Protein**	41 g	**Protein**	8 g
DAY 6	• 2 **Biscuits** • 2 tbsp. peanut butter • 1 tbsp. honey		• 1 **Flatbread** • 1 svg. **Black Beans** • ½ pk. taco seasoning		• 1 svg. **Black Beans** • 1 pk. taco seasoning • 1 svg. **Rice** • 1 slice **Cornbread**		• 1 slice **Brownie**	
	Calories	650	**Calories**	345	**Calories**	479	**Calories**	270.25
	Carbs	69 g	**Carbs**	58.5 g	**Carbs**	86 g	**Carbs**	40.5 g
	Fat	59 g	**Fat**	8.1 g	**Fat**	10.5 g	**Fat**	10 g
	Protein	13.1 g	**Protein**	12 g	**Protein**	14.2 g	**Protein**	5.6 g
DAY 7	• 1 svg. **Grits** • 2 **Eggs**		• 1 can tuna • ½ can peas • 1 svg. **Rice**		• 1 can tuna • ½ can peas • 1 svg. **Potatoes**		• 1 can fruit cocktail • 1 oz pecans	
	Calories	219	**Calories**	295	**Calories**	215	**Calories**	540
	Carbs	29.2 g	**Carbs**	45 g	**Carbs**	27 g	**Carbs**	94 g
	Fat	7.1 g	**Fat**	2 g	**Fat**	2 g	**Fat**	20 g
	Protein	10.2 g	**Protein**	25 g	**Protein**	24 g	**Protein**	3 g

One serving of pecans

Spaghetti, with chicken, peas, tomatoes and carrots

Oatmeal, with Milk and raisins

Fruit cocktail

Tuna, with Rice and peas

Creamy Grits, with chicken

Potatoes, with sardines and green beans

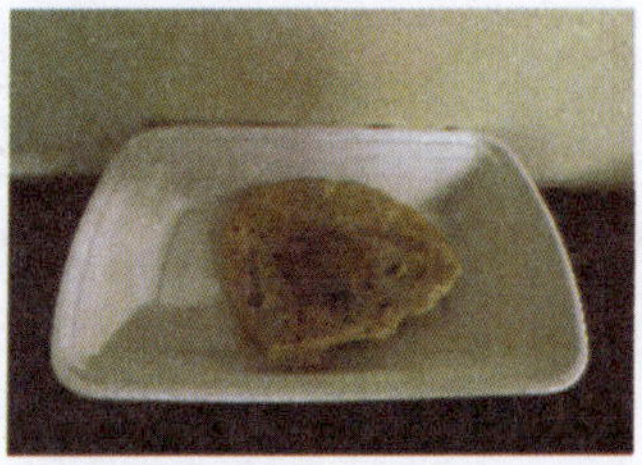

Flatbread, with peanut butter and honey

1st MONTH								
Week 3	**Breakfast**		**Lunch**		**Dinner**		**Snack**	
DAY 1	• 2 **Biscuits** • 2 tbsp. peanut butter • 1 tbsp. honey		• 1 **Flatbread** • 1 svg. **Black Beans** • ½ pk. taco seasoning		• 1 svg. **Black Beans** • 1 pk. taco seasoning • 1 svg. **Rice** • 1 slice **Cornbread**		• 1 serv. **Popcorn** • 1 oz pecans	
	Calories	650	**Calories**	345	**Calories**	479	**Calories**	300
	Carbs	69 g	**Carbs**	58.5 g	**Carbs**	86 g	**Carbs**	29 g
	Fat	59 g	**Fat**	8.1 g	**Fat**	10.5 g	**Fat**	21 g
	Protein	13.1 g	**Protein**	12 g	**Protein**	14.2 g	**Protein**	7 g
DAY 2	• 1 svg. **Oatmeal** • 1 tbsp. peanut butter • 1 tsp. cocoa • 1 tbsp. raisins		• 1 **Flatbread** • 1 svg. **Pinto beans** • 1 svg. **Small red beans** • 1 svg. **Rice**		• 2 **Eggs** • ½ can tomatoes • 1 svg. **Rice**		• 1 serv. **Popcorn** • 1 oz pecans	
	Calories	295	**Calories**	525	**Calories**	293	**Calories**	300
	Carbs	41 g	**Carbs**	103.5 g	**Carbs**	44.2 g	**Carbs**	29 g
	Fat	11 g	**Fat**	8.1 g	**Fat**	6.6 g	**Fat**	21 g
	Protein	9.5 g	**Protein**	23 g	**Protein**	12.2 g	**Protein**	7 g
DAY 3	• 2 **Biscuits** • 2 tbsp. peanut butter • 1 tbsp. honey		• 1 svg. **Lentils** • 1 svg. **Rice** • 1 **Flatbread**		• 1 svg. **Lentils** • 1 svg. **Potatoes** • 2 slices **Cornbread**		• 1 slice **Brownie**	
	Calories	650	**Calories**	455	**Calories**	409	**Calories**	270.25
	Carbs	69 g	**Carbs**	82.5 g	**Carbs**	68 g	**Carbs**	40.5 g
	Fat	59 g	**Fat**	7.6 g	**Fat**	10 g	**Fat**	10 g
	Protein	13.1 g	**Protein**	16 g	**Protein**	14.2 g	**Protein**	5.6 g
DAY 4	• 1 svg. **Creamy grits** • ½ can sardines		• ½ can sardines • 1 svg. **Potatoes** • ½ can green beans		• 1 svg. **Pinto beans** • 1 svg. **Rice** • 1 slice **Cornbread**		• 1 svg. **Cornbread Delight** • 1 oz pecans	
	Calories	290	**Calories**	195	**Calories**	479	**Calories**	553
	Carbs	41 g	**Carbs**	25 g	**Carbs**	86 g	**Carbs**	61 g
	Fat	6.5 g	**Fat**	6 g	**Fat**	10 g	**Fat**	30 g
	Protein	19 g	**Protein**	12 g	**Protein**	14.2 g	**Protein**	14 g
DAY 5	• 1 svg. **Oatmeal** • 1 svg. milk powder • ¼ cup raisins		• 1 **Flatbread** • 1 svg. **Pinto beans** • 1 svg. **Small red beans** • 1 svg. **Rice**		• 1 **Flatbread** • 1 svg. **Lentils** • 1 svg. **Rice**		• 1 slice **Brownie** • 1 oz pecans	
	Calories	370	**Calories**	525	**Calories**	455	**Calories**	460.25
	Carbs	72 g	**Carbs**	103.5 g	**Carbs**	82.5 g	**Carbs**	44.5 g
	Fat	2.5 g	**Fat**	8.1 g	**Fat**	7.6 g	**Fat**	30 g
	Protein	11.5 g	**Protein**	23 g	**Protein**	16 g	**Protein**	8.6 g

1st MONTH

Week 3	Breakfast		Lunch		Dinner		Snack	
DAY 6	• 2 **Biscuits** • 2 tbsp. peanut butter • 1 tbsp. honey		• 1 svg. **Lentils** • 1 svg. **Rice**		• 1 **Flatbread** • 2 tbsp. peanut butter • 1 tbsp. honey		• 1 serv. **Popcorn** • 1 oz pecans	
	Calories	650	**Calories**	270	**Calories**	439	**Calories**	300
	Carbs	69 g	**Carbs**	58 g	**Carbs**	49.5 g	**Carbs**	29 g
	Fat	59 g	**Fat**	0 g	**Fat**	21.6 g	**Fat**	21 g
	Protein	13.1 g	**Protein**	12 g	**Protein**	11.1 g	**Protein**	7 g
DAY 7	• 1 svg. **Grits** • 2 **Flatbreads** • 1 **Egg**		• 1 can salmon • 1 svg. **Potatoes** • 1 tbsp. coconut oil • ½ can green beans • ½ can carrots		• 1 pk. ramen • ½ can peas • ½ can carrots • 1 can salmon		• 1 slice **Brownie** • 1 oz pecans	
	Calories	544.5	**Calories**	479	**Calories**	663	**Calories**	460.25
	Carbs	78.1 g	**Carbs**	36 g	**Carbs**	70 g	**Carbs**	44.5 g
	Fat	19 g	**Fat**	20 g	**Fat**	20.6 g	**Fat**	30 g
	Protein	14.7 g	**Protein**	36 g	**Protein**	44 g	**Protein**	8.6 g

Week 4	Breakfast		Lunch		Dinner		Snack	
DAY 1	• 1 svg. **Creamy grits** • 1 can chicken		• ½ can chicken • 2 **Flatbreads** • ½ can carrots		• 1 svg. **Spaghetti** • ½ can chicken • ½ can carrots		• 1 serv. **Popcorn** • 1 oz pecans	
	Calories	491	**Calories**	540	**Calories**	375.2	**Calories**	300
	Carbs	41 g	**Carbs**	54 g	**Carbs**	39.75 g	**Carbs**	29 g
	Fat	6.8 g	**Fat**	18.2 g	**Fat**	3 g	**Fat**	21 g
	Protein	67 g	**Protein**	36 g	**Protein**	34.75 g	**Protein**	7 g

Oatmeal, with peanut butter, cocoa and raisins

Eggs, with Rice and tomatoes

Creamy Grits, with sardines

Flatbread, with Lentils and Rice

Lentils and Rice

Salmon, with Potatoes, green beans and carrots

Ramen, with salmon, peas and carrots

1st MONTH				
Week 4	**Breakfast**	**Lunch**	**Dinner**	**Snack**
DAY 2	• 1 svg. **Oatmeal** • 2 tbsp. peanut butter • 1 tsp. cocoa	• 1 **Flatbread** • 1 svg. **Pinto beans** • 1 svg. **Small red beans** • 1 svg. **Rice**	• 1 svg. **Black Beans** • 1 pk. taco seasoning • 1 svg. **Rice** • 1 slice **Cornbread**	• 1 slice **Brownie**
	Calories 360 Carbs 37 g Fat 18.5 g Protein 13 g	Calories 525 Carbs 103.5 g Fat 8.1 g Protein 23 g	Calories 479 Carbs 86 g Fat 10.5 g Protein 14.2 g	Calories 270.25 Carbs 40.5 g Fat 10 g Protein 5.6 g
DAY 3	• 2 svgs. **Grits** • 2 **Eggs**	• 1 **Flatbread** • 2 tbsp. peanut butter • 1 tbsp. honey	• 1 svg. **Lentils** • 1 svg. **Potatoes** • 2 slices **Cornbread**	• ½ cup raisins
	Calories 349 Carbs 58.2 g Fat 7.6 g Protein 13.2 g	Calories 439 Carbs 49.5 g Fat 21.6 g Protein 11.1 g	Calories 409 Carbs 68 g Fat 10 g Protein 14.2 g	Calories 240 Carbs 64 g Fat 0 g Protein 2 g
DAY 4	• 1 svg. **Creamy Grits**	• 2 **Biscuits** • 2 tbsp. peanut butter • 1 tbsp. honey	• 1 svg. **Pinto beans** • 1 svg. **Rice** • 1 slice **Cornbread**	• 1 serv. **Popcorn** • 1 oz pecans
	Calories 460 Carbs 70 g Fat 15 g Protein 14 g	Calories 650 Carbs 69 g Fat 59 g Protein 13.1 g	Calories 479 Carbs 86 g Fat 10 g Protein 14.2 g	Calories 300 Carbs 29 g Fat 21 g Protein 7 g
DAY 5	• 1 svg. **Oatmeal** • 1 svg. milk powder • ¼ cup raisins	• 1 svg. **Lentils** • 1 svg. **Rice** • 1 **Flatbread**	• 1 svg. **Pinto beans** • 1 svg. **Rice** • 1 slice **Cornbread**	• 1 svg. **Cornbread Delight** • 1 oz pecans
	Calories 370 Carbs 72 g Fat 2.5 g Protein 11.5 g	Calories 455 Carbs 82.5 g Fat 7.6 g Protein 16 g	Calories 479 Carbs 86 g Fat 10 g Protein 14.2 g	Calories 553 Carbs 61 g Fat 30 g Protein 14 g
DAY 6	• 1 **Flatbread** • 2 tbsp. peanut butter • 1 tbsp. honey	• 1 **Flatbread** • 1 svg. **Pinto beans** • 1 svg. **Small red beans** • 1 svg. **Rice**	• 1 svg. **Black Beans** • 1 svg. **Rice** • 1 slice **Cornbread**	• 1 serv. **Popcorn**
	Calories 439 Carbs 49.5 g Fat 21.6 g Protein 11.1 g	Calories 525 Carbs 103.5 g Fat 8.1 g Protein 23 g	Calories 48 Carbs 86 g Fat 10.5 g Protein 14.2 g	Calories 110 Carbs 25 g Fat 1 g Protein 4 g

1st MONTH								
Week 4	**Breakfast**		**Lunch**		**Dinner**		**Snack**	
DAY 7	• 2 svgs. **Savory grits** • 2 **Eggs**		• 1 can tuna • ½ can peas • 1 svg. **Rice**		• 1 can tuna • ½ can peas • 1 svg. **Potatoes**		• 1 slice **Brownie** • 1 oz pecans	
	Calories	304.5	**Calories**	295	**Calories**	312.5	**Calories**	460.25
	Carbs	58.1 g	**Carbs**	45 g	**Carbs**	17.5 g	**Carbs**	44.5 g
	Fat	5.5 g	**Fat**	2 g	**Fat**	2 g	**Fat**	30 g
	Protein	9.6 g	**Protein**	25 g	**Protein**	25 g	**Protein**	8.6 g

Week 5	**Breakfast**		**Lunch**		**Dinner**		**Snack**	
DAY 1	• 2 **Biscuits** • 2 tbsp. peanut butter • 1 tbsp. honey		• 1 **Flatbread** • 1 svg. **Black Beans** • ½ pk. taco seasoning		• 1 svg. **Black Beans** • 1 pk. taco seasoning • 1 svg. **Rice** • 1 slice **Cornbread**		• 1 slice **Brownie**	
	Calories	650	**Calories**	345	**Calories**	479	**Calories**	270.25
	Carbs	69 g	**Carbs**	58.5 g	**Carbs**	86 g	**Carbs**	40.5 g
	Fat	59 g	**Fat**	8.1 g	**Fat**	10.5 g	**Fat**	10 g
	Protein	13.1 g	**Protein**	12 g	**Protein**	14.2 g	**Protein**	5.6 g
DAY 2	• 1 svg. **Oatmeal** • 2 tbsp. peanut butter • 1 tsp. cocoa		• 1 can tuna • 1 **Flatbread** • ½ can peas		• 1 can tuna • 1 svg. **Potatoes** • ½ can peas		• 1 serv. **Popcorn**	
	Calories	360	**Calories**	370	**Calories**	312.5	**Calories**	110
	Carbs	37 g	**Carbs**	34.5 g	**Carbs**	17.5 g	**Carbs**	25 g
	Fat	18.5 g	**Fat**	10.6 g	**Fat**	2 g	**Fat**	1 g
	Protein	13 g	**Protein**	36 g	**Protein**	25 g	**Protein**	4 g

Chicken, with carrots and Flatbread

Spaghetti, with chicken and carrots

Grits and Eggs

2nd MONTH

Week 1	Breakfast	Lunch	Dinner	Snack
DAY 1	• 1 svg. **Blueberry Oatmeal**	• 1 svg. **Potato carrot soup**	• 1 svg. **Veggie bean soup with cornbread**	• 1 serv. **Popcorn**
	Calories 370	Calories 212	Calories 370	Calories 110
	Carbs 73 g	Carbs 42 g	Carbs 62 g	Carbs 25 g
	Fat 2.5 g	Fat 4 g	Fat 10.5 g	Fat 1 g
	Protein 13 g	Protein 11 g	Protein 13.2 g	Protein 4 g
DAY 2	• 1 svg. **Breakfast rice porridge**	• 1 svg. **Black-eyed peas** • 1 svg. **Rice** • 1 slice **Cornbread**	• 1 svg. **Southwest pizza**	• 1 oz pecans
	Calories 240	Calories 489	Calories 614	Calories 190
	Carbs 37 g	Carbs 85 g	Carbs 12 g	Carbs 4 g
	Fat 0 g	Fat 10 g	Fat 16 g	Fat 20 g
	Protein 11 g	Protein 14.2 g	Protein 25 g	Protein 3 g
DAY 3	• 2 **Pancakes** with honey drizzle	• ½ can chicken • 2 **Flatbreads** • ½ can carrots	• 1 svg. **Spaghetti** • ½ can chicken • ½ can tomatoes • ½ can peas • ½ can carrots	• 1 slice **Pecan raisin bread**
	Calories 343.67	Calories 542.5	Calories 540	Calories 208.5
	Carbs 40.56 g	Carbs 58.25 g	Carbs 80 g	Carbs 28.9 g
	Fat 16.6 g	Fat 17.2 g	Fat 4 g	Fat 10.4 g
	Protein 3.35 g	Protein 35.85 g	Protein 41 g	Protein 2.23 g
DAY 4	• 2 **Biscuits** • 2 tbsp. peanut butter • 1 tbsp. honey	• 1 svg. **Lentils** • 1 svg. **Rice**	• 1 svg. **Pinto beans** • 1 svg. **Rice** • 1 slice **Cornbread**	• 1 serv. **Popcorn**
	Calories 650	Calories 270	Calories 479	Calories 110
	Carbs 69 g	Carbs 58 g	Carbs 86 g	Carbs 25 g
	Fat 59 g	Fat 0 g	Fat 10 g	Fat 1 g
	Protein 13.1 g	Protein 12 g	Protein 14.2 g	Protein 4 g
DAY 5	• 2 **Biscuits** • 2 tbsp. peanut butter • 1 tbsp. honey	• 1 **Flatbread** • 1 svg. **Black Beans** • ½ pk. taco seasoning	• 1 svg. **Navy beans** • 1 svg. **Rice** • 1 slice **Cornbread**	• 1 slice **Brownie**
	Calories 650	Calories 345	Calories 479	Calories 270.25
	Carbs 69 g	Carbs 58.5 g	Carbs 85 g	Carbs 40.5 g
	Fat 59 g	Fat 8.1 g	Fat 10.5 g	Fat 10 g
	Protein 13.1 g	Protein 12 g	Protein 14.2 g	Protein 5.6 g

2nd MONTH

Week 1	Breakfast		Lunch		Dinner		Snack	
DAY 5	• 1 svg. **Oatmeal** • 1 svg. milk powder • ¼ cup raisins		• 1 can tuna • 1 **Flatbread** • ½ can peas		• 1 can tuna • 1 svg. **Potatoes** • ½ can peas		• 1 svg. **Cornbread delight**	
	Calories	300	Calories	370	Calories	312.5	Calories	363
	Carbs	71 g	Carbs	34.5 g	Carbs	17.5 g	Carbs	57 g
	Fat	2.5 g	Fat	10.6 g	Fat	2 g	Fat	10 g
	Protein	14 g	Protein	36 g	Protein	25 g	Protein	11 g
DAY 7	• 1 svg. **Rice** • 2 **Eggs** • 1 tbsp. soy sauce		• 1 svg. **Potato carrot soup**		• 1 svg. **Pinto beans** • 1 svg. **Small red beans** • ¼ pk. taco seasoning • 1 svg. **Rice** • 2 slices **Cornbread**		• 1 slice **Pecan raisin bread**	
	Calories	254	Calories	212	Calories	808	Calories	208.5
	Carbs	37.2 g	Carbs	42 g	Carbs	141 g	Carbs	28.9 g
	Fat	6.6 g	Fat	4 g	Fat	20.5 g	Fat	10.4 g
	Protein	11.2 g	Protein	11 g	Protein	24.5 g	Protein	2.23 g

Week 2	Breakfast		Lunch		Dinner		Snack	
DAY 1	• 2 **Biscuits** • 2 tbsp. peanut butter • 1 tbsp. honey		• 1 svg. **Lentils** • 1 svg. **Rice**		• 1 svg. **Pinto beans** • 1 svg. **Rice** • 1 slice **Cornbread**		• 1 serv. **Popcorn**	
	Calories	650	Calories	270	Calories	479	Calories	110
	Carbs	69 g	Carbs	58 g	Carbs	86 g	Carbs	25 g
	Fat	59 g	Fat	0 g	Fat	10 g	Fat	1 g
	Protein	13.1 g	Protein	12 g	Protein	14.2 g	Protein	4 g

Blueberry Oatmeal

Potato Carrot Soup

Veggie Bean Soup with Cornbread

Breakfast Rice Porridge

Black-Eyed Peas, with Rice and Cornbread

Southwest Pizza

Pancakes, with honey drizzle

Tuna, with Flatbread and peas

2nd MONTH				
Week 2	**Breakfast**	**Lunch**	**Dinner**	**Snack**
DAY 2	• 2 **Pancakes** with honey drizzle	• 1 **Flatbread** • 1 svg. **Pinto beans** • 1 svg. **Small red beans** • 1 svg. **Rice**	• 1 svg. **Veggie bean soup with cornbread**	• 1 slice **Pecan raisin bread**
	Calories 343.67 Carbs 40.56 g Fat 16.6 g Protein 3.35 g	Calories 525 Carbs 103.5 g Fat 8.1 g Protein 23 g	Calories 370 Carbs 62 g Fat 10.5 g Protein 13.2 g	Calories 208.5 Carbs 28.9 g Fat 10.4 g Protein 2.23 g
DAY 3	• 2 **Biscuits** • 2 tbsp. peanut butter • 1 tbsp. honey	• 2 **Eggs** • ½ can tomatoes • 1 svg. **Rice**	• 2 **Eggs** • ½ can tomatoes • 1 svg. **Rice**	• 1 oz pecans
	Calories 650 Carbs 69 g Fat 59 g Protein 13.1 g	Calories 293 Carbs 44.2 g Fat 6.6 g Protein 12.2 g	Calories 293 Carbs 44.2 g Fat 6.6 g Protein 12.2 g	Calories 190 Carbs 4 g Fat 20 g Protein 3 g
DAY 4	• 1 svg. **Blueberry Oatmeal**	• 1 can tuna • 1 svg. **Rice** • ½ can carrots	• 1 can tuna • 1 svg. **Potatoes** • ½ can carrots	• 1 slice **Brownie**
	Calories 370 Carbs 73 g Fat 2.5 g Protein 13 g	Calories 321 Carbs 49 g Fat 2 g Protein 24 g	Calories 241 Carbs 31 g Fat 2 g Protein 23 g	Calories 270.25 Carbs 40.5 g Fat 10 g Protein 5.6 g
DAY 5	• 1 svg. **Cornbread delight**	• 1 svg. **Taco soup**	• 1 svg. **Veggie bean soup with cornbread**	• 1 slice **Pecan raisin bread**
	Calories 363 Carbs 57 g Fat 10 g Protein 11 g	Calories 382 Carbs 63 g Fat 1.5 g Protein 17 g	Calories 370 Carbs 63 g Fat 1.5 g Protein 17 g	Calories 208.5 Carbs 28.9 g Fat 10.4 g Protein 2.23 g
DAY 6	• 1 svg. **Rice** • 2 **Eggs** • 1 tbsp. soy sauce	• 1 svg. **Black-eyed peas** • 1 svg. **Rice** • 1 slice **Cornbread**	• 1 svg. **Navy beans** • 1 svg. **Rice** • 1 slice **Cornbread**	• 1 serv. **Popcorn**
	Calories 254 Carbs 37.2 g Fat 6.6 g Protein 11.2 g	Calories 489 Carbs 85 g Fat 10 g Protein 14.2 g	Calories 479 Carbs 85 g Fat 10.5 g Protein 14.2 g	Calories 110 Carbs 25 g Fat 1 g Protein 4 g

2nd MONTH

Week 2	Breakfast		Lunch		Dinner		Snack	
DAY 7	• 1 svg. **Oatmeal** • 2 tbsp. peanut butter • 1 tsp. cocoa		• 1 svg. **Potato carrot soup**		• 1 svg. **Pinto beans** • 1 svg. **Small red beans** • ¼ pk. taco seasoning • 1 svg. **Rice** • 2 slices **Cornbread**		• 1 oz pecans	
	Calories	360	**Calories**	212	**Calories**	808	**Calories**	190
	Carbs	37 g	**Carbs**	42 g	**Carbs**	141 g	**Carbs**	4 g
	Fat	18.5 g	**Fat**	4 g	**Fat**	20.5 g	**Fat**	20 g
	Protein	13 g	**Protein**	11 g	**Protein**	24.5 g	**Protein**	3 g

Week 3	Breakfast		Lunch		Dinner		Snack	
DAY 1	• 1 svg. **Oatmeal** • 1 svg. milk powder • ¼ cup raisins		• 1 svg. **Lentils** • 1 svg. **Potatoes** • 2 slices **Cornbread**		• 1 svg. **Taco soup**		• 1 serv. **Popcorn**	
	Calories	300	**Calories**	409	**Calories**	382	**Calories**	110
	Carbs	71 g	**Carbs**	68 g	**Carbs**	63 g	**Carbs**	25 g
	Fat	2.5 g	**Fat**	10 g	**Fat**	1.5 g	**Fat**	1 g
	Protein	14 g	**Protein**	14.2 g	**Protein**	17 g	**Protein**	4 g
DAY 2	• 2 **Pancakes** with honey drizzle		• 1 svg. **Potato carrot soup**		• 1 svg. **Southwest pizza**		• 1 slice **Pecan raisin bread**	
	Calories	343.67	**Calories**	212	**Calories**	614	**Calories**	208.5
	Carbs	40.56 g	**Carbs**	42 g	**Carbs**	12 g	**Carbs**	28.9 g
	Fat	16.6 g	**Fat**	4 g	**Fat**	16 g	**Fat**	10.4 g
	Protein	3.35 g	**Protein**	11 g	**Protein**	25 g	**Protein**	2.23 g
DAY 3	• 1 svg. **Oatmeal** • 2 tbsp. peanut butter • 1 tsp. cocoa		• 1 svg **Creamy grits** • ½ can sardines		• 1 can sardines • 2 **Flatbreads** • ½ can green beans		• 1 serv. **Popcorn**	
	Calories	360	**Calories**	290	**Calories**	565	**Calories**	110
	Carbs	37 g	**Carbs**	41 g	**Carbs**	56 g	**Carbs**	25 g
	Fat	18.5 g	**Fat**	6.5 g	**Fat**	27.2 g	**Fat**	1 g
	Protein	13 g	**Protein**	19 g	**Protein**	26.1 g	**Protein**	4 g

Tuna, with Rice and carrots

Tuna, with Potatoes and carrots

Taco Soup

Egg, with Rice and soy sauce

2nd MONTH

Week 3	Breakfast		Lunch		Dinner		Snack	
DAY 4	• 1 svg. **Oatmeal** • 1 svg. milk powder • ¼ cup raisins		• 1 **Flatbread** • 1 svg. **Pinto beans** • 1 svg. **Small red beans** • 1 svg. **Rice**		• 1 svg. **Veggie bean soup with cornbread**		• 1 oz pecans	
	Calories	300	Calories	525	Calories	370	Calories	190
	Carbs	71 g	Carbs	103.5 g	Carbs	62 g	Carbs	4 g
	Fat	2.5 g	Fat	8.1 g	Fat	10.5 g	Fat	20 g
	Protein	14 g	Protein	23 g	Protein	13.2 g	Protein	3 g
DAY 5	• 1 svg. **Grits** • 2 **Flatbreads** • 1 **Egg**		• 1 svg. **Lentils** • 1 svg. **Potatoes** • 2 slices **Cornbread**		• 1 **Flatbread** • 1 svg. **Pinto beans** • 1 svg. **Small red beans** • 1 svg. **Rice**		• 1 serv. **Popcorn**	
	Calories	544.5	Calories	409	Calories	525	Calories	110
	Carbs	78.1 g	Carbs	68 g	Carbs	103.5 g	Carbs	25 g
	Fat	19 g	Fat	10 g	Fat	8.1 g	Fat	1 g
	Protein	14.7 g	Protein	14.2 g	Protein	23 g	Protein	4 g
DAY 6	• 1 svg. **Rice** • 2 **Eggs** • 1 tbsp. soy sauce		• 1 **Flatbread** • 1 svg. **Pinto beans** • 1 svg. **Small red beans** • 1 svg. **Rice**		• 1 svg. **Navy beans** • 1 svg. **Rice** • 1 slice **Cornbread**		• 1 slice **Pecan raisin bread**	
	Calories	254	Calories	525	Calories	479	Calories	208.5
	Carbs	37.2 g	Carbs	103.5 g	Carbs	85 g	Carbs	28.9 g
	Fat	6.6 g	Fat	8.1 g	Fat	10.5 g	Fat	10.4 g
	Protein	11.2 g	Protein	23 g	Protein	14.2 g	Protein	2.23 g
DAY 7	• 1 svg. **Breakfast rice porridge**		• 1 svg. **Navy beans** • 1 svg. **Rice** • 1 slice **Cornbread**		• 1 svg. **Veggie bean soup with cornbread**		• 1 oz pecans	
	Calories	240	Calories	479	Calories	370	Calories	190
	Carbs	37 g	Carbs	85 g	Carbs	62 g	Carbs	4 g
	Fat	0 g	Fat	10.5 g	Fat	10.5 g	Fat	20 g
	Protein	11 g	Protein	14.2 g	Protein	13.2 g	Protein	3 g

Flatbread, with sardines and green beans

Navy Beans, with Rice and Cornbread

Pecan Raisin Bread

2nd MONTH

Week 4	Breakfast		Lunch		Dinner		Snack	
DAY 1	• 1 svg. **Rice** • 2 **Eggs** • 1 tbsp. soy sauce		• 1 can salmon • 1 svg. **Potatoes** • 1 tbsp. coconut oil • ½ can green beans • ½ can carrots		• 1 pk. ramen • ½ can peas • ½ can carrots • 1 can salmon		• 1 slice **Pecan raisin bread**	
	Calories	254	Calories	479	Calories	663	Calories	208.5
	Carbs	37.2 g	Carbs	36 g	Carbs	70 g	Carbs	28.9 g
	Fat	6.6 g	Fat	20 g	Fat	20.6 g	Fat	10.4 g
	Protein	11.2 g	Protein	36 g	Protein	44 g	Protein	2.23 g
DAY 2	• 1 svg. **Blueberry Oatmeal**		• 1 svg. **Potato carrot soup**		• 1 svg. **Pinto beans** • 1 svg. **Small red beans** • ¼ pk. taco seasoning • 1 svg. **Rice** • 2 slices **Cornbread**		• 1 serv. **Popcorn**	
	Calories	370	Calories	212	Calories	808	Calories	110
	Carbs	73 g	Carbs	42 g	Carbs	141 g	Carbs	25 g
	Fat	2.5 g	Fat	4 g	Fat	20.5 g	Fat	1 g
	Protein	13 g	Protein	11 g	Protein	24.5 g	Protein	4 g
DAY 3	• 2 **Pancakes** with honey drizzle		• 1 svg. **Black Beans** • 1 pk. taco seasoning • 1 svg. **Rice** • 1 slice **Cornbread**		• 1 svg. **Grits** • 2 **Flatbreads** • 1 **Egg**		• 1 oz pecans	
	Calories	343.67	Calories	479	Calories	544.5	Calories	190
	Carbs	40.56 g	Carbs	86 g	Carbs	78.1 g	Carbs	4 g
	Fat	16.6 g	Fat	10.5 g	Fat	19 g	Fat	20 g
	Protein	3.35 g	Protein	14.2 g	Protein	14.7 g	Protein	3 g
DAY 4	• 1 svg. **Cornbread delight**		• 1 svg. **Taco soup**		• 1 svg. **Southwest pizza**		• 1 slice **Pecan raisin bread**	
	Calories	363	Calories	382	Calories	614	Calories	208.5
	Carbs	57 g	Carbs	63 g	Carbs	12 g	Carbs	28.9 g
	Fat	10 g	Fat	1.5 g	Fat	16 g	Fat	10.4 g
	Protein	11 g	Protein	17 g	Protein	25 g	Protein	2.23 g
DAY 5	• 1 svg. **Rice** • 2 **Eggs** • 1 tbsp. soy sauce		• 1 svg. **Black Beans** • 1 pk. taco seasoning • 1 svg. **Rice** • 1 slice **Cornbread**		• 1 svg. **Grits** • 2 **Flatbreads** • 1 **Egg**		• 1 oz pecans	
	Calories	254	Calories	479	Calories	544.5	Calories	190
	Carbs	37.2 g	Carbs	86 g	Carbs	78.1 g	Carbs	4 g
	Fat	6.6 g	Fat	10.5 g	Fat	19 g	Fat	20 g
	Protein	11.2 g	Protein	14.2 g	Protein	14.7 g	Protein	3 g

2nd MONTH

Week 4	Breakfast		Lunch		Dinner		Snack	
DAY 6	• 1 svg. **Breakfast rice porridge**		• 1 svg. **Lentils** • 1 svg. **Potatoes** • 2 slices **Cornbread**		• **1 Flatbread** • 1 svg. **Pinto beans** • 1 svg. **Small red beans** • 1 svg. **Rice**		• 1 slice **Pecan raisin bread**	
	Calories	240	Calories	409	Calories	525	Calories	208.5
	Carbs	37 g	Carbs	68 g	Carbs	103.5 g	Carbs	28.9 g
	Fat	0 g	Fat	10 g	Fat	8.1 g	Fat	10.4 g
	Protein	11 g	Protein	14.2 g	Protein	23 g	Protein	2.23 g
DAY 7	• 1 svg. **Rice** • **2 Eggs** • 1 tbsp. soy sauce		• 1 can sardines • **2 Flatbreads** • ½ can green beans		• 1 can sardines • 1 svg. **Potatoes** • ½ can green beans		• 1 oz pecans	
	Calories	254	Calories	565	Calories	275	Calories	190
	Carbs	37.2 g	Carbs	56 g	Carbs	25 g	Carbs	4 g
	Fat	6.6 g	Fat	27.2 g	Fat	12 g	Fat	20 g
	Protein	11.2 g	Protein	26.1 g	Protein	20 g	Protein	3 g

Week 5	Breakfast		Lunch		Dinner		Snack	
DAY 1	• 1 svg. **Grits** • **2 Flatbreads** • **1 Egg**		• 1 svg. **Navy beans** • 1 svg. **Rice** • 1 slice **Cornbread**		• 1 svg. **Veggie bean soup with cornbread**		• 1 oz pecans	
	Calories	544.5	Calories	479	Calories	370	Calories	190
	Carbs	78.1 g	Carbs	85 g	Carbs	62 g	Carbs	4 g
	Fat	19 g	Fat	10.5 g	Fat	10.5 g	Fat	20 g
	Protein	14.7 g	Protein	14.2 g	Protein	13.2 g	Protein	3 g
DAY 7	• 1 svg. **Breakfast rice porridge**		• **1 Flatbread** • 1 svg. **Black Beans** • ½ pk. taco seasoning		• 1 svg. **Taco soup**		• 1 slice **Brownie**	
	Calories	240	Calories	345	Calories	382	Calories	270.25
	Carbs	37 g	Carbs	58.5 g	Carbs	63 g	Carbs	40.5 g
	Fat	0 g	Fat	8.1 g	Fat	1.5 g	Fat	10 g
	Protein	11 g	Protein	12 g	Protein	17 g	Protein	5.6 g

3rd MONTH

Week 1	Breakfast		Lunch		Dinner		Snack	
DAY 1	• 2 **Biscuits** • 1 **Egg**		• 2 **Eggs** • ½ can tomatoes • 1 svg. **Rice**		• 2 **Eggs** • ½ can tomatoes • 1 svg. **Rice**		• 1 oz pecans	
	Calories	440.5	Calories	293	Calories	293	Calories	190
	Carbs	44.1 g	Carbs	44.2 g	Carbs	44.2 g	Carbs	4 g
	Fat	47.3 g	Fat	6.6 g	Fat	6.6 g	Fat	20 g
	Protein	9.6 g	Protein	12.2 g	Protein	12.2 g	Protein	3 g
DAY 2	• 1 svg. **Blueberry Oatmeal**		• 1 svg. **Veggie ramen**		• 1 svg. **Veggie bean soup with cornbread**		• 1 serv. **Popcorn**	
	Calories	370	Calories	525	Calories	370	Calories	110
	Carbs	73 g	Carbs	77 g	Carbs	62 g	Carbs	25 g
	Fat	2.5 g	Fat	14.5 g	Fat	10.5 g	Fat	1 g
	Protein	13 g	Protein	15 g	Protein	13.2 g	Protein	4 g
DAY 3	• 2 **Pancakes** with honey drizzle		• 1 svg. **Southwest pizza**		• 1 svg. **Black-eyed peas** • 1 svg. **Rice** • 1 slice **Cornbread**		• 1 slice **Brownie**	
	Calories	343.67	Calories	614	Calories	489	Calories	270.25
	Carbs	40.56 g	Carbs	12 g	Carbs	85 g	Carbs	40.5 g
	Fat	16.6 g	Fat	16 g	Fat	10 g	Fat	10 g
	Protein	3.35 g	Protein	25 g	Protein	14.2 g	Protein	5.6 g
DAY 4	• 1 svg. **Breakfast rice porridge**		• 1 can salmon • 1 svg. **Potatoes** • 1 tbsp. coconut oil • ½ can green beans • ½ can carrots		• 1 pk. ramen • ½ can peas • ½ can carrots • 1 can salmon		• 1 can fruit cocktail	
	Calories	240	Calories	479	Calories	663	Calories	350
	Carbs	37 g	Carbs	36 g	Carbs	70 g	Carbs	90 g
	Fat	0 g	Fat	20 g	Fat	20.6 g	Fat	0 g
	Protein	11 g	Protein	36 g	Protein	44 g	Protein	0 g
DAY 5	• 2 **Biscuits** • 2 tbsp. peanut butter • 1 tbsp. honey		• 1 svg **Veggie fried rice**		• 1 svg. **Taco soup**		• 1 slice **Pecan raisin bread**	
	Calories	650	Calories	495.5	Calories	382	Calories	208.5
	Carbs	69 g	Carbs	67.1 g	Carbs	63 g	Carbs	28.9 g
	Fat	59 g	Fat	17.3 g	Fat	1.5 g	Fat	10.4 g
	Protein	13.1 g	Protein	12.6 g	Protein	17 g	Protein	2.23 g

3rd MONTH

Week 1	Breakfast	Lunch	Dinner	Snack
DAY 6	• 1 svg. **Grits** • 2 **Flatbreads** • 1 **Egg**	• 1 svg. **Potato carrot soup**	• 1 svg. **Veggie spaghetti** • 1 tbsp. soy sauce	• 1 serv. **Popcorn**
Calories	544.5	212	355	110
Carbs	78.1 g	42 g	67 g	25 g
Fat	19 g	4 g	2 g	1 g
Protein	14.7 g	11 g	13 g	4 g
DAY 7	• 1 svg. **Rice** • 2 **Eggs** • 1 tbsp. soy sauce	• 1 svg. **3 Bean Pitas**	• 1 svg. **Veggie spaghetti** • 1 tbsp. soy sauce	• ½ cup raisins
Calories	254	670	355	240
Carbs	37.2 g	113 g	67 g	64 g
Fat	6.6 g	16.2 g	2 g	0 g
Protein	11.2 g	32.1 g	13 g	2 g

Week 2	Breakfast	Lunch	Dinner	Snack
DAY 1	• 1 svg. **Oatmeal** • 2 tbsp. peanut butter • 1 tsp. cocoa	• 1 svg. **Southwest pizza**	• 1 svg **Veggie fried rice**	• 1 slice **Brownie**
Calories	360	614	495.5	270.25
Carbs	37 g	12 g	67.1 g	40.5 g
Fat	18.5 g	16 g	17.3 g	10 g
Protein	13 g	25 g	12.6 g	5.6 g
DAY 2	• 1 svg. **Breakfast rice porridge**	• 1 can salmon • 1 svg. **Potatoes** • 1 tbsp. coconut oil • ½ can green beans • ½ can carrots	• 1 pk. ramen • ½ can peas • ½ can carrots • 1 can salmon	• 1 can fruit cocktail
Calories	240	479	663	350
Carbs	37 g	36 g	70 g	90 g
Fat	0 g	20 g	20.6 g	0 g
Protein	11 g	36 g	44 g	0 g

Veggie Ramen

Veggie Fried Rice

Veggie Spaghetti

3 Bean Pitas

3rd MONTH								
Week 2	**Breakfast**		**Lunch**		**Dinner**		**Snack**	
DAY 3	• 2 **Pancakes** with honey drizzle		• 1 svg. **Veggie spaghetti** • 1 tbsp. soy sauce		• 1 svg. **Taco soup**		• 1 serv. **Popcorn**	
	Calories	343.67	**Calories**	355	**Calories**	382	**Calories**	110
	Carbs	40.56 g	**Carbs**	67 g	**Carbs**	63 g	**Carbs**	25 g
	Fat	16.6 g	**Fat**	2 g	**Fat**	1.5 g	**Fat**	1 g
	Protein	3.35 g	**Protein**	13 g	**Protein**	17 g	**Protein**	4 g
DAY 4	• 1 svg. **Grits** • 2 **Flatbreads** • 1 **Egg**		• 1 svg. **Veggie bean soup with cornbread**		• 1 svg. **Black-eyed peas** • 1 svg. **Rice** • 1 slice **Cornbread**		• 1 oz pecans	
	Calories	544.5	**Calories**	370	**Calories**	489	**Calories**	190
	Carbs	78.1 g	**Carbs**	62 g	**Carbs**	85 g	**Carbs**	4 g
	Fat	19 g	**Fat**	10.5 g	**Fat**	10 g	**Fat**	20 g
	Protein	14.7 g	**Protein**	13.2 g	**Protein**	14.2 g	**Protein**	3 g
DAY 5	• 2 **Biscuits** • 2 tbsp. peanut butter • 1 tbsp. honey		• 1 svg. **3 Bean Pitas**		• 1 svg. **Potato carrot soup**		• ½ cup raisins	
	Calories	650	**Calories**	670	**Calories**	212	**Calories**	240
	Carbs	69 g	**Carbs**	113 g	**Carbs**	42 g	**Carbs**	64 g
	Fat	59 g	**Fat**	16.2 g	**Fat**	4 g	**Fat**	0 g
	Protein	13.1 g	**Protein**	32.1 g	**Protein**	11 g	**Protein**	2 g
DAY 6	• 1 svg. **Blueberry Oatmeal**		• 1 can tuna • 1 svg. **Rice** • ½ can carrots		• 1 can tuna • 1 svg. **Potatoes** • ½ can carrots		• 1 slice **Pecan raisin bread**	
	Calories	370	**Calories**	321	**Calories**	241	**Calories**	208.5
	Carbs	73 g	**Carbs**	49 g	**Carbs**	31 g	**Carbs**	28.9 g
	Fat	2.5 g	**Fat**	2 g	**Fat**	2 g	**Fat**	10.4 g
	Protein	13 g	**Protein**	24 g	**Protein**	23 g	**Protein**	2.23 g
DAY 7	• 2 **Biscuits** • 1 **Egg**		• 1 svg. **Potato carrot soup**		• 1 svg. **Veggie spaghetti** • 1 tbsp. soy sauce		• 1 serv. **Popcorn**	
	Calories	440.5	**Calories**	212	**Calories**	355	**Calories**	110
	Carbs	44.1 g	**Carbs**	42 g	**Carbs**	67 g	**Carbs**	25 g
	Fat	47.3 g	**Fat**	4 g	**Fat**	2 g	**Fat**	1 g
	Protein	9.6 g	**Protein**	11 g	**Protein**	13 g	**Protein**	4 g

3rd MONTH				
Week 3	**Breakfast**	**Lunch**	**Dinner**	**Snack**
DAY 1	• 1 svg. **Rice** • 2 **Eggs** • 1 tbsp. soy sauce	• 1 svg. **Veggie bean soup with cornbread**	• 1 svg. **3 Bean Pitas**	• 1 oz pecans
	Calories 254 Carbs 37.2 g Fat 6.6 g Protein 11.2 g	Calories 370 Carbs 62 g Fat 10.5 g Protein 13.2 g	Calories 670 Carbs 113 g Fat 16.2 g Protein 32.1 g	Calories 190 Carbs 4 g Fat 20 g Protein 3 g
DAY 2	• 1 svg. **Grits** • 2 **Flatbreads** • 1 **Egg**	• 1 svg. **Taco soup**	• 1 svg **Veggie fried rice**	• 1 slice **Pecan raisin bread**
	Calories 544.5 Carbs 78.1 g Fat 19 g Protein 14.7 g	Calories 382 Carbs 63 g Fat 1.5 g Protein 17 g	Calories 495.5 Carbs 67.1 g Fat 17.3 g Protein 12.6 g	Calories 208.5 Carbs 28.9 g Fat 10.4 g Protein 2.23 g
DAY 3	• 1 svg. **Cornbread delight**	• 1 svg. **Veggie bean soup with cornbread**	• 1 svg. **Black-eyed peas** • 1 svg. **Rice** • 1 slice **Cornbread**	• 1 serv. **Popcorn**
	Calories 363 Carbs 57 g Fat 10 g Protein 11 g	Calories 370 Carbs 62 g Fat 10.5 g Protein 13.2 g	Calories 489 Carbs 85 g Fat 10 g Protein 14.2 g	Calories 110 Carbs 25 g Fat 1 g Protein 4 g
DAY 4	• 2 **Biscuits** • 2 tbsp. peanut butter • 1 tbsp. honey	• 1 svg. **Veggie ramen**	• 1 svg. **Veggie bean soup with cornbread**	• ½ cup raisins
	Calories 650 Carbs 69 g Fat 59 g Protein 13.1 g	Calories 525 Carbs 77 g Fat 14.5 g Protein 15 g	Calories 370 Carbs 62 g Fat 10.5 g Protein 13.2 g	Calories 240 Carbs 64 g Fat 0 g Protein 2 g
DAY 5	• 1 svg. **Blueberry Oatmeal**	• 2 **Eggs** • ½ can tomatoes • 1 svg. **Rice**	• 2 **Eggs** • ½ can tomatoes • 1 svg. **Rice**	• 1 slice **Brownie**
	Calories 370 Carbs 73 g Fat 2.5 g Protein 13 g	Calories 293 Carbs 44.2 g Fat 6.6 g Protein 12.2 g	Calories 293 Carbs 44.2 g Fat 6.6 g Protein 12.2 g	Calories 270.25 Carbs 40.5 g Fat 10 g Protein 5.6 g

3rd MONTH

Week 3	Breakfast		Lunch		Dinner		Snack	
DAY 6	• 1 svg. **Cornbread delight**		• 1 svg. **Southwest pizza**		• 1 svg. **Veggie spaghetti** • 1 tbsp. soy sauce		• 1 oz pecans	
	Calories	363	Calories	614	Calories	355	Calories	190
	Carbs	57 g	Carbs	12 g	Carbs	67 g	Carbs	4 g
	Fat	10 g	Fat	16 g	Fat	2 g	Fat	20 g
	Protein	11 g	Protein	25 g	Protein	13 g	Protein	3 g
DAY 7	• 2 **Pancakes** with honey drizzle		• 1 can salmon • 1 svg. **Potatoes** • 1 tbsp. coconut oil • ½ can green beans • ½ can carrots		• 1 pk. ramen • ½ can peas • ½ can carrots • 1 can salmon		• 1 slice **Pecan raisin bread**	
	Calories	343.67	Calories	479	Calories	663	Calories	208.5
	Carbs	40.56 g	Carbs	36 g	Carbs	70 g	Carbs	28.9 g
	Fat	16.6 g	Fat	20 g	Fat	20.6 g	Fat	10.4 g
	Protein	3.35 g	Protein	36 g	Protein	44 g	Protein	2.23 g

Week 4	Breakfast		Lunch		Dinner		Snack	
DAY 1	• 1 svg. **Breakfast rice porridge**		• 1 can salmon • 1 svg. **Potatoes** • 1 tbsp. coconut oil • ½ can green beans • ½ can carrots		• 1 pk. ramen • ½ can peas • ½ can carrots • 1 can salmon		• 1 can fruit cocktail	
	Calories	240	Calories	479	Calories	663	Calories	350
	Carbs	37 g	Carbs	36 g	Carbs	70 g	Carbs	90 g
	Fat	0 g	Fat	20 g	Fat	20.6 g	Fat	0 g
	Protein	11 g	Protein	36 g	Protein	44 g	Protein	0 g
DAY 2	• 1 svg. **Grits** • 2 **Flatbreads** • 1 **Egg**		• 1 svg **Veggie fried rice**		• 1 svg. **Southwest pizza**		• ½ cup raisins	
	Calories	544.5	Calories	495.5	Calories	614	Calories	240
	Carbs	78.1 g	Carbs	67.1 g	Carbs	12 g	Carbs	64 g
	Fat	19 g	Fat	17.3 g	Fat	16 g	Fat	0 g
	Protein	14.7 g	Protein	12.6 g	Protein	25 g	Protein	2 g

3rd MONTH

Week 4	Breakfast		Lunch		Dinner		Snack	
DAY 3	• 2 **Pancakes** with honey drizzle		• 1 can tuna • 1 **Flatbread** • ½ can peas		• 1 can tuna • 1 svg. **Potatoes** • ½ can peas		• 1 serv. **Popcorn**	
	Calories	343.67	**Calories**	370	**Calories**	312.5	**Calories**	110
	Carbs	40.56 g	**Carbs**	34.5 g	**Carbs**	17.5 g	**Carbs**	25 g
	Fat	16.6 g	**Fat**	10.6 g	**Fat**	2 g	**Fat**	1 g
	Protein	3.35 g	**Protein**	36 g	**Protein**	25 g	**Protein**	4 g
DAY 4	• 2 **Biscuits** • 1 **Egg**		• 1 svg. **Veggie ramen**		• 1 svg. **Taco soup**		• 1 slice **Pecan raisin bread**	
	Calories	440.5	**Calories**	525	**Calories**	382	**Calories**	208.5
	Carbs	44.1 g	**Carbs**	77 g	**Carbs**	63 g	**Carbs**	28.9 g
	Fat	47.3 g	**Fat**	14.5 g	**Fat**	1.5 g	**Fat**	10.4 g
	Protein	9.6 g	**Protein**	15 g	**Protein**	17 g	**Protein**	2.23 g
DAY 5	• 1 svg. **Blueberry Oatmeal**		• 1 can sardines • 2 **Flatbreads** • ½ can green beans		• 1 svg **Creamy grits** • ½ can sardines		• 1 oz pecans	
	Calories	370	**Calories**	565	**Calories**	290	**Calories**	190
	Carbs	73 g	**Carbs**	56 g	**Carbs**	41 g	**Carbs**	4 g
	Fat	2.5 g	**Fat**	27.2 g	**Fat**	6.5 g	**Fat**	20 g
	Protein	13 g	**Protein**	26.1 g	**Protein**	19 g	**Protein**	3 g
DAY 6	• 1 svg. **Rice** • 2 **Eggs** • 1 tbsp. soy sauce		• 1 svg. **Potato carrot soup**		• 1 svg. **Black-eyed peas** • 1 svg. **Rice** • 1 slice **Cornbread**		• 1 slice **Brownie**	
	Calories	254	**Calories**	212	**Calories**	489	**Calories**	270.25
	Carbs	37.2 g	**Carbs**	42 g	**Carbs**	85 g	**Carbs**	40.5 g
	Fat	6.6 g	**Fat**	4 g	**Fat**	10 g	**Fat**	10 g
	Protein	11.2 g	**Protein**	11 g	**Protein**	14.2 g	**Protein**	5.6 g
DAY 7	• 2 **Biscuits** • 2 tbsp. peanut butter • 1 tbsp. honey		• 1 svg **Veggie fried rice**		• 1 svg. **Veggie bean soup with cornbread**		• 1 serv. **Popcorn**	
	Calories	650	**Calories**	495.5	**Calories**	370	**Calories**	110
	Carbs	69 g	**Carbs**	67.1 g	**Carbs**	62 g	**Carbs**	25 g
	Fat	59 g	**Fat**	17.3 g	**Fat**	10.5 g	**Fat**	1 g
	Protein	13.1 g	**Protein**	12.6 g	**Protein**	13.2 g	**Protein**	4 g

3rd MONTH								
Week 5	**Breakfast**		**Lunch**		**Dinner**		**Snack**	
DAY 1	• 1 svg. **Creamy Grits**		• 1 svg. **Lentils** • 1 svg. **Rice** • 1 **Flatbread**		• 1 svg. **Pinto beans** • 1 svg. **Rice** • 1 slice **Cornbread**		• 1 svg. **Cornbread delight**	
	Calories	460	**Calories**	455	**Calories**	479	**Calories**	363
	Carbs	70 g	**Carbs**	82.5 g	**Carbs**	86 g	**Carbs**	57 g
	Fat	15 g	**Fat**	7.6 g	**Fat**	10 g	**Fat**	10 g
	Protein	14 g	**Protein**	16 g	**Protein**	14.2 g	**Protein**	11 g
DAY 2	• 1 svg. **Blueberry Oatmeal**		• 1 svg. **Southwest pizza**		• 1 svg. **Veggie spaghetti** • 1 tbsp. soy sauce		• 1 oz pecans	
	Calories	370	**Calories**	614	**Calories**	355	**Calories**	190
	Carbs	73 g	**Carbs**	12 g	**Carbs**	67 g	**Carbs**	4 g
	Fat	2.5 g	**Fat**	16 g	**Fat**	2 g	**Fat**	20 g
	Protein	13 g	**Protein**	25 g	**Protein**	13 g	**Protein**	3 g

Recipes

Egg

Makes 1 egg

Calories	44.5	Carbs	0.1 g
Fat	3.3 g	Protein	3.6 g

Ingredients

- 1 tbsp. egg powder
- 1.5 tbsp. water

Steps

1. Mix 1 tbsp. of egg powder with 1.5 tbsp. water to make one large egg.
2. Stir and scramble on medium heat.

Milk

Makes 1 cup milk

Calories	80	Carbs	12 g
Fat	0 g	Protein	8 g

Ingredients

- 1/3 cup dry powder
- 7 oz. water

Steps

1. To make 1 cup of milk, add ⅓ cup dry powder to 7 ounces of water and stir until dissolved.

For best flavor, store in a tightly sealed glass container and refrigerate overnight before serving.

Spaghetti

Makes 1 serving (1 cup cooked)

Calories	210	Carbs	41 g
Fat	2 g	Protein	7 g

Ingredients

- 2 ounces spaghetti

Steps

Boil spaghetti in water until you've reached desired softness.

Oatmeal

Makes 1 serving

Calories	150	Carbs	27 g
Fat	2.5 g	Protein	5 g

Ingredients

- ½ cup oats, dry
- 1 cup water or milk

Steps

1. Boil 1 cup water or milk.
2. Stir in oats.
3. Cook about 5 minutes over medium heat, stirring occasionally.

Rice

Makes 1 serving (¾ cup cooked)

Calories	160	Carbs	36 g
Fat	0 g	Protein	3 g

Ingredients

- ¼ cup rice, dry
- ½ cup water

Steps

1. Bring water to a boil.
2. Add rice and boil for one minute.
3. Turn down heat low and cover with a lid.
4. Simmer until water is absorbed.

Mashed Potatoes

Makes 1 serving (1 cup cooked)

Calories	80	Carbs	18 g
Fat	0 g	Protein	2 g

Ingredients

- ⅓ cup potato flakes
- ⅔ cup water
- salt to taste

Steps

1. Bring water to a boil.
2. Add 1 pinch of salt.
3. Remove from heat.
4. Stir in potato flakes with a fork until potatoes are desired consistency.

Popcorn

Makes 1 serving

Calories	124	Carbs	17 g
Fat	5.5 g	Protein	2 g

Ingredients

- 1 tsp. coconut oil
- 2 tbsp. kernels

Steps

1. Add coconut oil to a skillet and turn on medium heat.
2. Add 2 tablespoons kernels and cover.
3. Let pop and shake until kernels expand.

Grits

Makes 1 serving

Calories	130	Carbs	29 g
Fat	0.5 g	Protein	3 g

Ingredients

- ¼ cup quick grits, dry
- 1 cup water
- salt to taste

Steps

1. Slowly stir grits and salt into boiling water.
2. Reduce heat and cover.
3. Cook 5-7 minutes or until thick, stirring occasionally.

*For savory grits, add ½ bullion cube to grits while boiling.

*For creamy grits, add one svg. of dry milk.

Flatbread

Makes 6 pieces

Calories*	185	Carbs	24.5 g
Fat	7.6 g	Protein	4 g

Ingredients

- ¾ cup dry milk
- 3 ½ tsp. coconut oil
- 2 cups flour
- ½ tsp. salt

Steps

1. Combine prepared cup dry milk and coconut oil.
2. Combine flour and salt. Pour wet ingredients into dry ingredients.
3. Knead for 2 minutes. Add extra salt if the dough is too sticky.
4. Wrap with cling wrap or enclose in a plastic bowl to rest for 30 minutes.
5. Cut dough into 6 pieces and roll into balls.
6. Roll balls out until they're about 8 inches.
7. Place one flatbread in a pan. For 60-90 seconds. It should be puffy.
8. Flip it and cook for another 45-60 seconds. Repeat until all dough is cooked.

*Nutritional values are calculated per slice.

Biscuits

Makes 8 slices

Calories*	198	Carbs	22 g
Fat	22 g	Protein	3 g

Ingredients

- 2 cups flour
- 1 tbsp. baking powder
- 2 tsp. sugar
- ½ tsp. salt
- 1 cup milk
- ¼ cup coconut oil

Steps

1. Combine all the dry ingredients.
2. Combine the milk and coconut oil.
3. Combine all ingredients.
4. Use a spoon to make 8 dropped biscuits.
5. Bake at 420 degrees until light brown.

Cornbread

Makes 10 slices

Calories*	219	Carbs	28 g
Fat	10 g	Protein	3.2 g

Ingredients

- 1 cup milk
- 1 tbsp vinegar
- 1 cup cornmeal
- 1 cup flour
- ⅓ cup sugar
- 2 tsp. baking powder
- ½ tsp. baking soda
- ½ tsp. salt
- 1 tsp coconut oil

Steps

1. Combine all the dry ingredients.
2. Prepare the powdered milk with water, mix in the vinegar, and set aside for 5 minutes.
3. Stir milk and coconut oil into the dry products and whisk.
4. Pour mixture into pan and bake until golden brown.

*Nutritional values are calculated per slice.

Lentils

Makes 1 serving

Calories	110	Carbs	22 g
Fat	0 g	Protein	9 g

Ingredients

- ¼ cup lentils, dry
- 1 cup water
- ¼ bouillon cube for taste

Steps

1. Rinse lentils.
2. Add one cup of water.
3. Simmer gently with lid tilted until desired tenderness is reached, about 1 hour.
4. Add ¼ bouillon cube for taste.

Black Beans

Makes 1 serving

Calories	100	Carbs	22 g
Fat	0.5 g	Protein	8 g

Ingredients

- ¼ cup black beans, dry
- 1 cup water
- ¼ bouillon cube for taste

Steps

1. Rinse beans.
2. Add one cup of water.
3. Simmer gently with lid tilted until desired tenderness is reached, about 1 hour.
4. Add ¼ bouillon cube for taste.

Navy Beans

Makes 1 serving

Calories	100	Carbs	21 g
Fat	0.5 g	Protein	8 g

Ingredients

- ¼ cup navy beans, dry
- 1 cup water
- ¼ bouillon cube for taste

Steps

1. Rinse beans.
2. Add one cup of water.
3. Simmer gently with lid tilted until desired tenderness is reached, about 1 hour.
4. Add ¼ bouillon cube for taste.

Black Eyed Peas

Makes 1 serving

Calories	110	Carbs	21 g
Fat	0 g	Protein	8 g

Ingredients

- ¼ cup black eyed peas, dry
- 1 cup water
- ¼ bouillon cube for taste

Steps

1. Rinse beans.
2. Add one cup of water.
3. Simmer gently with lid tilted until desired tenderness is reached, about 1 hour.
4. Add ¼ bouillon cube for taste.

Small Red Beans

Makes 1 serving

Calories	80	Carbs	21 g
Fat	0.5 g	Protein	8 g

Ingredients

- ¼ cup small red beans, dry
- 1 cup water
- ¼ bouillon cube for taste

Steps

1. Rinse beans.
2. Add one cup of water.
3. Simmer gently with lid tilted until desired tenderness is reached, about 1 hour.
4. Add ¼ bouillon cube for taste.

Pinto Beans

Makes 1 serving

Calories	100	Carbs	22 g
Fat	0 g	Protein	8 g

Ingredients

- ¼ cup pinto beans, dry
- 1 cup water
- ¼ bouillon cube for taste

Steps

1. Rinse beans.
2. Add one cup of water.
3. Simmer gently with lid tilted until desired tenderness is reached, about 1 hour.
4. Add ¼ bouillon cube for taste.

Pancakes

Makes 2 pancakes

Calories*	343.67	Carbs	16.6 g
Fat	40.56 g	Protein	3.35 g

Ingredients

- 1 cup all-purpose flour
- 2 tsp. baking powder
- 2 tbsp. brown sugar
- ½ tsp. salt
- 1 large egg
- 1 tsp. vanilla extract
- ½ to ¾ cup water
- 2 tbsp. coconut oil

Steps

1. Add flour, baking powder, sugar, and salt to a large mixing bowl and combine.
2. Add the egg, vanilla extract, and 1/2 cup of water and whisk again to combine until smooth.
3. Heat your frying pan over medium heat with about 1 tablespoon of coconut oil.

The coconut oil should be melted, and the pan should be nice and hot before you start to pour your pancake batter in. This will help you get that perfect golden-brown crispy exterior on your pancakes and make sure they don't spread and flatten too much.

4. Once your pan is hot and oil melted, fry your pancakes. Each pancake will take about 3 minutes on each side over medium heat. Cook until they are golden brown.

Brownie

Makes 8 slices

Calories*	270.25	Carbs	40.5 g
Fat	10 g	Protein	5.6 g

Ingredients

- 3 tbsp. coconut oil
- 1 cup granulated sugar
- 1 cup cocoa powder
- 1 ½ tsp. vanilla extract
- ¼ tsp. salt
- ⅓ cup of prepared dry milk
- ½ cup flour
- 4 tbsp. peanut butter

Steps

1. Combine coconut oil, cocoa powder and sugar. Stir until liquid.
2. Add the vanilla, salt, and milk. Stir just to combine.
3. Add the flour to the bowl.
4. Stir briskly for at least 30 seconds.
5. Add peanut butter and stir again.
6. Scrape the brownie batter into the prepared pan, and bake for 32-34 minutes.
7. Test with a toothpick before removing from the oven. The toothpick should be moist, not wet.
8. Cut into 8 slices.

*Nutritional values are calculated per slice.

Pecan Raisin Bread

Makes 12 slices

Calories*	208.5	Carbs	10.4 g
Fat	28.9 g	Protein	2.23 g

Ingredients

- 2 cups all-purpose flour
- 1½ tsp. baking soda
- 1 pinch salt
- 1 cup granulated sugar
- ½ cup vegetable oil
- 2 Eggs
- 1 teaspoon vanilla extract
- 1 cup pecans
- 1 cup raisins

Steps

1. Preheat oven to 350 degrees F.
2. Grease two 8×4-inch loaf pans; set aside.
3. In a medium bowl, whisk together the flour, baking soda and salt.
4. In a large bowl, whisk together the sugar, oil, eggs, vanilla extract, pecans, and raisins.
5. Add the flour mixture and stir until completely blended.
6. Divide the mixture into the two loaf pans.
7. Bake for 35 to 45 minutes, or until a thin knife inserted into the center comes out clean.

Blueberry Oatmeal

Makes 1 serving

Calories	370	Carbs	73 g
Fat	2.5 g	Protein	13 g

Ingredients

- 1 svg. Oatmeal
- 1 cup Milk
- 1 svg. sweetened dried blueberries

Steps

1. Prepare 1 svg. oatmeal accordingly.
2. Add 1 cup prepared milk while cooking.
3. Top with sweetened dried blueberries.

Breakfast Rice Porridge

Makes 1 serving

Calories	240	Carbs	37 g
Fat	0 g	Protein	11 g

Ingredients

- ¾ cup cooked Rice (1 svg.)
- 1 cup Milk
- ½ can fruit cocktail
- cinnamon to taste

Steps

1. Prepare the Rice.
2. Add 1 cup of prepared Milk and stir.
3. Top with the fruit cocktail.
4. Sprinkle with cinnamon.

Cornbread Delight

Makes 1 serving

Calories	363	Carbs	57 g
Fat	10 g	Protein	11.3 g

Ingredients

- 1 slice of cornbread
- 1 cup milk
- 1 tbsp. honey

Steps

Combine all ingredients in a bowl and serve.

Taco Soup

Makes 1 serving

Calories	382	Carbs	63 g
Fat	1.5 g	Protein	17 g

Ingredients

- 1 svg. Black Beans
- 1 svg. Navy Beans
- 1 svg. Small Red Beans
- ½ can tomatoes
- 1 tbsp. taco seasoning
- ½ tbsp. ranch dressing powder

Steps

1. Prepare black beans, navy beans, and small red beans.
2. Stir in tomatoes, taco seasoning, and ranch dressing powder.
3. Serve warm.

Veggie Bean Soup with Cornbread

Makes 1 serving

Calories	370	Carbs	62 g
Fat	10.5 g	Protein	13.2 g

Ingredients

- 1 svg. Small Red Beans
- ½ can carrots
- ½ can green beans
- ¾ cup cooked Rice (1 svg.)
- 1 slice Cornbread

Steps

1. Prepare Small Red Beans accordingly, in broth if preferred.
2. Add carrots and green beans.
3. Finally, add the prepared rice.
4. Serve with 1 slice Cornbread.

Potato Carrot Soup

Makes 1 serving

Calories	212	Carbs	42 g
Fat	4 g	Protein	11 g

Ingredients

- 1 svg. Mashed Potatoes
- 1 svg. Milk
- 1 tsp. coconut oil
- ½ can carrots

Steps

1. Prepare Mashed Potatoes accordingly, adding the milk and coconut oil.
2. Stir.
3. Add carrots.

Veggie Ramen

Makes 1 serving

Calories	525	Carbs	77 g
Fat	14.5 g	Protein	15 g

Ingredients

- 1 pk. ramen noodles
- ½ can carrots
- ½ can peas

Steps

1. Prepare ramen according to the package.
2. Add carrots and peas.

Veggie Spaghetti

Makes 1 serving

Calories	350	Carbs	66 g
Fat	2 g	Protein	12 g

Ingredients

- 1 svg. spaghetti
- ½ can carrots
- ½ can peas

Steps

1. Prepare 1 svg. of spaghetti according to the package.
2. Add carrots and peas.

3 Bean Pitas

Makes 1 meal

Calories	670	Carbs	113 g
Fat	16.2 g	Protein	32.1 g

Ingredients	Steps
• 2 Flatbreads • 1 svg. Black Beans • 1 svg. Pinto Beans • 1 svg. Navy Beans • 1/6 pk. taco seasoning	1. Prepare black beans, pinto beans, and =navy beans. 2. Add taco seasoning. 3. Prepare the flatbreads, but slit them down the middle to create pitas. 4. Stuff the pitas with the beans.

Southwest Pizza

Makes 1 meal

Calories	614	Carbs	102 g
Fat	16 g	Protein	25 g

Ingredients	Steps
• 2 Flatbreads • 1 svg. Black Beans • 1 svg. Pinto Beans • ½ can tomatoes • 1 tsp. taco seasoning	1. Prepare the flatbreads, black beans, and pinto beans. 2. Once everything is prepared, top each flatbread with the bean, tomato and taco seasoning mixture.

Veggie Fried Rice

Makes 1 serving

Calories	495.5	Carbs	67.1 g
Fat	17.3 g	Protein	12.6 g

Ingredients	Steps
• 1 svg. Rice • 1 Egg • ½ can carrots • ½ can peas • 1 tbsp. coconut oil • 1 tbsp. soy sauce	1. Prepare your peas, carrots and Egg. 2. Add in one serving of prepared rice. 3. Stir in coconut oil along with 1 tablespoon of soy sauce and heat.

Honey

1 serving

Calories	64	Carbs	17 g
Fat	0 g	Protein	0.1 g
Ingredients	• 1 tbsp. honey		

Peanut Butter

1 serving

Calories	95	Carbs	4 g
Fat	7.5 g	Protein	3.5 g
Ingredients	• 1 tbsp. peanut butter		

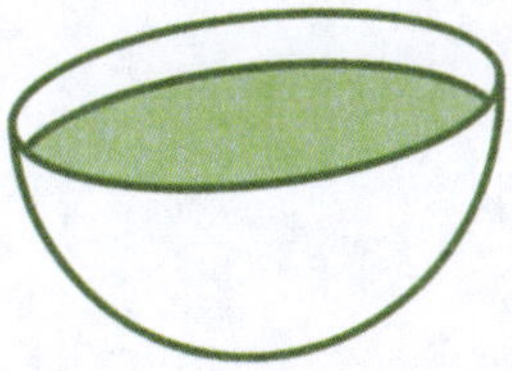

What Storage Looks Like

As you can see, our 3-month food stockpile includes many different kinds of foods and we use many different kinds of storage methods to assure our stockpile is safe in the short term and the long term. No matter when we have to call on our shelf stable food stockpile it must be ready to eat.

Sometimes we have foods like flour and sugar that we set in a "staging area" until we get a quantity that requires repackaging. Other foods like beans can be stored directly in buckets with oxygen absorbers and the bucket itself offers protection against threats from the outside world, like pests and moisture.

Let's take a look at the many ways we store the different types of foods in our stockpile.

Canned Goods

Canned goods are going to be organized either on a shelf or in a can rack with a focus on FIFO.

Fats

Our fats are stored to with a focus on protecting them from direct sunlight.

Grains

Grains, like rice, oats, and cornmeal, are stored in a number of ways. When shopping in a supermarket you are not going to buy enough grains each week to seal them up in Mylar bags. We use a shelf for "staging" these smaller batches of grains before storing them in mylar bags.

Dried Fruits

These are a pantry item that store really well as is. Truth be told it is the amount of sugar that keeps them safe over time.

Pasta

Your 12lbs of pasta can be taken from the box and stored in Mylar bags with Oxygen absorbers. You can also leave it on the shelf because rotating every 3 months means it will not go bad.

Potato Flakes

These are a very unique case because they come to us already in Mylar bags! I actually fill shopping bags with potato flakes and hang them on wall hooks in the pantry. It keeps these bags out of the way, off the ground, and easy to get to for meals.

As Is

Things like salt, baking soda, drink mix, peanut butter, coffee, and ramen are going to store on pantry shelves just the way they are. While you could repack them, if you like, we leave them just the way they are because they are really safe.

When People Ask Questions

As you start filling buckets and packing that pantry with a 3-month stockpile of food your home is going to look different. It might just be in a few spaces. However, when someone opens the pantry or walks into the storeroom, they might have questions.

Of course, this brings up all kinds of issues. How do you answer questions like:

- "Why do you guys have all this food?"
- "What's in all of these buckets?"
- "What are you some kind of crazy prepper?"

There are a few ways to handle these kinds of questions. The way you answer will affect your OPSEC (operational security), in a very big way. I am going to show you the three ways that you can answer these questions:

1. Lie
2. Stretch the Truth
3. Be Completely Honest

The reality is that every one of these options comes with its own set of consequences. To lie is always an ugly decision to make. To stretch the truth can still be a strain on your own morality and to tell the truth can put your stockpile and overall preparedness at risk.

LIE

- "My wife/husband just got into couponing. We are going to donate most of this to the local food bank."
- "The buckets are filled with holiday decorations/crafts/ something else/ and they stack really well so we leave them like this."

Stretch the Truth

- "There have been some great deals, lately! I don't know how high food prices are going to go, so we just took advantage of the sales. Now we have all this food! Yikes!"

Honesty

- "The world is getting weird and we just want to make sure we have enough food to stay fed no matter what happens. You remember 2020. It got crazy fast!"

The way you handle these questions is very personal. It might also depend on who you have in your home. I am sure you will explain your food stockpile to your mother a much different way than you explain it to the parent of one of your child's friends.

The Only Seeds You Need to Stockpile for a Crisis

While it is possible to stockpile enough food to last your family several months or even a year, at some point you're going to run out of both money and storage space. In order to have enough food to last several years, you'll need to be able to grow and produce your own food.

Growing your own food isn't as hard as many people think, if you've got the right seeds and good soil. Back during World War II, the government encouraged civilians to start "Victory Gardens", so that the produce grown on farms could be used for the war effort.

Granted, most people were closer to their agricultural roots back then, than we are today; but still, even city dwellers were growing most of their own produce, even raising chickens for eggs.

Of course, like everything else you need for survival, you're going to have to start preparing now, if you're going to grow your survival vegetable garden. Along with the food you are stockpiling, you're going to want to stock seeds as well.

But Just What Sort of Seeds Do You Need?

The first thing to consider is the growing zone you live in. The USDA has broken the country up into 10 growing zones, by average annual temperatures. Different plants need different climate conditions to grow. If you try growing lettuce in the south, you won't be successful, as lettuce requires a cold temperature to grow. So do many types of fruit, like cherries and apples. On the other hand, citrus fruit, grapes and olives require hot temperatures to grow.

You can find the latest version of this map on the USDA website at: https://planthardiness.ars.usda.gov/. It allows you to input your zip code and find what growing zone you are in, as well as the temperature range of your growing zone. Seed packs normally have the growing zone printed on them, usually on the back, making it easy to find which seeds grow well in your growing zone.

Also, you must pay attention to the growing season of each particular plant. Some you should plant early in the spring to maximize growing season, while others you should plant in late summer because they need cold to thrive. I planted cabbage in the spring one year and learned the hard way that they needed cooler temps! It's also worth investing in a seed mat to start some plants indoors to get a jump on things. A heating pad on a timer works also, but you can get an inexpensive seed mat for under $20.

Since you're going to be growing these plants to live on, you'll want to grow plants which give you the highest yield for your efforts. Growing something like pineapple, where you get one fruit from a six-foot diameter plant is not efficient use of your garden space. Ideally, you want fruits and especially vegetables which will give you a lot of food, for the space they are taking. One way to get this is from plants that continue to bear fruit, another is through plants that mature quickly, allowing you to replant and get more than one growing season in a year.

Here Are Some of the Highest Yield Plants You Can Grow:

Zucchini

Each plant provides roughly 10 pounds of fruit. Be sure to give them plenty of room to avoid fungi.

Summer Squash

Same as zucchini.

Tomatoes

Stick with indeterminate varieties, as they give the higher yield. They will continue to produce until the first frost. You should get about 8 pound per plant.

Cucumbers

These can either grow on a bush or vine, depending on the variety. Be sure to use a trellis, if you have the vine type. Most plants produce about three pounds.

Spinach

Like lettuce, spinach grows best in cold climates. It grows quickly, allowing you to begin harvesting in a little over a month. If you cut the leaves, while leaving the root intact, it will continue to grow more leaves.

Butternut Squash

Like many other types of squash, butternut grow on a vine, needing a trellis. One plant can produce 20 squashes, which can mean as much as 60 pounds of food.

Beets

These grow rather quickly, being ready for harvest in about two months, allowing multiple plantings in a growing season. Both the root and the leaves are edible.

Arugula

Another fast grower, which will continue to grow after partial harvest. You can start picking the leaves off of arugula in about a month.

As long as you don't kill the root, picking too much, it will continue to grow, providing more food.

Potatoes

As long as potatoes are planted in loose soil, they should produce a big crop; but that soil needs to drain well, so that they don't rot. When in doubt, grow them above ground in a raised bed.

You can get as many as 10 potatoes per plant, cutting up an old potato, with one eye per piece to grow into a new plant.

Turnips

One of the few plants which will actually grow well in the winter. Both the root and the greens can be eaten. Also a great cover crop that is edible for winter.

Carrots

You can plant carrots one inch apart, giving them the highest planting density of any vegetable. Planting a few rows every week will allow you to stagger your harvest.

Leaf Lettuce

A cold weather plant, lettuce can be grown early and late in the year in warmer climates. It will grow just about anywhere and be ready to begin harvesting in about 30 days.

Okra

This plant requires warm temperatures, so don't plant it early, even in the south. As you pick the fruit from the plant, it encourages the plant to produce more.

Kale

Compared to other leafy greens, like lettuce and spinach, kale is hardier, making it more filling. It also holds up under colder temperatures, allowing earlier planting and later harvests. Like other leafy greens, you can continue harvesting from the same plant, as long as the roots are intact.

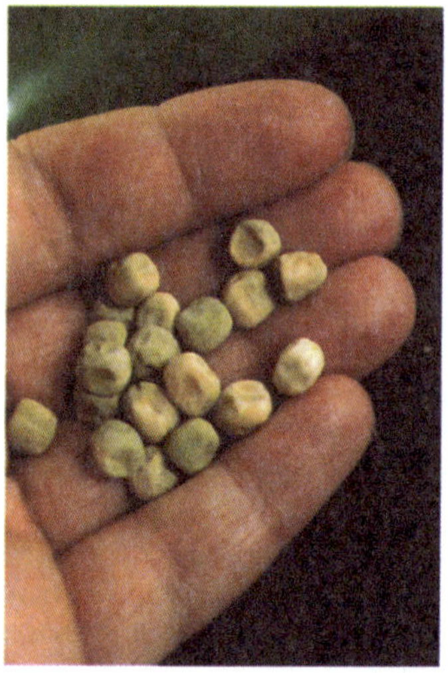

Peas

Peas must be grown vertically, on a trellis to avoid rotting. Pick when the vegetable is young and tender.

Pole Beans

One of the top producing bean varieties, these plants can grow to 10 feet tall, requiring a good trellis to grow on. They will produce about 20 beans per plant, about two months after planting.

Swiss Chard

Another leafy green, with similar growing characteristics, Swiss Chard will provide different nutrients than other greens.

Radishes

One of the faster growing vegetables, which can be ready for harvest in 30 to 45 days. Radishes can be planted close together, allowing a lot of plants in a small area.

One way of maximizing space is to plant radishes between other plants, like tomatoes, especially while those other plants are maturing.

You may notice that I have not included any fruit in this list. That's because fruit comes from trees and bushes, all of which need a few years of growing, before they produce any fruit.

As I am concentrating on what seeds you should stockpile, stockpiling seeds for fruit trees would not be effective for survival. But you might want to consider planting some fruit trees now, so that they will be ready when you need them.

Seed Types

Now we get down to buying the actual seeds. When you look at seeds online or in a store, you find that all seeds fall into three basic categories.

You want to be sure to buy the right category of seed, as it is the only one which will serve you well for a survival garden.

Heirloom Seeds

This is the type of seed that you want. Heirloom seeds are the old, naturally existing varieties of the plants. There are literally thousands of these, giving you a much better selection than you would believe. There are even online compa-

nies which sell heirloom seeds, allowing you to pick from 700 varieties of carrots, for example. Of all the types of seed out there, heirloom seeds are the only ones you can harvest the seeds from for the next year's planting.

Hybrid Seeds

Hybrid seeds are created by cross-breeding (or cross-pollinating) two different varieties of the same plant, such as two different varieties of carrots. While some are very tasty, when you harvest the seed and save it for the next year's planting, you will not have the same thing. The seed produced will be from one of the two varieties used to breed the hybrid.

GMO (Genetically Modified Organisms) Seeds

Much of the produce we buy in the grocery store today is GMO produce. These are laboratory produced seeds, which have been modified at the genetic level, in order to produce a higher yield, prevent insects from eating the produce or some other desirable trait. Unfortunately, to get these things, they often sacrifice taste, nutrition and of course the ability to reproduce.

It is clear that heirloom seeds are the only possible seeds to use for survival gardening. But there's more to it than just buying heirloom seeds. You're going to need to harvest the seeds, as you harvest your produce. Depending on the type of plant, that seeds may be inside the fruit, attached to the plant's stalk, outside the fruit, or in some other form.

Potatoes, as I've already mentioned, are planted from cutting up old potatoes which have grown eyes. Garlic is grown from individual garlic cloves.

Any seed that you harvest from your garden will need to be dried, in order to save it for the next year. You should see a 95% or higher germination rate on the seed that you harvest and save. However, that germination rate starts to drop as time goes on. As long as you have electricity, you can store your seed in the freezer, preventing it from going bad.

While good seeds are critical to growing a survival garden, it is not the only thing you need. As everyone knows, you'll need water as well, so make sure that your plan for harvesting water takes that into account, providing enough water for both your family and your garden. Fortunately, you can recycle grey water for gardening, saving on your overall water needs.

Careful watering can make a huge difference in how far that water goes. Israeli farmers have pioneered the use of drip irrigation, watering exactly at the base of the plant, rather than watering indiscriminately. While you can't use a drip irrigation system without power to provide water pressure, you can still take advantage of that principle, watering exactly at the root of the plant, and water at times when the water won't evaporate before the plant can take it in, making the most of your water.

The other really important thing is the quality of your soil. Plants receive nutrition and water from the soil, so good soil is critical to a good harvest. Yet most people's backyards don't have good soil.

So, in addition to stockpiling seeds for your garden, it would be a good idea to start fortifying your soil, adding nutrients to it, so that it will be ready for when you want to plant.

There are several ways of going about this, like fertilizing your entire yard with composted manure. But if you want to do it the easy way, build some raised garden beds and fill them with good potting soil.

There are many recipes for good garden soil online, allowing you to pick one that meets your needs and your budget. Make sure it has a good quantity of organic matter, as decomposing organic matter is where most of the nutrients come from.

Add a healthy population of worms, so they can get to work, breaking down that organic matter and making it ready for your seed.

Other Important Things to Keep in Mind as Far as Food Goes

The Under $1 Walmart Cans You Absolutely Need to Add to Your Food Reserves

Stocking up your pantry doesn't have to cost a lot. In fact, you can stock up on some items that you can keep on the shelf for a longtime, for very little money.

I am going to address some of the least expensive canned goods that you can stock up on, along with how you can use them some day.

Having a good stock of inexpensive non-perishables is always a great idea. Inexpensive will help with the budget. And, non-perishable is a must when stocking up, especially when a budget or crisis is a concern.

Here are a few items that I have discovered at Walmart that are under $1.

1. Beans

You can get an off brand can of beans, of many varieties, for just over $0.60 per can, such as the appropriately named brand, Great Value. And, Rosarita is often under $1 per can as well.

There is a good variety of beans to choose from:

- Pinto beans
- Kidney beans
- Black beans
- Great Northern
- Refried Beans

I tend to like the Bush brand for beans. So, I look for sales on that brand and stock up when I find a good sale. But, when used with other ingredients, Great Value works just fine.

Also, keep in mind that beans are a great source of fiber and protein. So, if you are in a SHTF situation, a can of beans can be a decent choice for nutrition, as well as be far more satisfying for filling you up quicker and longer than other canned choices.

2. Canned Pineapple and Other Fruit

Once in a while you can find a great deal on canned fruit, making it less than $1 per can. When you do, stock up on the fruit you like. I find that I am often able to get the Great Value brand of canned pineapple for under $1. For most other canned fruits, I wait until they are on sale or can use coupons to get it under a buck.

3. Canned Vegetables

Canned vegetables can be found under $1 each, but you might have to shop sales. However, they also might come in packages of 4-6 cans and are sold cheaper that way.

The Libby's brand is a popular brand that will sell in bulk for a better value for the customer. So, while the actual purchase is over $1, each can could be less than $1. For example, these veggies are often grouped for a good deal:

- Corn
- Beans
- Peas

But, other single cans of veggies can be found, well under $1 each, especially if you go with an off brand such as Great Value. These include the following:

- Corn
- Beans
- Peas
- Spinach
- Hominy
- Mixed veggies (typically corn, peas, carrots, etc.)
- Carrots
- Potatoes
- Beets
- Cabbage
- Mushrooms
- Green chilis

Some of the brands to look for in canned vegetables under $1, or just over, are: Great Value, Del Monte, Libby's, and Margaret Holmes (cabbage),

I also want to share some of the other canned veggies I noticed that are slightly over $1 each, because if they go on sale, or you find a coupon, they could easily fall under $1 each. You can then stock up on them at that point. I have spotted the following (brands including Bruce, Glory, and Great Value):

- Sweet potatoes or yams
- Collard greens
- Turnip greens
- Mixed greens
- Asparagus

You will find a better price with off brand items, most of the time. Just look for coupons and sales.

If you are like me, you probably strongly prefer fresh over canned when it comes to fruits and veggies. But when SHTF, we might not have the luxury of being picky, or salvaging a garden, or have the time to freeze or can produce fresh food ourselves.

4. Canned Meat

There are some meats that you can find in a can that will also be under $1. But, just like the others, you might have to purchase in bulk to get the better price. Some of these meats include from the brand Armour and Butterfield Farms:

- Vienna sausage
- Ham
- Potted meat

Lately, I have been able to find tuna in a pouch for $1 in a single-single serving size. Now, I have stretched that to 2 servings, when I add it to something else, such as a salad or pasta.

Again, watch for sales and coupons, because you might even be able to get canned chicken at a really good price at times.

5. Canned Soup

If you look for off brand, you can find canned soup for under $1 each, especially the following from Great Value:

- Walmart Cans under $1 Chicken noodle
- Cream of chicken
- Cream of mushroom
- Tomato
- Broth (chicken, beef, or vegetable)

Once in a while I find a really good sale for more hearty soups. The Campbell brand will often have a good sale or some good coupons. And, then I stock up.

6. Canned Meals

This might not be my ideal meal, if I had the time and resources to cook whatever I want. But, in a pinch both financially and circumstantial, I know I can turn to the following inexpensive canned choices:

- Walmart Cans under $1 Ravioli
- Macaroni and cheese
- Hash
- Beefaroni
- Spaghettio's

Brands to look for in this category are Campbell and Great Value.

Canned goods can easily be stored up to 5 years without reducing quality, if kept in a relatively cool and dry place, such as the pantry. After 5 years, they don't necessarily go bad, but they start to lose flavor.

In addition to loss of quality when not used in time, there are some other mistakes we could be making when storing canned goods. Common mistakes in storing canned goods include:

- Not Rotating Cans: Store newly purchased cans in back of existing can, based on expiration date so the older gets used first.
- Not Organizing: In order to best use product in a timely manner, as well as save money, keep your cans organized and grouped together. This will help you know what you have, what you need, and what you don't need.
- Buying Large Cans: Unless you are going to use the entire can right away, it is often a big waste to buy large cans. If you really want to make sure you save money, or not waste product, buy single serving cans. You can always open 2 if you need more. But, it's more difficult to save excess when you don't need the entire can.

Also, make sure to avoid any can that is leaking, rusty, or swollen!

You might want to do more than simply open a can and eat the contents. So, a recipe for these canned goods would be helpful. But, whether you are interested in inexpensive canned foods for financial reasons, or for survival, those recipes need to be simple. I have a few ideas for utilizing the canned goods, with adding maybe 1 or 2 other ingredients, if that.

For example, open a can of beans and mix it with rice and some seasoning of your choice. I tend to go with Mexican flavorings when it comes to beans and rice. So, open a pack of taco seasoning and mix it with the beans and rice. That will make a hearty meal without meat. Or, add meat if you want.

Canned fruits can make a decent sweet treat all on their own. Or, you can add them to cottage cheese for a salad, or mix them together.

One dish I like to make out of mostly canned items is:

Ingredients	Steps
• 1 can black beans and 1 can corn, drained • 1 can diced tomatoes, drained • ½ lemon, juice only • ½ onion • salt and pepper	Mix it all together for a tasty side dish, or even a meatless main dish. Add a packet of taco seasoning for more flavoring, or add some cooked meat and serve it warm.

A veggie soup or stew is an easy option for canned goods if you don't have the resources:

Ingredients	Steps
• 1 Can of tomatoes, undrained • 1 Can of beans and 1 Can of peas, drained • 1 Can of corn, undrained • 1 Can of carrots, drained	Just open the cans and mix, then add whatever seasoning you prefer or have on hand. You could also add a can of broth. Another option would be, if you want some more substance to it, to add a can of meat that I mentioned above, such as vienna sausage or ham.

Make a taco soup with the following:

Ingredients	Steps
• 1 Can of black beans, drained and rinsed • 1 Can of corn, undrained • 1 Can of beef broth • a jar of salsa • Seasoning, such as taco seasoning, salt, and pepper.	Mix all this together for an easy, quick, and inexpensive taco soup. If you want more substance, and have the resources, add some beef or chicken. You could also drain all cans, then add some rice for a taco bowl.

Another quick fix...make some mac-n-cheese and add a can of green chilis to it. There are other things you can make with canned goods. But, it is up to personal preference and what you like, or don't like.

Get creative and save some money and peace of mind by being prepared for anything!

Must-Have Canned Foods You Didn't Know Existed

If you're looking to add some unique and exotic foods to your food storage for either variety in your diet or for trading, you'll find below some canned goods you didn't know existed.

1. Bread

Canned bread is totally a thing, and it's available in several different varieties. While it's likely more practical to store ingredients to make your own bread for the long-term, canned bread could be a tasty, quick way to a full belly and to get some carbohydrates into your system. You can find Original and Raisin Brown Bread by B & M in many stores or online.

2. Butter

Would you miss butter if you suddenly didn't have access to the supermarket? No big deal, you can get that canned, too. There are a few brands of canned butter available, and it's rather expensive since it's not canned in the US. However, it'd be a lovely treat in a SHTF situation, and fat is a crucial part of the diet. For a less expensive canned butter, you can opt for powdered butter, instead.

3. Pudding

Canned pudding is more often found in Europe. But you can find it in stores in the US, too, as any buffet or cafeteria worker attest. Whatever your favorite type of pudding, it's likely available in a can.

4. Cake

A pudding in the European sense that refers more to a dessert dish in general, you can get canned Spotted Dick Sponge made by Simpson's. It's essentially a sponge cake with spices and raisins.

This canned cake doesn't quite fit into what we think of as a cake in everyday life. However, I bet it'd be an incredible birthday treat in a SHTF situation.

5. Bacon

Very few people don't like bacon. So it's great that Yoder makes it in a can for long-term storage. It's salty, fatty, and flavorful, which makes it great for spicing up boring food made from more traditional prepper food items. You don't need much of it to transform a pot of soup or some powdered eggs.

6. Cheese

Making your own cheese isn't rocket science. However, there is a lot of actual science involved, and the raw materials needed may not be easy to come by.

So, there's canned cheese. Check out Kraft's Prepared Pasteurized Cheddar cheese or Heinz's Macaroni Cheese for reasonably priced options.

While it's not quite like what we think of as 'real' cheese, canned cheese has plenty of fat and flavor to be a worthwhile addition to your prepper's pantry.

7. Hamburger

Generally, people think of canned hamburger being home-canned. However, it's available in cans from both Yoders and Keystone. There are even pre-seasoned canned hamburger products available, like the taco meat by Yoders.

8. Whole Chicken

Canned whole chicken, like those available from Sweet Sue, are good for more than just the meat.

When the entire chicken is canned, all the gelatin and fat is preserved, allowing you to make a fantastic chicken soup. This makes it a great survival food, especially in an SHTF situation.

9. Potato Salad

Who knew this traditional, delicious picnic side was available in a can? Canned potato salad would be a good way to add a little flavor into your preps.

10. Tamales

Simply heat these canned tamales up, maybe add some fresh veggies or canned cheese to them, and voila! You've created an entire meal by simply opening the can.

These provide a ready-made meal in a solid form, which can have profound positive psychological impacts.

While canned soup is great for filling you up and providing a decent balance, it's simply not the most satisfying food out there.

It can be eaten warm or chilled, making it a more versatile side dish than you'd possibly realized.

11. Cheeseburger

Made in Switzerland, these rather expensive canned cheeseburgers aren't very practical. But they're a fun addition to your preps.

You simply boil the whole can and open for a tasty (that's subjective, of course) cheeseburger.

Better than Walmart: Cheapest Survival Foods You Can Find

Anyone who has even thought about prepping quickly came to realize that it's not a hobby for the faint of heart. One look at what it costs to build a stockpile is all it takes to send many potential preppers packing.

I personally know quite a few people who have expressed interest in prepping, but haven't started. Their reason, in every case, is not having the money to do it.

Keep in mind that none of these people have actually sat down to calculate the cost of prepping. Nor have any of them looked at how to make prepping any cheaper. They are all basing their opinion on a vague idea of how much they spend per month on their grocery bill.

That alone has been enough to relegate prepping to the "nice to do if I can afford it someday" pile.

The difference between those people and us is that we've found a way to make prepping an integral part of our lifestyle. For some, that has meant making some pretty heavy sacrifices in other areas of their lives. For others, it's about finding a way to make prepping cheaper.

Still, others have found ways of integrating their prepping in with other areas of their lives, making the overall cost something that they can handle.

Regardless of which group you fall in, we can all use a bit of savings on our prepping efforts now and then.

So, whether you're a new prepper starting out or you're looking to expand your stockpile so that it has enough to last you a year, I've searched out the best bargains in foods that you can stockpile.

Keep in mind that we're talking about a survival diet here, not a normal every day one. Its intention is to keep you alive, hopefully while providing enough nutrients that you can continue to function.

It's probably not going to be the foods you like or provide convenient foods to eat; but it will put calories in your belly, so that your body can keep on going.

1. Lentils

While any sort of beans can be good, lentils seem to be a great choice. Not only are they high in calories, but they're high in carbohydrates and protein as well.

Some people consider them a superfood for their high nutritional value. Most often used in soups, there are actually a number of different things you can do with them.

You can find dried lentils in your local grocery store for about $0.99/lb.

2. Chick Peas

Also known as "garbanzo beans", chick peas are a common food in Mediterranean countries, with a lot of different recipes made from them, like humus.

While not as high in protein as pinto beans, they do pack some protein, as well as a variety of other nutrients.

Just make sure you find recipes you can make out of them, so that you can get the most mileage out of your chick peas.

A one pound can of chick peas or garbanzo beans should cost $0.99 at your local grocery store.

3. Turkey

If you want some real animal protein in your survival diet, then I'd recommend buying turkeys at Thanksgiving time and converting them to jerky.

Most grocery stores have a sale on turkeys right before Thanksgiving, selling them at a considerable discount.

While some grocery chains will limit the number of turkeys you can buy per trip, they won't limit the number of trips you make; nor will they limit how many family members can buy a turkey.

One year I bought a dozen 25-pound turkeys in the before Thanksgiving sale. That gave us one turkey per month, for the next year, saving us quite a bit on our grocery bill. But that was before I was doing my own dehydrating. Now, with a dehydrator, I can turn that turkey into jerky, packing it away as part of my stockpile.

Raw turkey can be extremely difficult to cut, especially if you want to cut it neatly. What I recommend is to make the cutting a process, as the turkey thaws. Only cut off what you can cut easily; ideally the part which isn't quite frozen, but isn't quite thawed either. Then allow it to thaw a little more, offering you more meat that is easy to cut.

Keep going in this manner, until you've stripped the meat off the bones. Currently the average price for turkey is $1.60/lb. but if you catch it before Thanksgiving, it's about $0.79/lb.

4. Pork

I hesitate to put pork on this list, simply because it has to be very well cooked to kill off parasites. Having said that, I've been getting some amazing deals on pork lately; approaching $1 per pound.

More than anything, I've been buying pork loin, because it is a large piece, with almost no fat. This makes it ideal for slicing up and making jerky out of.

What? You didn't know that you can make pork jerky? Well, you can. You just need to be careful to dehydrate it fully and use plenty of salt. Once dehydrated, it will store for years, as long as it is kept in an airtight package. Then, when you're ready to use it, you can rehydrate it in soups and other recipes.

I just checked and Sam's Club has whole pork loins for $1.68/lb.

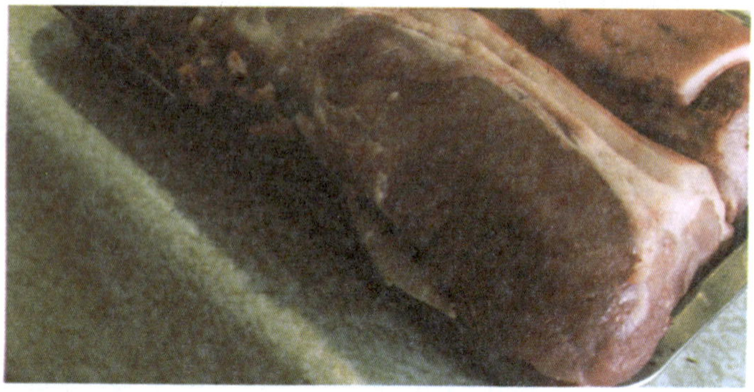

5. Drying Your Own Foods

Just as with that turkey, there are many other foods which you can dehydrate inexpensively, storing them away as part of your prepping stockpile.

The real savings is that you're doing the dehydrating yourself.

But in doing so, you store foods away that you might not otherwise be able to store, as well as doing it at a price that's hard to beat. That's even more true when you catch the foods in season and on sale.

Here's a sampling of foods I'm recommending and their prices in my local grocery store:

- Potatoes – Russet potatoes go for about $0.35/lb.
- Sweet potatoes – A little more expensive, at $0.88/lb.
- Carrots – You can get them for less than $0.99/lb. if you buy them in five-pound bags.
- Bananas – Typically run at about $0.48/lb. Banana chips are great.

Of course, if you grow your own fruits and vegetables, then dehydrate them, you'll be getting an even better price on them.

How to Preserve Eggs for Years Without Electricity

It's incredible just how versatile eggs are and just how much we depend on them. Whether over easy, hard-boiled, baked in a cake or cookies, or used as a binder, it's unlikely that a week goes by when you don't use what might just be the world's perfect food.

But you know what makes me sad? The idea that those of us who raise chickens for eggs may end up wasting some of them in the spring and summer because of over-production. We might then have to buy the much-inferior grocery store eggs in the winter when our hens have slowed down laying.

Fortunately, there are numerous ways—some far better than others—to preserve eggs for anywhere from a few weeks to several years.

And if you would like to add to your long-term pantry to have fresh eggs available in a natural disaster or other crisis, there is one method of preservation that stands above the rest: lime-water preserving.

But first, let's take a quick look at the other options for preservation.

In addition to lime-water preservation, there are many other methods used over the last several hundred years to keep eggs longer than they could last naturally.

DRYING

With this method, eggs are cracked, beaten, and then dehydrated either in a commercially purchased dehydrator or in an oven.

However, a potential problem with this method is that the eggs must be dried at a heat of 165°F or more. With most dehydrators, that isn't possible. Without being heated to that temperature, you're risking salmonella—and that's not a good idea.

When done correctly and at appropriate temps, this method is acceptable, although the eggs yielded are better for cooking with than eating. Dried eggs can be vacuum sealed for even longer, safer storage.

FREEZING

To freeze eggs, you start the same way as drying: out of the shell and beaten. The biggest drawback to freezing eggs is that the process requires electricity—a freezer—for storage, and depending on your circumstances, electricity may not always be available.

MINERAL OIL (or cooking oil, butter, or lard)

With this method, you are essentially sealing the pores of the eggshell so that no bacteria can permeate it and thus contaminate the egg. But the fat source usually needs to be heated on a stovetop or in a microwave to melt it or purify it, and that requires electricity.

It's also messy and, in the case of butter, can turn rancid. Storage may also attract rodents or insects.

SALT OR WOOD ASH

Another preservation method is to store eggs in a box or crate willed with salt or wood ash. This should get you through winter but isn't a viable longer-term solution. And both substances can permeate an eggshell and alter an egg's flavor.

WATER GLASS

Water glass preservation is a chemical means for sealing and insulating whole eggs in a gel-like mixture of water and sodium silicate. For this method, the eggs must be very fresh—no more than 24 hours old. They become very slippery and potentially messy and should be pinpricked to prevent the eggs from exploding!

Not only will lime-water preserved eggs last for two or more years, but they are also preserved in the shell, so they are much more versatile when it comes time to use them. The taste and consistency of such eggs are nearly identical to fresh eggs.

Preserving eggs this way is super economical and a fantastic way to use all those eggs you can't use as quickly as your chickens can lay them. They do not require heat or refrigeration for storage and will be an excellent option, should access to power be lost. Neither will they attract rodents or bugs.

If you're thinking "citrus" when you hear lime water, well, let's clear that up right now. What we are actually talking about is slaked lime—a mineral commonly used in building for centuries. Also known as "hydrated lime", it is different than the lime one might use in the garden.

Today, you can ask for slaked lime at a building supply store. But it is also used in pickling as an agent to "crisp up" cucumbers. Which means you might be able to find it in the canning section of your local grocery store. And of course, there are always online stores available.

Just remember, the product you want is PICKLING LIME; the ingredient label should list CALCIUM HYDROXIDE and nothing else.

Even though it's called pickling lime, you aren't pickling your eggs when you do this. Pickling lime firms up and seals the eggshells.

What You Will Need

Here is a list of everything you will need:

- Fresh eggs—ONLY fresh laid, unwashed eggs will work. Grocery store eggs are washed, and during washing, the natural "bloom" that prevents bacteria from entering through the pores in an egg's shell is removed.

Furthermore, store-bought eggs are not sustainable outside of a refrigerator. (I bought mine from a kind neighbor.)

- Glass jar with a lid (or another water-tight container with a lid)
- Slaked lime or pickling lime (CALCIUM HYDROXIDE) and measuring spoon
- Bowl or jar for mixing lime solution
- Water

How to Lime-Water Preserve Eggs

1. In a large jar, mix room temperature water with one ounce (about two heaping tablespoons) of calcium hydroxide. You can adjust or multiply this ratio to suit your needs. It's VERY IMPORTANT to mix this solution well before adding eggs. If the lime isn't well dispersed in the water, it might not seal your eggs, and they will go bad! I write from experience unfortunately.
2. Shake or stir to mix. The mixture will be milky white.
3. Choose eggs without cracks or any other issues and that are as fresh as possible. They should be clean but unwashed. Fill the jar with the eggs.
4. Pour the lime-water solution over the eggs, ensuring they are completely submerged.

5. Cap the jar tightly.
6. Store in a cool, dry location for up to two years.

When you're ready to use your preserved eggs, remove them from the solution and rinse. (Rinsing ensures the lime solution will not affect the flavor of the eggs.) Then crack them as use them as desired.

When you preserve eggs with lime water, you are:

- Ensuring a nutritious, versatile food source is available when you need it.
- Making the most of the eggs your chickens produce. (I hate wasting food, and I'm sure the same is true for you.)

Eggs preserved using this method:

- Do not require electricity for storage.
- Will not attract rodents or insects.
- Will remain viable for at least two years.

Preserving eggs for future use, whether for self-reliance, homesteading, or disaster preparation, is easy and smart.

The Meal in a Jar That You Need to Add to Your Stockpile

While canning vegetables and sauces at home is a fairly common activity, most people don't realize that canning meat is just as easy, safe, and delicious; if you take the right steps.

If you don't believe me, then just ask the Amish; they have been off-grid for literally hundreds of years and are one of the healthiest people in the US.

Here I am going to share with you one of their recipes for canned meat, that is simple and delicious: Amish Poor Man's Steak. As with all recipes, you can tweak this one any number of ways but the key to this steak lasting a long time in your pantry is the canning method at the end.

Simply put, Amish Poor Man's Steak is seasoned ground beef patties smothered in gravy. Pair a couple of these patties with some home-canned green beans and carrots and some instant mash potatoes and you have a proper meal.

Unlike others, I will not be relying on store-bought soup and gravy packets to season my food. So here is what you are going to need. For this recipe I am going to use 2.5 pounds of ground beef. All the ingredients listed below can easily be found at your neighborhood grocery store. If they don't have dried mushrooms, they can easily be found at any Asian food market.

Ingredients Needed

For the steak you will need:

- 2.5 pounds of lean ground beef
- 2 stalks of celery
- 1 carrot
- 1 large onion
- ½ cup bread crumbs
- 2 eggs
- ½ tsp. black pepper
- 1 tsp. salt
- 1 tsp. dried herbs mix
- ½ cup milk

For the gravy you will need:

- Beef bullion
- 3 Tbsp. flour
- 3 Tbsp. butter
- ½ tsp. pepper
- ½ tsp. salt
- 1 cup dried mushrooms
- 1 tsp. dried herbs mix
- 4 diced garlic cloves or 2 tsp. dried garlic powder
- 2 cups milk

The Recipe

Preparing the Steak

1. Dice up all your vegetables as seen below. The dice should be fairly fine, not blender fine, but close to it.

2. Put all those vegetables in a bowl/container big enough to hold them and all the remaining ingredients.

3. Add in your salt, pepper, eggs, dried herbs mix, breadcrumbs, and milk. Stir together.

4. Next, add your ground beef. I like to mix it with my hands. Mix until all the ingredients are evenly integrated.

5. Take the lid of your canning jar as a mold and start making "steak" patties.

6. Place them on an oven tray, preheat your oven to 375 degrees Fahrenheit and cook them for 40 minutes.

Preparing the Gravy

1. Rehydrate and dice finely your mushrooms.

2. Peel and fine chop your garlic.

3. Add mushrooms and garlic and cook until garlic and mushrooms brown slightly.

4. Make your roux by melting butter and add about 2 tablespoons of flour and stir vigorously until they are mixed.

5. Pour in milk and continue stirring until gravy just begins to boil and thicken.

6. Lower the heat and season with salt, pepper, and dried herbs.

Canning Your Amish Poor Man's Steak

Now that you have your steaks and gravy, it's time to can them. Begin by stacking your steaks inside your mason jar all the way to the top. Then pour in your gravy, again all the way to the top. Firmly cap your jar.

Sterilize your jars of delicious canned Amish Steak. To do this, you need to grab a pot big enough to hold your mason jar. Fill it with water and get that water up to a nice rolling boil. Then gently place your mason jar into the water making sure it is completely submerged.

Once the water gets back to a rolling boil, leave your jar to sterilize in the water for at least 3 hours. Unlike fruits or some vegetables, which usually only require 10 or so minutes in the boiling water bath, here we are dealing with meat, so the longer the better.

At the end, remove your jar and let it cool.

As it cools, the "button" on the top of the jar should compress down. This is your signal that the contents inside are sealed and that your canning was a success. If it doesn't, the sterilization process didn't work so either you have to start over, or you can eat those steaks over the next couple of weeks, as long as you keep them refrigerated.

Some people may think that when dealing with meat, you always need to pressure can it. However, the Amish do water bath canning when it comes to meat and doing it safely for hundreds of years. I follow in their footsteps, particularly for this recipe, but this does not mean I encourage you to do the same.

Do the research and decide for yourself.

Either way, Amish Steak makes an undeniably delicious meal in a jar. Give it a try!

WATER

How to Stockpile a Ton of Water for 365 DAYS Without It Going Bad

It is common knowledge that water is one of the most important resources for survival. In a disaster scenario, where your situation starts to deteriorate very quickly, having a large stockpile of water is crucial to staying alive.

Considering that water is not only needed for drinking but for hygiene purposes also, it is estimated that the average person will use roughly 1-1.5 gallons (4-5 litres) of water a day; therefore, in the event of a catastrophic disaster, having 1 ton of water at the ready will help you stay alive for upwards of 6 months to a year. (It is useful to note that 1 litre of water is equivalent to 1 kilogram in weight).

The first step in stockpiling 1 ton of water is to identify what container you are going to use. You essentially have two options here: either four separate 55-gallon barrels (250 litres) or one large 220-gallon water tank (1000 litres).

The choice here is yours; however, four individual barrels may potentially be safer, as if one of your barrels was to somehow become damaged - then you would still have three more barrels to survive with.

But if you chose to use one large water tank, and it somehow became damaged (for instance, from a natural disaster such as an earthquake), then you would be stuck without any water at all - which could be devastating.

For these reasons, I recommend that you use multiple barrels to store your water. When choosing your barrels, ensure that they are BPA- free and UV- resistant; this is typical of water barrels, however, you must ensure that this is the case, otherwise, your water may start to develop an unwarranted plastic flavour.

When you first acquire your barrels, make sure to clean the insides thoroughly. I recommend using a diluted solution of bleach and water for this (with a ratio of 1:32 of bleach to water).

It is also highly recommended that you buy brand-new barrels, as it can be risky to store water in second-hand barrels, as you cannot be certain as to what someone may have used them for in the past.

Before you start filling your barrels, you must consider their location carefully - you don't want to start having second thoughts after you have already filled your barrels with water. When thinking about where to store your barrels, consider **the factor of safety** of the utmost importance; this means not only from the elements but from other people as well.

In a true disaster scenario, where the water which flows from the taps comes to a halt, the majority of people will have little to no stockpile of supplies at all - let alone enough water to last them any significant amount of time. This means you must consider that if anyone knows about your stockpile, or has any vision of it, then you may start to attract some unwanted intruders. Therefore, it is important that you choose your location wisely with this in mind.

The best option here will be different for everyone, as it is highly dependent on your situation, however, try to be inventive, and make sure to consider your best options carefully.

Another thing that you must consider, is whether your stockpile is at risk from its local environment - ask yourself the following questions:

- Are my barrels in a cool, dry location, out of direct sunlight?
- If there was a natural disaster, would my barrels be at risk from any local objects which may fall onto my stockpile and cause any damage?
- And most importantly - Are there any toxic substances nearby which may contaminate my water?

The last thing you want is for your stockpile to become contaminated at the very moment a disaster strikes. If you are unsure as to whether a substance is toxic or not, ask yourself if it would be problematic if the substance somehow found its way into your water supply, if the answer is yes – then move it elsewhere!

To fill your barrels, it is recommended that you use water-specific tubing made safe for drinking water (BPA-free).

Simply attach the tubing to your tap (using an adapter if needed) and lead it safely to your container; then, wait for them to fill (it will take approximately one hour, depending on your water pressure).

At this stage, you may also want to consider buying a small water pump, this ensures that you can get your water out of the barrels with ease, and without the risk of unnecessary contamination.

There are many different options here to choose from, however, sometimes the simplest option can be the best, and using a small hand pump will save you from having to submerse more complicated pumps into your water supply - further minimising the risk of contamination.

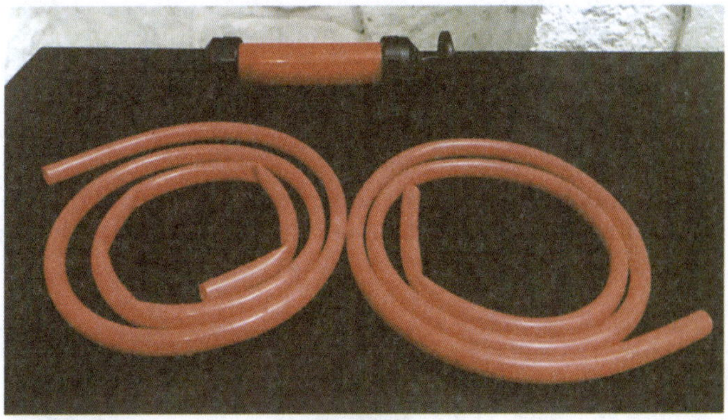

Once you have successfully filled your containers with water, the next step is to sanitise them. This will ensure that your water is safe to drink for up to one year.

Although tap water has already been chemically treated by your local water companies, it is important that you do so for yourself as well. This removes any risk of contamination that may have occurred during the filling process.

The best way to sanitise a large quantity of water is by using chlorine bleach - this is the same stuff that you use around the house for cleaning, however, it's important to find the right stuff.

Make sure to use regular, unscented and un-thickened bleach, which has the active ingredient of sodium hypochlorite - with concentrations between 5% and 9%.

Some products may also have instructions for disinfecting water printed on their labels, which is useful so you know you are using the right stuff.

When adding the chlorine bleach, you may wish to use a dropper to be more precise, however, a simple teaspoon will do the job nicely.

Use the following proportions to carefully add the bleach to your water supply:

- 1 teaspoon for every 10 gallons (45.5 litres) of water
- Or 80 drops for every 10 gallons

So, for each 55-gallon barrel (210 litres), you would need roughly:

- 5 and a half teaspoons
- Or 440 drops
- And for a 220-gallon water tank (1000 litres), you would need approximately:
- 22 teaspoons
- Or 1760 drops

After you have treated the water, be sure to stir thoroughly with a clean utensil and secure the top lid tightly so that nothing can get inside or out until it is needed.

To finish, it is also a good idea to label your water barrels with a name and date. This ensures that you don't mistake your liquid gold for anything else, and so that you know exactly when they were stockpiled (this is in case you felt the need to rotate your water supply after a long period of time).

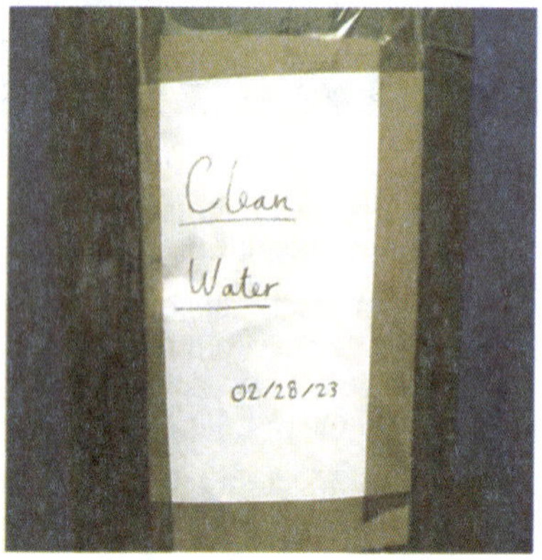

Although some people may recommend that you do this (rotating your water inside the barrels), it isn't particularly necessary, as water itself doesn't go 'bad' per se. The only risk of water becoming unsafe to drink is from local contaminants (bacteria), which may disturb the water's purity - however if you have treated your water correctly and the containers have been sealed tight, then your water will be safe to drink for a very long time.

Here is a list of all the needed materials for this project:

55-Gallon Water Barrel — **$138.98**

https://us.amazon.com/Gallon-Water-Barrel-FreshStorage/dp/B07B68CVRD

I bought 4 barrels, so I paid $559.92

Hand Pump — **$17.45**

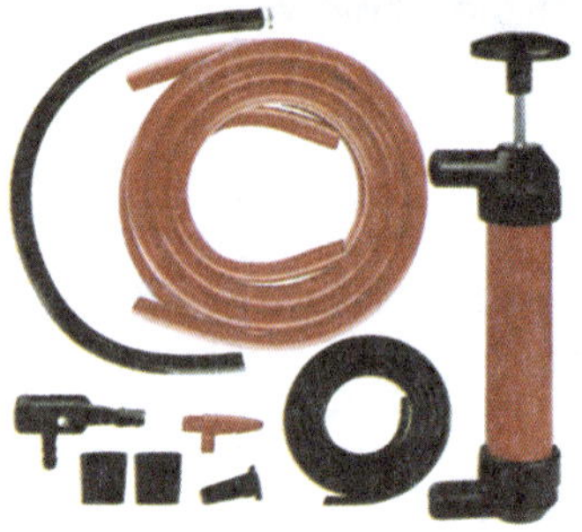

https://us.amazon.com/Vila-Heavy-Duty-Pumping-Variety-Automotive/dp/B07GR1HSR7

Bleach — **$25.99**

https://www.amazon.com/dp/B0BKR89BNR?pd_rd_i=B0BKR89BNR

Water-Safe Tubing — **$7.99**

https://www.amazon.com/Flexible-Lightweight-Plastic-Chemical-Resistant/dp/B07HF648M5

Water Faucet Adapter — **$7.99**

https://us.amazon.com/HZFJ-Swivel-Fitting-Irrigation-Adapter/dp/B089Y3M2FV

Total Cost of Project — **$619.34**

Deadly
Water Storage Mistakes
to Avoid

The value of water storage extends far beyond hydration. In a bug in situation, you are always going to worry about hydration because we have but three short days without water before our bodies shut down. This is something we cannot take for granted.

Still, we may also have gardens to water, we have bathing and hygiene to worry about. How we store and use our water is of the utmost importance.

Any mistakes made could affect the quality and quantity of water available during the bug in.

We must be careful about things like waste; we have to be careful about things like contamination. The only thing worse than running out of water in a bug in situation is drinking from a contaminated water storage, which can result even in death.

There are few natural water sources on this planet that are not contaminated. There is a good chance that you will get ill from drinking water directly from a river or a creek.

Water contamination is not only the fault of man, but also occurs from animals defecating into lakes and streams.

Natural water contamination includes things like algae growth and pathogen growth in water sources. Even a pristine and clear mountain creek is going to contain pathogens like cryptosporidium and giardia.

These pathogens can make you very sick with symptoms like stomach cramps, vomiting, and diarrhea.

This is the last thing you will want to deal with if you are bugging in during some kind of national emergency.

Of course, mankind has done plenty to poison the waters we depend on. There is no denying the chemical runoff from things like agriculture and mining. These things have had terrible effects on our water resources and aquatic life.

Chemical contamination comes from runoff, dumping into water sources, or poorly managed chemical additives, like chlorine.

Chemical contamination can also occur from parts of your water collection system that are not managed properly or maintained. Things like rust and leaching chemicals are both examples of this kind of contamination.

That said, there are a variety of mistakes you can make that will radically affect your chances of survival. The good news is these mistakes are easy to avoid once you understand them.

The Most Common Deadly Water Storage Mistakes

Dirty Water Storage Containers

Whether we are talking about juice and milk containers that haven't been washed properly or containers that are not food safe, storing water in dirty storage containers is very dangerous. By doing this you are going to create immediate contamination of the water source.

The longer water is stored in dirty water storage containers the more contaminated that water source can become. Both chemical and natural bacterial contamination from doing this can be deadly.

Direct Sunlight

A mistake that is easy to make is for your water storage to be exposed to direct sunlight. This will create a variety of problems for you. The biggest is that the direct sunlight will promote algae growth, which makes your water dangerous to drink.

Poor Maintenance Of Water Containers

Water containers need to be maintained. They can be made of different types of plastics and maybe have metal spigots that need to be maintained. You should wash out your water storage containers at least once per year.

Not Storing Enough Water

You will need at least 1 gallon of water per person per day in order to stay hydrated. I would recommend storing even more than that to aid in cooking and personal hygiene, as well.

You will also need a plan to water animals and gardens, should these be part of your bug in plan.

Not Testing Water

If you are pulling water from a new source, you should be testing the water. If it is your first-time filtering water from a river or pulling water from a rain barrel, then take the time to test it to ensure there are no life-threatening contaminants.

Poor Rotation

Long term water storage needs to be rotated over time. Use your stored water to drink, cook, and clean over time so that you can rotate in fresh water either from the tap or in the form of bottled water.

Improper Chlorine Use

One of the most common and simplest ways to make water safe to drink is through chlorination.

However, if you do not know how much unscented bleach to add to your water, then you can either not kill enough of the pathogens or over-chlorinate the water and make your family sick.

6886 Rule for Water Sanitization

- 6 drops of 8 percent bleach per gallon of water
- 8 drops of 6 percent bleach per gallon of water

Not Explaining the Water Storage Procedures to Your Family

All of the information above and all the water preps you have acquired until now are of the utmost importance. Still, what if something were to happen to you?

Does your family know how much bleach to add to rain barrel water to make it safe to drink? Do they know how to test water quality?

No matter how well prepared you are, you can only be as strong as your weakest link. Maybe the biggest mistake you can make is not training your family how to use water filters, bleach, and teaching them to avoid all the mistakes we have just mentioned.

How to Test Water Before Drinking It

Whether you are pulling water from a lake, a rain barrel or a well, you want to have confidence in that water source and its safety. Sure, it may need to be filtered and even boiled to be ready to drink, clean, or to cook with.

How do you test your drinking water after a serious disaster or emergency? How do you know if your water is safe to drink during your bug in?

Consider the Disaster

Ground Water Contamination

There are all kinds of disasters that can affect the quality of groundwater. If you are dependent on a well for your water or even an inground pool or body of water, it could easily get contaminated.

Disasters like earthquakes and floods can easily contaminate the ground water and if you do not have a way to test your water sources, then you will not know they are contaminated.

Radiated Water

There are some radiological disasters and of course nuclear war, which could very well contaminate your water sources, too. The problem with this is that common water testing methods are not going to work to tell you about the radiation levels in the water.

Drinking radiated water is going to make you very sick and eventually kill you. You will need a dosimeter or Geiger counter to know whether or not your water source is contaminated by radiation. The good news is that water does not stay radiated for long unless the radiation exposure is continual and if that is the case, then bugging in will likely not be an option for survival.

So, measuring contamination and having a backup plan like water storage indoors, is going to make all the difference.

Water Testing Kits

For everything else you should use trusted water quality testing kits. Remember, testing water quality is a tried-and-true process that is conducted all the time in every place that provides the public with water. Water testing kits are the in-home version of that process and do a great job of telling you if your water is safe to drink.

The great thing about these water testing kits is they often come with 100 test strips for your water so you can test regularly, if you like. The Fresh Water Analysis Kit is a great option that comes with 100 strips for testing water quality and 2 bacteria tests that you could use immediately following a natural disaster.

Remember that water filtration and boiling water will eliminate natural contamination. What you are most worried about after a disaster are chemical contamination levels in the water.

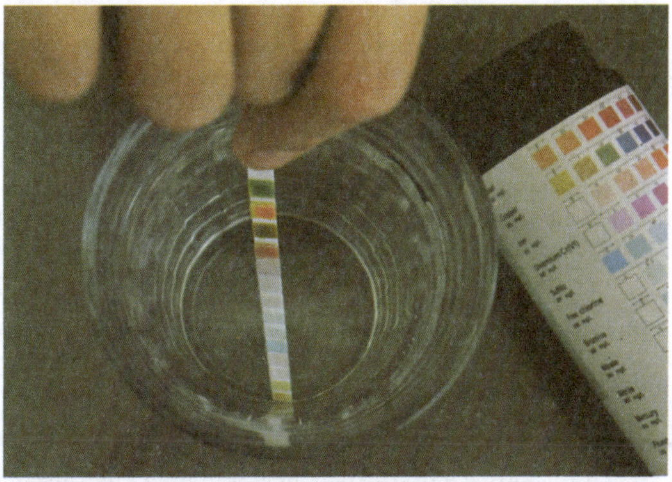

An example of an easy to use water testing kit

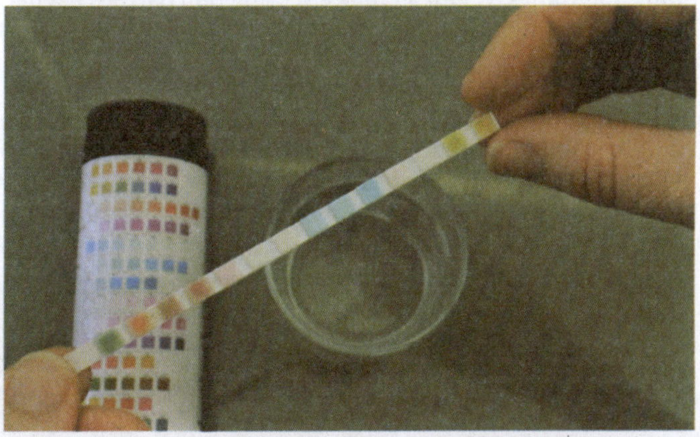

Consult the product instructions when reading the results.

Test your water stockpile regularly and only drink it if it's still good.

A Simple and Cheap Device That Can Filter Huge Quantities of Water

There are a variety of water filters on the market today. You can have a tabletop water filter in your home, and you might even pack a straw type of water filter in your bug out bag. However, there is one type of water filter that you MUST have as part of your bug in water storage solution.

I am talking about a hand pump water filter. This type of water filter allows you to put a tube into a water source and then pump that water through the filtration system and out the other end comes clean water.

The Survivor Filter Pro is one of the best and most affordable handheld pump water filters on the market. Weighing in at just 12.8 oz., this filter is also very easy to carry and store.

The three-stage water filtration system is comprised of a pre-filter, carbon filter, and an ultrafilter. This filtration system is USA Tested to remove 99.999% of tested Virus, Staph, Bacteria and Protozoa and reduces heavy metals according to NSF/ANSI Standards.

The Survivor Filter Pro — **$69.95**

https://amzn.to/44qTyac

When you have a powerful handheld water filter like this one for a bug in situation, you will be able to use it for several different things. When it comes to using rain barrels, having a pump water filter makes drinking that water much safer and easier.

If you plan on pulling water from a pool, creek, or pond in a bug in situation, then having a hand pump water filter will make sourcing water much easier. Your other alternatives are hauling dirty water back to your home to filter and sanitize as you see fit.

Not only will this water filter remove 99.999% contaminants, but it does this so fast that it is hard to believe. Just by using the hand pump you can pump a standard 16.9 oz. bottle of water per minute. That is 500 ml of water every minute with a simple hand pump.

These are long lasting water filters that are used by the military to purify water all around the world.

Everything this affordable water filter offers you, and you get a lifetime guarantee!

Why You Should Put A Silver Coin In Water

Basic Container Hygiene

Clean water is essential for survival, and it is vital to ensure water safety. One way to do this is to ensure that water bottles and containers are kept clean and free from bacteria by regularly washing them with hot, soapy water and giving them a thorough rinse afterward.

It is also essential to ensure the bottles are completely dry before storing them away, as dampness can create an environment where bacteria can thrive. By taking these simple steps, you can ensure that your equipment does not contaminate your water supply.

But what about the water itself?

Bacteria can be present in water at its source, introducing bacteria into your equipment.

Silver as Water Preservation Agent

Silver is known for its anti-bacterial properties, as it can kill bacteria, fungi, and other microorganisms. Silver ions penetrate bacterial cells when released into liquids and surfaces and disrupt the metabolic processes that allow them to survive.

Silver ions bind to the bacteria's cell membranes, blocking the cells from receiving nutrients and causing them to die. Silver is an excellent tool for preppers and survival enthusiasts looking to stay off-grid and live a more sustainable lifestyle.

Silver can be used to treat water, preventing the growth of bacteria that can make it undrinkable. It can also create anti-bacterial surfaces, providing hygiene and protection from disease.

Is Silver Safe?

Silver has long proven to be an effective tool for water purification. Silver is non-toxic and can purify large volumes of water quickly and easily.

Additionally, silver is more affordable than many other water purification methods, making it an ideal choice for preppers and homesteaders.

Silver has been used since antiquity as a natural antimicrobial agent, and by placing a solid silver coin into a water bottle, you can help to kill any bacteria that may try to form.

In addition, silver coins are a lightweight and cost-effective way to ensure that the water you have with you is always safe to drink, and it's a great way to stay prepared for any situation.

The silver from a silver coin will not contaminate the water in the bottle; instead, it will remain safe for human consumption. Therefore, water with a silver coin in it will remain safe from microbial contamination and will remain safe for drinking.

Only the Real McCoy Will Do

Knowing if a coin is solid silver or merely silver-plated is vital for preppers. Silver-plated coins could lose their plating, which can release other metals into the water.

Therefore, it is essential to use a solid pure silver coin. To test the authenticity of a coin, you can use a magnet. If the coin is attracted to the magnet, it is not pure silver, as silver is not magnetic.

Additionally, you can use a nitric acid test to see if a coin is a silver or merely silver-plated.

This test involves rubbing a small drop of nitric acid onto the coin. If the coin is silver, the acid will not react, and the coin will remain unchanged.

However, the acid will create a dull spot or discolor if the coin is silver-plated.

Getting Hold of Real Silver

Preppers and survival enthusiasts looking to acquire solid silver coins can find them in many places. Online retailers often offer a wide selection of silver coins in various sizes, denominations, and styles.

Coin dealers and pawn shops are also great places to buy silver coins, as they often have a good selection of rare and collectible coins.

Additionally, many banks and credit unions offer silver coins, making them an excellent and easily accessible choice for those looking to purchase them.

Lastly, many local coin shows and conventions provide a wide selection of silver coins, allowing preppers to find the perfect ones for their needs.

Other Silver Options

Silver coins were traditionally used to purify water, but several other options are available to preppers and survival enthusiasts. For example, silver metal drops, also known as colloidal silver, can kill bacteria in water.

This method is relatively easy to use and requires only a few drops of silver in a water container. However, colloidal silver can be expensive and must be used carefully, as it can cause water discoloration if too much silver is added.

Another option for purifying water is to use silver wire.

Silver wire has been used for centuries to purify drinking water and can be fashioned into a wide range of shapes and sizes. In addition, silver wire is relatively easy to use and can be fashioned into various shapes to suit the user's needs.

Finally, silver-lined water bottles are an excellent option for purifying water. This method requires a special water bottle with an interior silver lining. The silver kills the bacteria in the water and makes it safe to drink.

Silver-lined water bottles are easy to use and do not require any additional equipment. Regardless of your chosen method, it is essential to remember that silver effectively purifies water.

Each of the above methods has its benefits and drawbacks, so it is vital to research each option before deciding which one is best for your survival needs.

How Much to Use

In terms of quantity, the amount of silver needed to keep a given amount of water pure can vary depending on the application. For general use, an approximate guideline is that 2 grams per gallon is sufficient for keeping bacteria and other contaminants at bay.

Silver can also be used in reservoirs, but it is essential to remember that silver is not a filter and should be combined with other filtration methods to ensure the water is entirely free of contaminants.

You can learn here how to build a rainwater harvesting and purification system that will give you an endless supply of clean water to drink and cook with.

Is One Coin Enough?

A silver coin can keep water fresh for an extended period, but the amount of silver needed depends on how much water you want to stay fresh. Generally, 3 liters of water would require around 3-6 grams of silver.

Therefore, if using a silver coin, you will want to choose a coin that is at least one ounce in weight, or 28.35 grams.

When Not to Use a Coin

Silver coins are not recommended for camelbacks since they can be difficult to remove and may damage the material.

Instead, you can use a silver wire or silver mesh. Silver wire is a thin strand of silver that can be woven into a mesh and placed in the water container to keep it fresh.

Silver mesh is a more durable option and can be reused. Both silver wire and silver mesh can be purchased from various online retailers.

HOME SECURITY

How to Make Your Property LOOTER-PROOF

In the military we are really good at defense. We have the resources, the manpower and the training to do so. In your case, you might not have any of those things. Though in a collapsed society the challenges you face could be similar to those we face in a warzone.

When the hungry and desperate people in the neighbourhood find out that you have a stockpile of supplies, they will consider stealing it to feed their families.

It may seem like the best defence in cases like this would be a good offence. However, I can assure you that if you plan to defend your home with force as the first line of defence, you will find out too late why that strategy is flawed. What we need is a multi-layered approach to securing our homes against looters, with violence being the last resort.

The military uses procedures to help deal with people approaching our bases. We do things like identify and establish communications. Even soldiers have protocol to follow before they jump on a weapon and neutralize a target. We have rules of engagement.

We have seen many instances of mob rule turning ordinary people into mindless looters. All it takes is a few bad actors to rile up a crowd, and chaos will ensue.

Anyone can become a looter, be it a riot or full-blown SHTF; many individuals who have never so much as had a parking ticket will be smashing the windows of the nearest Best Buy to steal anything not bolted to the floor.

Desperate people who want to feed their families will be a significant threat, but one that will not be well organized or particularly dangerous. Instead, these individuals will be looking for empty homes they can ransack rather than weaving their way through a maze of alarms and traps to attack a fortified house.

Desperate individuals and ordinary people caught up in the situation are only one group you need to be concerned about. Local gangs and organized crime have the resources to take whatever they want from whomever they wish. These groups are the ones that you want to avoid crossing at all costs.

At the elite levels of special operations forces, we conduct what is known as an Area Study. The area study, while not always conducted the same way, is designed to give our men on the ground a better understanding of all manners of the environment they are operating in.

You can conduct your own area study and research things like demographics, political geography, social structure, crime, gang activity, resources and routes of travel. This information will help you better understand exactly who those larger groups are in your area and likely approach vectors.

Local Police and FBI websites can be a great place to get information about gangs in your area.

Sun Tzu said:

"The greatest victory is that which requires no battle."

When looters descend on your home, it seems logical that opening fire on those trying to break in would deter most of them and prevent anyone from entering your home.

Unfortunately, the reality is that anyone you wound or kill will have friends and family that will probably want to seek vengeance. It also emphasizes to anyone in the area that you have stuff worth killing to protect.

All you are doing by shooting first is turning your home into a larger target and opening yourself up to future prosecution if the SHTF situation turns out to be temporary.

You will also be forced to live with the psychological consequences of your actions, especially if they turn out to be the wrong choice.

Before any trigger is pulled, you must be 100 percent sure there is no other option; the same goes for deploying traps or devices that can critically wound or kill.

Don't Be a Target

The best way to deter looting is to give the impression that there is nothing of value inside your home. This is a tricky proposition, especially when we must rely on our stockpile of supplies to survive. It takes a lot of effort and discipline to keep others from realizing the extent of our preparedness supplies.

One of the first things we can do is exercise solid Operational Security (OPSEC). There is no reason that your neighbours should know the details of your preps, and you should make every effort to hide the fact that you are ready for SHTF.

Clandestine missions are a great comparison to your own operational security. Covert and clandestine missions are a vital part of any military operation. These are missions that very few ever know about.

You should look at things like deliveries, training, and adding fortifications to the home as clandestine missions of your own.

Once we are in an SHTF situation, there are other measures that we can take to make looters move along.

Noise and Light Discipline

When the grid fails, the world will become very still, dark and quiet; any disruption to this new reality will stand out like a sore thumb.

It is important to keep any noise that is artificial or obviously generated by electronic devices to an absolute minimum. Running a generator will attract the attention of those around you who are desperate for power. The sounds of music, radio communications, appliances, power tools, etc., will attract much-unwanted attention.

While it is still a bit of an investment, night vision has become much more reasonable in price. When the Navy SEALs operate at night our targets have trouble seeing us but with night vision tech they stick out like a sore thumb.

You might consider adding a simple night vision monocular lens to your gear so that you can avoid using the flashlights at night and instead strap on something like those created by Nightstar.

If you have a battery bank that allows you to have power during dark hours, be sure that you are blacking out windows so that no one can see inside your home and you have electricity and are running lights indoors.

LED Strip Lights	$15.40

https://t.ly/WGhMY (Amazon)

Battery powered LED strip lights can be run up railings, behind televisions and in bathrooms essentially lighting up any room with the press of a button and just 3 AA batteries in each.

Keeping Preps Out of Sight

If you are forced to bug in and start using your stockpile of gear and supplies, it is vital to keep any desirable items out of sight. If you must use your solar panels, keep them out of sight from anyone who may be walking past. Equipment desirable to looters should always be kept out of sight from anyone who is not in your immediate family.

A Navy SEAL mission can begin with a night jump and then traversing water. In these conditions, we are donning camouflage, our boats are black, and the night keeps us concealed. We use camouflaged tarps, nets, and—the best option—natural vegetation in the light of day to hide things from the enemy. Camo netting can be used to cover up chicken coops and water storage or even vehicles!

Dogs

If you have a dog, you should encourage them to bark at anyone approaching the house. Even if the dog doesn't have a mean bone in their body, the barking from your home will deter many people who may be looking at your home as an easy target. None of us want to be attacked by a dog, and the same goes for looters.

Dogs are the absolute BEST alarm and deterrent! If you have some land, consider getting some guinea fowl. They are self-sufficient, eat thousands of ticks, are good meat birds, produce eggs, and are crazy loud! ANYTHING approaching your property will get called out, and no one will miss the alarm!

Police Your Trash

It is hard to say that you don't have food when your neighbours can see the empty canned goods in your trash. Remember that no one is coming to bring your trash to the dump. The stuff you throw away may betray you. Searching someone's trash is a well known surveillance technique.

The bottom line is that the best defence for your home is never to be attacked by looters in the first place.

Making It Difficult for Looters to Approach Undetected

A well-known military weakness is that we lack the foresight to know what the next conflict will look like, both in environmental factors and the evolving generations of warfighting techniques. We are always training and designing gear and tactics based on the last conflict. After years of fighting with counterinsurgency in mind, the U.S. military is beginning to shift expectations back to peer warfare missions. The threat is no longer in the sands of the Middle East but in the Far East in places like China and Russia. These militaries are much more comparable to that of the US.

Before doing anything else, you need to take a good look at the property from a defence perspective. Look out all the windows and see if any locations offer concealment from the view of people inside the home. Unfortunately, there may not be anything that you can do about these spots.

It could be time for you to change tactics, too! Install countermeasures to either deter looters from using them or at least alert you that someone is using the area to conceal themselves.

Areas around doors and windows must be free of shrubs and bushes that offer hiding places. Make sure you can walk out of any entry door and not run the risk of being ambushed by someone hiding in the shadows. Ensure that each window you use for defence and observation has clear sightlines and minimal areas to the front where looters could find cover.

After you have viewed the property from a defensive standpoint, view it from an attacker's perspective. Approaching your home as if you are about to loot is the best way to assess the defence plans' effectiveness and determine what changes need to be made.

An inexpensive commercial/subscription-based or home-built closed circuit television setup is worth investing in. Mine chimes when it detects anyone in its field of view, and I can then use my phone to view the feed if I'm not near the base unit.

Layers of Defence

The trick is to lay out multiple overlapping layers of defence from your property line to the walls of your home. The goal is to deter anyone from attempting to loot in the first place, but if they decide to breach the perimeter, there should be measures in place to slow them down.

Fencing

A tall fence around the property line is an excellent first line of defence. Still, most single-family homes only fence the backyard leaving the front wide open. If it is practical, consider running a chain-link fence or picket fence around the front of the property. Shorter fencing will not be as effective but will slow down a looter's advance.

Placing razor blades, broken glass, nail boards, or razor wire on top of a fence will make it very difficult for a looter to climb over the top. Even placing these types of deterrents on shorter fencing will help to prevent looters from climbing over.

It's a very good idea to make these fence deterrents easy to see as it's best to have people decide NOT to attempt to break in rather than to have them learn the hard way, which can have unintended consequences.

Even if the fence line does not cover the entire property line, it will help funnel looters through the gaps, making their movements predictable and allowing you to place early warning alarms and traps.

In combat tactics this is a defensive strategy that we call creating a CHOKE POINT or forcing movement into a channelized area.

Early Warning

Placing alarms, cameras, and other early warning devices around the property will alert you to anyone trying to breach the perimeter. You can also place alarm devices that are loud and disruptive, which can also act as a deterrent.

For example, when a looter trips a tripwire alarm and is met by a loud bang from an empty shotgun shell or primer going off, they will think twice about continuing.

Installing cameras is also a great early warning system as well. Cameras should cover all entry points into the building and provide general coverage over the front, back, and sides.

While modern security cameras get all the glory for home security, don't forget about the hunters trail cameras which come camouflaged and can be hidden in places that give you greater time to react. Just because you don't have satellite imagery doesn't mean you can't see the threats coming.

The best way to monitor cameras is to have all the live feeds displayed on the same screen of screens directly adjacent to each other. Couple cameras with a good comms plan; you can direct other family members to where they should mount their defence in real time.

Traps

Deploying traps on your property should not be taken lightly. In most cases, doing so is illegal. It opens you up to the possibility of legal ramifications once everything returns to normal.

In addition, you should not deploy traps designed to kill or critically injure. Doing so will cause more problems than it is worth, and there is a significant probability that these traps will inflict collateral damage.

Depending on the size of your property, there are many types of traps and obstacles that you could set out to secure your land. When deciding what to place and where to, consider how these traps will affect approaching looters.

For example: If there is an open area that looters may run through, stringing a tripwire or laying loose coils of barbed wire would be effective at slowing their advance. Where someone may vault over a fence would be a good spot for a nail board or punji stick trap.

The best way to plan the placement of traps and alarms is to draw a scale map of the property, including all fencing, trees, shrubbery, gardens, neighbouring properties, entry points, etc. Then you can decide where to place devices to alert you or to trap the looters.

After you have decided on placement and deployed the alarms and traps, approach the property as if you are a looter and test the effectiveness of the layers of security you have built. Doing this is an excellent way to determine whether the traps and alarms will be effective and if there are any gaps in coverage.

If cameras are a part of your security, take a walk around the property and have someone watch the camera feed and let you know where all the blind spots are. Then adjust the camera angles to provide as much coverage as possible.

Securing the Entry Points

Looters may navigate the maze of traps and alarms that you have placed. In this case, you will find that these desperate people will try to enter your home through any weak points they can find. Therefore, these points must be secured and hardened against attack.

Windows

Windows are the weakest link in the entire home. All it takes is a well-placed brick, and looters can access the inside of the building.

Installing bars on the windows is a good option but one that is not aesthetically pleasing. Most people will not want to install bars on each window, but one option is to purchase bars and store them until you find yourself in a bug in scenario. A problem with bars is that they also make it difficult to exit the home through the window.

If the steel bar route is not an option for your home, polymer or plastic film can be installed on glass windows which helps to prevent them from shattering. These films will be almost invisible and make the windows challenging to break.

3M makes an incredible clear tape for windows that makes them much harder to break. This will not only alert you but it will also take the easiest way into your home and make it much more difficult.

Placing nail boards or punji stick traps below windows will make it exceedingly difficult for looters to get close enough to make entry through a window. They will also act as a last line of defence when looters rush to the window without paying attention.

Stepping in a Punji stick trap will stop almost anyone in their tracks, much like stepping on a nail board. Unfortunately, this leaves you with the problem of a wounded looter.

Doors

Doorways are where most looters and others will make their first attempts at breaking in. The problem with doors is that they are designed to open inward, making them vulnerable to being kicked or bashed in. Doorways are also the points that you will be using for ingress and egress into your home.

The first step is installing only the highest quality entry doors you can afford. The best main entry doors are steel, which is almost impossible to break down. However, we should not lull ourselves into a false sense of security.

Most doors are designed to stop a burglar who is trying to break into a home quickly so they can avoid being arrested. They are not intended to stop a mob of looters in a world without law and order.

Most doors are not secured properly when they're installed. They just use nails to secure the jams. Kicking the door is very easy. To fortify our homes, we can add more elements that secure our homes' entry points further.

Doors hang on hinges which allow us to open and close them easily. These hinges, however, represent a weak link in the door's ability to secure the home. Therefore, buy upgraded hinges whenever possible and replace the included screws with longer, stronger ones. Drill in 3-inch screws right into the frame.

Being a Navy SEAL I take my home fortifications very seriously. I installed a product called door armor on my main doors. This fortifies multiple parts of the door and the door frame. It makes your door much harder to break into using tools like a crowbar or a saw.

To secure doors against being kicked in, the first line of defence is the highest quality deadbolt you can afford. The locking mechanisms for your entry doors are not the area to try and save money. Do not install smart locks or any devices that use Bluetooth or Wi-Fi. These locks could be hacked and disabled even in a grid-down scenario.

Along with an upgraded deadbolt, you need to also reinforce the door jam as well. Add a reinforcement lock that blocks the door from the inside. Make sure to add this at the point of impact, which is usually at the middle. Most people install this in the upper corner of the door frame, which does not help much if anyone tries to break open your door.

Securing the door with a heavy board or steel bar is another way to prevent the door from being broken down. These bars or boards are held in place with purpose-built brackets fastened to the studs on either side of the doorway. When reinforcing a door this way, you must use lag screws rather than wood screws to fasten the brackets to the wall.

Use as many lag screws as possible to ensure that the brackets will not be ripped from the wall if the door is hit with sufficient force.

Garage Doors

Many break-ins occur through garage doors because they can often be opened by criminals who can figure out the code that garage door openers use to activate the motor, or they either drive a vehicle into the garage door or pull the door off the tracks. Many garage doors are made from thin sheet metal, which is easy to cut into or bend enough to push it inward and off the tracks.

There is no really good way to secure the actual door against being pushed in or pulled out. Likewise, not much can be done to stop someone from cutting their way through the door.

To this end, the best solution is to secure the doorway from the garage to the home like all the other entry doors and to keep the garage empty of anything you do not want to fall into the hands of looters.

Installing early warning systems on the garage door will alert you that the door has been compromised and allow you to mount a defence.

Booby traps are not a straightforward tactic. They can be exceptionally effective and can also be counter-productive in this particular scenario. As much as I love using them, they are rife with liabilities and must be employed with extreme caution and a well-thought-out strategy. Without that, you will open yourself up to strategic, tactical, and legal ramifications.

To be specific, putting in an injurious trap on your property in a SHTF situation to deter/take out looters or enemies also has the potential to hurt or kill a neighbor, their pet or livestock, or a child, which will likely turn your neighbors (an extremely important asset) completely against you, screwing up your overall strategy.

Additionally, booby traps are a (mostly) set and forget tool, so after you set them, you lose the ability to identify your target before triggering. And you will have little to no control over the target. Friendlies, pets, livestock, and children are all potential casualties. So you MUST have a clear understanding of the intended target(s), who and what travels on that route, and where to place the trigger.

This brings up a multitude of potential legal liabilities. Just because potential victims are trespassing does NOT give you the right—either morally or legally—to set intentionally injury-causing traps to cause harm, and after the SHTF situation has passed (which it will), you will be open to legal action, both criminal and civil.

In Manhunt, I set booby traps and early warning systems all the time. However, it was a television show, and none of my traps had a kinetic component that could actually injure my opponents. That being said, the goal of those traps was to slow down pursuers, to make them feel hunted as well, and to get in their heads. No one wants to be the dude who triggered the trap on a global television show! In the SEAL teams, booby traps and stay-behinds (another name for a quickly deployed deterrent) were used to injure, not kill. When you injure an enemy, you then take that person out of the equation; they're usually in great pain and mental anguish, so they're freaking everyone else out with them. They're noisy, and now someone else needs to carry and attend to them and a third person needs to take their load and areas of responsibility. So with a properly executed booby trap, you have the potential to take three (or more) enemies out of the fight as well as slowing down pursuit, crippling their effectiveness and getting in their heads! So early warning systems and deterrents are in many cases a better choice than a trap designed to injure or kill.

Now that we've gotten the cautionary part out of the way, we can get to the good stuff!

There are many different types of traps and primitive tech that are generally just traps used for hunting game scaled up to man size. There are also modern self-contained stay-behinds like the PDM and other explosive, kinetic types. There are three main components to a good dynamic trap: the payload (the injury-causing or noisemaking part), the energy supply (what powers it, whether electricity, a tension rod or spring, a counterweight, or a person's own weight/gravity/momentum), and the most important part of the trap, in my opinion, the trigger.

There are five general types of trigger actuation: pull, pressure, pressure release, tension, and tension release. Most triggering systems fall into one of these categories. For home defense scenarios like this, I prefer static traps such as tangle using netting or, even better, concertina (razor) wire or barbed wire if concertina wire is hard to source. Chicken wire or plastic bird netting will work as well but are less durable. Pulling a roll of concertina wire loosely across routes of approach is incredibly effective and can be easily pulled back away from driveways or other routes of approach. Not only is it painful to run into even if it's not anchored but it is very difficult to see, will entangle a person nearly inextricably, is impossible to move through, and is very simple to attach noisemakers to. The best technique for this, in my opinion, is to use three coils, two next to each other on the ground and one loosely stacked on top, like a pyramid. The problem is that the coils will become entangled with each other, making it difficult to roll back up, but in this manner, it can't really be jumped over or pulled apart to get by. You can use dynamic noisemakers such as shotgun primers, battery-operated doorbell chimes or alarms from any home improvement store, cowbells, or simply empty bottles or cans that are attached to it. This is an exceptionally effective and cheap deterrent and alarm. I used a variation of this technique in the South Korea episode of Manhunt, and it worked well.

I prefer noisemakers and lights as my primary deterrents as these allow me to then see what is occurring and then use my judgment to determine how I want to engage. It's also not damaging for animals or friendlies.

Whatever traps you choose, you must MARK THEM and attend to them, just like a trapper. There is nothing more irresponsible than setting a trap or snare and then not checking on it.

Inside the Home

Once a group of looters is at your door, there is a possibility that they may eventually make their way into the home. This is the time when defending oneself becomes a necessity but depending on the number of looters and the situation, you may need to take other actions.

Fighting Inside Your Home

The SEALS use a wide variety of defensive strategies. We have already discussed choke points and your front door or windows become a perfect choke point. So for this next section, let's talk about cover versus concealment really quickly. Simply put, cover is "They can't shoot me," while concealment is "They can't see me." For example, cover would be a brick wall, and concealment would be behind a door.

Fortification is another defensive strategy. To fortify our home, you will need bullet stopping cover. Sandbags are best, and you can easily keep a stack of empty bags on hand. You can fill these bags with sand, dirt, solid, rocks, etc. and stack them in areas you intend to use as defensive positions.

However, once you set a fortified barrier up, you are bound by it unless you are going to set up overlapping and fallback defensive positions. (Who wants to do this in their home?) It's much better to be mobile unless you have the high ground and clear fields of fire with overwhelmingly superior firepower. For this reason, I prefer body armor. You can get Level 3 plates (protection from most commonly used rounds) for less than $100 each! I use 3A front and back plates from AR500 Armor (currently about $129 each). While body armor won't protect your lower body or head, you will remain mobile, and it will protect your vital organs and keep you in the fight longer. I keep mine by my bed so I can throw it on quickly and engage! You can spend much more and get lightweight ceramic or even flexible plates, but unless you are using them for eight-plus hours a day, 3A steel plates and a decent plate carrier are fine.

If you are going to set up a defensive position in your house, it's better to set up a trap to pin the bad guys down rather than pinning yourself down with a fortification. One incredibly effective one I learned from LAPD SWAT that they were dealing with back in the eighties and nineties was the chain-link box. Essentially, you build a chain link-box just inside the entry point of your home. It can be as simple as an anchored roll of chain link, but it's better to have it secured with posts to create a small foyer of sorts just as you enter through the door. The better constructed ones would have tubular metal fence posts anchored to the floor and ceiling, with a door that is able to be padlocked leading into the actual living space. This maintains the functionality of your home while also giving you complete control over everyone coming in that door, invited or not! When the LAPD would raid, the cops stacking on the door would find themselves stuck in a cage with more cops entering behind them and preventing their exit, and they were in a Keystone Kops shooting gallery of sorts. You could also deploy chemical spray, such as bear or pepper spray, or other nonlethal techniques here. If the threat is great enough, one man could leisurely pick off all the attackers from behind cover/concealment. If you don't want to fight, it also buys time for you to exit out the back.

A trap like this is easily built and, while ugly, doesn't compromise the livability of your home. It is also incredibly effective and cheap! This was causing one of the best-trained, -experienced, and -equipped SWAT teams in the world no end of problems back in the day! It will work for you.

Aside from sandbags, not many household objects will block bullets. One item that has been shown to be effective against small arms fire is books or stacks of paper. It is unlikely that anyone would have enough paper on hand to form a barricade thick enough to be effective.

Cinder blocks, brick, and cement are viable options if you have a surplus of those materials. Railroad ties are also a good option going the fortification route, if you find you have access to them.

It is important to remember that modern western homes are usually wood frame construction with plywood, thin siding, and drywall as the only things standing between you and gunfire. Most bullets will easily pass through a home's walls, making it exceedingly challenging to harden a house against gunfire.

Don't bother unless you have LOTS of money and are willing to completely remodel your house around a potential firefight. Learn about the fatal funnel (doorways), and how bullets travel down walls, and adjust your tactics accordingly: Stay at least a foot off of walls as bullets tend to ricochet and travel down the wall. If you are leaning on the wall, you will get hit.

People who aren't well conditioned to violence will often break mentally and stop or flee when confronted with death or maiming. Factor this into your own anticipated behavior and that of potential invaders.

I would also consider buying frangible rounds for your weapon. Frangible rounds will break apart into powder when hitting interior walls instead of passing through unscathed. That way you don't have to be as concerned about your own gunfire penetrating too far into the interior of your home and hitting a loved one.

Depending on how many people are attacking, it may be best to withdraw from the situation rather than stand fast and mount a defense. In the military, we have what are considered acceptable casualties. Who in your family would you consider an acceptable casualty? Avoid firefights at MOST costs because bullets go both ways.

This is a good place to talk about something I always bring up in escape and evasion. In the military, we are taught to resist and escape and to evade up until the point of injury or death. They teach that it is better to be captured than to succumb to the elements or experience great injury. I generally disagree. Personally, there are many instances where I would much rather die than be captured. The Japanese did terrible things to the Filipinos in WW2, and many other countries have treated POWs very badly. I say that to illustrate that if my home were being invaded, in most circumstances—although the situation ALWAYS dictates—I will stand my ground.

I do not lightly say "the situation dictates." This is an exceptionally important piece. There is NEVER a one-size-fits-all solution to a problem. There is no one best tactic, knife, gun, etc. The real-world situation; the varying circumstances and conditions; and your varying abilities, assets, and goals will always affect your answer—and they should. So always adapt whatever knowledge and assets you have around the situation, not the reverse. We MUST stay flexible. In this book, we are presenting lots of options. It is up to YOU to be discerning and choose what best serves your abilities, desires, budget, and training and then to implement those.

The key to this is that you MUST decide ahead of time what your plan is. Decide when you are at your best, not when you are cold, wet, tired, hungry, or just pulled out of a sound sleep by a home invasion. You must make a plan when you are thinking clearly, communicate it to all concerned, then trust it!

In the SEAL teams, because we are a small, unconventional force and don't utilize numbers or very many conventional assets, we can win most engagements with violence of action, meaning ruthless, aggressive, unyielding violence and firepower.

Yes, avoid firefights as much as possible, especially if you are not well acquainted with or conditioned to violence; however, once the first effective shot is fired, you are in it, and you best win it!

In a raid or engagement, there are three winning strategies: speed, surprise, and violence of action. You must have two of these to expect victory. In this scenario, you will likely not have surprise (but the attackers might), so you must use speed of movement/reaction and return fire—overwhelmingly return effective fire—utilizing shock value and violence. Set yourself up to neutralize any surprise the attackers might have as much as possible. Like I mentioned before, people not intimately conditioned to violence will often recoil and lose their motivation when it becomes real.

This is a good place to speak about the reactionary gap. A reactionary gap is simply the time between someone violating your personal space in some manner and your mental and physical process to react to it. This can be trained. Condition yourself to take an unexpected punch if possible, and accustom yourself to gunfire, especially in an enclosed place. Running drills in your home is a great way to train this.

Mike Tyson:

"Everyone has a plan until they get punched in the mouth."

You should not overlook the military strategy of withdrawal. Live to fight another day. Everyone must sleep, even the bad guys. There could come a better time to attack.

You need to have several routes which you can use to escape the property in the event a swarm of looters funnels through your front door. If your home has multiple stories, you need a plan and a route to escape from each floor. This includes the basement or crawlspace.

No matter where you are in the home, you should have a couple of ways to get out, and you should plan your defenses so that an invader will never block your only path to an egress or a weapon. No matter where they are or I am in my home, I can exit and circle back behind them, and I always have access to a firearm.

For higher floors, you can purchase roll-up ladders mounted underneath the windows. These ladders can be deployed rapidly, allowing a quick exit from the upper floors. For the ground floor or basements, you should plan on using windows as an exit since looters will probably enter through the doorways.

An escape plan also needs to include a rally point where everyone will meet after the escape. It may not be possible for everyone to exit the house simultaneously, so it is vital to establish a rally point far enough away from the home that you can be out of sight of the looting.

If forced to flee, you'll want several caches of food, water, ammo, medical supplies, and fuel stored outside the home. Even small hidden caches with food, water, and other critical supplies will be helpful if you are forced into a bugout.

Bugging In for Apartment Dwellers

So many of us live in urban areas and cannot live in a single-family home or on a property of any significant size. Therefore, the prospect of a remote off-grid location is also out of reach for the average family. What this means is that a considerable number of people will be stuck in a tall concrete tower when SHTF hits.

Bugging in a condo or apartment building is going to be one of the most challenging environments to do so. While you are stuck inside your unit, getting water or food will require imagination and creativity. The only advantage is that the concrete walls will provide good ballistic protection. There are a few things that you can do if you are forced to bug in while living in an apartment or condo.

Join Forces with Your Neighbours

There is strength in numbers, and one of the best ways to get through SHTF is to join forces with those around you. Surviving in an apartment building alone is almost impossible. However, if the residents of the building organize to mount a unified defence, it is entirely possible to repel attacks from looters.

It is very common for the Navy SEALs to build and train allied militaries in other countries. This comes down to having a plan and the knowledge to pull this off. Consider writing up a simple plan for defending your neighborhood and print copies that can be handed out to neighbors.

This will give them instant confidence in you, and make them feel much better. Even if it is not the best plan, it will be much better than not having one at all.

Denying access is a strategic essential when it comes to defending any location.

If it is an actual SHTF situation and there is no escape, the best way to keep looters away from your front door is to isolate the floor you live on.

If the grid is down, the elevators will not function, leaving the stairways as the only avenues of attack. Collect as much furniture as you can from abandoned units and push them down the stairwell, creating a massive, chaotic obstacle. Be careful not to block your only exit, though.

Think about Escape

Apartments are another place where roll-out ladders could be used to access units on lower floors. If you live low enough, you could get a ladder that you could lower all the way to the ground. Fire escapes are also an option for egress, but they are also ways looters could gain access to your unit.

If adjacent buildings are close enough, you could bridge the gap with an extension ladder, but this should be considered a last resort.

Hunkering down in a condo or apartment is far from ideal and will present problems that seem insurmountable, but with a bit of imagination and some help from your neighbours, it is possible to make the situation work during an SHTF situation.

Bugging in opens you up to a wide range of problems you would not likely face if you had a well-stocked and remote location. However, even with the cards stacked against you, you can see that it is possible to do things to shift the odds in your favour.

If you are willing to learn how, rappelling is a great option for quick egress from upper floors or roofs. You can buy static rope for about $1 per foot, and with a figure 8 climbing device and carabiner (about $10), you can effectively and quickly descend from windows and roofs. You will need a harness (less than $20), but you can learn to make an improvised harness called a Swiss seat or use a very sturdy belt in emergencies. You can get a large number of people out of a building quickly this way. You can go to any climbing gym and learn the basics in an afternoon.

Silent Alarms and Traps

Securing our property is paramount during an SHTF situation and one that requires planning and preparation. Traps and alarms are all part of a comprehensive readiness plan and defensive strategy. The 4 Pillars of Army Readiness are, manning, equipping, training and leadership.

The moment you begin to employ things like traps and alarms you need those in your home to understand them, be trained how to use them, and even how to fix them. Otherwise, these devices could become more of a problem than anything else.

When we think of traps and alarms, we usually think of them as loud and disrupting, which alert both the intruder and those inside the home.

While loud alarms and traps have their place, sometimes we should deploy either silent or nearly silent devices to keep the element of surprise on our side. The more notice we have the better we can prepare for the threat.

The terms trap and alarm are sometimes used interchangeably, but they serve different purposes. Traps are designed to deter, delay, or detain any would-be intruders on your property. On the other hand, alarms are meant to detect and to warn those inside the building that the perimeter has been breached.

Alarms should be placed at the perimeter of a property, on or near entryways, or at the access points for any blind spots that you may have.

Traps are best suited to areas that intruders would use as ingress points and areas that provide cover and concealment. However, ingress points and cover and concealment are places we will frequent also, so be very wise with the placement!

Physically walk your property and identify some of the best places for these types of traps and alarms. A simple hand drawn diagram can be a great tool for this and you can simply put an X on the locations where traps should be set. Sharing this with family and neighbors will make them aware of the traps, too.

Using Silent Alarms

When it comes to silent alarms, there are many types and styles that you can use; what you decide on is dependent mainly on your budget and the size of your property. What is compiled here is a list of alarms you can either purchase or, in some cases, build yourself.

This is by no means an exhaustive list; there are many more silent alarms that are available and that can be created with a bit of imagination.

Cameras

Cameras are used to secure almost everything these days! Today's technology delivers a wide range of wired and wireless security cameras, some of which are inexpensive. In fact, there is little excuse not to establish cameras around your property to keep a watchful eye.

Most cameras come with the ability to detect motion built into the software, making them fantastic silent alarms. Using a camera as a motion-sensing alarm also has the advantage of showing you who triggered the alarm.

In addition, many modern security cameras have excellent night vision.

That being said, there are problems with using cameras that require mentioning. I see two major issues with using cameras as a part of your security post-SHTF. Firstly, these cameras require electricity to operate, so you need a power source to run them when the grid is down.

The second is that many wireless cameras require Wi-Fi and mobile apps, so you must keep your Wi-Fi router powered. Steps also need to be taken to ensure that any app associated with the camera can function correctly without direct internet access.

The power issue can be solved by installing a battery bank and solar panels, providing electricity for your camera system and the router. The potential issue of the camera's app not working without the internet can be tested by attempting to use it with internet access temporarily turned off.

Motion Sensors/PIR Sensors

Sensors are a good way to keep a watchful eye on the shadows. Most of these devices use a PIR (Passive Infrared) sensor to detect motion.

The PIR has two sensors placed side by side and the difference between the sensors is monitored.

The unit is triggered when the sensors detect a difference between the two. In addition, the PIR sensor can be a trigger for various electronic devices such as lights, alarms, locks, etc.

There are also wireless motion sensors that you can purchase through online retailers that have transmission ranges of over a hundred feet. These are often meant to be used at the end of a driveway to alert the homeowner that a vehicle has pulled in.

Pressure Plates

Pressure plates are essentially a switch triggered when someone steps on them. You can repurpose pressure switches often used in Halloween displays or build one yourself reasonably quickly.

Pressure plates can be placed underneath mats or camouflaged beneath grass or dirt. A pressure plate does not need to be sophisticated; a pushbutton switch placed in the right location and well concealed is very effective.

A well-designed and placed pressure plate has the advantage of being triggered without the intruder ever realizing that they tripped the alarm. They do, however, have a couple of disadvantages.

One major disadvantage to using pressure plates is that they are challenging to effectively conceal. In some instances, such as along a dirt path, you can cover the pressure plate with soil.

The problem is that many places where you want to place a pressure plate are going to be areas covered in concrete or grass, which are not suitable places to conceal a pressure plate.

Depending on which style of pressure plates you use, the switch may need to be reset each time it is triggered. This may seem like a nit-picky annoyance, but when you're in an SHTF environment, leaving the safety of your home to reset any alarm or trap is risky business.

There is an often overlooked aspect of trap and snare placement that is essential to efficacy, and that is making sure your quarry steps where the trigger is located. With a pressure plate, this is a little easier as the surface area is larger, but it is still not guaranteed. This can be addressed using a tracking principle I use all the time and one we all are familiar with: the path of least resistance. Animals—and humans—all else being equal, will always unconsciously take the path of least resistance, that is, we will use the trail or route that costs the least perceived energy in our travels. We do this subconsciously, so when walking on a trail, we will place our feet in the most efficient manner. Simply put, we step where it's clear and dry. So by using rocks, twigs, and bits of vegetation starting ten to fifteen feet back, we can direct people's footfalls right into the trap. This is easy to learn and doesn't take much practice to get the hang of. Grab a friend, and give it a try. Take small twigs with a bit of greenery on them, and place them in the path, sticking them in the dirt like they are growing there naturally, and watch what happens to your footsteps. Or use stones—whatever is natural to the area is most important.

Magnetic Door Contact Sensors

No matter how many layers of security you place around your home, you must also consider setting alarms around doors and windows. A Magnetic contact sensor is one of the most common sensors used for this purpose. These sensors use magnets to determine whether a door or window is closed or open.

These sensors can be placed on doors, windows, gates, garages, and sliding doors. When the two sides of the sensor are pulled away, the circuit is completed. It can activate a buzzer, alarm, light, or many other electronic devices.

One disadvantage of these sensors is that they can often also be bypassed using a magnet, which is why you should not rely on these for the security of the entry points of your home.

Trip Wire Alarms

Trip wire alarms don't have to go beep or boom. There are a lot of ways to set up a silent tripwire alarm. You can use something as simple as clothes peg or mouse trap as the trigger mechanism, or there is the option to purchase devices that are purpose-built as tripwire triggers.

Tripwires are a great way to provide coverage across areas that are likely avenues of approach. You can place them across trails, paths, driveways, gaps in treelines, or anywhere else you suspect someone may approach.

Clothes peg tripwire

Mouse trap tripwire

One downside of tripwires, like motion sensors, they are not selective about what they are triggered by. Unlike motion sensors, however, once a tripwire is activated, someone must go out and reset the wire and trigger.

There is an often overlooked aspect of trap and snare placement that is essential to efficacy, and that is making sure your quarry steps where the trigger is located. With a pressure plate, this is a little easier as the surface area is larger, but it is still not guaranteed. This can be addressed using a tracking principle I use all the time and one we all are familiar with: the path of least resistance. Animals—and humans—all else being equal, will always unconsciously take the path of least resistance, that is, we will use the trail or route that costs the least perceived energy in our travels. We do this subconsciously, so when walking on a trail, we will place our feet in the most efficient manner. Simply put, we step where it's clear and dry. So by using rocks, twigs, and bits of vegetation starting ten to fifteen feet back, we can direct people's footfalls right into the trap. This is easy to learn and doesn't take much practice to get the hang of. Grab a friend, and give it a try. Take small twigs with a bit of greenery on them, and place them in the path, sticking them in the dirt like they are growing there naturally, and watch what happens to your footsteps. Or use stones—whatever is natural to the area is most important.

Monitoring Alarms and Traps

One of the 4 pillars of tactical readiness is Manning. You need people and eyes on the things that are important. The best way to monitor these devices is to set up a command post (CP) in a central location in your home where anyone can get access to it within seconds, regardless of where they are inside the house.

It is essential to consider that many of the devices you buy will not work together cohesively. You may have several devices or apps that you'll need to set out and watch to keep an eye on your property.

This command post should also be a central hub for communications. This will give you the ability to stay in touch with whoever addresses trip alarms and traps. Ham radio base stations, two-way radio chargers and other emergency comms resources should be situated in this room, too.

When it comes to sensors, trip wires, pressure plates and other alarms, one of the better ways to monitor them is to create a map of your property and indicate the locations of all the sensors, tripwires, and other devices. You can then place a light or LED through the board, which lights up as they are tripped.

In most cases, there will be no legal repercussions from securing your property and home with silent alarms. However, there are a few things that you must take into consideration when placing these types of devices around your property.

1. False alarms

Any device you set out as silent alarms will get triggered unintentionally. Wildlife will be a primary culprit in false alarms. Still, PIR sensors can be activated for various reasons that do not include human or four-legged intruders.

2. Monitoring

When establishing a multi-layered system for securing your property, you will also require a way to monitor all the sensors clearly, concisely, and efficiently. You will also need someone awake and watching for the system to be effective. Alternatively, you could have an audible signal to wake you up, resulting in much-lost sleep due to false alarms.

In the SEALs we have a security detail. It takes a lot more people to run a 24/7 security detail than you think. Keep that in mind. If you want to truly be secure you should consider adding people to your group.

In the military, we utilize a watch bill. Depending on how many people are available, people "stand watch" for various windows of time. The watch periods are usually two to twelve hours. The watch bill is filled out weekly and posted. The person on watch is responsible for monitoring and addressing anything that occurs. We also use a notebook, called a "pass down log," that has the time and date of your watch, and you notate anything of interest in it; then subsequent watch standers can read back and identify potential shortfalls or equipment failures before they occur. It's wise to make daytime watches eight to twelve hours as those are pretty easy. You go about your business—staying onsite of course—yet monitor all the applicable things. At night, make them two to four hours so people can be effective without getting sleepy.

3. Wires and power

The problem with almost everything I've mentioned is that they mostly require electricity to work. This means that you are going to have a lot of wires. This also provides a security vulnerability; if an intruder found the cables, he could simply cut the wire and render that sensor useless. Wi-Fi is an alternative to wired and what I mostly run my place on. Providing power is also an issue in a grid-down situation.

You will need a battery bank because using a generator would not be practical since it would need to run all day and night to power devices with a low power draw, unless there is a way to store the excess generated electricity. Solar panels are a great way to keep battery banks topped off as well.

Traps

Using alarms as early warning is excellent, but you may sometimes want to set out some traps as deterrents against looters or intruders attempting entry. However, you should consider carefully whether you set traps on your property.

The first consideration is that, in most cases, doing so is probably illegal and could result in injury or death to those caught. Therefore, you mustn't ever deploy any traps on your property except in an SHTF scenario, where there is no longer any rule of law.

Deploying traps on your property will delay, deter, and detain intruders. What type of trap you decide to place in a particular location depends a lot on the purpose that trap is going to serve.

If you want to prevent intruders from gaining access to your property, selecting traps designed to deter intruders would be advisable. If your goal is to slow down intruders already on your property, then traps designed to delay are best. Finally, if your goal is to capture the intruder, traps intended to detain a human are the best option.

There are a lot of different types of traps that you can deploy on your property. With some imagination and ingenuity, you can create a wide range of unique and effective traps beyond the ones I will mention here.

Deterrent Traps

Deterrent traps are designed to be seen by intruders, causing them to re-think their plan to come on your property.

RAZOR WIRE

Razor wire comes in rolls which are pulled out to coils of wire with sharp blades attached to them. The wire can be deployed and then recoiled when not in use. When coiled, it has a small footprint, making them easy to store. You will often see razor wire atop chain link fencing or used extensively by the military for the hasty creation of obstacles to prevent the enemy from advancing on friendly positions.

Placing coils of razor wire on the top of fencing around your property is a great way to deter intruders from trying to scale your fence. You can also lay a couple of coils across your driveway to discourage people from advancing along it.

One point of note is that you must have special gloves for handling razor wire or run a significant risk of being cut. Concertina razor wire is also more "stabbing" than "cutting" and is nearly impossible to get free from once it gets caught on your clothing. It's very good at stopping a person from walking through an area. Its effect is that of hundreds of fishhooks in your skin and clothing, shutting you down hard. Ask me how I know. I still have scars on my kneecaps, and that was more than twenty years ago.

TRENCHES

Digging a trench is not easy, but if you have a large enough property and equipment available to make the digging easy, it is something to consider. Trenches are especially good at deterring vehicles; if you want to prevent vehicles from accessing your property, they can be an excellent option. You must establish a plan for entering and leaving your property using your vehicle, if you use trenches to stop unfriendly vehicles.

Trenches should be wide enough that the average person couldn't jump across easily and be deep enough that an intruder would be slowed down while traversing the obstacle.

A disadvantage of trenches is that they provide cover from view and fire to anyone inside them, so it is important to consider this when selecting positions for trenches.

Delaying Traps

Delaying traps are great for slowing things down. Once your perimeter is breached, you'll have to get into a position to defend your home. In these cases, time is a critical resource and anything you can do to slow down the advance of intruders will give you precious minutes to prepare for them to arrive at your door.

TRIP WIRES

You can use trip wires to activate an alarm, but you can also string a wire at ankle height to actually trip intruders. This is called low wire entanglement in special operations and on your own property you should positively festoon the areas around your main walking paths with these ankle height trip wires.

Whatever cordage you decide to deploy as a trip wire needs to be strong enough to not break when a fully grown adult runs into it at a full sprint.

When deploying trip wires, you can also set out stuff for the intruders to fall into. Broken glass, loose coils of razor wire, sharpened stakes, or anything else you can think of that anyone would not want to land face first on top of.

If they cannot walk through your property without falling over or getting tangled up then then you can funnel them to an easier path free of trip wires. You are again creating a choke point to bring the bad guys right where you want them.

You can funnel people into a choke point using traps only if they are easily seen visual deterrents. If funneling is your goal, use obvious methods. Be judicious. Everything has a purpose and is better than others for certain results. You are again creating a choke point to bring the bad guys right where you want them. Also, all these traps you are thinking of creating will work on you and your loved ones just as well as the bad guys, so consider that while under duress, it's likely you will run into these yourself. Use lots of caution.

BARBED WIRE

Many types of obstacles can be created with barbed wire and fence posts. Strands of wire can be strung long distances as a fence, but you can also string barbed wire at shin height in a random pattern over open area.

This creates an obstacle that intruders will likely choose to avoid or take time to traverse.

You can also string barbed wire in loose coils on the ground. When someone runs into this trap, the barbed wire gets tangled in the intruder's legs and will either cause them to trip and fall or get cut up pretty bad in the process.

A succession of trip wires and razor wire is a real life nightmare and you will either deter people from your location altogether or you can easily force them to travel whatever paths you like as they will do anything to get out of that mess. At night, concertina wire and barbed wire are very hard to see while moving, This is a great option. It can be pulled out of the way or recoiled easily but is a fantastic trap and deterrent. You don't even need to anchor it unless you want to; it will work excellently just strung loosely across an area.

A Few Simple DIY Traps

DIY RAZOR WIRE

Screwing razor blades to the top of your fence so that the sharp edge is slightly higher than the top will slice up the hands of anyone trying to climb up and over.

Be advised, this will likely PERMANENTLY damage the nerves and ligaments of the hand and can cause you major legal and moral duress. Broken glass is decorative, just as effective, and a much better visual deterrent. I would much rather a threat see and ID my traps and decide to move along than have them be caught in my trap.

These traps are quick and easy to set and require only screws and razor blades. With all these traps, remember to designate a safe, clear spot that only you and your family are aware of. For instance, you could use pieces of aluminum foil to resemble razor blades and mark that section of fence so that you have a safe corridor if necessary.

NAIL BOARDS

Hammer a bunch of nails through a piece of lumber to stick out the other side and place the board nail side up in areas where intruders are likely to step or land when they jump over the fence.

You can also use nail boards to flatten vehicle tires as well.

Traps to Detain

When deterrence and delaying traps don't work traps to detain the intruders can be your next best option.

Before you set out traps such as these, you'll have to decide what you will do with anyone you capture. When a hurt and angry human is stuck in a trap on your property, you must be willing to be responsible for whatever happens to them.

SNARES

Snaring is a very effective way to trap animals; the same traps and techniques can also be effective against humans. The one caveat is that the cordage used in the snare needs to be stout enough to hold a struggling human.

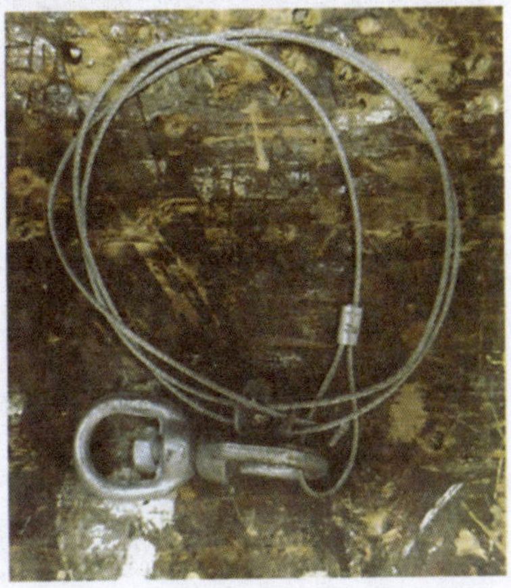

In addition, any snare you use will have to have some locking device to make it more difficult for the person stuck in the trap to loosen the snare and escape.

The best way to set a snare to trap a human is

to have some form of counterweight that will pull and tighten the noose. This will make it much more challenging for anyone to escape from it. Setting up a counterweight for a human-sized trap is very dangerous, and you have a small window to attend to the person as they will free themselves rather quickly. Those pesky opposable thumbs! I don't advise this. An animal caught in a trap is very dangerous; a human, possibly with a firearm, is doubly so.

PUNJI STICK TRAPS

A punji stick trap is a pit with spikes at the bottom. When someone steps into the hole, their leg and foot are either punctured and severely injured, or they end up with their leg stuck in the trap. Either way, there will be a hurt and immobile person for you to deal with.

The American forces dealt with these punji stick pits in the Vietnam War. They are battle tested and would be a nightmare to deal with for anyone trying to sneak onto your property.

These traps are designed to wound humans and, therefore, illegal to deploy, so keep this fact in mind when choosing the traps, you plan to place around your home. I would only consider traps with this level of damage in a Mad Max situation. The legal and moral ramifications are too great. Also, children and pets are vulnerable, and I don't want to risk that.

Net Traps

There are many ways that you can use a net to detain someone. A heavily weighted net will be difficult to get from under when it drops on top of them. The difficulty comes from suspending the net in such a way that it will fall on top of an intruder when triggered but also be concealed from view.

When setting up a net trap, you'll have to do extensive testing to determine the optimal positioning of the trigger and net to ensure that the trap is effective each time. I find that nets are more efficiently utilized by stringing them up along likely routes of travel. They are very entangling if you design them to be pulled along with and to entangle the target. They are also easy to attach noisemakers to for an audible warning.

PIT TRAPS

Digging a pit large enough to trap a human being is no simple feat. It will require a significant amount of time or heavy equipment to accomplish. You will also need a way to dispose of the soil from the hole without raising too much suspicion.

Then there is the matter of covering the pit effectively enough that an intruder will fall through the camouflage while keeping the open top of the pit concealed. Doing this is no simple feat and is probably well outside the scope of what the average homeowner would be able or willing to do. Even if you had the motivation for something like this, you time and energy are much better spent on a more effective and flexible deterrent, such as concertina wire.

Traps That You Should Never Use

Some traps should never be deployed regardless of the circumstances. Here are some traps you should never use. I mention these because some people may be tempted to set traps like them on their property without considering the consequences. What follows is a selection of traps that you should NEVER consider deploying.

1. Land mines

It is not challenging to improvise field expedient land mines. Still, there is no circumstance in which it would ever be acceptable to set out land mines around your property. The collateral damage these devices always brings is never worthwhile.

These devices are banned under international treaties and most people on this planet agree that land mines are despicable weapons with no legitimate use.

2. Killing traps

While it is possible to set out traps that could main or kill, you should not be doing this for much of the same reason you should never deploy a land mine.

3. Chemical Traps

It may seem like a good idea to set up a trap that will shower the person caught in it with chemical irritants, but it is another bad idea. Nothing good can come from trying to spray an intruder with a chemical concoction; anyone who has tried to use bear spray will attest to the unpredictability of wind.

A Few Things to Consider

Placing traps on your property is never something you should take lightly. There are a lot of considerations to make before you start constructing these devices to protect your home.

Final Considerations When Setting Silent Alarms and Traps

The First Thing to Consider

One of the first considerations is that when intruders see that your property is well defended, they will assume that there is something within the walls of your home worth protecting. This circumstance is where many traps and alarms could make you a bigger target rather than deter those who want your supplies.

The Second Thing to Consider

The second consideration is that you, family members, pets, and animals may also trigger your alarms and traps. Alarms do you no good if they are always tripping. I go back to our militaristic pillars of preparedness to remind you of training and leadership. Make sure those you are leading understand the situation and are trained on the tripping and setting alarms.

The Third Thing to Consider

The third thing to consider is that in a post-SHTF situation, your property may be surveilled before intruders attempt to raid your home. When I was a Navy SEAL we relied heavily on surveillance of individuals, operations, and locations. We used everything from drone footage, to satellite imagery, even down to boots on the ground intelligence to learn about a target. We knew almost everything about the person and the place LONG before even starting the mission.

It is vital in this case to be very aware of how you are moving around the property and if your movement may be betraying the location of your traps and alarms.

For example, suppose you deliberately step over an otherwise invisible tripwire every time you walk up your driveway. In that case, someone watching you will deduce that there is something there that they want to avoid.

Defensive strategy is not just about waiting for an attack from your fortifications but gathering intelligence and conducting counter tracking and counter surveillance in your area can tell you a lot about what's happening on your property and community.

Last but Not Least

The final consideration is that you need to plan for having routes in and out of your property that effectively bypass your system of traps and alarms. These routes also need to be disguised so that intruders do not recognize that they are safe passage into and out of the property.

You'll also need to monitor these pathways in the event intruders discover them and place their own traps along your entrance and escape routes. Even soldiers have to plan for overwhelming force and retreat. Having a couple escape routes with silent alarms only will allow for rapid egress but can still help to secure your home. Caching things like weapons and clothing along the escape route will help you in a surprise attack, too.

The placement of silent alarms and traps is an excellent way to keep your family and supplies safe when you are forced to bug in during an SHTF event. You can deploy as many or as few traps and alarms as your property size allows and tailor the information in this chapter for your situation.

Security Mistakes You're Probably Making on Your Property

Many of us think that security is a series of physical and technological interventions that we place between ourselves and criminals. Almost like an obstacle course.

These interventions are not "security", but simply aids. They will help you maintain safety easier and help you maintain a higher level of safety. But passive security is the same as no security. Any system is dependent on being "actively worked".

Security starts and ends with you. All of the most spectacular security breaches happened because of two things:

- Human Action (error, negligence, stupidity, or intent but seldom purely accident)
- Underestimating human ingenuity (obstacles are simply challenges)

I will toggle between the two, alternatively offering high-level and practical advice while priming your thought process on practical ways to implement conceptual considerations.

Thinking You Are Safe

Most think that because we have addressed security concerns, we are safe. It's the same as thinking that a gym membership will increase your fitness. What increases your fitness is going to the gym and working out.

Your security is not "created" through measures but constant vigilance.

Putting This into Practice:

If you don't have a security routine, you are not safe.

Are you checking doors and windows before you go to sleep?

Do you have a procedure for how you approach your house after work and let yourself in?

Pro Tip

Pro's vary their routines. They don't follow the same route every night when checking the house for lockdown. They approach their property from different directions.

They drive past their entrance for a mile and then backtrack. When leaving for work, they drive for 5 minutes, then head back to do a surprise inspection.

Trusting Your System

Complacency is the biggest safety risk. Security is an arms race between predators and prey. Every innovation in security will be matched by an innovation amongst criminals.

Switching your system on at night should not fill you with a sense of absolute safety.

Even redundancy within your system should not fill you with complacency.

Assume that something can and will go wrong. Assume that someone has hacked your home security system and can deactivate it at will.

Assume that the gardener is an enemy agent that has systematically been sabotaging your motion sensors.

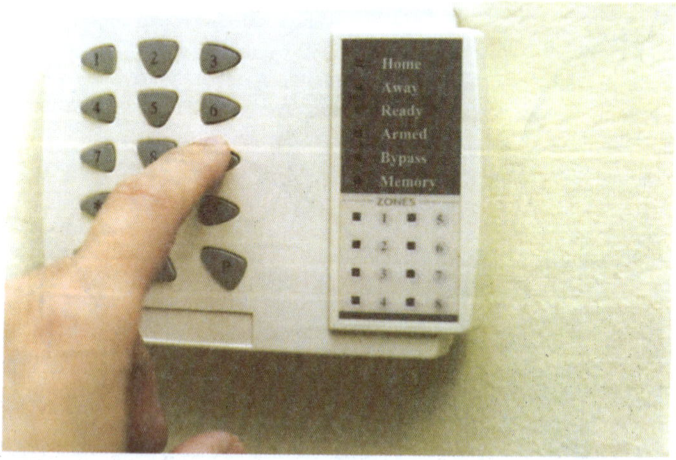

Putting This into Practice:

Paranoia is a heightened state of awareness of how events can go wrong or how systems can fail.

Don't trust anything. Verify everything. Think like a highly motivated criminal.

Think of how you would breach your security system if someone took your family hostage in your home, and you needed to get past your security measures to infiltrate your house.

Find the point of a breach, consider the method of a breach and then take measures against that.

This could mean opening motion sensors to see if duct tape has been used to create blind spots. Put recognizable objects in view of security cameras that you regularly move around to see if your feed has been hacked or if you are getting a delayed feed.

Pro Tip

Analog backup. Determine the most likely points of entry and identify your most vulnerable spots.

Use analog backup devices to create offline redundancy that cannot be compromised from the outside. Pro's know that two measures are one, and one is none.

Analog or mechanical backup can be strings attached to buckets filled with stones to tripwires attached to flares or stun-grenades.

Profiling Wrong

Whenever psychopaths or child abusers are captured and brought to justice, a common refrain from witnesses at their trial is that they were such pleasant people and everyone liked and trusted them.

If you are realistic about statistics and profiling, you will be wary of people who seem trustworthy and close to you.

The person you see and think is not a threat, is more likely to be a threat than someone walking around in rags, talking to themselves, and acting weird. People who intend to harm you, come as wolves in sheep's clothing.

Try the following for some time and you will be amazed at the results.

Don a hardhat and a high-visibility jacket with visible identification. Have a clipboard in your hand, and look like you are about to solve an impending problem. You will meet very little resistance from ordinary folk.

Putting This into Practice:

It is essential to verify that the work crew is indeed who they say they are. If they are outside your property, don't let them into you if you cannot verify their credentials. If they flag you down while driving, don't stop. If you have to stop, keep your window up and your finger on the trigger of your mini Glock.

Pro Tip

Don't allow any unscheduled or unplanned entry into your property. As a rule, don't let anyone into your house. If this cannot be avoided, keep a distance of at least 7 feet between you and the person, and never turn your back on them.

Also, don't allow lost drivers' cars or un-summoned delivery vehicles onto your property. Let the person walk from the gate to the house. They will be less inclined to do anything bad since they will need to carry stolen items or kidnapped people to the vehicle.

Defensive versus Offensive Security

Most security measures are like static obstacles. Tripwires. Motion sensors. Motion-activated cameras. Infrared devices.

All these are like landmines.

They are generally immobile and act as early warning systems.

But let me ask you the following question: What do you do when the alarm goes off? You check to see if there is anything there. Right? And then?

Most of us have pretty clear plans up and till we detect an intruder. But what then? And let's add, that in most cases, you will have been awoken and still be groggy when you need to go into full defensive or offensive mode.

I call these offensive security measures, although they are not just about attacking. The reason I call them offensive measures are that these are not static but active, proactive, and responsive.

Putting This into Practice:

You need an action plan. This will differ for everyone and every situation. I evaluate my possible and ideal responses based on two criteria: the proximity to the danger, and the level of threat.

A guy walking in the garden is different than an armed guy walking in the garden. This can escalate to a masked task force with automatic weapons outside your bedroom door.

You need a response, broadly speaking, for when to wait and see, when to warn, when to engage and when to hide.

Your family and other occupants of the house must know how these plans are put into action, and what part they play.

Pro Tip

Pro's never leave anything to chance or get themselves into situations where they have not only pre-decided what to do but have trained and worked scenarios.

What do you do if the intruders cut the power? What do you do if some of your family members get separated and are not in the safe zone?

I also recommend practicing this and practicing it under stress. Let someone set an alarm and wake the family up at 02:00 AM and see how fast everyone can get their act together.

Safe Zones

The worst possible situation to find yourself in is waking up to an attacker holding a gun to your child's head.

Sleeping areas have to be fortified and impossible to access even if you are out cold.

Think prison. Steel bars, bulletproof glass, self-sufficient and cut off from the rest of the house.

Putting This into Practice:

The ideal situation is to have your sleeping rooms together, with only one access route in and out. You need an escape route in case of a fire, or if attackers trap you, but that must not be an option available as an entry route.

Install a security door between the sleeping areas and the rest of the house. Make sure all your people are safely behind the door before you go to sleep.

Pro Tip

I have a steel bar door mounted just around a corner in the passage that leads to the bedrooms. Shots fired through the door don't have a direct line of sight to occupants. Anyone entering through the door cannot charge in a straight line but needs to take a turn. This is my kill zone where anybody entering will come under severe fire.

Security is all about safety. Be prepared to lose property in order to stay alive. Early warning is essential. Constant vigilance exponentially increases your chances of surviving a breach.

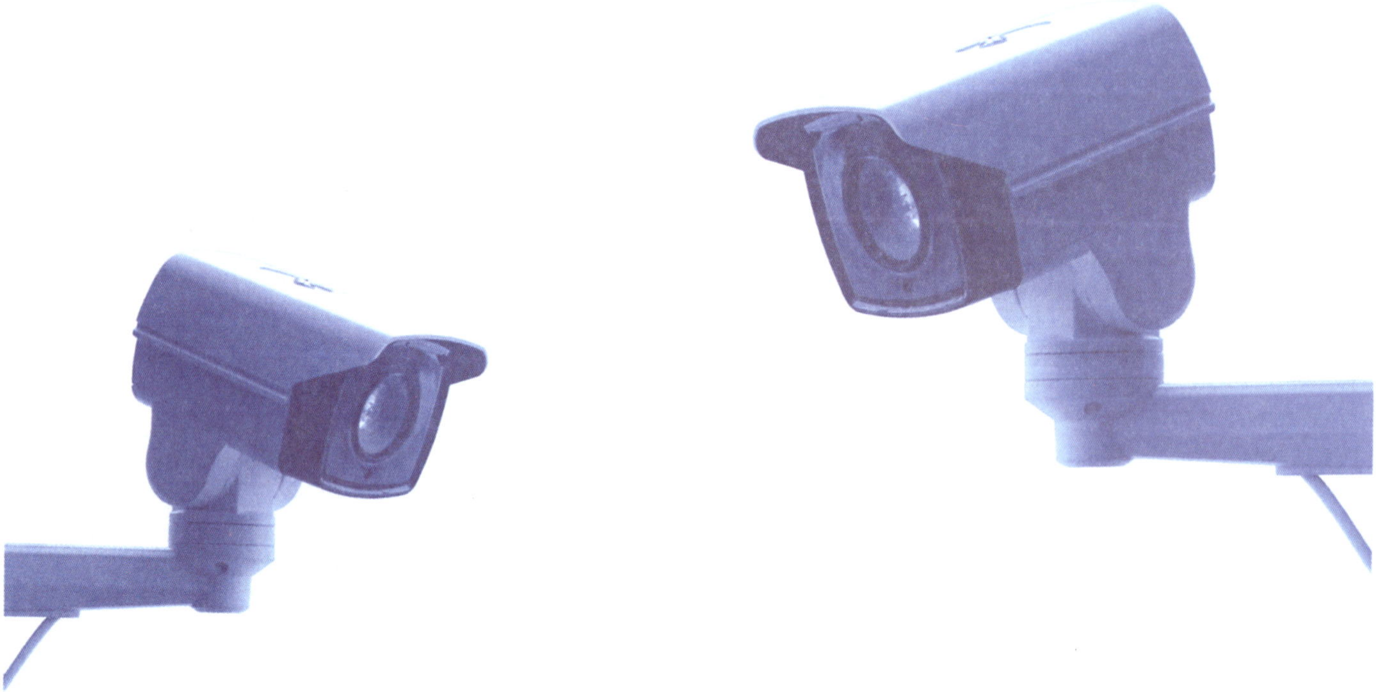

Best Guns For Self-Defense to Have at Home

The reason you decided to bug in is that your home is the best place to survive in. Familiar and well stocked, it has all the advantages. The problem is, other people know that too. If desperate refugees can see that you're getting through the crisis, there's a good chance some of them will decide to try to get their hands on what you have. That means you need to be ready to defend your home against anyone who tries to take it from you.

The first step in defending your home is to conceal the fact that you're living there and have the resources to survive; but while that might deter casual looters, it's never going to be foolproof. Sooner or later, somebody is going to figure out that you're in there.

You might be able to deter them with barriers, dogs and alarms, but if they're really determined, they're going to try to get in. At that point you're going to have to either persuade them to leave, or fight them off – and to do that you'll need weapons.

When it comes to defensive weapons, nothing beats a gun. Only bows come close to matching their efficacy, and compared to guns they're bulky, slow to load, and poor at penetrating barriers.

With a gun you can keep attackers at a distance, hold your own against multiple opponents, and neutralize an enemy's superior strength. Without a gun, you're vulnerable.

So, you need a gun to protect yourself in a crisis, but it's not as simple as digging out your shopping list and adding "a gun" to the bottom. There are thousands of different guns available, covering several main types and a lot of variations. All of them are better than nothing, but some are a lot better for self-defense than others.

What's the best gun for you? This comes back to "the situation dictates." The best weapon or firearm is the one you have. The ideal firearm is the one you are most comfortable with and trained on. That's a very personal decision; you really need to try a few and decide what you're most comfortable with. If you're already an experienced shooter, of course, you probably know what guns you prefer.

On the other hand, if you're not too familiar with firearms but want one to protect yourself, this chapter is for you.

Guns can be split, roughly, into two types: handguns and long guns. There are subcategories inside each type, though, plus some weapons that sit in a gray area between the two.

For home defense, the choice really comes down to handguns, rifles, or shotguns. All three have good and bad points, and how those fit with your personal circumstances will help make the decision as to what suits you best.

Let's look at all three in detail.

1. Handguns

Handguns are the smallest firearms. They're the most common choice of self-defense gun by a long way, and if you're looking for a weapon to protect yourself, a handgun can seem like the obvious choice. It might be the best option for you, but then again it might not.

Here are the pros and cons:

PROS

Size: A handgun is the most compact type of gun, and the lightest. If you're busy working, you can carry a handgun without it getting in the way. You can also usually conceal it fairly well under normal clothing.

One-handed: You can fire a handgun effectively with one hand. It's possible to fire long guns with one hand, but accuracy will drop off sharply. With a handgun there's much less of an accuracy penalty, and that's a real edge if you only have one hand free.

Convenience: Many handguns are designed so they can be carried, relatively safely, with a round in the chamber and ready to fire; there's often no safety catch to worry about. Any handgun can be carried ready to fire, but a lot are specifically intended to be carried that way and have features to make that a safer option.

CONS

Low Power: Except for a few exotic rounds – and you don't want to be using one of those – no handgun comes anywhere near the power of a long gun. They're certainly viable as a self-defense weapon, but they just don't have the punch or effective range of a rifle.

Short Range: Handguns are fine at close range, but they don't have a lot of reach. In combat conditions you're not likely to hit anything more than about 50 feet away. This isn't a problem indoors, but if you're trying to keep an enemy away from your home, they're a lot less capable than a rifle.

Accuracy: With a short barrel and short sight radius, handguns just aren't that precise. That's even more true in a combat situation.

Safety: The short barrel means it's a lot easier for a handgun to end up pointing at things you don't want it to point at, for example your own leg. Most accidental shootings involve handguns.

Types of Handguns

There are two main types of handguns – revolvers and semi-automatics. As always, there are pros and cons to each, and a lot of people have strong preferences one way or the other. Here's the background.

REVOLVERS

Revolvers of some kind have been around for centuries, but the basic design that's still around today first appeared in the 1830s. Revolvers were the first modern handguns, and dominated for close to a hundred years. They still have some advantages, and many people rely on them – but handgun technology has come a long way in a century, so revolvers have been left behind in some ways.

PROS

Simplicity: The actual mechanism of a revolver is quite complicated, but it doesn't need a lot of maintenance – just keep it clean and oiled – and they're extremely simple to operate. Once it's loaded, all you usually have to do is aim and squeeze the trigger. Most revolvers don't have safety catches, but modern ones with a transfer bar are safe to carry. Even accidentally hitting the hammer on something won't fire a round.

Reliability: Revolvers are generally extremely reliable. There's not much to go wrong with them, and if you have a misfire all you need to do is squeeze the trigger again and move on to the next round. With a semi-automatic, a misfire causes a stoppage that needs cleared. It might only take a couple of seconds to do that, but in a close-range gunfight fractions of seconds count. Another advantage of revolvers is that there's no magazine spring to weaken under pressure, so you can leave them loaded for years at a time without doing any harm.

Versatility: A lot of semi-automatics can be finicky about the ammunition you feed them, but a revolver will fire anything that fits down the barrel. That means you can fire any bullet type, or even shot cartridges, without worrying about reliability issues.

Multiple calibers: Some revolvers are able to chamber and fire multiple calibers. For instance, an S&W 686, the revolver we used in the SEAL teams, can fire .357 Magnum (all varieties, an exceptionally potent round), all .38 special ammunition (a cheaper option for target shooting but still effective), and, in a pinch, 9mm parabellum ammunition, probably the most common pistol ammunition in the world and very easy to find. This is not an approved caliber, and while I've done it myself, no manufacturer or person will recommend this, for liability reasons—but it can be done! The cartridge is a little differently sized, so it has a tendency to expand and not be easily removed from the wheel after firing, but in a SHTF situation, this is a strong characteristic to have.

CONS

Capacity: Most revolvers have a six- or seven-shot capacity; some compact or large-caliber ones drop down to five. Six shots was a lot in 1836, but compared to modern high-capacity semi-autos packing 15 rounds or more it's a lot less impressive.

Bulk: Revolvers can be compact, but the cylinder means they're never going to be as flat as a semi-auto. The cylinder tends to "print" on whatever clothing is covering the gun. That makes revolvers harder to conceal.

SEMI-AUTOMATICS

Semi-automatic pistols first appeared in the late 19th century and by WWI they were starting to take over from revolvers. Now, most handguns are semi-auto, including just about all military and police ones.

PROS

Capacity: A typical modern 9mm pistol holds around 15 rounds even without an extended magazine.

Reliability: Semi-automatics might not be quite as reliable as revolvers, but they're reliable enough, and most stoppages that do happen can be cleared very quickly.

Concealability: Because they feed from a magazine instead of a cylinder, semi-autos have a much flatter profile than revolvers. This makes them easier to conceal. Compact pistols with lower capacity single-stack magazines are the most concealable handguns.

CONS

Sensitivity: Depending on the model, semi-automatics can have reliability issues with some ammunition types. Military-style full metal jacket bullets will feed reliably in any pistol, but many shooters feel these lack performance on the target. Hollow point rounds don't work well in all pistols, though. Also, semi-auto pistols are dependent on springs, both in magazines, which can cause feeding issues, and in internal mechanisms, which, over time, will inevitably fail

Handgun Calibers

There's a vast array of handgun calibers to choose from, but preppers should quickly narrow it down to just a handful.

For revolvers, .357 Magnum is the obvious choice. A .357 handgun can also fire .38 Special, which is adequate, while in a Magnum loading it's a very powerful weapon. Also, a good .357 can chamber and fire the world's most ubiquitous round, the 9mm parabellum.

In semi-automatics the choice comes down to 9x19mm NATO, also known as 9mm Parabellum or 9mm Luger, and .45 ACP. Both calibers have their fans, and they're prone to fierce debates, but for a prepper the 9mm is a better choice. In military loadings it's often as powerful as .45, and ammo capacity is much higher.

The most popular .45 handgun is the M1911, a big, heavy pistol with a seven-round magazine. While the 1911 has its die-hard fans, it's a very old design—you guessed it, 1911—and while a good gunsmith can hot rod one out, it's not the most reliable choice. The best-selling 9mm right now is the Glock 43X, which holds ten rounds – but is a pound lighter and two inches shorter.

Its bigger brother is the Glock 19, which is still more than an inch shorter than the 1911, almost a pound lighter and takes a 15-round magazine. Loaded with 9mm hollow points – which it will fire flawlessly – it gives over twice the capacity of the 1911 in a smaller, lighter package.

9mm handguns tend to have softer recoil. That makes accurate follow-up shots much easier, and improves general accuracy – especially when you're under stress. The US military and most police departments also use 9mm, so the ammunition will never be hard to find. The .45 round is bigger, slower, and heavier, so it tends to impart more kinetic energy into the target, improving stopping power, even though with modern ballistic technology, the difference between .45 and 9mm is much smaller than it used to be.

Recommended Handguns

GLOCK 19

The Glock 19 is a compact version of the Glock 17 service pistol. It's a polymer-framed, striker-fired semi-automatic that's designed to be carried safely with a round in the chamber.

There's no safety catch; instead there's a trigger safety that prevents the gun firing unless the trigger is correctly pulled.

This pistol needs to be kept well away from children, but apart from that, it's an extremely safe gun. It's also compact and light, at 7.4" long and 23.7 ounces, and holds 15 rounds of 9mm NATO with a standard magazine.

COLT KING COBRA

If you prefer revolvers, the King Cobra is a good choice. It comes in two versions, with exposed or concealed hammers; the concealed hammer is a good choice for a carry gun, as there's no risk of the hammer (or the low-profile sights) snagging on clothing.

The 2" barrel makes it reasonably compact, and it holds six rounds of .357 Magnum. The S&W 686 is another great choice with lots of barrel lengths to choose from. A longer barrel = greater accuracy.

That's obviously nowhere near the capacity of the Glock, but it's a simple and completely reliable. Plus the .357 magnum is a very hard-hitting round.

2. Rifles

Rifles are high-velocity weapons that can hit accurately and powerfully at a distance. Modern designs are becoming very popular for home defense, and they have a lot to offer in that role. Of course, they're not perfect. Here are their plus and minus points:

PROS

Power: Rifle bullets carry a lot more kinetic energy than any standard handgun, so they're much more likely to stop an attacker quickly and effectively.

Accuracy: Your chances of hitting what you aim at are far higher with a rifle than with a handgun.

Range: Whatever target-shooting enthusiasts tell you, handguns are essentially useless beyond 15-20 yards. Any rifle can reach more than 200 yards effectively, and many hunting rifles are capable of good accuracy at five times that. If your home is isolated and you want to keep enemies at a distance, a rifle is the tool you need.

Capacity: A modern sporting rifle will take 30-round magazines, far more ammunition than any standard handgun can hold. You can get a 30-round magazine for some semi-automatics, but the whole point of handguns is they're compact. With a ridiculously long magazine, they're not.

CONS

Bulk: Rifles are much longer and bulkier than pistols. A modern sporting rifle with a carbine barrel and collapsible stock is a fairly small package, but it's still much bigger than a handgun. If you're working, you'll probably sling it over your back, and that makes it slower to get into action.

Weight: The weight of rifles varies wildly, from under six pounds loaded to well over double that. In either case, compared to a handgun it's significant – and, at over a pound a piece, spare magazines bump the weight up even more.

Length: Rifles aren't just more awkward to carry around; their length is also a disadvantage in confined spaces. A pistol is much handier indoors.

Types Of Rifles

There are three common types of rifles. There are also a few uncommon types, but none of them are worth considering for self-defense. Here are the practical options:

BOLT ACTION

Bolt action rifles appeared in the late 19th century. Most military rifles were bolt action until the early 1950s.

PROS

Reliability: A bolt action is very reliable, with few moving parts. They're quite resistant to dirt and fouling.

Accuracy: With almost no mass moving as a shot is fired, a bolt action makes a very steady platform. Most sniping rifles are still bolt action.

Strength: The bolt action design is inherently very strong, and can handle extremely powerful calibers.

CONS

Rate of fire: While a bolt action can almost match anything else for aimed fire at long range, at close quarters they're relatively slow – and easily outmatched by a handgun or semi-automatic rifle.

Magazine capacity: For a bolt action, ten rounds is a large magazine. Five – or even fewer – is more typical.

LEVER ACTION

Lever actions were first developed in the 1850s, and were some of the earliest practical repeating rifles. They were widely used during the Civil War and in the settlement of the West, and they're still popular sporting rifles today.

PROS

Compactness: A lever action is short, reducing the length of the rifle. As most of these rifles are chambered in pistol calibers they're usually compact, handy weapons that are relatively easy to use even indoors.

Reliability: A lever action can be more finicky than a bolt gun, but if you have a misfire there's no need for stoppage drills – just work the lever to eject the round and chamber a fresh one.

CONS

Rate of fire: Like a bolt action, a lever is slower than a semi-automatic.

Magazine capacity: Lever actions usually hold more rounds than a bolt action, but they're still nowhere close to a modern sporting rifle with a 30-round magazine.

Power: Some lever actions are chambered for rifle cartridges like the classic .30-30, but most of them are in handgun calibers. Their longer barrels mean they hit harder than a pistol, but they're still anemic compared to a real rifle round.

SEMI-AUTOMATIC

The first semi-automatic rifles appeared in the early 20th century, and they started to be widely used during WWII. By the 1950s most major armies were using them, and now they're the most popular rifles in the USA.

PROS

Rate of fire: A semi-automatic can fire as fast as you can pull the trigger. If you're taking deliberate aim the rate of fire drops off, but they're still a bit faster than a bolt action.

Consistency: Because the rifle automatically ejects the empty case and chambers the next round, there's no disturbance to your position between shots. Follow-up shots are also faster.

Ammunition capacity: Most modern semi-automatics can take high-capacity magazines, usually holding 30 rounds. Magazine changes are quick, too.

Modularity: Modern sporting rifles, particularly the AR15 style, are incredibly customizable. There's a huge range of accessories available for them, and whole subassemblies can be swapped out. It's often possible to change barrel length and even caliber relatively easily.

CONS

Reliability: This isn't actually much of a problem; modern semi-automatic rifles are very reliable. They're not quite as reliable as a bolt action, though. If a round fails to fire, you'll need to carry out a stoppage drill, whereas with a bolt action you just work the bolt like you were going to anyway.

Legality: Anti-gun states focus most of their dislike on semi-automatic rifles, especially modern sporting rifles. If you live in California, for example, there are very restrictive laws on these guns.

Rifle Calibers

Rifles come in an even more bewildering array of calibers than pistols. In general, for a survival weapon it's best to stick to commonly available ones to make finding ammunition easier.

The three most common rifle calibers in the USA are .308 Winchester (7.62x51mm NATO), .223 (5.56x45mm NATO) and .22LR. While .308 is a great hunting round, it's overpowered for self-defense. It's a big, powerful cartridge and most rifles that fire it are also heavy. The .308 round is also extremely good at barrier penetration; if you have to use the rifle inside your home, a gun that's capable of killing someone through two thicknesses of brick isn't a good thing.

The little .22LR isn't an ideal self-defense round, but fired from a semiautomatic rifle it can do the job. A single round will often fail to stop an assailant, but a rimfire semi can deliver accurate follow-up shots very quickly – and if you hit your assailant with a swarm of angry .22 bees that will stop him. Ammunition is also ridiculously cheap.

If you want an effective rifle for self-defense, though, it's best to go for the middle option - .223. Much smaller and lighter than the .308, with much lower recoil, it's still effective to around 500 yards from a long rifle barrel and around half that from a carbine.

The AR-15 platform, the most popular 5.56/.223 carbine and with a large buffer assembly, is also very easy to shoot with very little perceived recoil. Most children are able to effectively handle one of these.

That lets you keep enemies at a distance, but if you do have to fight in your home you still have a relatively light, handy weapon that won't get in your way. It does penetrate, and will rip through most modern house construction (consider frangible ammo), but its overpenetration is nowhere near as extreme as the .308's. It's also the most popular rifle caliber in America, so ammo should always be easy to find.

Recommended Rifles

RUGER AR-556 MPR

This AR15-style rifle comes in several calibers and versions, but the one to go for as a home defense weapon is the AR-556 MPR in 5.56mm NATO with a 16.1" barrel. The barrel is free-floated inside an aluminum handguard with M-Lok accessory attachment points.

Picatinny rail on the upper receiver makes it easy to mount a red dot sight – ideal for close quarters shooting – or a scope. Another short length of rail at the front of the handguard gives you space to fit a forward iron sight. There's a Magpul-stype collapsible butt and the rifle comes with a 30-round Magpul PMAG.

This isn't the cheapest AR15 clone on the market, but it's still at the affordable end and it's a high-quality rifle with many Mil-Spec components.

There are many manufacturers of the AR-15 design, and you can spend as much as you like. My personal rifle is one by Sons of Liberty Gunworks. The owner is a friend of mine, and he builds the most robust and reliable AR-15/M-4s on the market, in my opinion. I personally prefer a shorter barrel; mine is 13.7". The original M16, which these are based off of, came with a 16" barrel, and in the SEAL teams, we had an option of a 10" barrel for close quarters work. The shorter barrel was more maneuverable and much louder, so these days I have a happy medium at just under 14".

CZ BREN 2 MS

Not everyone loves the AR15's direct-impingement gas system, or the recoil buffer than means it can't take a folding stock, but it does generally come with a collapsible stock.

The Bren 2 Ms, from Czech manufacturer Česká zbrojovka – the creator of the legendary Bren gun – is a good alternative that offers all the compactness and firepower of an AR15 carbine, combined with a traditional gas system and length-adjustable folding stock.

Chambered in 5.56 NATO, it takes standard AR15-style magazines. It also features a full-length Picatinny rail along the top, aluminum handguard with M-Lok slots on the sides and bottom, one-piece polymer lower and excellent ergonomics – the layout of its controls beats an AR15 hands down. This rifle is becoming very popular, and don't write CZ off as a small foreign company – they own Colt.

The primary advantage of the AR design is its modularity and plethora of accessory manufacturers, which is a huge advantage. The AR is the only long gun you can infinitely customize and find spare parts for in all conditions.

3. Shotguns

If you can only have one gun, there are plenty reasons to make it a shotgun. When we watch Westerns the most common firearms are always revolvers, with lever-action rifles in second place – but the reality is that most people in the Old West couldn't afford these expensive weapons, and probably wouldn't have bought them even if they could.

A cheap and simple shotgun was far more useful to them, able to hunt anything from small birds to deer and packing a formidable punch if self-defense was needed.

Shotguns are still an excellent choice for preppers; here's why:

PROS

Versatility: Shotguns can fire an incredible range of ammunition, from less lethal rounds and sall birdshot (or even rock salt) to heavy slugs. You can also stack your shells in the tubular magazine so you can increase lethality at will. You can effectively select what round you want to use in any given situation. Snooper? #9 birdshot. Threat? 00 buck. Kill shot? 1 oz. slug. There are also all kinds of exotic rounds, like flechettes, incendiary rounds, literal flamethrowers, and flash bangs for disorientation.

Effectiveness: Inside its range, a shotgun can be devastatingly powerful. You can also combat reload a shotgun in the heat of battle, so you effectively never run dry.

Safety: With the right ammunition a shotgun can have much less penetration than a rifle or handgun, reducing the risk of hitting someone on the other side of a wall. Small shot will generally penetrate less than buckshot, but is still devastating at close range.

CONS

Length: Like rifles, shotguns are long-barreled weapons. That makes them less than handy indoors.

Weight: Most shotguns aren't light. If you find one that is light it's going to be extremely unpleasant to fire, because of...

Recoil: Recoil is an equal and opposite reaction; as the projectile travels up the barrel, the gun moves in the opposite direction. Shotguns can launch some very heavy projectiles – and come back at you hard. If you're lightly built, a shotgun can be punishing.

Range: While a shotgun can reach out further than a handgun, it's no match for a rifle. Unless you have a very specialized hunting shotgun with a rifled barrel, even a slug is only effective out to about 100 yards.

The higher energy of buckshot can be canceled out by the smaller number of pellets and the reduced chance of any hitting the target if you're not set up right. This is an advantage if you prepare correctly. Shotgun barrels are fitted with chokes that thread into the end of the barrel, which affects the dispersion pattern of the projectiles. You can set up your shotgun to spread, for close range, for multiple targets close together, or to keep a tighter pattern out to distance. In Vietnam, SEALs used duck bill chokes, which would spread the shot pattern out horizontally. This worked to great effectiveness in the close-range jungle fighting.

Types Of Shotguns

Again, there are three types of shotguns. Two of them are worth looking at for a self-defense gun.

BREAK-OPEN

These are the classic sporting shotguns. They can be single or double-barreled, with doubles either over and under or side by side.

PROS

Reliability: There's very little to go wrong with these guns. The box lock action is well sealed against dirt and debris, and the loading mechanism is as simple as it gets – just operate the lever and break the gun open.

Versatility: All shotguns can fire a wide range of ammunition, but with a break-open gun there's no limit on the length of the round. As long as it fits down the barrel, you can fire it. If for some reason you want to fire a round with a foot-long dart sticking out the front, you can.

CONS

Ammunition Capacity: At most, a break-open shotgun holds two rounds. They're fast to reload, but when you're fighting for your life two shots isn't much.

PUMP ACTION

The first pump action shotgun was developed by firearms legend John Browning in 1893. They're now the most popular choice for tactical shotguns.

PROS

Ammunition Capacity: A pump action's magazine usually holds between four and eight rounds, depending on the length of the magazine and the length of the shells.

Rate of fire: Pump shotguns are very fast to cycle, so it's easy to manage a quick follow-up shot.

Round selection: A pump-action shotgun can cycle through a chambered round without firing it, so for instance, you can have a flash bang round loaded first to distract or deter an intruder then #9 birdshot loaded in the next two rounds, which won't penetrate interior walls but is still effective at close range; then have several rounds of #00 buck, which is devastating, and the rest loaded out with 1 oz. slugs for longer, better aimed finishing shots. You can cycle to any one of these to escalate your engagement without firing them.

Deterrence: I don't care what language you speak. The sound of a cycling shotgun is universally recognized and best avoided.

CONS

Reliability: Pump actions are pretty reliable, but if the action isn't operated firmly and positively, they can malfunction. Usually people short stroke (meaning not cycle the pump action far enough back, which will eject the spent shell but fail to pick up the next one) the pump mechanism when they're excited and can fail to chamber the next round. Practice!

SEMI-AUTOMATIC

The first semi-automatic shotgun was designed in France in 1891. They hit the US market when John Browning – of course – designed the Auto-5 in 1900.

PROS

Ammunition Capacity: Like pump actions, semi-autos are magazine fed. Standard tube magazines hold up to eight rounds; some guns have box or drum magazines with more capacity.

Rate of Fire: Like semi-automatic rifles, these shotguns can fire as fast as you can pull the trigger.

CONS

Reliability: Again, these are fairly reliable guns, but they can be sensitive to ammunition. Some need adjustment if you change ammunition types.

Shotgun Calibers

There are many shotgun calibers, but far and away the most popular is 12-gauge. Anything smaller than that starts to lose out on power; anything larger has brutal recoil.

If you're lightly built a 20-gauge could be worth considering, but for most people a 12-gauge is the best bet.

For home defense, a 2¾" shell loaded with #4 buckshot is a good choice. It minimizes overpenetration, but inside 30 yards it will do massive damage to an attacker.

For outdoor use consider 00 buckshot instead; the larger pellets will retain their energy further, to 50 yards at least. If your shotgun has rifle-style sights slug rounds will extend its reach to 100 yards.

Recommended Shotguns

REMINGTON MODEL870

The 870 has been in production since 1950 and is the best-selling shotgun of all time. They are VERY affordable. It's also probably the most popular pump-action shotgun worldwide among law enforcement and military users. This is my personal favorite and the one I used regularly in the SEAL teams. Consider the Marine Magnum version.

There's a huge range of aftermarket accessories for it, so it's easy to customize into a home defense gun. The Tactical model comes with an 18.5" barrel and an extended magazine that holds seven rounds of 2¾" 12-gauge. There's also a folding stock version, which makes the gun more compact to carry and store, but make sure to unfold it before shooting – and avoid pistol grip-only shotguns. The recoil is too heavy to use them accurately. They are strictly conceal and close range weapons.

KEL-TEC KSG

This gun is radically different from the Remington. It's a bullpup design, allowing it to fit an 18.5" barrel in a very compact weapon that's just 26" long. It also has two tube magazines, each holding seven rounds of 2¾" 12-gauge. You can quickly switch between the magazines, allowing you to load two different kinds of ammo or just go for a massive 14+1 capacity. It also has a long Picatinny rail on top for sights, and a shorter one underneath for a grip or tactical light.

Not everyone loves its ergonomics, but if it works for you this is a very handy weapon.

In an emergency any gun is better than no gun, but having a firearm you're familiar and comfortable with, that was chosen to suit your own circumstances, makes a huge difference.

Many people make the mistake of buying too much gun – handguns in massively powerful Magnum calibers, for example, or semi-automatic .308 carbines. These guns have their uses, but home defense isn't really one of them. A reliable, easy-to-use and compact gun in one of the most common calibers – 9mm NATO, 5.56mm NATO or 12-gauge will serve you well and be easy to find ammunition for even in a major crisis.

The First Thing You Should Do If Martial Law Is Declared

Executive order 9066 is not the first thing that comes to mind when you think of Martial Law, though it is to this date the most extreme example in the USA history. Following the attacks on Pearl Harbor 120,000 Japanese were relocated and interred for 4 years under Martial Law.

The military assumed control over these areas and civilian government was suspended. What would you do if something like that happened in your area?

If Martial Law is declared, the first thing you should do is go through these 7 steps to make sure that you are prepared to deal with a suspension of your civil rights and military occupation.

Executive order 9066 is not the first thing that comes to mind when you think of Martial Law, though it is to this date the most extreme example in the USA history. Following the attacks on Pearl Harbor 120,000 Japanese were relocated and interred for 4 years under Martial Law.

The military assumed control over these areas and civilian government was suspended. In the Navy SEALs we train for a variety of scenarios, but urban warfare training is an important part of what we do.

What would you do if something like that happened in your area?

If Martial Law is declared, the first thing you should do is go through these 7 steps to make sure that you are prepared to deal with a suspension of your civil rights and military occupation.

STEP ONE: VERIFY MULTIPLE SOURCES

Where did this declaration of Martial Law come from? Where did you hear it? This day and age we must be very careful about news sources and the further we get down the path with AI, the more careful we will have to be.

As with any information, verifying with more than one source is essential. Intelligence gathering is an essential duty of a Navy SEAL. We spend a lot of time talking to sources, watching/surveilling for intel, and we even go undercover to seek out the intel we need.

While it might be tempting to look for answers in the national news, I would suggest immediately looking to local resources in a situation where Martial Law is involved.

You could call first responders on the non-emergency line to get information about something like this. Turn on local radio and local news.

Remember, a declaration of Martial Law will have to be local for it to affect you. If the major city down the road is under Martial Law, the rules and enforcement will likely not touch you.

All branches of the military, especially Special Operations forces like the SEALs, only have so many resources. In a national breakdown we would only have so many soldiers to commit to each region and city.

STEP TWO: DEFINE THE AREA

Intel through local news is also the best resource to find out if your community or neighborhood are part of the perimeter defined by this declaration of Martial Law. Your experience could be that local law enforcement has simply created curfew for everyone.

As I mentioned, this is a game of manpower, and the manpower will be concentrated where it is needed most.

It might be that your city or town is under martial law, but the manpower is far too limited to reach your community or neighborhood.

It may take more digging to get this kind of information, but it will be well worth it. This is where a phone list of people from different neighborhoods could help. If you have a good relationship with police, that could help you, too.

STEP THREE: LEARN THE RULES

By bugging in during a Martial Law scenario, you may not have to be subjugated by the rules of Martial Law compared to those who must traverse this scenario. The best defense against Martial Law is to not be visible or be around while it is happening.

Still, it will be in your best interest to learn about the restrictions that are being put in place.

Should the threat increase, and you decide to bug out, you will have better luck if you know the types of restrictions that are in place.

Here is a list of things you can expect under Martial Law:

- Suspension of civil liberties
- Curfews
- Military presence
- Communications restrictions
- Arrests and detentions
- Transportation restrictions
- Temporary closure of business
- Suspension of Habeas Corpus in the US

A population being subjected to a simple curfew and some business closures will react differently than a population that is dealing with arrests, transportation, and communications restrictions along with a suspension of habeas corpus.

STEP FOUR: COMMUNICATE

At this point, assuming communications are allowed, you should open communications to the people around you. Start with the people closest to you. You can visit your neighbors and talk to them about the situation, make calls to others in your neighborhood or community. You could also create a group text or feed into your already existing group text.

In the Navy SEALs communications are paramount to every mission. We employ multiple methods of communication in case something goes wrong with our primary communications method. We also keep communications brief and secure. This assures that our messages are not listened into by bad guys.

Whenever the dynamic of life has changed this much, you need to communicate with those around you. This could be your neighbors, community, family, or your MAG (mutual assistance group).

I would recommend communicating with everyone. Get everyone in your life on the same page in case further steps need to be taken.

STEP FIVE: LOCKDOWN

In a serious Martial Law situation, it will be best to stay out of sight and out of mind. By preparing to bug in you have the option of initiating your own lockdown process.

A lot of what we do in the Navy SEALs is covert. We keep to the shadows and stay hidden. Sometimes we use influence and similar tactics to achieve goals without ever using violence. Your own covert operations are important and the less visible you can be in chaos the better.

Having communicated with everyone you might find it best to stay put in your home for the foreseeable future. This lockdown mentality will keep you from meeting the military or LEO (law enforcement officers) element.

STEP SIX: HIDE VALUABLES AND FIREARMS

With so many of your civil rights removed, you need to understand that some unthinkable things can happen. The need for things like warrants goes out the window. They are no longer an issue. This means that a heavily armed military presence can take anything they want from your property, and they can do it by force.

While it might hurt your ego, a small, trained fighting force is going to take whatever they want from you. That is not to mention if they are capable of things like calling in backup and resupply. The devastation that a 16 man platoon of Navy SEALs is capable of can be mind boggling.

So, hide your firearms, food, valuables, precious metals, and anything else you do not want taken from you.

STEP SEVEN: WATCH THE WATCHERS

With optics or plain sight, you should spend some time watching the people who are conducting Martial Law in your area. Watch their demeanor and their integrity. Watch how they deal with the people of your community.

Keeping an eye on where they are and what they are doing at various times of the day will give you an idea of how the operation is going. You want a Martial Law situation to be swift. Should this drag on, then you may begin to see the people with the power start to abuse that power. Have you ever considered what you would do if Martial Law turned into something more? What if the people with the guns and the power started committing terrible acts?

Do you know anything about guerilla warfare? The SEALs' counterparts, the Green Berets, are notorious for training local forces in guerilla warfare. You might consider reading the book Total Resistance by H Von Dach.

If Martial Law becomes something more, something worse, you might have to change your plans or at least adjust how you deal with this evolving Martial Law scenario.

What to Do If Neighbors or Friends Come Asking for Food in a Crisis

Anyone who gets involved in prepping eventually ends up hearing, "Oh, I'm not worried about a disaster coming, I'll just go to your house.". That comment usually comes from a friend or family member, just after they find out you're a prepper.

They'll talk about how they don't have the time or money needed to get into getting prepared themselves, so they think they have some right to expect you to take care of them, when a disaster comes and they don't have any food to eat.

There's just one little problem with their idea; you and I don't have the time and money to prepare for them either. It's hard enough for most of us to prepare for our own families, let alone prepare for extra people who show up at our doorstep.

Giving food to them, no matter how desperate their personal situation might be, can literally mean taking that food from your own children.

When we go into an operation, we have a certain number of resources to conduct that mission. The food rations, medical resources, ammo, and so forth are all part of the planning for that mission. Anything we give away, damage, or lose, puts the mission in jeopardy.

You have a mission, also. That mission is to keep your family alive during the chaos.

It's hard to quantify, since most preppers are rather secretive about their activities, but less than two percent of the population truly qualifies as preppers and thinks of themselves that way. That's up from pre-COVID times, when it hovered around one percent.

We can probably add another couple of percentage points of people who have some extra food in their homes, while not really being preppers. Still, that means that less than one in twenty households have enough food to last more than a week.

According to FEMA statistics, the average family has three days' worth of food in their homes. The average grocery store only has three days' worth of food on the shelves. So, at the most, we're looking at six days' worth of food, even though the grocery stores don't have three days' worth of food for everyone.

It doesn't take long to start feeling desperate when your belly is empty. That time is cut considerably when your children are crying because they are hungry. What parent can stand to hear their child cry because they don't have food to eat?

Desperate people, it is said, will do desperate things. That applies directly to what we're talking about here. Just what desperate things they will do, will depend on the individual.

Some will resort to begging; others to stealing; still others will sell their bodies to get something to eat. The worst will turn to violence, willing to kill in order to steal what they need.

They don't need to know that you're a prepper in order to come knocking on your door. While those that do know will come knocking, there will be plenty of others who just start knocking on doors, hoping to find someone who can help them out.

Then there will probably be some who will talk about "sharing resources," so that they can skim off the top.

All three of these categories are equally dangerous; because all three can turn violent. The real question is just how capable they are at violence.

YOU'VE GOT TO DECIDE NOW

You and I have to make up our minds now, as to what we're going to do when people come knocking on our doors. That's especially important if our decision is to not share what we have with them. If we haven't already made up our minds on what our reaction will be and what we will say, we will hesitate, causing them to think that we have food. Even if we say that we don't, they won't believe us.

As an elite fighting force the SEALs have rigorous operating procedures. There is a way things should be done. And it should be done the same way every time. That is procedure and it is documented.

I want you to write out your own SOP (Standard Operating Procedure) for someone coming to your door and asking for food.

1. Who are they?
2. Do you have resources to help?
3. Are you going to help?
4. Identify what FOOD HELP is. (1lb bag of rice and a can of green beans ex.)
5. What are the stipulations of your help?
6. What do you do if they get hostile?

At a minimum your process should detail these things.

As I mentioned earlier, agreeing to give anyone food out of your family's stockpile can mean that you're taking food out of your own children's mouths to feed others. That won't happen if the disaster and its aftermath is over quickly and things return to normal before you run out of food.

But unfortunately, that's something that none of us can know. We keep adding to our stockpiles, because we don't know how long any coming disaster will last.

Looking at it that way, there is no way I can personally justify taking food that my children need and giving it to someone who didn't prepare.

Regardless of who they are, they had the same opportunity to prepare that I have, even if finances are a problem for them. Prepping is a financial strain for my family too.

My greater responsibility is to my wife and children. Therefore, the only real answer I can have in that situation, is to tell people no, that I don't have any food I can give them.

WHEN THEY DON'T BELIEVE YOU

There's a good chance that people aren't going to believe that you don't have food or don't have food that you can share. Their desire to think that you have food will be largely driven by their own hunger and desperation. It's easy, in such a situation, to convince yourself that others have what you need, even if they don't.

So, the question is then, what are those people going to do?

You can be sure that they will be back. In fact, you can be sure that they will continue coming back until the crisis is over. They will continue trying different tactics, with you, as well as with others, to get what they need.

The real problem isn't that these people will keep asking, it's that they will do when they get tired of asking. The more desperate these people become, the greater the likelihood that they will turn to violence.

You can expect that they will attack your home at some point in time, when you least expect it. They will do so with the intent of getting your food; but they probably won't be particularly concerned about whether they hurt or even kill you in the process.

Prisoners of War are something that Navy SEALs might have to deal with. Informants and such might need to be held and interrogated. You, too, might need to consider some kind of punishment, jail, or other repercussions for someone that keeps showing up on your property.

I know the popular answer to this death by rifle but if we are in a Martial Law scenario or if you expect life to go back to some semblance of normal, a body count could put you securely in the jailhouse.

This is also why home defense is so important. If you're not ready to defend home and family, then someone who is more desperate than you is likely to come along, either running you out of your home or killing you to get what you have.

This is also why a survival team is important, as that team, working together, has a much better chance of defending your home. Of course, that only works if your team is close enough to gather together for defense, so you want to think that through.

Don't just assume that beating any attackers once will be enough either. There's nothing to say that a victory will be final. If you defeat them, there's a fairly good chance that they will gather together with others and come back. This is especially true of those who live in the edge of the law to start with. They'll keep coming back with bigger and more violent groups, until they defeat you.

Look at our time in the Middle East. As a part of one of the most elite fighting forces on the planet we beat back the very definition of evil. Time and time again we have seen that these evils can be brought down but are never out of the fight completely.

This may end up being a trigger for you bugging out, escaping to a survival retreat before it is too late. That's one of the many scenarios you have to think about and plan for. You should also have an escape route planned and prepared, just in case you have to bug out in the midst of an attack. Remember, "He who fights and runs away, lives to fight another day.".

But being ready to defend home and family isn't all that you need to think about. You should also do whatever you can to hide as much of your food stockpile as possible. Better yet, split it up in several different hiding places. That way, if they do run you off and get into your home, hopefully they won't find all your food. That way, you can go back for it.

ANOTHER OPTION

There is another way to look at this problem. That's to prepare for those people who are going to come around asking for food, by having something to give them. Now, I know that might sound a bit radical; but hear me out. It might be much more beneficial to befriend someone in need, turning them into an ally, than it would be to turn them into a potential enemy.

I'm not talking about stockpiling the same level of food for these people, as I stockpile for my own family. As we've already discussed, it's unlikely that any of us can afford doing that. But stockpiling a few hundred pounds of rice and beans really isn't all that expensive. Bag it up in five-pound bags when the time comes, so that you can dole it out as necessary.

Don't just give that food away though. Rather, barter with them. Either trade for something useful that they have or if they don't have anything you can use, have them work for it.

Pulling weeds in your garden or hauling water from the local pond or stream in exchange for your rice and beans may seem unfair, but so is expecting you to give them food for nothing. They won't appreciate it anywhere near as much if you give it to them, as they will if they work for it.

The other thing to have on hand is a lot of seed, so that you can help those people start growing their own food. Until they are at a point where they are able to take care of themselves, they are going to keep coming back, looking for more. Helping them to start growing their own food will both eliminate their dependence on you and hopefully leave them feeling indebted, so that they will remain a valuable part of your survival team.

Keeping a Low Profile: Operational Security

A big part of being prepared is having the tools and supplies you need to get you through a crisis. What separates preppers from most people is that we have those supplies and they don't. That doesn't mean they don't need those supplies, of course; it just means that, for whatever reason, they don't think they do. Of course, when disaster strikes, they're going to realize that they're wrong, and a lot of them are going to start wondering where they can get all the stuff they should have been stockpiling before they need it.

One of the biggest differences between the average prepper and a Navy SEAL is that we can call for reinforcements and we can call for resupply. We can call for air support. You cannot call for much so, you need to have the things you need on hand and keep quiet about it!

Of course, in a major SHTF situation there's going to be widespread looting of stores, warehouses, and even food processing plants. All those locations will quickly be swamped by desperate mobs, and it's likely they'll become extremely dangerous to be around as people fight over supplies and federal agents try to restore order and protect the supplies.

People who weren't smart enough to be prepared, but are smart enough to stay clear of the chaos around obvious stocks of food, will soon start thinking about another source of supplies they could pillage – you.

If society breaks down and hungry neighbors know about your preps, they're going to start thinking about how useful your stockpile would be to them. They might ask you to help them. They might offer to trade money or valuables for some of your food. Or they might decide to grab a gun and take what they need by force.

In fact, it isn't just hungry neighbors that might do that. There isn't really a risk of federal agencies going door to door, confiscating food from preppers. They'll head straight for the source, requisitioning warehouses and whole farms.

What about local officials, though? If your town is collapsing into chaos, and food supplies have been cut off as supply chains fall apart, can you guarantee that local cops won't show up at your home and order you to "share" the supplies you've built up with your own hard work and money?

Any sensible prepper has thought about how they're going to defend their supplies – and their life – from looters in the aftermath of a disaster, but we have to be realistic here: There's a limit to how well you can defend yourself. If you're attacked by a gang of armed looters there's a good chance you'll lose; even if you don't, you could be injured, and your home will almost certainly take damage. Alarms to warn you of intruders, and hopefully scare them off, are a great idea. Fences and barriers to deter the curious are also a big help. A gun and the skill to use it effectively are essential. But, at the end of the day, it's much better if nobody even tries to steal your supplies because they don't know they're there.

Former special operators all over the nation are giving civilian training on how to use a rifle, how to secure an area, and how to patch up someone who is injured. These training courses are open to all and some are even conducted by former Navy SEALs.

Some that come to mind are Sheepdog Response Training and Fieldcraft Survival.

Be sure to take into account the immediate area in which you live. I left California three years ago and relocated to rural Tennessee. While my house is set back a good half mile from the road, we have a prominent garden and chicken coop as well as a barn and outbuildings. However, so do all of my neighbors! We're all farmers, own livestock, and are very self-sufficient, and the entire state is very much this way. Big cities are very different. We grow most of our food out here, and there is no shortage of cattle and other livestock and produce. The result of this is that the likelihood of neighbors not having access to food and other essentials is much lower. We are also all well armed out here; if people from the cities come up here, they are going to have a tough time if they're aggressive! If you don't live rurally, especially if you're in a big city, the scenario under martial law or any kind of unrest will be much different. PLAN! If all your food is shipped in and you live within a high population density, someplace gun control is harsh, expect a very different experience.

The best defense is to not be a target in the first place. If looters or local authorities don't know you have a valuable stockpile of food and equipment, they won't try to take it. Hiding all your preps can be a challenge, but it's definitely possible. In this chapter we'll look some ways you can do it.

What Is Operational Security (OPSEC)?

In the Navy SEALs, OPSEC is part of everyone's life. It's short for Operational Security, and it's all about hiding important information from the enemy. You might not be in the military, but in a crisis, you'll certainly have enemies – all the people who might try to take your food, for example. The same principles that protect soldiers, and let them hide their plans from the enemy, will also protect you.

Start Close to Home

The people most likely to know you're a prepper are, unfortunately, also the hardest to hide it from – your neighbors. We often socialize with our neighbors. We visit each other's homes, and can have a pretty good idea of what's in there. Even if relations are just at the saying hello level, we notice a lot of what's going on next door. This means your neighbors are likely to know you're a prepper and have a stockpile of useful supplies – unless you're very careful about your preps.

Some things just can't be hidden. If you've turned your entire yard into a vegetable garden that's pretty obvious, for example. Other preps are easier to conceal. The key to good OPSEC is to conceal what you can, and either distract attention from the rest or give it a different explanation that won't drop you in hot water when a crisis arrives. There are plenty of ways to do both – and of course if you manage to hide a lot of your preps from your neighbors, that gives you a huge head start on hiding them from anyone else that might come along, too.

The first step to take in hiding your preparations – and especially your supplies – from your neighbors is to not tell them you're prepared. If you already have told them, stop. Now. Don't actively tell them you've stopped prepping, because they might wonder why you felt the need to tell them that. Just stop talking about it and let the subject fade away. If they ask if you're still prepping, don't make a big deal about it. Say you've been doing other stuff and haven't really bothered with it for a while. If you can fit in a joke about having to eat 96 cans of chili before it went out of date, that can give the impression that your stockpile isn't such a valuable asset. The main thing is to make sure that, in an emergency, the fact you're a prepper isn't taking center place in your neighbors' minds. And, of course, the easiest way to do that is to just not tell them in the first place.

The art of deception is the art of war. The act of deception is not just about standing in front of someone and telling them 'I AM NOT A PREPPER,' when they know you are. In war you might assure that the enemy gets its hands on false information so that he can make plans on this false information.

Your neighbors are not your enemies, just yet. The goal of solid OPSEC is to keep it that way! The last person they will expect to be a prepper is the person always borrowing things.

Something as simple as borrowing things from your neighbor can put you in the other category very quickly. Borrow tools, food items, and such to present to them a neighbor that does not always have the things he/she needs.

What if you're trying to persuade your neighbors to be prepared, too? There are a lot of advantages in having prepper neighbors. You can trade supplies, share some of the time-consuming jobs that need done in a crisis – things like security or radio watch – and just generally share the load. Two households working together will achieve a lot more than twice as much as one on its own. You have to be careful, though. If you think a neighbor could be interested in preparing, sound them out without letting them know you're already prepared.

Discuss the world situation, or the risk of a crisis. Comment on how you can see advantages in being prepared. If they agree, that's your opening to talk about getting started. You can talk about working together to get more done. Once they start actually prepping – not just talking about it – then you can progressively reveal your own preps. That way they don't know what you have until they're invested in prepping too – and in a crisis they'll see you as someone to cooperate with, rather than attack and rob.

There are three things that can get the wheels spinning in your own community:

1. Start a Community Garden
2. Create a Neighborhood Communications Network (text groups, email group)
3. Reinvigorate the Neighborhood Watch

If your neighbors aren't interested in being prepared you need to hide as much of your prepping from them as possible. If you can't hide it, explain it away. That vegetable garden in the yard? It's obvious you're growing your own vegetables, but come up with a different reason for why you're doing it. Unless you're conspicuously wealthy (and as a prepper you shouldn't be – we'll cover that later) the obvious explanation is that you're growing produce to save money on groceries. That's something that anyone can understand, and it won't raise any suspicions that your basement is stuffed with MREs and medical supplies. You could also hint that you don't approve of modern farming methods, and prefer your own organic produce.

If you have the space, you might also consider a smaller vegetables garden in liu of a food forest. Growing a food forest uses permaculture principles that focus on perennial foods that return each year. These collections of plants and trees start to tangle together and look much more like a forest than a row of vegetables in a garden. The food forest is a very convert means of growing lots of food.

Anytime you make some preparations that involve having stuff outside, think about OPSEC before doing anything. If you want to install a generator or ham radio antenna, look for a location that isn't visible from the street or a neighbor's property. If you can't find one, create one. A generator can be housed in a small shed; this will also protect it from the weather. Just make sure there's plenty of ventilation. Think about noise, too. It doesn't matter how well hidden your generator is, if the whole neighborhood can hear it running.

Fuel or other supplies that you don't want to store in the house can also go in a shed. Keep outbuildings as ordinary-looking as possible; you don't want people looking at them and wondering what they're for. A little set dressing can help; a couple of old garden tools next to a shed's door suggest it's used for storing garden tools and deflect people from its real purpose.

Again, we return to the art of deception. In the SEALs you become well versed in the art of deception as your very existence is in the shadows. In your case you merely need to cast shadows over certain aspects of your life. You can do it!

OPSEC Works Indoors, Too

Some of us socialize with our neighbors. If they're regular visitors to your home, how can you prevent them realizing that you're a prepper? Actually, it can be done. If your neighbors visit it's likely they'll see the living room, the bathroom, and perhaps the kitchen. Realistically, most preppers don't keep part of their stockpiles in the living room or bathroom anyway, so there's no risk of them being seen by visitors.

Just make sure there isn't any prepper literature lying around; if your guests spot a copy of The Lost Ways, or a book on building fallout shelters, that's likely to get them thinking. If you then start work on a new root cellar, they'll probably manage to put two and two together and assume you also plan to use it as a fallout shelter (which you should). Keep prepping literature with your supplies, in a part of the house visitors won't see.

Kitchens can be trickier. Often, we do keep a significant part of our supplies there. A vegetable garden can be put down as a source of cheap, healthy food, but if a visiting neighbor sees shelves loaded with cases of ramen and hundreds of tins that's a bit harder to explain. Try to keep bulk food supplies out of sight. Use cupboards instead of shelving racks; keep bulk rice, pasta or flour in the basement in rodent-proof bins, and have normal kitchen containers for daily use. Try to make your kitchen look like you'd be running short of food if you missed the weekly grocery shop. In general, if you look around it and see something that gives you a moment of pride at how well prepared you are, that's something that should

probably be moved out of sight.

There are really two methods to consider when hiding preps.

METHOD ONE: They can be hidden in another location in the home where people do not go.

METHOD TWO: Preps can be integrated into the home using hidden storage and creativity. Places under steps, under beds, in closets, and behind secret doors and mirrors are some examples.

Hiding your preps from your neighbors takes some work; there's no way around that. It's definitely achievable, though. You don't have to hide everything - just enough that people can't put things together and realize you're prepared for a crisis. As long as the people next door don't actually see a huge stash of supplies, the chances are you can give them an innocent explanation for anything else.

What About Everyone Else?

Your neighbors are the people most likely to realize you're a prepper, but there's a whole world out there – and you have to hide it from them, too. Whether it's people that drive past your home every day on the way to work, or desperate refugees in a crisis, anyone that looks at your house and sees something unusual about it is a threat to your OPSEC.

If your neighbors can't see your preps, they should be well enough hidden from everyone else, too; so, your priority is not looking distinctive in any other way. Look around your neighborhood and see how well your home blends in. If everyone else has a nicely landscaped yard but yours looks utilitarian, that stands out. If all the other houses in your street have crabgrass lawns and an old rusty truck on blocks, but yours is immaculate, that stands out too. You don't need to exactly match all your neighbors' homes – good news if they're the crabgrass and junker type – but you don't want your place to look so radically different that it grabs people's attention.

Not standing out also applies to obvious security measures. If yours is the only home in the neighborhood with a ten-foot fence, barred windows and security lighting, people are going to wonder what you're so worried about protecting. Your visible security should match what your neighbors have. Don't have a more impressive fence than them. Don't go overboard on warning signs – stick to a low-key "Beware of the dog". If nobody nearby has visible security at all, keep yours low-key.

In the Navy SEALs one of our great strengths is how we move like ghosts in an operation. We are quiet and invisible. While you cannot make your home disappear, you can blend in as just another home and another homeowner.

If a security fence is too visible, set up less noticeable alternatives. Dense bushes planted around your house, especially under windows and in any corners that can't be easily seen from inside, will deter potential thieves. An ordinary garden fence can be discreetly reinforced with barbed wire in a way that won't be obvious to anyone driving past, but will deter intruders who get close enough to take a good look.

What if a crisis has struck and refugees are moving through your area? This is the moment of greatest danger for any prepper. These are people who're already desperate, and they'll be on the lookout for food, clean water, and other supplies. Worst of all, they could have the numbers to overwhelm you.

Whatever security measures you've taken to protect your home, if a couple hundred hungry refugees want to force their way in, the chances are they're going to succeed. To put it in perspective, when the US military defends a location they have numbers, training, and weapons to get the job done. Unless you can match that level of firepower, a couple of dozen armed attackers are going to be hard to keep out. When desperate mobs are looking for food, the only hope of hanging on to yours is to make your home unobtrusive and just a little more secure-looking than the neighbors. Looters will usually go for the easier target, but if the harder target also looks like it could be a lot more profitable all bets are off.

So, what sort of signs can give you away to a hungry horde? If the power is down, but your home still has electric lights, that's a sign that you're at least somewhat prepared for a crisis – and that makes you a likely source of food. Keep your generator as inconspicuous as possible – remember the noise problem – and disguise the fact you still have power. Only use electric lighting if you need to; if foragers see the same candle or oil lighting in your windows as everyone else's, you're not standing out. Blackout curtains are also an option. Close them at sunset, before any lights get switched on.

Any sort of visible vegetable garden is an obvious target. Even if looters leave your home alone, you're going to lose any visible crops. Do all you can to hide them. Where possible, grow food on parts of your property that aren't visible from the road. Otherwise, use your imagination to find creative solutions. Drug producers often grow marijuana plants between rows of a taller crop, like corn. Obviously, you don't want to plant corn around your garden because refugees will just try to steal the corn then discover everything else, but consider planting something taller than your crops but not obviously food. A row of flowering bushes might be all you need – the message that sends is that your yard is more ornamental than edible.

Think outside the box. Grow food indoors with grow lights, store preps underground in water tight caches. What's most important is to understand the lengths those willing to find your preps will go. Chances are no one is willing to dig up your whole backyard to find a PVC pipe full of packaged white rice.

Online OPSEC

The internet has been an amazing boost for preppers. It gives us a way to stay in touch with each other, share tips and help newcomers. Unfortunately, it's also a massive OPSEC risk. If we're not careful with what we do online, we can reveal all the information someone needs to work out not just what supplies we have stored, but exactly where to find them.

Intelligence agencies use a concept called "aggregation" to build up very detailed pictures of what's going on from tiny scraps of information. None of these scraps, on its own, tells you anything useful. Collect enough of them, though, and the picture starts to emerge.

Imagine you're on a prepper forum and pull up a list of someone's posts. Among them you find:

- A complaint about a new gun law their state – which they don't name – has passed.
- A review of a ham radio set.
- A photo of their vegetable garden. In the distance is a water tower and you can see half the town name that's painted on it.
- Photos of their food stockpile.
- A discussion of EMP-proof vehicles, where they mention that a 1960s pickup truck is the ideal survival vehicle.

This probably isn't enough to pinpoint their home exactly, but it might be – and even if it isn't, it's a very good start. A quick Google search for recent gun control laws will identify the state they live in. From there, Wikipedia will probably be enough to identify the town based on the half of its name you already know.

Google Earth will locate the water tower, and if it shows up on Street View then it could be possible to work out the direction from it to the prepper's home by looking at the orientation of the town name. That's already enough to give you a general area to search – and if you drive round that area, and spot a house with a radio antenna on the roof and an old truck parked outside, there's a good chance you now know where a large stash of food is hidden.

Elite units like our own gather intel in much the same way. If we are seeking out terrorists, we are going to utilize a collection of information in the flesh and blood world as well as the digital. It's much easier to narrow down someone's location than you might think.

Now go and look at your own posts on prepping forums. Consider them from a curious, and potentially hungry, stranger's point of view. How much information are you giving away? Is it possible to get a general – or exact – location of your home or bug-out location from the details you've mentioned online? If the answer's yes, then it's time to think about editing or deleting some of your posts.

When you're working out what pieces of information could give away your location and the extent of your preps, be imaginative and think laterally. Anything you say about your neighbors is describing their home – but it's also describing a home that's close to yours, and if an online watcher finds one, he's very close to finding the other. Is there a stream, pond or cornfield bordering your property? Don't mention that online. Planning to bug out in a crisis because your home is nine miles from the Minuteman missile silos at Minot AFB? Remove some details from that and just say you live a few miles from an Air Force base. It gets the point across, without revealing your location.

In fact, it's a good idea to never give distances from your home to anywhere. Do it once and there can be a pretty big circle to search, but do it with two different locations and the area shrinks dramatically; add a third, and anyone with a map can locate you quite precisely.

The final piece of the puzzle is surveillance and recon. While the SEALs get most of their credit for daring missions in the dark of night that make headlines, we also do a lot of surveillance. We seek out targets for airstrikes and these can have a serious impact on the battlefield.

If someone is narrowing down your location to find food or resources, they might spend time surveilling your property. How can you know? Well, conduct a little counter surveillance of your own. Using binoculars or IR optics you can scan your property from time to time. This is also when those trail cameras can come into play.

Counter surveillance can give you the upper hand in a situation like this.

A Picture Paints a Thousand Words

It's easy to share photos on the internet, and it can also be really useful. Why settle for a description of your preps when you can show people exactly what you've done? The problem is, photos can also do serious damage to your OPSEC. Every time you post a picture of your preps, you're potentially showing people not just what you have, but where it is and how to get at it. The good news is that you don't have to stop posting photos; you just have to be careful about what they show.

Photos can compromise your OPSEC in a couple of ways. The first is by revealing where you live. There are a few obvious things to avoid here, which most preppers do; for example, a street sign will tell people what street you live on, and if they already know the town you're in – which is usually much easier to work out – that lets them pinpoint you. For security it's best to avoid any sign with place names on it. A highway sign that shows distance to other locations, especially if it has distances to two or more places, is very helpful to anyone who's trying to find you. Even business signs can give away a lot, because the internet makes it easy to search for businesses.

Signs are fairly obvious, and any reasonably OPSEC-aware prepper is going to avoid including them in photos, but there are more subtle ways to give your location away. Apps like Google Earth let anyone access high-quality satellite – or even ground-level – imagery of almost anywhere in the world. If you post a photograph of your yard, and in the distance I can see a very tall, slim arch rising above a city, I know that you live somewhere near St Louis, Missouri. I can then use Google Street View to narrow down the search area based on the angle the arch is shown from and how it relates to the buildings around it. Combined with closer objects that could be enough to let me identify your location quite precisely.

If you're taking outdoor pics, keep the horizon close. Even the internet won't let me find you based on a photo that just shows your yard – but as soon as the horizon starts expanding, you risk revealing clues. I picked St Louis's Gateway Arch as an extreme example but there are all kinds of things that are big enough to be visible in the background of your pics and recognizable enough to be found online. Bridges, prominent buildings, water towers, even mountains or water features can give your location away.

Indoor photos are a lot less likely to give away your location, but the risk is non-zero. Before posting a pic taken inside your home, check it for anything that could tell a watcher where you live. Local newspapers, phone books or even takeout menus can all provide clues. Anything with readable phone numbers is a danger, because that shows your local area code.

There are two other problems with indoor photos, though. One is simply that they tempt thieves. You're showing exactly how valuable your supplies would be, and that value isn't just something that matters during a crisis. Prepping can be expensive, and your stockpile probably has a significant cash value. It's fine to show people what you have, but this makes it extra important to keep your location private.

The other issue with indoor pics is that, once someone's identified where you live, photos of the inside of your home can be a huge help to a thief. An innocent photo might reveal alarm sensors, details of window latches, even where security locks are placed inside your door. That's all-valuable information for a potential intruder. Make sure none of your snapshots show entry points to your home.

Online OPSEC Is Vital!

Don't be fooled into thinking that online security doesn't

matter, because in a crisis the internet will be down anyway. Yes, it will be down – in large areas, at least – if we've suffered a nuclear strike or EMP attack. A major natural disaster, like an eruption of the Yellowstone super volcano, could also take out the web across large parts of the country. On the other hand, there's plenty potential for a crisis that doesn't shut down the internet. Remember the panic buying during the COVID pandemic? Well, believe it or not, that was minor. When the coronavirus hit, the US economy was still in fairly good shape.

Just imagine if another virus came along in late 2022, with the country already staggering under high gas prices and runaway inflation, and the government decided to push through the same measures as it did in 2020/21. Many people already struggle to afford the essentials; a new supply chain breakdown, and the surging prices that causes, would mean they simply couldn't buy food and other basics. If someone has lost their job to a government-mandated lockdown and is living on the last few dollars of their savings, but they still have an internet connection, they have the time and tools they need to locate resources to steal – maybe your resources. You have to make sure you don't provide those tiny shreds of information they can weave together into a detailed picture of what you have, where it is, and how it's protected.

Here's another thought: What if it's the government that's looking for preppers? There isn't much risk of FEMA coming looking for your supplies – they'd rather requisition a food-processing plant, so they can roll trucks in and load them up with bulk goods – but what will your town county officials do when food's running low and supply chains are breaking down? There's a good chance that once they've seized and emptied local stores, they'll start looking for preppers, so you can "do your fair share" by "donating" your food supplies. The thing about governments, even local ones, is they always have the time and resources to interfere in people's lives, so you don't want to leave a trail of online breadcrumbs for them to follow.

This goes back to dealing with trained forces like the Navy SEALs. You must understand how outgunned you will be. Even local resources like State Police or SWAT, if they come in force, you will be overwhelmed. Best to conceal as much as you can. Stay quiet, stick to the plan, and survive!

ENERGY

How to Choose the Best Generator for Your House

During most SHTF situations, grid power will be unreliable or lost altogether. The absence of reliable power from your wall sockets is more than an inconvenience; it is a serious problem for which you need a reliable alternative.

For many years, gas or diesel generators have been the mainstay emergency power option for homeowners. Gas or diesel generators have several serious problems associated with them and they are simply not a great option for backup power if you are bugging in.

The good news is that technology has advanced far enough to bring the size and cost of solar power options to a level accessible to the average prepper.

Gas or diesel generators have several problems, making them less suitable for use during any SHTF scenario. These problems are not easy to overcome and can potentially place you and your family at serious risk from those around you who will be desperate for your power.

Problem number 1

One of the biggest downfalls of a generator is that they are loud, and that sound carries over great distances. Even smaller inverter-style generators, while quieter than their larger counterparts, are still loud enough to draw unwanted attention.

There are many ways to deaden the sound of a generator, but these often only reduce the sound, not cut it completely. Anyone passing by the house will know that you are running a generator. These individuals will be tempted to steal your generator, potentially using force.

Problem number 2

The gas or diesel that is the lifeblood of a generator is expensive, requires safe storage, and may not be available during or after SHTF. If fuel is stored for more than a few months, it will start to break down and oxidize.

The result is that when you try to use it in your generator, it may not start, or if it does start, the fuel will clog up the engine. So, both gas and diesel must be stabilized for long-term storage. Even if you have stabilized fuel, storing enough for long-term emergencies is difficult.

Problem number 3

Any generator that runs on fuel will emit harmful fumes. This means that you cannot bring them into the home. You must keep the generator outside the house, which is problematic in a SHTF scenario.

Problem number 4

Since you must run these generators outside the home and they make a lot of noise, you are opening them up to the possibility of theft. In fact, it is almost certain that someone will try and steal your generator straight out of your backyard.

What Is a Solar Generator?

A solar generator is a portable battery bank that is designed in such a way that it is easily charged through solar panels. The size of solar generators is determined by the amount of power the batteries can deliver. The larger the capacity, the bigger the generator and the higher the output.

Since these units are battery-powered, they are silent, do not emit fumes, and require no fuel. These factors make solar generators far superior to gas or diesel generators for most families looking for backup power when bugging in.

Solar generators have one serious drawback that you will need to consider. Since these are battery packs that require solar charging, you are extremely limited in the amount of power you will have available.

Most large solar generators have a capacity of around 3000 watt-hours of power before needing a recharge. This means you will be very limited in how many devices you can power with a single solar generator.

Some solar generators can add additional battery packs to the system to expand the capacity, which may be an option to consider. Still, given that these generators are so small, investing in two or three solar generators may be better rather than creating one large one using additional batteries.

Basic Electrical Terms and Definitions

Before we get too far into choosing a solar generator, knowing the terminology we will be using will be helpful.

- Volt (V) – A measure of electrical force. In North America, the voltage from the wall plugs is 120V
- Amp (A) – The flow of current
- Watt (W) – A measure of electrical power
- Watt-hours (Wh) – The number of watts used in one hour

How Much Capacity Will You Need?

Before purchasing a solar generator, you must know how much capacity you need. This can be confusing, but it is the most critical step in planning your backup emergency power.

Since a single solar generator will only provide about 3000Wh of power, you must be realistic about what appliances you will power. The critical things you will want to power are your fridge/freezers, lights, smartphones, and charging batteries.

Your first step is to make a list of each of the appliances that you want to power. Then beside each appliance, create three columns, one for watt-hours, one for hours, and one for the totals. Use this to calculate the total energy requirement of the devices you want to power for 24 hours.

Appliance	Watt Hours	Hours	Total
Fridge			
Smartphones			
Lights			
Battery Chargers			
Total Watt Hours Required			

You can then fill in the table to determine what a single solar generator will power.

CALCULATING YOUR POWER REQUIREMENTS

Each appliance you want to run will have specific power needs you must consider.

1. Refrigerators/Freezers

Your fridge and freezers will not run at full power 24 hours a day. They turn the compressor on only long enough to cool the inside to the right temperature. You could use a generator or a solar generator to keep your fridge and freezers powered all day, but this is unnecessary.

Instead, you should monitor the internal temperature with a wireless thermometer and plug it into your solar generator when the temperature rises. This way, you may only need to have it plugged in for a few hours a day.

To calculate the number of watts your fridge uses, simply multiply the amperage by the input voltage, you can find this information on the information decal that your fridge should have. In the case of my refrigerator, it draws an average of 3 amps and uses 120 volts of electricity.

To determine the number of watts my fridge uses, I multiply the volts by the amps.

3 Amps x 120 Volts = 360 watts

Let's assume you will be plugging it into power for at least 6 hours every 24 hours. This would mean that you would plug your fridge into the generator every three hours for an hour. This should keep everything inside the fridge cold and safe to eat.

To figure out the watt/hours required to power this fridge, you must multiply the number of watts it draws by the number of hours it will be plugged in for.

360 watts x 6 hours = 2160 watt/hours

In the case of freezers, they usually keep everything inside frozen for 24 and 48 hours before the food inside thaw. If you monitor the temperature, you should only plug it into power once daily for an hour or two. Figuring out the watt hours for your freezer is the same as for the fridge.

2. Devices

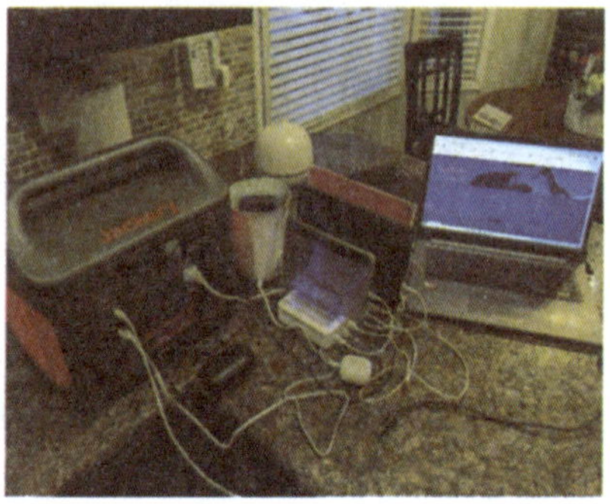

Charging devices, such as smartphones, require negligible amounts of power but still need to be considered.

The average smartphone needs to be charged daily, and you may rely on it as your only means of communication, if the cellphone towers are still active.

The average smartphone will draw between 5 and 30 watts per hour when charging and usually must be charged for around three hours daily. This means you will use 15 – 90 watt-hours of power per phone for a family of four, which could be up to 360 watt-hours a day.

3. Lights

It is best to always use the most energy-efficient light bulbs you can, regardless of whether the world is ending. The problem with using a solar generator is that you can only power lights that you can plug into it.

You would likely be running no more than one or two lamps to light up a room so your family can read, play games, or work on household projects.

For this example, let's assume you want to power two lamps with 60-watt incandescent bulbs for three hours each night.

120 watts combined power x 3 hours = 360 watt-hours of power

If you were to use a LED light bulb that is 9 watts, which is the equivalent of a 60-watt bulb, your energy requirement would be:

18 watts combined power x 3 hours = 54 watt-hours

As you can see, switching to LED bulbs is a big benefit.

4. Charging Batteries

Flashlights and headlamps will require batteries to run. If you have rechargeable batteries, you can use a solar generator to charge them. Every battery charger is different; you must determine how many watt-hours yours will draw.

For a family of four, you can count on needing at least four flashlights, four headlamps and four lanterns, all powered by either AA or AAA batteries. For example, you can assume that each headlamp takes 3 AAA batteries, each flashlight has two AA batteries, and the lanterns have four AA batteries. We can also assume you would want a backup set of batteries for each.

This family of four would have 24 AAA and 48 AA batteries to keep charged. To make the math easy, assume that at least half of the batteries you hold in reserve will need charging at any given time; in this case, that would be 18 batteries.

I found a charger online that will charge 4 AA or AAA batteries in three hours using 7 watts of power. In this case, to charge 20 batteries, you would use 140 watt-hours of power.

Appliance	Watt Hours	Hours	Total
Fridge	360	6	2160
Smartphones	120	3	360
Lights	120	3	360
Battery Chargers	21	3	140
Total Watt Hours Required			**3020**

As you can see, a 3000wh solar generator will barely cover the energy costs for these appliances, and I haven't even included a second fridge or a freezer in these calculations.

The problem with fridges and freezers is that once the compressor turns on to start cooling, there is a momentary power surge. This surge can be 2000 – 3000 watts, and if you have two such appliances plugged into one solar generator, it will trigger it to shut down. It is for this reason that I would suggest a separate solar generator for each fridge or freezer.

What Solar Generators Are Available, and What Features Should You Look For?

Many companies are producing solar generators, and their products are remarkably similar. A few notable solar generator companies are Jackery, BougeRV, Bluetti, and Goal Zero. Any of these companies will give you a well-built and functional solar generator, but there are a few features that you should be looking for:

Included solar panels

Your solar generator will need charging and is pretty useless unless you have enough solar panels. Look for portable panels to move them to the best locations on your property for sun exposure.

Pass-through charging

The ability to run appliances while the solar generator is being charged is a handy feature that you should be looking for.

Lots of USB ports

For charging smartphones, it is much better to do so through a USB port than to plug a charger into the AC outlet.

If you use the AC outlet, the generator must convert the DC power from the battery to AC power, resulting in some of that power being lost.

Able to take a brief surge of power

Fridges and freezers will have surges of power when the compressor activates, and any solar generator you choose needs to be able to handle it.

Multiple charging options

You should buy a solar charger that can be charged through solar power and standard household AC power. This way, you can keep it charged when the grid is up and know you have a fully charged solar generator when it fails.

Some of these solar generators can be charged using the 12V outlets on a vehicle.

Portability

You are going to be lugging your solar generator around the house, so having one that is light enough to carry and small enough to fit in most spaces is important.

Multiple AC outlets

You'll want enough AC outlets to power the things you wish to during a grid-down scenario, so make sure the solar generator you buy has enough plugs.

High watt-hour capacity

You should know what capacity you need and buy a solar generator that exceeds this capacity. I would recommend getting the largest one that you can afford.

Fast solar charging

You only have a limited amount of full sunlight each day, so you'll also want to consider the speed of solar charging in your decision.

The company that I believe has the best solar generator for bugging-in is Jackery. Their largest model is the Jackery 3000 Pro, which has 3024Wh of power and can power devices that use up to 3000W. It can be charged in as little as 6 hours with solar panels or 2.5 hours with AC power.

I currently own a Jackery 1500 solar generator and four 100W solar panels. I have found that the stated charging times have been very accurate, and it was easy to set up and carry around. Even though this solar generator will run my fridge, it cannot do so for a long time. Compared to the Jackery 3000, the 1500 has just over half the available battery capacity.

You can purchase the Jackery 3000 pro from their online store. At the time of writing this, the Jackery 3000 Pro was $3999.00 USD, and you'll need to buy the solar panels separately.

The panels are $389.99 USD and can be found online on their website. In total, you'll need 6 solar panels to properly charge the Jackery 3000 Pro.

One cool feature of the Jackery solar panels is their built-in USB port, so you can charge USB devices straight from the panel. This allows you to use the panels to charge anything that uses USB, such as smartphones, tablets, or rechargeable batteries.

A Few Important Things to Consider

1. Should You Get One Large Solar Generator or Several Smaller Ones?

There are several factors in deciding whether to invest in one larger solar generator or several smaller ones. You'll need to carefully consider them before making a purchase.

2. How Much Sun Does Your Property Get?

You'll need to keep the solar panels hidden from view when charging the solar generator. The second anyone sees you have solar panels, they will know you have power and want to take it from you. You'll have to assess how much sun the concealed areas on your property get and whether or not you can get enough sun to charge the generator fully.

It doesn't make sense to buy a solar generator that is so large you cannot charge it using the sunlight available. In these cases, having several smaller units that rotate between charging and powering your appliances might make sense.

3. How Many Large Appliances Will You Be Running?

I recommend getting a solar generator for each fridge and freezer. This way, you don't have to worry about the strain on the generator when two or three fridges are plugged into it at one time.

4. What Is Your Budget?

This is a significant consideration. If you only have enough free cash to buy one solar generator, your decision has been made for you. Having a second or third generator will always be good if you can afford it.

5. Two Is One, and One Is None

It is unlikely that your solar generator will fail, but you should still be ready if it happens. Having a backup solar generator will be a lifesaver. Even if the second generator is smaller, it will still be a good investment.

6. Using a Solar Generator for Bugging-In

Once the grid goes down, it's time to start using a solar generator. For the most part, using a solar generator is as simple as placing it next to the device you want to bring power to and plugging it into the solar generator. There are, however, several critical things you must do in a bug-in scenario when using your solar generator.

7. Close the Blinds

In a grid-down bug-in situation, you will want lighting inside your home. Unfortunately, having a working electric light is a massive sign to outsiders that you have a source of electrical power. Keep the blinds open during the day to use natural light but once the sun goes down and you start plugging lamps into your generator, keep the blinds shut so no one walking past can see that you have power.

8. Find a Concealed Spot for Your Panels

Solar panels are a big sign that you have power, so you will need a spot on your property that is concealed from the view of your neighbours but still gets enough sunlight. This can be challenging but it is essential if you want to keep your solar generator from being stolen.

Often, just placing panels in your backyard is enough to keep them out of view, but you can also hang them on fences or place them on top of awnings or deck covers. In some cases, putting them on your roof may work out.

9. Use Extension Cords

You should pick a solar generator with pass-through charging; if the sun is out, it should be plugged into the solar panels. You should always take advantage of sunlight when you can, but you may also need to run your fridge while charging the generator. In this case, run extension cords from the generators to the appliances you want to charge. This way, you are charging the batteries and providing power simultaneously.

10. Set Timers

It is easy to forget that something is plugged into your solar generator. To prevent this, set timers to remind you to unplug them.

11. Conserve Power

Having power in a grid-down scenario does not mean you can waste it. Use low-wattage bulbs, conserve battery-operated devices, and if you need to go into the fridge or freezer, do so when it is plugged into the generator.

Also, keep the door to fridges and freezers closed as much as possible between the times you have them plugged in. Keeping the inside cold will mean that you must provide less electricity when it's plugged in.

12. Keep it a Secret

Do not tell anyone that you have power. People you think are your friends may stop at nothing to take what you have when the grid is down.

Solar generators are a great way to provide power during any emergency, especially when bugging in. The energy provided by these generators is clean, quiet, and renewable, which makes them a great alternative to traditional gasoline or diesel generators. If you are preparing for a long-term grid-down, bug-in, situation, a solar generator should be at the top of your list of products to invest in.

The Best Way to Protect Your Electronic Devices Against an EMP

An electromagnetic pulse (EMP) or coronal mass ejection (CME) are massive threats to the power grid throughout the world. If either event happens, the power grid may be disabled for months or years. Every prepper should have backup power in case of an EMP or CME, but those generators are also vulnerable to these events.

An EMP or CME will overload and destroy the circuitry inside your gas, diesel, or solar generator, making it useless. To prevent this from happening, you should protect your generators by placing them inside a Faraday cage. A Faraday cage is an enclosure covered in metal or conductive mesh that will absorb the high-energy particles that EMPs and CMEs release.

The problem with a Faraday cage is that they are difficult and expensive to build in the sizes required to protect a generator.

What Is an EMP Cloth?

A better and more affordable alternative to a Faraday cage is the EMP cloth. The EMP cloth is a blanket with copper and nickel mesh sandwiched between polyester layers. The cloth measures 3.5 ft. x 15 ft. and is designed to be able to cover any portable generator that the average homeowner would own.

The EMP cloth will protect against the E1, E2, and E3 waves of an EMP and the low-frequency waves of a CME.

Buying an EMP cloth is much more affordable than building a Faraday cage which is large enough to protect a generator.

You can order the EMP cloth using this link or by scanning the QR code: https://www.theempcloth.com/bug-in-guide/

How to Use an EMP Cloth

Using the EMP cloth is quite simple, but there are a few things that you need to consider first:

- Whatever you are trying to protect must be covered on all sides, including the bottom.
- There cannot be any gaps in the protection; if you can see the generator, it is not protected.
- Before trusting this product to protect your equipment, you can test it with a radio and cellphone.

To use the EMP cloth, follow these simple steps:

1. Lay the cloth out. You should do this in the final location where you will be storing the generator, but if you can easily move the items after wrapping, you can lay the cloth out in any location with enough room.

2. Place the generator in the center of the cloth.

3. Pick up the ends and lay them one at a time over the generator.

4. Allow the sides to drape over. Feel free to use Scotch Tape to secure the ends of your EMP cloth in place.

For other smaller items, such as cellphones, laptops, walkie talkies, ham radios, credit cards, key fobs, and any other electronics, you can cut the EMP cloth to fit your needs.

You can wrap them up in the cloth by rolling, folding over, or any other method that gives you 100% coverage.

To test the EMP cloth, follow these steps:

1. Before wrapping the item, place a smartphone that is turned on and an AM radio tuned to a strong radio station next to whatever you are covering.
2. Wrap the object as you normally would.
3. If the cloth provides protection, the AM radio will stop receiving the station, and you should not be able to call or text the cell phone.

If the test fails, you might need to take greater care in the wrapping. In my testing, I found that the EMP cloth blocked electromagnetic radiation very effectively and passed both the radio and the cell phone test.

What Should You Cover in the EMP Cloth

Any item that could be affected by an EMP or CME should be wrapped in an EMP cloth, but here are some notable examples of things you could protect:

- Generators
- HAM radios
- Electronics
- Vehicles

What Else Can an EMP Cloth Be Used For?

There are other uses for the EMP cloth; other than wrapping generators and electronics. You can use the EMP cloth to block the electromagnetic radiation from 5G, Wi-Fi, or radio waves. If you bought enough EMP cloth, you could line the walls of a room to make it an oasis from EMF.

Your smartphone is tracking you even when it is off, so cutting a small section of this cloth out and using that to wrap your phone can make you invisible from Big Brother.

We all need some kind of protection for our electronics in case of EMP and CME. Many of us do not want to or don't have the skills to build Faraday cages, making the EMP cloth a great option to get the protection you need without spending much money. I use my EMP cloth to protect my solar generators and some HAM radio gear from damage by EMP or CME, and you should do the same.

Close-up picture of an EMP cloth

How to Heat Your Home When You're Bugging In

A wood burning stove can be a great asset in an emergency. It provides a reliable source of heat and light, and can be used to cook meals and boil water for drinking. It is also much more affordable than electric and gas stoves, especially if you have access to free firewood.

In addition, a wood burning stove is easy to operate and doesn't require electricity to run, which is an important factor if the power goes out.

Finally, it can help reduce the cost of energy bills, as it is often more efficient than other types of stoves.

However, it's important to take the time to properly install your stove to ensure that it functions safely and efficiently. In this chapter, I'll take you through the step-by-step process of how to install a wood burning stove with a "through the roof" stove pipe set up.

For this install we chose 'The Englander' wood burning stove, which is rated to heat up to 2000 square feet when burning seasoned cordwood. It is a freestanding design which allows versatile placement and also with a large firebox; it holds logs up to 18 inches in length.

It's also an EPA certified stove, which comes with some advantages. EPA certified wood stoves are more economical to run for several reasons.

First, they are designed to burn wood more efficiently, resulting in less fuel being used.

The stoves are also designed to capture more of the heat generated and direct it into the room instead of up the chimney. This allows you to heat a larger area with less fuel.

In addition, the stoves are designed to generate less smoke and reduce creosote buildup than the older type of non-certified stoves, making them safer, more economical to run, and also more environmentally friendly.

Finally, EPA certified stoves are designed to last longer and require less maintenance, making them even more economical to operate over time.

We installed our stove 2 years ago and have been very pleased with it. We use it to heat the main living space of our temporary shed house, which measures 500 sq. ft. and the stove has performed very well, easily maintaining the indoor temperature at 75 degrees F or higher during outdoor winter temperatures of down to -20 degrees.

It would easily heat a larger open plan living space. When dampened down it will also burn for 8-10 hours overnight making it easy to re-start in the mornings.

Heat does not travel well through doorways to adjoining rooms so installing a blower can help with this. Do note that although this stove comes with a blower, you have to send off for the blower separately; for some reason it doesn't arrive with the stove itself.

Stove Choice

Taking time to choose the right stove for you is very important. When choosing a stove, here are some things to consider:

1. What type of fuel does it burn?
2. Does it need an air intake installing?
3. What size is the firebox / what size logs will it hold?
4. How efficient is the stove (cost of fuel consumption)?
5. What size room will it heat?
6. Do I need to use the stove top for cooking?

Cooking on a wood stove is another huge benefit to consider when choosing which stove to install. It is important to understand the difference between wood burning stoves and dedicated wood burning cook stoves.

The primary function of the wood burning cook stove is to behave more like an oven and so its capacity for heating a room is not equal to a regular wood burning stove.

It is possible to use most regular wood burning stoves for basic cooking, to boil water, and cook stews. You can even bake pies and make cookies simply by using a few additional tools.

However, the location of the chimney pipe will limit the stove top area in terms of the available space on which to place cookware and in this instance selecting a stove with an offset or rear exit chimney pipe might become a priority.

See end of chapter for additional resources and stove alternatives.

Materials Needed

Before you start the installation process, you'll need to gather some tools and materials. Below I've put together a list of materials and tools needed.

- A wood burning stove (We paid $1499 for ours.)
- Fire resistant floor pad (We built our own concrete pad and it cost us $60.)
- Ceiling support box (Home Depot Kit - $359)
- Stove pipe adaptor (comes in kit)
- Chimney flashing kit (comes in kit)
- A chimney cap (comes in kit)
- Chimney Pipe (triple wall 36" section - $140)
- Chimney pipe extension (24" section - $91; this project needed 3 sections)
- Stove pipe (up to 68" double wall pipe - $173)
- Stove pipe extension (24" per section - $50)
- High-temperature silicone sealant (through the roof silicone - $11.00 per tube)
- Screws, bolts, and other hardware as necessary

Tools Needed

- A plumb line or laser
- Stud finder
- An oscillating tool or drywall knife
- A drill
- Angle grinder or tin snips
- A reciprocating saw
- Tape measure
- A level
- Indoor ladder and roof ladder
- Safety gloves and goggles
- A dust mask
- A helper

Once you have all of the necessary tools and materials, you're ready to get started. This project can be successfully completed in one day. The total project cost was around $2500.

Installing Your Wood Stove

Step 1: Choose the Location for Your Stove

The stove should be placed in a central location in your home, away from walls and other combustible materials; refer to manufacturer's instructions for clearance measurements.

Allow enough height for an effective chimney flue; the recommendation is at least 15 ft. of stove pipe between the top of your stove to the exterior chimney cap to create a good enough draw to efficiently burn fuel.

Use a stud finder to mark the location of your roof trusses to ensure the chimney will go between them. Outside, the chimney's shortest side will need to be 3 ft. above the roof penetration. The chimney cap must be 2 ft. higher than any part of the building that's within 10 ft.

Step 2: Install the Floor Pad and Stove

Place the stove on top of a non-combustible surface, such as a concrete or tile pad. Wood stoves require pads 48" and larger, at least 12 mm thick to protect from falling embers. Consult your stove dealer or stove manual for your stove's specific requirements.

Once the floor pad is installed, situate the stove in place.

Step 3: Install the Ceiling Support Box (On a Dry Day!)

The hole should be cut to the size of the ceiling support box that will be inserted.

Start indoors and use a plumb line or laser to mark the center of the area where the chimney will penetrate the roof and from there use a pencil to trace out the area where the support box will go.

Cut away the drywall, push any insulation material aside (or remove). Use a drill to make holes in the roof at the 4 corners of the area you traced out.

Now go up onto the roof and cut the roof open using the drill holes as a guide. Slide the ceiling support box in place and secure it with screws.

Note: If the ceiling support box is too deep, cut it down to size using tin snips. Fold excess tin backwards to make flaps but make sure that they go under the shingles or roof tin and not over it. The excess tin can also be removed if referred.

Step 4: Install the Chimney Pipe Section 1

Next, insert the first section of the chimney pipe into the support box. Be sure to follow the manufacturer's instructions for securing the pipe in place. This model is a twist lock.

Step 5: Install the Chimney Flashing

With the chimney pipe in place, you can now install the chimney flashing boot. The flashing boot will prevent water from coming through the roof.

To install the flashing boot, apply roofing tar or sealant around the hole, then place the flashing boot over the hole and secure it in place using screws or other hardware as necessary. Install the chimney collar or cuff over the top of the flashing boot and seal in place to stop rain water running into the ceiling support box from above.

Use sealant around the edges of the flashing or anywhere that water might be able to get in. The top half of the flashing should sit under the shingles while the lower half should remain on top of the shingles.

Install the remaining sections of chimney and chimney cap. Follow manufacturer's instructions to lock them together correctly.

Step 6: Install Stove Pipe Adaptor

The transition from triple wall chimney to double wall stove pipe is made by a stove pipe adapter. With the arrow pointing towards the ceiling, install the stove pipe adaptor into the hole in the ceiling box.

Step 7: Connect Stove Pipe to Adaptor

Double wall stove pipe is designed with the crimped end of the pipe always being the top end which inserts inside the opening of the pipe above - in this case the stove pipe adapter. Always follow the manufacturer's arrows on the stove pipe instructions which indicate the directional flow of the flu.

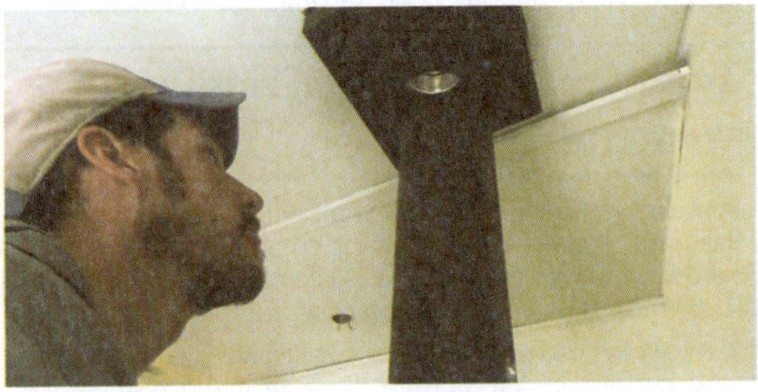

Step 8: Connect Stove Pipe to Stove Pipe

When joining two sections of double wall stove pipe, insert the crimped end of the lower section upwards and in between the two walls of the above section.

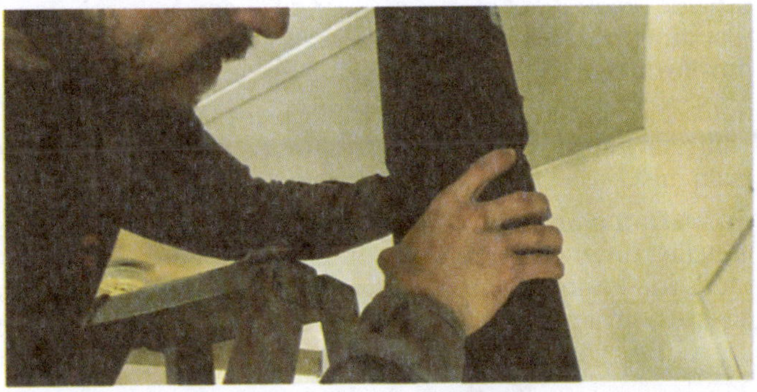

Step 9: Secure the Stove Pipe Joints

Use small screws that come with the stove pipe to connect any sections of pipe. These small screws go through the outside wall but not the inside wall of the double wall stove pipe.

Step 10: Install Ceiling Flashing

Install any ceiling flashing or locking bands to cover joints and seams to give a more decorative finish.

The First Burn

Don't forget to read the manufacturer's instructions about the best way to break in your stove; this stove gave off a chemical smell for about the first 6 hours of burn time, which is due to factory paint fumes curing with the heat. It can be an overpowering smell, so make sure you're able to be out and have the doors and windows open for some good ventilation!

Tools for Cooking on a Traditional Wood Burning Stove

You can use any normal pots and pans on the wood stove. Pans with thinner walls will heat up more quickly and cook food faster, however this can also cause food to burn or stick if the bottom of the pan becomes too hot.

Placing your pan on top of a cast iron 'trivet' will help to avoid food burning on the bottom of a pan if the surface of the stove is too hot. Cooking with cast iron cookware is more suitable for wood stove cooking, as the cast iron absorbs heat evenly and spreads it gently while cooking. The drawback to using cast iron is that care must be taken to season the cookware properly before use to avoid the cast iron from rusting.

Enamel coated cast iron gives the ideal 'nonstick' solution if you don't want the hassle of seasoning traditional cast iron; however this cookware carries a higher price tag.

Should you want to bake something (bread/ pie/ cookies) on your stove top, you can create an oven by placing a dutch oven upside down over your food.

It is also important to understand that not all wood burns equally, different types of wood burn at different temperatures. It is therefore useful to have an instant thermometer to give you an accurate reading of the temperature of your stove top before you begin cooking.

Here is a list of alternative recommended wood burning cook stoves:

1. Baker's Choice Wood Cookstove

https://us.amazon.com/Gallon-Water-Barrel-FreshStorage/dp/B07B68CVRD

$2459

2. La Nordica Rosa

https://www.woodcookstove.com/wood-burning-cooking-stove-62.html

$3600

3. Pioneer Princess Amish Wood Burning Cookstove

https://us.amazon.com/Gallon-Water-Barrel-FreshStorage/dp/B07B68CVRD

$3980

Items to Stockpile
for the Next US Blackout

Losing power affects much more than the lights in our home. When the power goes out, pretty much everything stops working. If the power stays out as little as just a few days, it can become life-threatening, especially if there is bad weather to go with it.

We won't be able to just go to the store and get what we need either, as stores can't function without electricity to power their computerized cash registers and inventory management systems. Considering that the incidence of long-term power outages is on the rise, we need to be prepared for those long-term power outages, with everything we need on-hand so that our families can survive.

Apart from stockpiling food and water, we need to consider such things as light, first-aid, fire, communications, and self-defense. There are so many things we use every day, which are part of our survival, even though we don't think of them that way.

Producing Electricity

The first thing we want to consider for power outages is some means of producing our own electricity. While gas-powered generators aren't effective for long-term survival situations, they're ideal for short-term ones, lasting up to a couple of weeks. Depending on the size of the generator, you can keep your refrigerator running to preserve food, have some lighting, and recharge portable devices, like phones.

Our big restriction with generators is the gasoline. Not only can gasoline be dangerous to store, but it has a limited shelf-life. It is possible to extend that shelf-life by keeping it in metal gas cans, rather than plastic ones.

There are also additives that can be put in the gas, extending its shelf life from six months to a year. But the best thing to do is rotate your gasoline stock, using it as it starts getting old and replacing it with fresh gasoline.

The other big and better way of producing electricity for your home using a solar generator and solar panels. While these are expensive, especially if you want to have enough to provide power to your whole home, a few panels, connected to a solar generator, should give you enough to keep your refrigerator running and allow you to recharge phones and other portable electronics.

Heating

There's a reason why heating is our biggest survival priority. During Winter Storm Uri, 246 people died from hypothermia, just in Texas, due to not having electricity for heat. Even if a home has gas heat, it still needs electricity for the controls and blowers. About the only people who would have heat in their homes during a blackout are those who have fireplaces and wood-burning stoves.

Of course, installing a wood-burning stove is a very good idea; but what if you can't? What can you use for an alternate means of heating, which doesn't require electricity and is safe for use indoors?

There are a number of small propane heaters which can be used indoors; just be careful to buy one that is rated for indoor use; as not all are. You'll also need a supply of the small propane tanks that they use.

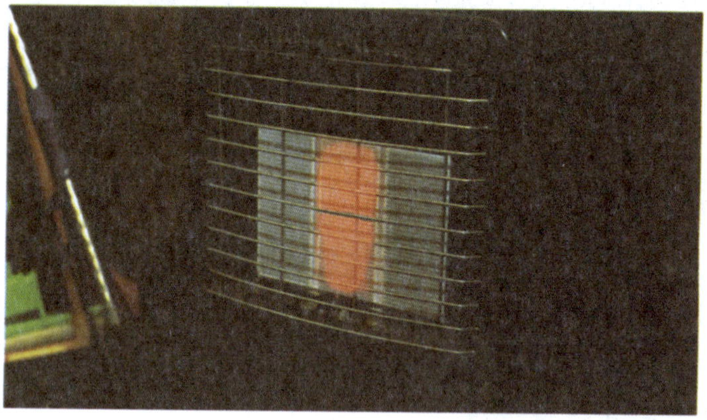

Rather than spending $5 each on a bunch of those tanks, buy a few and an adapter which will allow you to fill them off a standard 20-pound propane tank, like you would use on a propane barbecue grille. That cuts the refill charge down to roughly $1 per small tank.

Insulation

Along with providing yourself with heat, you want to do whatever you can to make sure that the heat you have can't escape from your home. Our homes are fairly well insulated, but heat can still escape from the windows and doors, the least insulated parts of most homes.

There are several things that can be used to cover those windows and doors, some of which you may already have sitting around the house. Extra blankets are the easiest thing to use. You can tape them in place with duct tape.

If you don't have enough blankets to cover all your windows and doors, foam rubber or Styrofoam work well. You can buy Styrofoam in four by eight-foot sheets at lumberyards and home-improvement centers; it's used for sheathing on houses and only costs about $10 per sheet.

Since we're talking about covering windows and doors, that insulation is going to provide another advantage, helping to keep noise from escaping from your home. But we can take that one step further, taping plastic sheeting (often called visqueen by contractors) under the insulation, sealing off the windows and doors. That will help prevent food odors from escaping from your house, to be smelled by others and attract them to come beg or steal your food.

Lighting

Probably the first things that most people think about, when talking about the power going out is light. While light is not normally considered a survival requirement, there are an awful lot of things we need to do, which require light so that we can see to do them.

The typical solution for light is to use flashlights. There's nothing wrong with that, especially if you have the newer LED tactical lights. Not only do they produce more light, but they are also less susceptible to breaking.

Make sure that you have enough for every member in the family, locating them in various parts of the house, so that there is always one readily available, regardless of where you are.

An alternative to tactical flashlights is the LED headlights that they are now producing. These are essentially an alternate form of the tactical lights, with a headband that allows you to wear it on your head, so that the light is shining where you are looking. This also has the added advantage of leaving your hands free to work.

Both of these types of lights are power hungry and will go through batteries quickly. You'll need to make sure that you have plenty of batteries on-hand for them. Better yet, get rechargeable batteries and a solar charger to recharger to keep them charged.

Most take lithium-ion batteries, rather than the more common AA or AAA batteries, so you'll need to find the right equivalent rechargeables.

At the same time, stock up on AA and AAA batteries, both alkaline and rechargeable, as there are other things that need them. Fortunately for us, battery manufacturers are now saying that alkaline batteries have a shelf-life of 10 years.

Of course, rechargeable batteries indicates that we have to have a way of recharging them as well; one that doesn't require being plugged into an electric outlet. If you have solar power or a generator already as part of your survival plan, then you can use that for recharging your batteries as well.

Non-Electric Lighting

Skipping electric lighting altogether, we can go to old-fashioned solutions, like candles and oil-lamps. Both are effective, although they don't produce as much light. Nevertheless, there are a lot of situations where we need lighting, but don't need a lot of lighting. In those situations, candles and oil-filled-lamps are ideal.

The Coleman company still produces their old gas lantern, which will run off of gasoline. This is a great option, being simple to use and reliable, while producing quite a bit of light. Just make sure you have lots of the mantles for the lantern, as they are consumable and the lantern won't work without them.

Don't forget to buy plenty of fuel and wicking/mantles for the oil lamps and/or Coleman lanterns.

Communications

Finally, you'll want to be able to maintain both incoming and outgoing communications when the power is out. For the most part, we can do that with our cell phones. Today's phones not only allow us to call people, but also provide us with access to a broad range of information and other means of communications.

But they do have a weakness, if the local cell tower doesn't have power, we won't have the ability to use those phones.

The other problem with them is that they are power hungry. Phone batteries have gotten bigger and bigger, while engineers have worked to make them run more efficiently, so those batteries will last longer. But you're going to need to be able to recharge them eventually.

Unless you have a generator or solar power for your home, then that means having a solar phone charger. Don't buy one of the little pocket versions though, as they will take three to four days to recharge your phone. You're better off with a larger charger, like the folding type. Better yet, get a folding type which also has a battery inside, so that the charger can charge its own battery and then you can charge your phone off the charger's battery. That should keep your phone running all the time, throughout the blackout.

Don't just count on your phone for communications though. You'll want a simple radio, so that you can hear what is happening, including news about restoring power. That means either a battery-operated radio or one that has a hand-crank generator. In either case, conserve power, as you don't know just how long the power outage will last.

How to Draw Electricity Out of Dead Batteries

With so many electronic devices in our daily lives, anyone who doesn't have a good stockpile of common sized batteries is asking for trouble. While it is still possible to live without those electronic devices, we've become so accustomed to using them and the convenience that they provide, that it would be difficult to get by without them, especially in the event of an emergency.

But there are more types of batteries today than ever before. So, between the increased types of batteries and the increased number of devices we all have, it can be challenging having all the batteries we need. If only we could make our batteries last longer; that would save us money, as well as allow us to use our survival devices longer in a crisis.

What if I were to tell you that you could? What if I were to say that "dead batteries" weren't really dead?

Let's talk a little battery theory for a moment. Small batteries fall into two basic categories: rechargeable and single use. Obviously, you can recharge batteries that are designed for it and continue using them. That's not what I'm talking about. What I'm talking about are the batteries designed for single use. We usually throw them away, once they are dead.

But what is dead?

For simplicity's sake, let's just talk about AA and AAA batteries. These are the most common sizes and whatever applies to them will also apply to all other single use batteries. These battery sizes, as well as C and D cells, are rated at a nominal 1.5 volts DC. I say "nominal" because new batteries actually have a higher charge, typically somewhere around 1.6 volts DC.

The devices we use generally have (use) a number of these batteries, as there is little that actually runs off of 1.5 volts (although there are some devices that do). To get more voltage, the batteries are connected in series.

That means that the positive end of one battery (the one with the nipple on it) is connected to the negative end of the next (the flat end). Whenever we do that, the voltage of the batteries is added, increasing the voltage. So, we'll put two batteries in to have a nominal 3 volts or four batteries to have a nominal 6 volts.

Batteries produce this electrical power by chemical reaction. As the device is used, it draws power from the batteries, gradually lowering the amount of available chemicals. As this level diminishes, the voltage that the battery produces drops as well.

So, that battery which started out somewhere around 1.6 volts, will keep dropping its voltage until it hits about 1.3 volts. At that point, the device usually stops working. This is the point at which we normally say that the battery is "dead". But it really isn't.

The battery just has less power than it needs to have, in order to power our device. But perhaps it can be used for something else.

Okay, so if those batteries still have some power in them, all we need is some way of getting it out. To do that, we're going to do the exact same thing that we did inside the device; we're going to connect the batteries in series.

The only difference is, we're going to connect more of them together, than we usually do. By doing this:

- 4 batteries provide us with 5.2 volts (1.3 x 4)
- 6 batteries provide us with 7.8 volts (1.3 x 6)
- 8 batteries provide us with 10.4 volts (1.3 x 8)
- 12 batteries provide us with 15.6 volts (1.3 x 12)

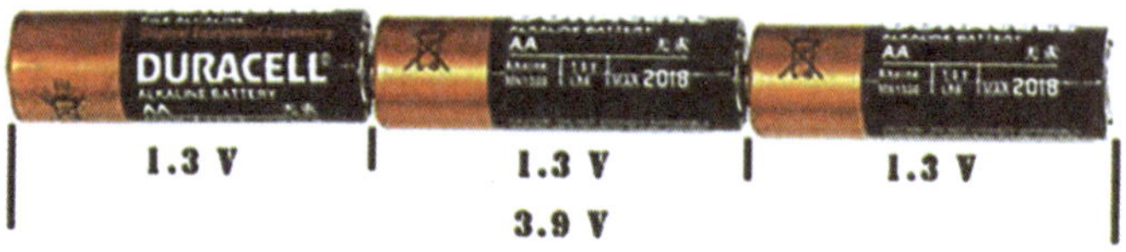

Obviously, these batteries can't be put in the device this way, because there isn't enough physical space for them inside the device. But many electronic devices have an external power connector, which we could connect to.

Many of today's electronics are designed to be able to be recharged by a computer; connecting it to the USB connector. The USB connector on your computer provides 5 volts. So do the USB chargers that plug into the wall.

The main difference is that the ones which plug into the wall will provide a lot more 5-volt power than you can pull out of a USB connector on your computer. That's why some devices won't charge when connected to a computer.

If you look at the battery in many of these devices (cell phones are a great example), it's actually not a 5-volt battery, but a 3.6 to 3.8-volt battery. So, as long as we are providing more than 3.6 volts to the device, it will work. We can get more than that much power out of 4 dead AA batteries.

All we need is a way of hooking all this up together; some sort of a battery pack that will allow us to connect the batteries together, along with a connector to attach to our electronic devices.

This battery pack holds 4 AA batteries. If we put in 4 dead AA batteries, that means we've got a total of 5.2 (1.3 x 4) volts available to us. There's an intermediate connector that I've attached to it, in order to allow the same battery pack to provide power through a variety of connectors.

Finally, since that's enough to run those devices that charge off of a USB connector, I've added a USB connector.

This device will now work to charge or power a cell phone, tablet or digital camera; amongst a host of other devices. All I need is a USB to micro USB adapter, something that is quite common. So, I can continue using those batteries, until their output voltage drops to 0.867 volts each. Then the batteries will have to be replaced.

Granted, 0.867 volts doesn't sound like much, but it's still a bit over half the battery's nominal rating. So, we should be able to continue using them a while longer, just by using more batteries connected together in series, than what we had before.

If we connect six of these batteries together in a battery pack, we'll be producing 5.2 volts. If we connect eight of them together, we'll be producing 6.936. Either of these would work for powering those same USB devices.

Since battery packs to hold six batteries are not that common, but battery packs for four and eight batteries are fairly common, we might be better off using the eight batteries.

Even though this sounds like too much power for the devices, it's not. All electronic devices have a voltage regulator in them. They have to, as the amount of power the batteries provide isn't constant. We've seen how it goes down. So, the "extra" voltage will be cut off, only allowing the amount of voltage that the device needs to pass through.

In real terms, there are limits to how much voltage we can give a device, before the voltage regulator can't do its job. But that's not a worry here, as we're not going over that limit. Were we to hook 12 volts to a 5-volt device, however, it would probably be too much.

So, there you have it, a great way to save money on batteries, but more importantly, a great way to get more mileage out of your batteries in an emergency survival situation.

HOW TO COMMUNICATE POST-SHTF

How to Communicate in a Blackout

When the grid goes down and we are plunged into darkness, communication becomes a necessity that many people will lose entirely. Therefore, one important but often overlooked aspect of preparedness is a solid plan for maintaining communication when traditional methods are rendered ineffective by blackouts or grid-down SHTF scenarios.

Many off-grid communications exist, and you could certainly find an option that fits your plans and requirements. However, the problem with off-grid communication is that there is no one-size-fits-all solution to suit every distance and situation.

Get an Amateur Radio Licence

The most effective means for grid-down communication is amateur radio, but you must become licensed to use it. It is true that you do not require an amateur radio license in an emergency, but if you do not practice and get to know other amateur radio operators in the area, attempting to use ham radios after SHTF is not practical.

Only through becoming licensed, practicing, and learning the ins and outs of your radios will you develop the skills needed for communications after SHTF. Also, unless you get your name and callsign out on the local repeaters, you will not be effective at communicating with other amateur radio operators in the area.

Each country has its levels of qualifications and testing procedures for licensed amateur radio operators, so I will not get into the specifics here. However, I suggest that you obtain the highest level of licensing that you can.

This will give you the greatest spectrum of privileges in the radio spectrum, which in turn grants you access to a wide array of communication methods.

While this is an effective way to communicate over very long distances, HF communication is tricky to learn, especially antennas. As a SEAL, we were all trained in comms but the knowledge would quickly fade, and it's not an easy skill to master. HF communication is way down my priority list, especially since my family on the West Coast is not trained at all.

Listening

Regardless of your plans for obtaining an amateur radio license, you must include the ability to monitor shortwave radio in your emergency communications preps. Many countries still broadcast news and other radio programs over shortwave radio bands, and the ability to listen to these broadcasts is critical after SHTF.

Depending on the disaster, there may be no information coming from the local or federal government, but foreign nations may have and be transmitting the news and information that they receive. This will give you an insight into what is happening and maybe what the response to the disaster is.

Most HF amateur radios will be able to receive transmissions on shortwave bands. However, having a good quality shortwave receiver in your preps is still a good idea. Many shortwave radios are designed for emergency use and battery-operated or powered through a hand crank or solar panels.

One radio listening option that should be considered is software defined radio (SDR) dongles that plug into the USB port on a computer. The radio frequencies are passed through the SDR dongle into the computer, allowing you to monitor a massive frequency space.

SDR receivers let us monitor from the lower High Frequency (HF) bands through to the Very High (VHF) and Ultra High (UHF) frequency bands. This gives you the ability to monitor a large amount of radio traffic.

A high-quality handheld scanner is important to create a well-rounded communications monitoring kit. In some areas, you may be able to still receive police, fire, and EMS with a handheld scanner, which would come in handy during an emergency.

Beyond that, many public services and commercial interests use trunked radio systems which you would need a scanner to listen to. You can check online for lists of the trunked radio systems in your area and purchase a scanner that would cover all or at least the most important ones. Many scanners will cover amateur radio bands, airband, military, marine and even CB radio frequencies.

PACE Plan For Emergency Communications

All the radios and communications gear in the world will be useless if you do not establish and practice a solid communications plan. While you can develop your own format for SHTF communication planning, I think it is best to use planning formats that have been tried and tested by those who rely on reliable communications for survival.

The military takes communication very seriously and uses the acronym P.A.C.E for emergency communications plans.

Primary

This is the easiest and most common communication method you would use in an emergency. Even in a grid-down scenario, mobile phones and landlines may still be operable for a period. Therefore, this will always be the first step in establishing communications.

I and my family on the West Coast are using Wi-Fi calling on the Starlink satellite network as our primary communication. The likelihood of enough satellites going down to severely disrupt service is very low, so as long as we have power to operate the Starlink antenna, our router, and the mobile phones, we're good. If that window is small, we can communicate long enough to make a plan and shift to secondary.

Secondary

This is an effective but more complex or less reliable method of communication. Satellite phones or messengers are an example of secondary communications because they can provide direct device-to-device communication.

Our secondary comms are Garmin InReach Explorer+ devices. These are robust GPS units with shareable location global SOS capability and extremely long battery life, and they have the ability to send texts and location both to cell phone numbers and other Garmin units using the Iridium satellite network. These will work anywhere in the world and are our plan for linking everyone back together. They require a subscription; I pay around $12 a month to keep mine active. I used the predecessor to this unit on *Manhunt* so the producers could locate me on a map in case something bad happened, and in fact, several times something bad *did* happen.

Contingency

Contingency communications require more skill or experience to master and require specialized equipment. Amateur radio falls into this category since it requires licensing and equipment to be effective.

Emergency

The last resort for communications in a crisis. This method is the most unreliable and difficult to work with but can still be used to get a message from point A to point B. One example is sending messages through people traveling in the direction of those you want to communicate with or leaving messages in a dead drop or bulletin board for the intended party to read.

You must develop and test your PACE plan before an emergency hits and ensure that every family member knows how the plan works and what is expected of them when it is put into play. In addition, all communication methods should be tested to ensure that they will be effective over the distances that you expect to need to communicate over.

I personally have been trained in HF and radio protocol, so my contingency (or tertiary) plan is that I will use relays and get a message to my family members.

An example of a PACE plan is as follows:

PRIMARY

- Use text messaging to establish contact with family members.
- Send a message immediately after the crisis, then every hour at ten minutes past the hour, and monitor for ten minutes.
- Turn phones off during the intervals where we will not be transmitting.
- If there is no contact for two hours or the network is unresponsive, move to secondary or contingency.
- Regardless of whether primary communication fails, monitor secondary and contingency.

SECONDARY

- Activate and attempt communication using satellite communicators.
- If device-to-device comms fail, attempt relays through a third party out of the area.
- Continue to monitor primary and contingency.

CONTINGENCY

- Switch the VHF radio on and to channel one.
- At ten minutes past the hour, attempt to establish communication for five minutes.
- If there is no response on channel one, switch to channel two and repeat the procedure for five minutes.
- If there is no response, switch the radio off and repeat this procedure every hour at ten minutes past the hour.

EMERGENCY

- When all other methods fail, establish communication by leaving messages at previously established locations or by reaching out via radio through the local repeater network.

PACE plans need to be tailored to your situation and the equipment which you have available to you. Therefore, what I have listed above should be considered a guide to developing your plan.

Emergency Communication Considerations

The chief consideration is the licensing level the people you intend to communicate with have or are willing to obtain. For example, if everyone you want to talk to when the grid goes down refuses to get an amateur radio license, then relying on amateur radio for your comms plan will not be effective.

One way around this problem is to form a network of licensed amateur radio operators throughout the area that you can then relay messages through. This is not ideal because it relies on the kindness of others as a cornerstone of your comms strategy. You also need to understand radio protocol in order to use the network. Ham radio operators live for emergencies—that's when all their skills come into use—so they are a fantastic option and will fight to help, but you need to know at least the basics of radio protocol.

A massive consideration is that much of this equipment is expensive and will need to be budgeted. There is also the problem of the technical aspects of radio communications. Buying a radio is rarely enough. It needs to be powered, have feed lines, and a properly matched antenna, which can be an art into itself.

The best radio in the world isn't going to work unless it is connected to a properly matched antenna. Unfortunately, the problem with antennas is that there is no do-it-all universal antenna.

For example, suppose you are planning on using VHF/UHF/CB radios. In that case, your antenna options are pretty narrow. However, antennas can be built inexpensively and have a small footprint in many instances.

When we start getting into HF radios, the antenna options increase, and the antennas become much larger. In many cases, an HF antenna will be simply a couple of lengths of wire attached to a matching unit. Many HF antennas can be home built, but you would be better off buying one in some cases especially when using high wattages.

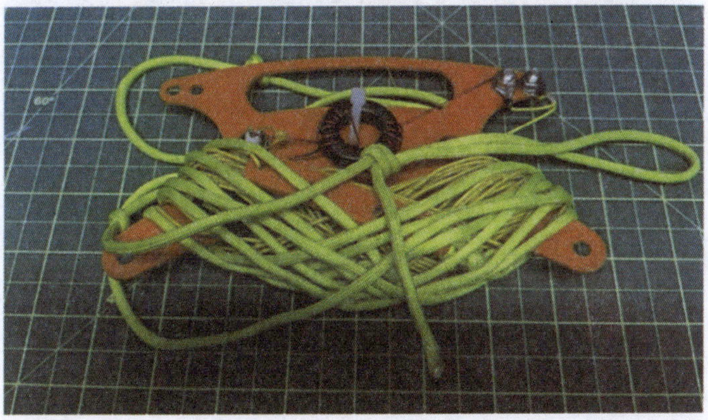

Antennas are built to resonate on specific frequencies, so the more radio bands you plan on using, the more antennas you will need to build or buy. While there are many multi-band antenna options, it is unwise to only have one antenna for your emergency communication needs. The best strategy is to have several antennas cut for many radio bands and of multiple styles.

The easiest way to start planning for emergency communication is to think about it in terms of the range that you would like to communicate over. So I like to break it down in terms of short-range, regional, and global communications.

Short Range Communications

We often want to maintain communication with neighbors and other people throughout a neighborhood. The good news is that most short-range two-way radio systems do not require you to get a license or require a license that does not need testing.

FRS/GMRS RADIOS

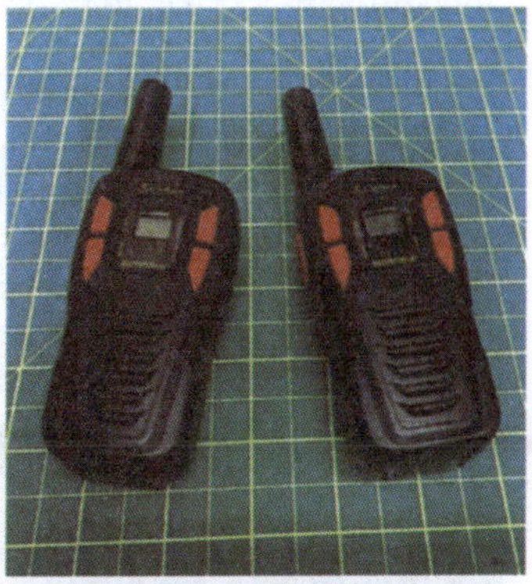

The easiest way to establish and maintain communication within a mile or less is by using Family Radio Service (FRS) or General Mobile Radio Service (GMRS) radios. You can find these radios at any big box store, and while the range is short, they are easily obtained and inexpensive enough to stockpile.

These radios operate on set FM frequencies that are represented as channels on the radio. The difference between FRS and GMRS radios is that GRMS radios require a license which does not require a test in the United States but does involve paying a fee.

One of the advantages of getting a GMRS license is that GMRS radios can allow for the use of repeaters that extend the effective communication range. They also allow for running higher power outputs than FRS radios.

CB RADIO

Citizens Band (CB) radio has seen its popularity decrease significantly in the past few decades. The introduction of cheap Chinese amateur radios and the greater accessibility of getting a ham radio license has led to many people getting rid of their CB radios. That being said, there are a lot of CB radios in garages, storage rooms, crawl spaces, and basements that can be put back into action without too much difficulty.

CB radio does not have a very impressive range. In optimal conditions, you could transmit up to 20 miles, but realistically, using a CB radio can get around a 3 to 5-mile range.

MURS RADIOS

Multi-Use Radio Service (MURS) is another channelized radio service much like CB radio and FRS/GMRS. They also do not require a license to operate and can have a range of 10 miles but a more realistic range of around 3 miles.

LORA

LORA devices are an interesting option for short-range communication. These devices create a mesh network where you can create a network of devices that communicate with each

other and allow for passing text messages between them. The good thing about LORA is that smartphones can be paired with them, and through apps such as Meshtastic, text messages and location data can be passed through the mesh network.

Many different LORA devices are available, but the TTGO Meshtastic T-Beam is one of the better options for anyone looking to build their mesh network.

However, there is one massive disadvantage to using LORA for short-range post-SHTF communications. These devices require significant knowledge and experience in electronics and software to be able to be set up and used.

Regional Communications

Getting an amateur radio license is required when we want to communicate outside the immediate neighborhood. One of the best things about amateur radio equipment is that most, if not all, of it is designed to be run off 13.8-volt DC power. This makes it perfect for off-grid communication because it allows for using battery banks and off-grid power options.

VHF/UHF RADIOS

Within the spectrum of options available to the amateur radio operator, Very High Frequency (VHF) and Ultra High Frequency (UHF) radios are the best starting point. VHF/UHF radios can be base station, mobile, or even handheld and transmit with much higher power than the license-free options. For example, handhelds usually have outputs of around 5 watts, the average mobile VHF/UHF radio is between 50 and 75 watts, and base stations can be 100 watts or more. This gives a much more extensive communication range and access to repeaters in the area.

Repeaters

VHF and UHF radios are 'line of sight", so the terrain and buildings around you will limit their range. This is why repeaters are used to extend the range of VHF and UHF radios. Repeaters are placed atop tall buildings or mountains around the area to provide broad coverage. Radios transmit into the repeater through one frequency and retransmit the signal through another frequency.

Most areas with a decent-sized amateur radio community will also have many repeaters surrounding the area. These repeaters are usually set up and maintained by amateur radio clubs and have the capability to operate absent of the grid.

One of the primary purposes of the amateur radio service is to assist emergency services with communication after a disaster. This is a bit of a double-edged sword. On the one hand, being a licensed amateur will grant you access to emergency communications after SHTF. But on the other hand, the airwaves will be very busy, and finding frequency space for your communications needs may be challenging.

Handheld radios are small and powerful enough to hit most repeaters in a line of sight from your location. Carrying a cheap handheld as a part of your EDC, vehicle kit, or get-home bag is the best first step in communication preparedness.

In addition, putting a mobile VHF/UHF rig in your vehicle allows for a greater communication range and the ability to maintain comms while on the move.

Antennas

If you have a mobile VHF/UHF rig, you will have already mounted an antenna on your vehicle. As far as base station units go, a few good options are available, some of which can be home built. For example, j-pole antennas can be built out of copper plumbing pipe, directional yagi antennas can be made from PVC and tape measures, and ground plane antennas require only stiff wire. For handheld radios, always upgrade the stock antenna to one that is longer and has more gain.

HF RADIOS

High frequency (HF) Radios are typically used for long-range communications beyond the line of sight. However, HF radios are great for regional communication if you understand how to use them. Normally, HF radio signals are bounced off the ionosphere and then returned to Earth, which allows the signal to travel considerable distances.

The problem is that these signals often skip over the areas we want to communicate with when thinking about regional communications. These few hundred-mile distances usually fall within traditional HF propagation's skip zone.

NVIS Antennas

Near Vertical Incident Skywave (NVIS) antennas are one way to use an HF radio for regional communication out to a couple of hundred miles. An NVIS antenna is a dipole antenna strung close to the ground, usually less than half a wavelength. When the antenna is close to the Earth, the signal is directed almost straight up rather than off at an angle which means that it will be bounced off the ionosphere and sent directly back down to Earth.

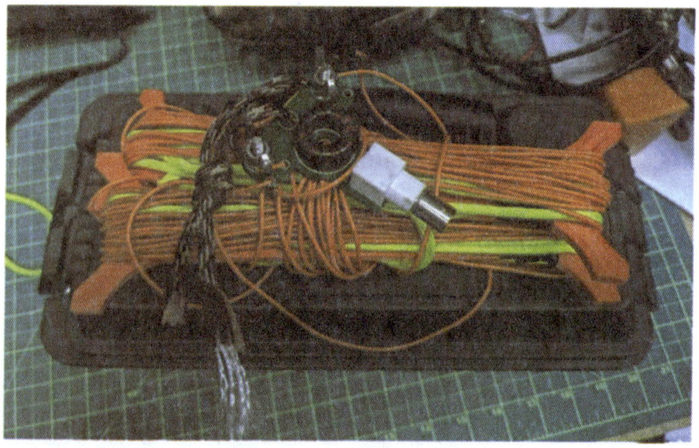

Global Communication

The only way to use radio to communicate globally is either through satellites or HF radios. Even though it is possible to establish effective global communication with a radio that operates on 5 or 10 watts, to be effective, you should consider a radio that has at least 100 watts of output power. You will also need a well-matched antenna that is elevated high enough to achieve peak efficiency.

Alternatively, you could use satellite communicators or phones to communicate globally. However, these come with an increased cost and can be at-risk during a global SHTF event. The other issue with satellite communications is that they require a clear view of the sky to work. Even heavy tree cover can be enough to delay or block your attempts to get a message out.

Morse Code

The problem with voice communications on the radio is that they take up a significant amount of bandwidth. In contrast, morse code occupies a far narrower section of the spectrum. If your goal is to transmit as far as you can on as little power as possible, Morse Code is one method that is worth a look. The largest issue with Morse Code is that you are learning another language, so it will be a difficult process that will take time to master. You will also need to practice regularly to maintain a reasonable level of proficiency.

Digital Modes

Communicating over the radio is not limited to voice or Morse Code. The amateur radio operator can use a wide array of digital data modes to send communications. To transmit using digital modes, you must connect a computer to your radio and have the appropriate software installed.

One of the good things about using digital modes is that, like Morse Code, they occupy a narrow bandwidth and allow us to transmit further than we could using voice.

Amongst the dozens of digital data modes available, a few notable examples are worth implementing.

- Winlink – RMS Winlink allows us to send emails over radio frequency. You can use this to send an email through a radio gateway and then onto the internet, or you can connect with another amateur radio operator directly to exchange emails.
- JS8 – The great thing about JS8 is that it is a keyboard-to-keyboard text messaging mode over the radio.
- FT8 – FT8 is a popular digital mode that radio amateurs use to make contacts and send each other signal reports. After a disaster, FT8 could be useful for people to check in with each other.
- RTTY/PSK31 – PSK31 and its predecessor Radio Teletype (RTTY) have been widely used in the amateur radio space for a long time. Like JS8, both these modes send text messages between stations. RTTY traditionally utilized machines to print out the message as it was received, but with computers, we can send and receive these messages digitally.
- SSTV – Slow Scan Television (SSTV) is a digital mode in which we can send pictures over the radio. One great use of this mode is to capture images from NOAA weather satellites which would be beneficial in a grid-down situation. The ability to get pictures straight from the weather satellites allows you to have a birds-eye view of the weather systems that are approaching your area, giving you the opportunity to prepare.

Digital radio modes are tricky to set up, but they have the advantage of giving you extended range on far less power than you would have using voice modes such as Single Side Band (SSB). The primary issue with digital communication is that it requires more components such as computers, soundcards, and radio interfaces, making operating portable using digital data modes difficult.

Communicating During a Blackout

When the lights go out, the only way that communications will be effective is if everyone involved is on the same page. When you establish a PACE plan, everyone involved must have a copy of that plan and understand how to implement it.

Carrying a radio as a part of our EDC is a great first step, but the people we want to contact also need radios and an in-depth understanding of how to use them. The communication component of EDC could involve amateur radio, FRS/GMRS, satellite communication, or possibly a burner phone. In addition, if practical, each vehicle should have a mobile radio installed, but this is not always possible.

Suppose you do not have radios permanently set up at home. In that case, you should create a communications kit in which there would be all the components to set up a radio station. This should also include other methods of communication such as burner phones or satellite communicators. The best way to store such a kit is inside a Faraday cage which will protect the devices within from an EMP.

Communication is a critical element of preparedness and one that you should not ignore. Regardless of whether it is a simple blackout, EMP, CME, or a natural disaster, you will be desperate to find out if your family and friends are ok. Setting up an effective comms plan will be difficult and complex, but the reward for your efforts will pay off a thousandfold when every member of your group checks in with each other after SHTF.

Essential Medical Pills and Supplies

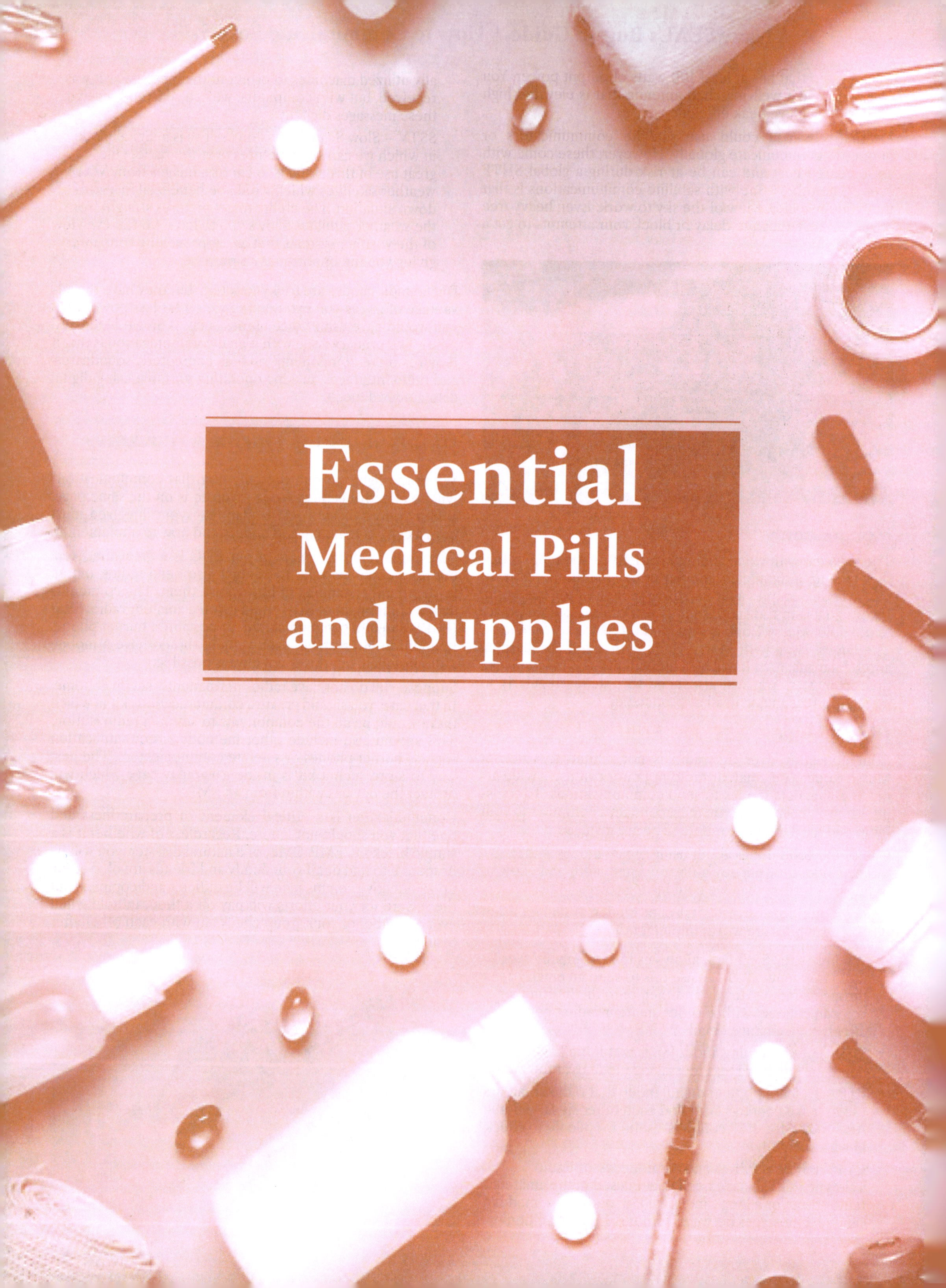

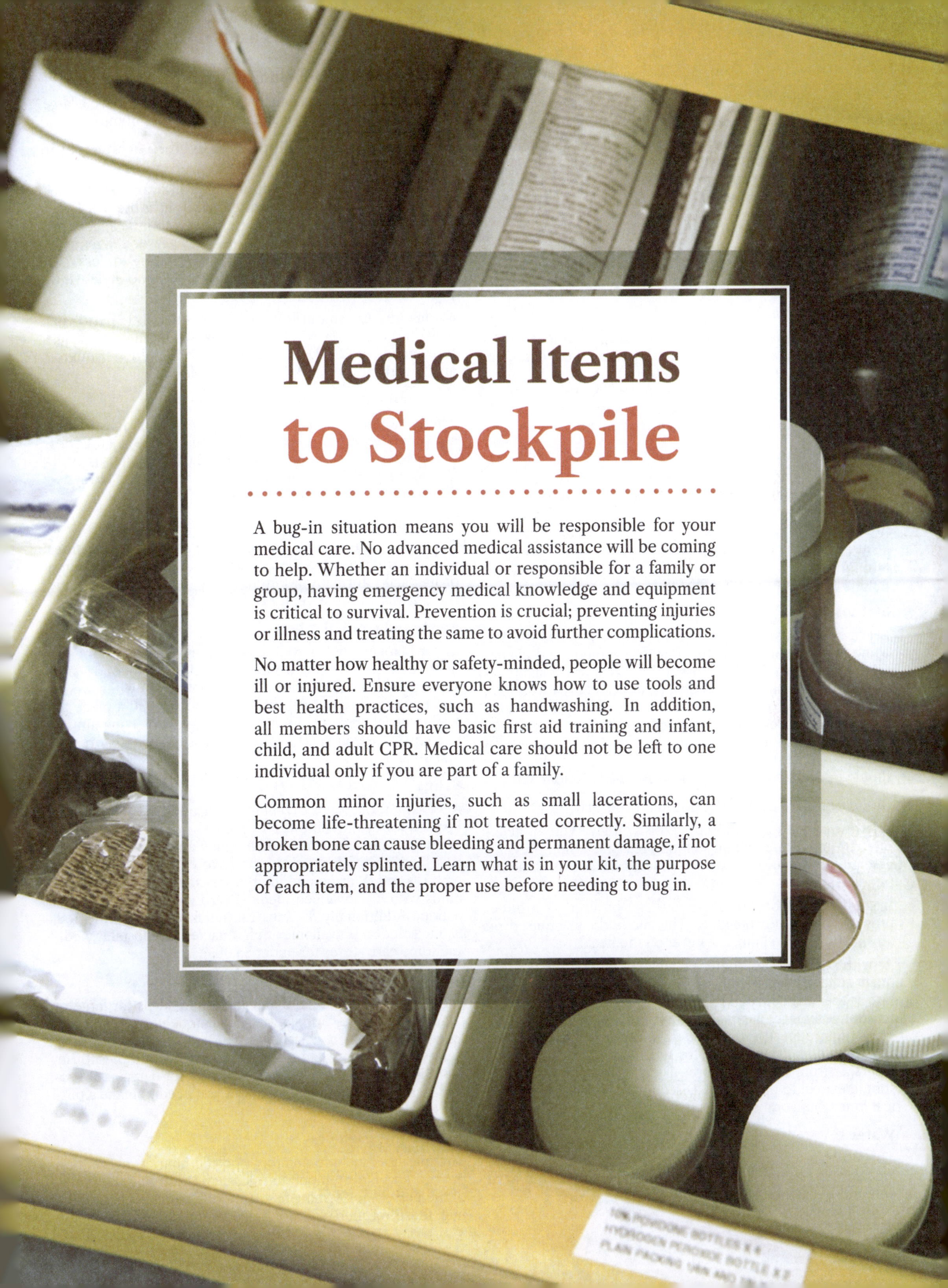

Medical Items to Stockpile

A bug-in situation means you will be responsible for your medical care. No advanced medical assistance will be coming to help. Whether an individual or responsible for a family or group, having emergency medical knowledge and equipment is critical to survival. Prevention is crucial; preventing injuries or illness and treating the same to avoid further complications.

No matter how healthy or safety-minded, people will become ill or injured. Ensure everyone knows how to use tools and best health practices, such as handwashing. In addition, all members should have basic first aid training and infant, child, and adult CPR. Medical care should not be left to one individual only if you are part of a family.

Common minor injuries, such as small lacerations, can become life-threatening if not treated correctly. Similarly, a broken bone can cause bleeding and permanent damage, if not appropriately splinted. Learn what is in your kit, the purpose of each item, and the proper use before needing to bug in.

Below is a list of the medical items you should consider having in your bug-in location.

Large waterproof bag or container to hold items

With no concerns about weight or size, find the item that best fits your supplies. How much you stock depends on how many people are in your group. Use what you have or buy a container for your supplies.

Smaller plastic bags to hold items

Your kit must be organized to be effective. Break up the supplies into categories. Use what you have or purchase specific containers, as with the first aid bag.

First aid manual

This is not a replacement for training! In an emergency, there is no time to read a training manual. Learn infant, child, and adult CPR and, at minimum, an introductory first aid course. Consider wilderness training or more extensive first aid classes. Recertify every year. Expect to spend $5.00 - $10.00 for a basic guide at a local bookstore or online.

CPR Mask

A mask protects you from many germs and viruses. Also, when you perform CPR, the patient will likely spit up or vomit. This response is normal because of the deep compressions. A mask will protect you from vomit but requires clearing before continuing CPR. A two-way valve CPR mask kit, including a mask for infant CPR, can be found at any medical store for less than $15.00.

Stethoscope

Learn how to use the stethoscope before you need it. Become familiar with the parts, how to use them, and change them if necessary. The stethoscope will give you valuable information on heart rate and quality, lung and breath sounds, and used with a blood pressure cuff, it provides a reliable blood pressure reading. Unless you use it daily, you do not need to spend much money on this item. To see a choice of products, you can go online and check different offers. You should be able to easily find a stethoscope for under $20.00.

Blood pressure cuff (Sphygmomanometer)

When used with a stethoscope, this will give you an accurate reading of the patient's blood pressure, which provides essential information related to shock, cardiac issues, or impending stroke.

In addition, a blood pressure cuff can be used as a direct pressure device for bleeding. This method can be used on any portion of the limb, but never on the neck.

As with stethoscopes, there is a range of blood pressure cuff quality and pricing. Blood pressure machines are not as accurate as the stethoscope and blood pressure cuff; they give no information on the heart rate or quality. In addition, the devices require electricity or batteries. Buy a cuff from a store that sells hospital products for the home, such as wheelchairs, or from an online source like allheart.com, where you should expect to pay $30.00. Discount stores often sell medical items, but good quality is better.

Water

This water is for first aid only; sterilizing equipment, sheets, etc. No need to purchase anything; use containers you have at home.

Small container for boiling water

This could be an extra pan, part of a mess kit, or even a large coffee can. Use what you already have in your home.

Waterproof matches/Zippo-type lighters, firestarter for boiling water

For waterproof matches, dip in nail polish and let dry before packing. Zippo-style lighters work in a breeze. Dryer lint makes an excellent fire starter, takes up little space, and weighs almost nothing. Pick up inexpensive wooden matches and nail polish from a discount or grocery store for less than $7.00. Expect to pay $30.00 and up for a Zippo-style windproof lighter.

My favorite fire starter is cotton balls with a little petroleum jelly on them. They will light reliably with a small spark, last forever, and are CHEAP. Couple this with a ferrocerium rod and striker for the spark, and you're golden.

Soap and antibacterial soap

These should be available both for the patient and the first aid provider. Regular soap can be purchased at groceries, pharmacies, and discount stores for $2.00. Hibiclens is available at some groceries and discount stores, but can always be found at pharmacies for around $5.00.

Waterproof notebook with permanent markers

Document date of injury or illness, vital signs, medications administered, instructions for care, or other significant health or medical information. Purchase the items from an online site like waterproof.com for about $20.00.

Mylar and wool blankets

Mylar blankets are incredibly lightweight and consume little space while working wonderfully to keep someone warm. Wool blankets will provide some warmth even when wet. If you buy in multiples, expect to pay about $2.00 a piece for quality mylar shelters. A wool blanket might be lying unused in a closet, or you can buy them at most discount stores for $20.00 and up.

Saline

A 9% saline solution is excellent for cleaning wounds and can be used for eye irrigation. This saline is not intended for use as an IV. Establishing and maintaining an IV is not practical in a bug-in situation unless you have extensive experience with IVs and IV drugs and their dosages. It is doubtful that IV fluids without advanced medical care will sustain a critical patient. Additionally, IV sites can quickly become infected. Saline solution is available at pharmacies and hospital medical home care stores for under $5.00.

Cotton sheets

These have multiple uses. Cut them into strips for large or triangular bandages for slings. They can be used to move or carry people. When wet, they can be used to cool body temperature. Use those old sheets you have around the house, there is no need to buy new ones. Check for bargains at second-hand stores and garage sales if you need to make a purchase.

Hand/body warmers

Multiple uses include comfort, specific injuries, prevention of core and limb temperature loss, and warming the hands of the person performing first aid. If the patient is hypothermic, these warmers will not make enough difference. Some brands will provide heat for 8 hours or more. These warmers can be found at many stores, including grocery, discount, and sports. In winter, the warmers can be purchased for 2/$2.00.

Hot/cold packs - gel and chemical

Heat and cold are first-line defenses for many injuries and some illnesses. Gel packs have the advantage of being reusable. If you have access to electricity, you can freeze them. People have had success also with keeping them in a cold stream. The hot packs can be reactivated as well. The chemical packs do not require anything to be used, but they cannot be reused.

Readily available at grocery and discount stores or pharmacies for two small or one large at $12.00 - $15.00 for the gel packs. Chemical packs are sold in grocery and discount stores, as well as pharmacies at $6.99 for a two-pack.

Gloves – surgeons and nitrile

Surgeons or surgical gloves fit the hand, are sterile, and are much easier to work with than the general boxed variety. Any work holding an instrument demands well-fitting gloves. For general first aid, nitrile gloves will work, but stock extras because you may need more than one pair per incident. Purchase surgical gloves from a shop that sells medical items or a pharmacy. Bulk purchases are less expensive, but one pair will cost approximately $1.00 depending on the material. Nitrile gloves are available at medical shops or pharmacies at 100 for $11.00.

Face masks

Face masks can help protect from germs, smoke, dust, and other contaminants. These can be used when working with a contagious patient to reduce contact with infectious material and prevent the first aider from exposing the patient. Medical or surgical face masks are easy to find at medical shops and pharmacies, as well as many discount stores, averaging $15.00 for 100 masks.

Safety pins

To hold bandages and slings, pin medical information to sleeping bags or clothes, and so many more uses. Available at grocery and discount stores costing $1.50 for an assorted pack of 50 pins.

Magnifying glass

Perfect for examining splinters and minor injuries, the area being treated as suturing, and can be used to start a fire to boil water. Discount stores have this product for $10.00.

Paracord

Make a stretcher with the cord between two poles/sticks or a drag-stretcher. The inner cord can start a fire to boil water, tie splints, and much more. One hundred-foot rolls are $10.00 at discount and sports stores and survivalist shops.

Cervical collar

When someone falls, has a motor vehicle injury, or has another violent accident, the cervical spine is likely to be injured. You cannot do repairs in the field, but you can limit further damage by using a cervical collar. Find this item at the first responder or medical supply store. There are two kinds of cervical collars soft and rigid. The soft collar will be $8.00 and a rigid one $12.00.

Swabs

Remove debris from wounds, and apply salves or ointments. Buy at any grocery or discount store for $3.50 for 500 swabs.

Analog thermometer

Do not count on batteries - use an analog thermometer instead. Also, include a rectal thermometer to check the core temperature for hyperthermia and hypothermia. Pharmacies are the place to shop for thermometers. The regular thermometer costs $4.00 and a core thermometer about $6.00.

Scissors – bandage, dressing, trauma raptor shears

You can survive with one pair of scissors, but since there is space and no weight limits, stock the best type for the job. Bandage scissors are for cutting off clothes and cutting dressing and bandages. (Purchase at a pharmacy or medical supply for $7.00 - $20.00). Dressing scissors are used for general purposes such as cutting sutures, tubing, skin, and tissue. (Buy at medical supply tore. Trauma raptors are multi-function shears with a ring cutter, strap or belt cutter, a ruler, and carbide glass breaker. (Purchase at a medical supply shop for $30.00.)

Tweezers – regular and tick

Standard tweezers remove small splinters, thorns, etc. Tick tweezers are designed to lift the tick instead of pulling, which can cause tick-borne illness. Standard tweezers are readily available at grocery, discount stores, and pharmacies for $2.00, while tick tweezers are a bit more expensive at $5.00 from a medical supply store.

Wire snips/cutters

For removing someone entangled in or removing wire from an injured person. Expect to pay $7.50 for a pair from a hardware store.

Tongue depressors

Not only can you use these for checking the throat or teeth, but they also make great finger splints. A box of 100 tongue depressors retails for $6.99 at pharmacies.

Sterile irrigation water

Can be used instead of saline solution for cleaning wounds of debris and before closing the wound. Found at pharmacies or medical supply stores for $2.75 a bottle.

Alcohol (Isopropyl) alcohol wipes

Sterilize and disinfect instruments and wounds and use as a handwash when no water is available. Around $1.00 a bottle at grocers and discount stores.

Hydrogen peroxide

This item is especially good for cleansing dirty wounds. Purchase at any grocery or discount store for less than $1.00 per bottle.

Hand sanitizer

When soap and water are unavailable for handwashing. Never use on wounds or open skin. A small bottle will cost $2.50 at any discount, grocery store, and pharmacy.

Eye drops

Dust, smoke, pollen, fatigue, and other issues can cause red, itchy, swollen eyes. Available for $3.25 at discount shops, grocers, or pharmacies.

Eyewash

For removing contaminants. Saline or sterile irrigation water can be used if not available. Buy this item at pharmacies or first responder stores for about $4.00.

Salt and salt tablets

Use cautiously in hot weather. Some people may have stomach cramps or nausea. When taken, consume plenty of water. Buy this item from a pharmacy or discount store for the least expensive options, such as 100 pills for $6.00.

Burn gel

Minor burns can be painful and present a threat of infection. Burn gel will relieve pain while covering the open area. It is much easier to find burn gel than in the past. Pick up a $12.00 - $15.00 package at pharmacies.

Burn kit

For more extensive burns, a burn kit is convenient. The dressings are coated with burn gel in different sizes, along with bandages and other items. It is not imperative to have the items in a purchased burn kit, as you can make one. If you buy the items separately, examine what is in the kits. A basic burn kit costs $20.00 - $25.00 at pharmacies or emergency medical supply shops.

Syringes

Use for cleaning wounds, flushing injuries, and eyes of contaminants. Also, it can be used with a hypodermic needle. A range of sizes is available for $.20 - $1.00 at pharmacies.

Hypodermic needles

Use a syringe for deep wound cleaning, intramuscular and subcutaneous injections of certain medications like antibiotics and analgesics. Only experienced medical personnel should inject a patient as severe or even fatal reactions may result.

Needles can be difficult to find in brick-and-mortar shops, and even pharmacies may not be able to sell them depending on the laws. The easiest way is to purchase online. Large gauges (10 - 12 needles) are suitable for wound irrigation. This size also works if a patient loses their airway, but the first aider should be extremely careful in its use and have previous knowledge of the maneuver. Injections require smaller gauges, usually in a 22 gauge or similar. If purchased separately, expect to pay $0.75 per needle.

The following items require medical knowledge for safe and appropriate use. If you are unfamiliar with precisely how to use the items, do not use them at all, as further injury or fatality may result.

Oral airways

Infant, child, and adult sizes for establishing and maintaining an airway. There are precise times when an airway is appropriate. Misuse can worsen the situation. If you do not have the training, do not use it. Buy a three-pack at first responder stores or websites for $15.00.

Scalpels

Some injuries may require a scalpel to enable removing a foreign object, cutting away dead or

damaged skin, or creating an area for sutures, only for those who have experience. An emergency is not the time to learn how to use a scalpel. Though it may seem simple, it is easy to do extensive damage, including excessive bleeding, tissue damage, and infection. Buy scalpels at a pharmacy or online for $15.00 for several size blades.

Sutures/kit

Lacerations are common occurrences and will be no different in a bug-in situation. Many cuts will only require a small covering, but sutures may be required for larger or deeper wounds. Stock 2-0 and 3-0 or smaller for delicate skin or where the sutures will show, such as the face. Choose regular or non-dissolving sutures to treat external wounds.

Sewing up a wound may sound simple enough, but if you have no experience, you are more likely to create more significant problems, including not closing the wound properly and infection. A basic suture kit costs $ 20.00 - $25.00 at first responder and prepper stores.

Forceps – Adson, Kelly, and tissue

Adson forceps are curved and slender at the tip for moving skin or dressings. Kelly forceps are used when a small tool is needed, and the handle locks, making it a clamp. Tissue forceps are used for holding or moving soft tissue. No need to spend a lot of money on forceps and clamps because you will not be using them often. Find these items at first responder stores or online medical equipment sites for $10.00.

Hemostats, straight and curved

Use for clamping bleeding, usually during surgery, but excellent when holding a small object or removing a foreign body. As with the forceps, basic hemostats will serve well at $10.00 from online medical or first responder shops.

Wound stapler/remover

An alternative to using sutures but requires a medically trained user. Another item at first responder or medical supply stores for under $15.00. You are wrong if you think anyone can use this stapler. If you are inexperienced, do not use it.

Medical grade adhesive

This product is made to seal wounds without using sutures or staples. Though it seems simple to use, it is critical the wound is thoroughly cleaned and disinfected before application. Never close a puncture wound with any method. Buy at pharmacies or first responder shops for $7.00.

Tourniquet

If you are going to have a tourniquet, it should be 1 1/2 to 2 inches wide. Once applied, the person will doubtless lose the limb and likely their life if advanced medical care is unavailable. Direct pressure combined with elevation is the best option. A tourniquet is $23.00 at first responder stores.

Ace Bandage

Brand name products are unnecessary, but this item can be confused with compression trauma dressing, which is different. Strains and soft tissue limb injuries, such as a sprained wrist or ankle, require compression. Include several in your kit. Attach safety pins to the outside because the clips tend to break. Find at pharmacies and sporting goods stores for $4.50.

Adhesive and paper tape

Include a few rolls of several types and sizes of medical tape. Caring for an injury can require multiple dressing changes requiring tape. Buy a few packages of quality waterproof tape from a pharmacy: a two-pack sells for $3.50. Include several rolls of duct tape for multiple uses, including removing splinters by placing them directly over the object and lifting and keeping splints together. Prevent blisters, keep a wound dry, and immobilize after clavicle fracture. There are numerous uses for duct tape in your first aid kit. Duct tape is available at grocery, hardware, and many other stores for around $5.00 a roll. Be aware that almost all duct tape contains latex.

Band-Aids (flexible adhesive bandages), knuckle bandages, and assorted

Flexible adhesive bandages are the most commonly used item in a first aid kit. Small cuts or nicks might seem minor, but in a bug-in situation, options are limited if there is an infection. Prevention is always critical, even more so when in a bug-in environment. Stock one assorted box for each person and use them consistently. Do not try to save on this item because inferior brands will fail. The cost will be $7.00 for one box at pharmacies or discount stores.

Wound pads - 2x2s, 4x4s

For minor or small wounds. Sterile 2x2s – 100 for $7.50, sterile 4x4s 100 for $16.00 at a pharmacy.

5x9 ABD pads (combine dressing)

These are much larger and thicker for more extensive wounds. Purchase at a pharmacy for around $17.00 for 20 pads.

Kling (rolled gauze)

Brand names are not always necessary, but Kling works well because it does not shed fibers as Kerlex and some cheaper brands often do. Buy at a pharmacy or online for $20.00 for 100 yards.

Butterfly bandages

For closing wounds. Before you think sutures, think waterproof butterfly bandages. These strips work well for closing small or shallow wounds. A box of 100 waterproof bandages will cost $7.00.

Steri-strips

Another alternative for closing wounds. Steri-strips are usually longer than butterfly bandages. Again, consider if waterproof Steri-strips will fill the need instead of sutures or staples. Purchase from a pharmacy at $22.00 for 50 strips.

Compression trauma bandages

These bandages are designed so that an injured person can apply them with one hand. The bandages can be cinched to create pressure or even a tourniquet. Purchase at a first responder or medical supply store for $11.00. If a tourniquet is applied without advanced medical care, the person will lose the limb and probably their life. Tourniquets cannot be left in place.

Cohesive dressing

One of the advantages of the cohesive is that it does not require additional tape and offers light compression. Buy from pharmacies and sports shops for $6.00.

SAM (structural aluminum malleable) splints

Lightweight, bendable into any shape, and sturdy, these splints are invaluable for any splinting need. There are different widths, which can be cut into lengths with scissors. Purchase in first responder or medical prepper site online for $20.00.

Trauma dressings

At the simplest, these are large, very thick sterile dressings. However, there is a range of trauma dressings, including abdominal and wraps for direct pressure over the wound. Find this item at first responder and medical supply shops for $5.00.

Chest seal kit (also used for neck and abdominal injuries)

The best option for severe neck, chest, and abdominal wounds. The kit includes an occlusive dressing for covering a hole in the lung. Find this item at first responder and medical supply stores for less than $20.00.

Eye trauma kit

Everything you need to treat eye trauma, including special-sized pads and an eye cup for protection while the injury heals. The kit is under $7.00 at a pharmacy or medical supply store.

All of these items are important to have in your bug-in location. But while you should start preparing as soon as humanly possible, here's what you should also know. The cost for these items can add up, so if it's too expensive for you to buy everything at once, pick up one or two items on the list to buy every time you go shopping.

You shouldn't rush to the pharmacy and get them all in one big shopping spree. Start with making a list of what you already have in your house – you probably have more than you think and there's no need to buy those again. Then, look for offers and sales in all the places you go shopping. There is a big chance you can find some great deals for most of the items listed here. That's the moment you want to buy it and if it's a big sale, you can buy them in bulk.

And probably the best thing is that once you have these medical items in your stockpile - if stored properly - you can use almost all of them forever. That's because they practically have an endless shelf life.

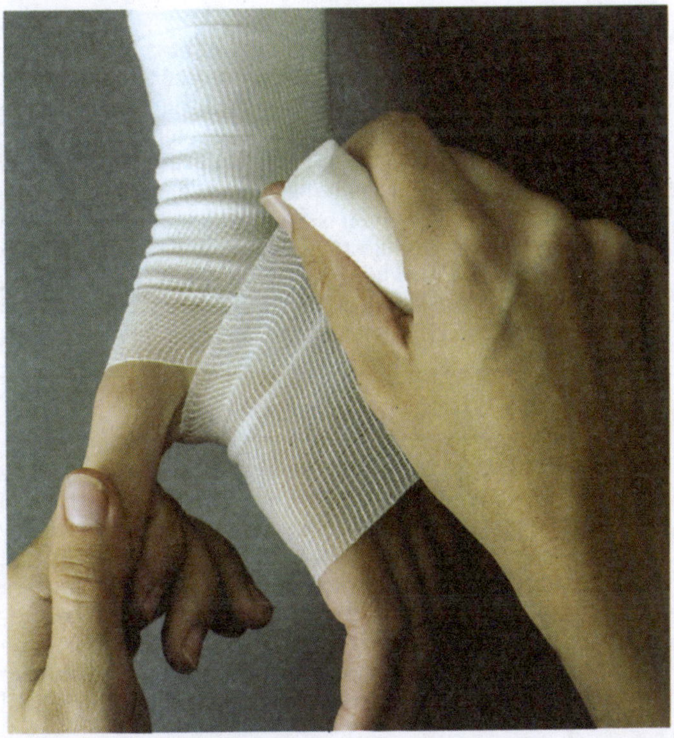

The Only 12 Medicines You Need to Stockpile

One of the best ways to prepare for an emergency is to make sure you have medications on hand to treat illness should it arise. There are certain illnesses we take for granted because we have the medications on hand to treat them and move on with our lives.

However, in a disaster situation, these medications may not be available. In fact, there is a good chance they will absolutely not be available. That is why you need to start putting together a stockpile of medications now.

This chapter will guide you through some common issues and illnesses that can arise and what medications you can have on hand to treat those issues. The problems below can turn very deadly if not treated and are the most important to address in a timely manner when you are in a survival situation.

The top medications to stockpile include medications to treat bacterial infection, viral illness, pain, parasitic infection, blood loss/anemia, allergic reactions, inflammation, cardiovascular issues, radiation exposure, dehydration, wounds, and poisoning. These are issues that can lead to death if not treated promptly. These will be discussed in more detail below, as well as the best way to store them so they are still good when you need them.

Something to look into now: if you have a preexisting condition or comorbidity, you are more likely to run into complications should a disaster arise. If you have the option to stockpile medications you take for a particular health issue, get as much in advance as you can just in case. Some people are able to get a three month's supply of their medication to save having to go to the pharmacy all the time. If you have this option, take advantage of it.

Perhaps most important: This very moment is the best time to start working on your health so you aren't in bad shape should a disaster occur. That means start watching your diet and eat less inflammatory foods. Lose weight if necessary. Start taking steps to mitigate stress in your life. Maintaining a healthy weight is crucial to helping with inflammatory issues like arthritis and joint pain. It is also crucial to having healthy blood pressure and cholesterol levels. Stress and anxiety lead to heart and organ damage. Do what you can to manage these. If you are already healthy and med-free when a disaster hits, you are much more likely to survive and even thrive.

Bacterial Infection: Antibiotics

One-hundred years ago, antibiotics weren't as widely used as they are today. As a result, many people died needlessly from seemingly minor wounds and infections that turned deadly without proper treatment. A simple cat scratch back then could mean death. Today, we are fortunate enough to have access to different kinds of antibiotics to treat various bacterial infections. The type of antibiotic used will depend on the type of infection. There are also natural antibiotics you can utilize in a pinch, if you don't have access to pharmaceutical antibiotics.

Pharmaceutical antibiotics are only administered by prescription from a doctor, so it can be difficult to stockpile these. Some people purchase fish antibiotics to stockpile instead. This is something you can look into, but make sure to research what is best. The best way to store any antibiotic for long-term use is to either refrigerate or freeze them. Freezing is the best way to keep them fresh longer.

Below are some useful antibiotics to keep on hand for emergencies, as well as what they can be used to treat. The antibiotics below can also be found in fish antibiotic form:

Amoxicillin: This is a common penicillin antibiotic that fights bacteria. Amoxicillin is used to treat many different types of infection caused by bacteria, such as tonsillitis, bronchitis, pneumonia, gonorrhea, and infections of the ear, nose, throat, skin, or urinary tract. Do not use penicillin-based antibiotics if you are allergic to penicillin.

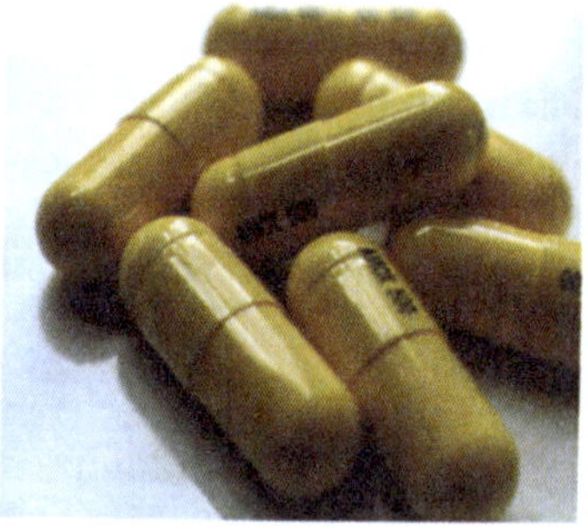

Ciprofloxacin: This antibiotic is used to treat a variety of bacterial infections of the bones and joints, endocarditis, gastroenteritis, malignant otitis externa, respiratory tract infections, cellulitis, urinary tract infections, prostatitis, anthrax, and chancroid. Ciprofloxacin belongs to a class of drugs called quinolone antibiotics. It works by stopping the growth of bacteria.

Cephalexin: This is a cephalosporin antibiotic. It works by fighting bacteria in your body. Cephalexin is used to treat infections caused by bacteria, including upper respiratory infections, ear infections, skin infections, and urinary tract infections.

Penicillin: This antibiotic was the first antibiotic that doctors used. There are several antibiotics in the penicillin class. In addition to pneumonia and blood poisoning, the major causes of death, in hospitals, during the war, strep throat, scarlet fever, diphtheria, syphilis, gonorrhea, meningitis, tonsilitis, rheumatic fever, and a host of other diseases were successfully treated using penicillin.

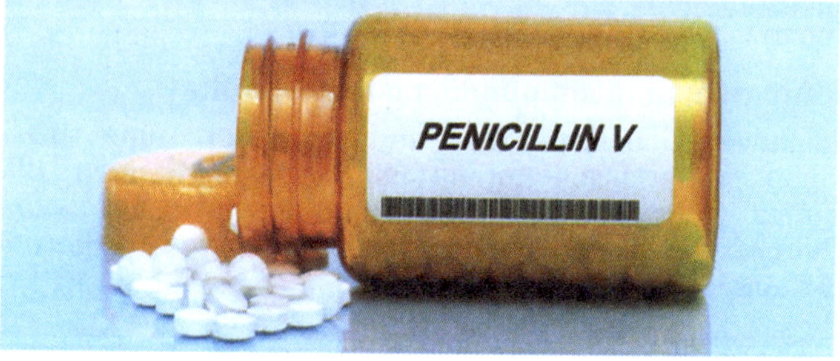

Over the past century, many doctors overprescribed antibiotics like this and some bacteria has found a way to evolve without being affected by this drug. It is still a good choice for a wide range of infections.

Before taking any antibiotic, make sure you are one-hundred percent certain that you have a bacterial infection. Make sure you are not allergic and take only what is needed. Antibiotics are often prescribed based on body weight, so you will need to take them regularly without missing a dose in order to see positive results.

Look for antibiotics in 500 milligram dosages, as this is a cheaper way to buy them. Additionally, most adults can be successfully treated with a dosage between 500-800 milligrams daily. You can open up the capsules to add the antibiotic powder to a liquid or food if this helps with ingestion and dosage.

Triple antibiotic ointment: For suspected skin infections, triple antibiotic ointment is an over-the-counter medication that can prevent worsening of an infection and calm red, irritated, feverish skin eruptions. After cleaning a wound, dry it and apply a liberal amount of triple antibiotic ointment to the area as needed. You can read more about wound care later in this chapter.

In addition to pharmaceutical antibiotics, you can also keep some natural antibiotics on hand just in case you find yourself in a situation where you are unable to get the antibiotics listed above. Some great natural antibiotics include goldenseal and usnea lichen. These can be tinctured and taken in extract form for best results. Take two dropperfuls of goldenseal or usnea lichen tincture up to three times daily for infections.

Viral Illness: Natural Antivirals

We all probably know what it feels like to suffer from a viral illness, whether it is influenza, a cold, or Covid. Some common symptoms to watch for include a fever, chills, congestion, and body aches. Make sure that you don't have an infection before starting treatment for a viral illness. Infections can have similar symptoms as far as a fever and pain. It is important to be as certain as possible, so you don't treat the wrong illness.

Most doctors will tell you that a virus will pass on its own and there is no real treatment for most viral illnesses. However, you can take steps to support your immune system as it works to fight off illness. There are several natural antiviral herbs you can utilize during viral illness to shorten the duration of illness, prevent viral replication, and ease symptoms so you can feel better faster.

Below are the best herbs to have on hand for viruses:

Elderberry: Elderberry is a popular remedy for viruses for a reason. It can reduce inflammation brought on by viral illness, as well as inhibit viral replication so the virus isn't able to thrive in the body as long. It has been shown to shorten the duration of some viruses.

Elderberry is best taken at the earliest sign of viral illness for quicker recovery. Because it contains quercetin, it is also a great choice for allergies and allergy-related congestion and inflammation.

Take two dropperfuls of elderberry tincture every three hours as needed until symptoms diminish. You can also take five milliliters of elderberry syrup every three hours until symptoms are gone. Again, the earlier you begin taking any viral remedy, the better the outcome.

Sweet wormwood: Sweet wormwood has been shown to inhibit viral replication with viral illnesses like Covid-19. This is no surprise, as this common "weed" has been used for centuries to treat a variety of issues, with viral illness being one. Sweet wormwood also happens to have antiparasitic and anticancer properties as well. Take two dropperfuls of sweet wormwood (Artemesia annua) tincture up to three times a day at the first sign of viral illness.

Japanese honeysuckle: This common and often invasive vining plant has a history of use in Asia for viral illness. It has plenty of studies to back this up and can prevent viral replication. It is really easy to make a tincture with this plant. It grows all over North America. Just make sure you have the right plant, as this particular species is a vining plant – not a bush.

Rip the vine out when it is flowering and chop everything thoroughly. Fill a jar with the chopped vine, leaves, and flowers. Completely cover this in at least 80 proof alcohol and allow this to sit and infuse for four to six weeks. Shake your jar daily to promote infusion. Strain out the liquid at the end of the allotted time period and bottle this in a labeled bottle.

Use this tincture-making technique to make medicinal extracts with all the plants mentioned in this chapter. Take two dropperfuls of Japanese honeysuckle up to three times daily at the first sign of viral illness. You can take this tincture with elderberry if you want.

For congestion and cough, you can take mullein tincture or stock up on decongestants and cough syrup in order to keep the airways clear and prevent infection from forming.

Important: Make sure that you are getting plenty of fluids when you are suffering from any type of affliction. Dehydration is one of the leading causes of hospitalization when one is suffering from viral illness. Drink fluids even if you don't feel like it. If a child is sick, make sure to push fluids often as well. You can read more about how to prevent dehydration below.

Pain Management

Pain can be a serious problem if you are in a disaster situation. When left untreated, it almost always raises blood pressure to a dangerous level. Not only that, but suffering in pain is no way to live. Different types of pain may need different medications.

Not everyone can take medications like the NSAIDs below, so make sure you avoid Aspirin-containing medications if you are already taking blood thinners or suffer from a bleeding disorder. If you have kidney or liver damage, you shouldn't take NSAIDs at all or for an extended period of time.

Pain in the body is a sign of something else going on. Your body is trying to tell you something. Pay attention and try to find the root cause of your pain before you begin treating it. Pain is just a symptom. Your pain may be the result of an infection or something serious, so make sure to determine the cause as soon as possible and treat it if you can. You can live your best life and mitigate pain by stocking up on the pain medications listed below. Store them in a cool, dark place and you can refrigerate or freeze them as well if you want to make them last longer.

Tooth pain: Tooth pain can get bad very fast due to the nerves in that area. To control tooth pain, you can apply benzocaine to the area as needed. Stock up on products like Ora-gel just in case. If you don't have access to this, you can chew on a clove, as this may help control tooth pain. Address tooth pain as soon as possible in a survival situation, as a tooth infection can turn into a brain infection if not treated. This may mean a tooth should be pulled or antibiotics administered.

Body pain: For body aches and pains, some great medications to stockpile include ibuprofen (contains Aspirin) and Tylenol (acetaminophen). Ibuprofen can help with pain and inflammation. It is good for helping with arthritis, sore muscles, sore joints, and soreness from trauma.

Make sure that you don't take this if you have a bleeding disorder or are on blood thinners, as it can thin the blood. It is not safe for infants.

Tylenol is a good alternative for those seeking pain relief who cannot have blood-thinning medications. Take these as directed on the bottle. Since these are over-the-counter medications, they can be stockpiled easily. Never take these for long periods of time, as they can harm the organs.

Natural alternative: If you find yourself in a situation where you do not have access to over-the-counter pain medications (NSAIDs), you can use natural pain killers instead. A great choice for natural pain relief includes white willow bark. Willow trees are abundant across North American and one simply needs to harvest some inner bark to create a pain-relieving extract.

Fill a jar with the bark from the inside of the white willow tree and then completely cover this in at least 80 proof alcohol. Allow this to sit for four to six weeks and then strain it out. Take two dropperfuls as needed for pain. White willow contains a compound called salicin. This compound is what is used to make Aspirin. For this reason, it may also have blood-thinning effects.

Parasitic Infection

Certain situations may put you at a higher risk for picking up parasites, such as eating meat that isn't fully cooked, working in the soil, and working with livestock. These are things that many people who live in a survival situation do, so this means that you may be at a higher risk for parasitic infection in a disaster scenario.

Having parasites may go unnoticed by some people, but it is a good idea to watch for signs of a parasitic infection, such as pain in the liver and gallbladder areas, abdominal pain, digestive issues, fatigue, fever, headaches, bloating, gas, and an increased or decreased appetite. Allowing parasites to continue doing damage in the body can result in major gastrointestinal damage, leaky gut, cognitive impairment, anemia, and more.

If you suspect a parasitic infection, it is crucial to start treating it right away to prevent further damage to the body. Thankfully, there are natural remedies you can take that have been proven to get rid of parasites. Native Americans used these remedies often to address parasitic concerns, and these remedies are still effective and useful today.

Below are some common plants you can tincture to make your own antiparasitic remedy (follow the steps above under the viral illness section of this chapter where Japanese honeysuckle is discussed). Choose a remedy from the ones below and take one to two dropperfuls up to three times daily for two weeks to address a parasitic concern:

Wormwood: Wormwood is a famous antiparasitic remedy that has been used for centuries. It is native to Europe, but it didn't take long for this plant to spread across North America during colonization. Wormwood is now found growing wild all over the place.

In addition to helping eliminate parasites, it can also help improve digestion and appetite for those suffering from parasitic infection.

Pumpkin seed: Save those pumpkin seeds when you are carving pumpkins! Not only are they a healthy snack, but they can be tinctured to create a great remedy for parasites. These seeds contain an amino acid called cucurbitine which has shown to possess antiparasitic properties. In studies, pumpkin seeds displayed a similar effect to a pharmaceutical drug called fenbendazole. This drug is often prescribed to eliminate Ascaridia galli parasites, so the fact that common pumpkin seeds can do the same thing is very promising.

Black walnut: Black walnut trees can be found throughout North America. The nuts from this tree are very nutritious and a great source of sustenance in a disaster situation. However, when you are hulling these nuts, save the green hulls.

The green hulls of the black walnuts that fall off this tree in autumn can be tinctured to treat a wide variety of parasites. This is a remedy used by Native Americans for parasites. The hulls are a powerful parasite remedy due to the presence of astringent tannins, iodine, and a compound called juglone. Because they are powerful for treating parasitic infection, take this with caution to avoid purgative effects like diarrhea.

Fungal infections aren't exactly the same as a parasitic infection, but are also worth addressing here. It can help to have over-the-counter antifungal cream on hand for external fungal issues. You can also stock up on tea tree essential oil to add to fungal infections like athletes' foot and ringworm.

Blood Builder/Anemia/Weakness

Weight loss, digestive diseases like IBS, Crohn's, and ulcerative colitis, blood loss, low iron, malnutrition, and a number of other factors can cause anemia. One can be at a higher risk of anemia and malnutrition in times of stress, low food supply, injury, etc.

To help build the blood, supply the body with vital nutrients like iron, and help your body recover faster from injury, blood loss and more; the remedies in this section can give you the strength you need to survive and thrive.

These remedies are also excellent for speeding recovery during and after illness, as well as after surgery.

Stinging nettle: Stinging nettle is a common and invasive plant throughout North America. This can be a good thing in a survival situation, as it is likely easy to find. Harvest this plant with gloves, as it has tiny hairs that cause the sting in those who touch it. Cooking the leaves can disarm these hairs and remove any danger.

This plant is a powerhouse of nutrition. It is a good source of vitamins A, C, K, and B. It also contains minerals like calcium, iron, magnesium, potassium, phosphorous, and sodium. Stinging nettle also contains amino acids, linoleic acid, palmitic acid, steric acid, oleic acid, various polyphenols, and beneficial compounds like flavonoids, quercetin, and coumarin. This amazing plant makes a great blood builder and provides an abundance of nutrition to improve overall health.

A great way to take this plant for health purposes is to add the leaves to bone broth. After cooking chicken, turkey, beef, or any other animal with bones, save the bones. Place them in a stock pot and completely cover them with water. Bring this to a boil and add a cup or two of stinging nettle leaves, as well as other beneficial herbs. You can also add garlic, onion, and anything else you desire to the pot. Let this simmer for 10-24 hours under low heat (after you have brought it to a boil initially). Keep an eye on it to make sure it doesn't boil over. Strain out the broth when it is finished and cooled. Drink a cup of this broth three times daily as needed to build the blood and recover faster.

Beet root: Beet roots are a great source of iron and since the blood needs iron to produce enough of a substance in red blood cells to help them carry oxygen. Anemia can result when one has an iron deficiency. When you have anemia, you may feel tired and short of breath. Beet roots can help give your body the iron it needs to correct the situation.

Beets are easy to grow in a garden, so consider planting and saving beet seeds for a survival situation. Boil them to soften them and then add them to a blender with some water until you have a liquid consistency. Drink three ounces of this daily for best results.

Allergic Reaction

If you are in a survival situation and you happen to have allergies to certain substances, making sure you have Benadryl and an EpiPen on hand should be at the top of your list. Some people need an EpiPen to mitigate a serious allergic reaction that can lead to anaphylaxis and death.

While it is important to do your best to steer clear of your allergic triggers, this is not always possible. Not everyone has allergies severe enough to warrant an EpiPen, but for those who do, it is crucial to make sure you have several on hand for an emergency situation.

Get as many pens as you can to stock up on. Unfortunately, EpiPens do expire and when they expire, they may not work as well or as fast. Keep this in mind when preparing for a disaster. Some people can mitigate an allergic attack by quickly taking two Benadryl tablets when they feel an allergic reaction coming on or they can even take the Benadryl before a situation they think may be triggering to mitigate a reaction.

Benadryl is an over-the-counter antihistamine that is great to stock up on for emergency situations. It can bring down swelling, lessen hives, and help keep a reaction from happening. It is also helpful for seasonal allergies and congestion caused by pollen, etc. Since it is over-the-counter, it is easy to stock up on. Store it in a cool, dark place and take it as directed in the event of an allergic reaction.

If you use an EpiPen for allergic reactions, use this first before trying Benadryl. EpiPens will work faster and more effectively for your allergic reaction. However, if you find yourself in an emergency situation without an EpiPen, take some Benadryl tablets and try to keep calm.

Hydrocortisone cream can be an additional option for skin rashes and hives. Sometimes, allergic reactions like hives cause severe itching. Hydrocortisone cream helps calm the itch and may even alleviate hive rashes. This cream can be purchased at most drug stores or pharmacies without a prescription.

Arthritis/Inflammation

If an inflammatory condition has you down, you may be able to control it with turmeric. Inflammatory conditions like arthritis, autoimmune disease, and areas that have experienced trauma can benefit from turmeric.

You can grow turmeric in pots, even if you don't live in a tropical location. If you happen to live in a warmer climate, you may have luck growing this rhizomatous plant outdoors. If not, you can stock up on turmeric powder or turmeric supplements to have on hand. Store these in the freezer to keep them fresher longer. Use a teaspoon or two of turmeric powder to make turmeric milk by heating milk and adding the powder until it dissolves. Drink one to two cups of this daily.

Take any turmeric supplement you purchase as directed. For fresh turmeric roots, you can dig them up as you need them and wash them well. Chop them and add them to a jar to make a tincture. Add a tablespoon of black peppercorns to make an even more anti-inflammatory and powerful remedy. Take two dropperfuls of this up to three times daily.

Turmeric is a great remedy to help with inflammation caused by trauma as well. For example, if you happen to twist or sprain your ankle in a disaster situation, start taking turmeric right away to help with swelling and pain. You can take turmeric with other pain relievers that contain acetaminophen if you are in severe pain. It is not a good idea to pair turmeric with aspirin because this can thin the blood too much.

Blood Pressure/Heart

There are many people who struggle with high blood pressure and other cardiovascular issues. For these people, a disaster situation may mean that they no longer have access to blood pressure medications they usually take daily. This can be very dangerous and cause a spike in blood pressure, as well as lead to stroke and other deadly events. If you happen to take daily blood pressure medication, try to see if your pharmacy can send you a three month's supply of your medications whenever possible, so you always have a bit in case an emergency should arise.

However, in the event you find yourself without your normal high blood pressure medications, there are some things you can do to keep your blood pressure down and mitigate any serious events.

Below are some natural remedies you can use to lower blood pressure and nourish the heart and cardiovascular system:

Motherwort: This plant's Latin name (Leonurus cardiaca) literally translates to Greek words meaning "lion tail" and "to the heart." This is because motherwort has been utilized for centuries to nourish the heart and cardiovascular system. Motherwort not only helps lower high blood pressure; it can also strengthen the heart and support cardiovascular health. It is a valuable remedy for those concerned about high blood pressure and heart health in an emergency situation.

You can tincture the aerial parts of this plant and take two dropperfuls up to four times daily or as needed for hypertension, stress, and to support cardiovascular health.

Lavender: Lavender is such a common and popular herb, but this is for good reason. It has been shown in studies to lower high blood pressure, while also calming stress and anxiety.

You can tincture the aerial parts of this plant and take two dropperfuls three times daily, or you can purchase lavender essential oil and inhale this as needed for stress and anxiety. Since stress and anxiety greatly contribute to high blood pressure, this is great news for those who have hypertension brought on by stress.

Garlic: Garlic is a common garden plant and is highly recommended for any survival garden due to its versatility of use. Not only is garlic great for adding to various dishes, it contains potent medicinal properties specific to heart health.

It has been shown to reduce high blood pressure and it can also thin the blood to prevent plaque buildup in arteries. Buildup of plaque can lead to blockages, heart attacks, and strokes. It also helps break down thrombi and clots in blood vessels to reduce your risk of strokes and heart attacks. These properties make garlic invaluable for cardiovascular health.

If you want to grow garlic, you can harvest the bulbs and add cloves to a jar. Completely cover this in raw honey and allow it to ferment for as long as you desire. Take a spoonful of this twice daily.

Another option is to purchase garlic extract supplements to have on hand in emergency situations. Store these in the refrigerator and take them as directed.

Keep in mind that these natural remedies are to be used in an emergency situation where you don't have access to your normal medications. If you have access to your usual medications, take them. Do not replace your medications with the remedies above unless you have no other choice.

Radiation Exposure

It pays to plan for every possible disaster scenario and radiation exposure is one such scenario. In the event of a nuclear disaster, it helps to be prepared with potassium iodine tablets and cilantro. This is especially critical if you live near a nuclear facility. Even if you live within 50-100 miles of one, it pays to have these remedies on hand just in case.

Potassium iodine tablets: Potassium iodine can act as a thyroid blocker to protect you against radiation poisoning. Your thyroid is especially susceptible to radiation damage because it is made to take up certain minerals from the body in order to function. Unfortunately, other more dangerous heavy metals are also taken in by the thyroid when we are exposed to them. Stock up on these tablets and take them as directed on the package for one to two weeks if you are exposed to radiation.

Cilantro: Cilantro is a common garden herb with the unique ability to remove heavy metals from the body. It acts as a heavy metal binding agent and mobilizer. It is a useful remedy in situations where you have been exposed to heavy metals and other toxins. Tincture cilantro and take two dropperfuls twice daily for three weeks. Some people advise to avoid using cilantro if you have mercury fillings in your teeth, as it attempts to pull the mercury from these, causing it to leach into the body.

Electrolytes

If you are suffering from a viral illness, injury, or an infection when you are in an emergency situation, you can put yourself at even greater risk if you aren't staying hydrated. Many people end up in the hospital when they are sick because they let themselves get too dehydrated. Dehydration is something you want to avoid at all costs if you are in a survival situation. Even if you don't feel like it, it is crucial to make yourself drink fluids. While water is the best fluid you can drink, make sure that if you don't have access to clean water, you boil your water before drinking it. If you have diarrhea or fever, you can become dehydrated even faster. Force yourself to drink fluids often in these situations.

Electrolytes: Electrolytes are a useful addition to any survival medication stockpile. These are sometimes called rehydration salts. You can keep a big stockpile of these in your

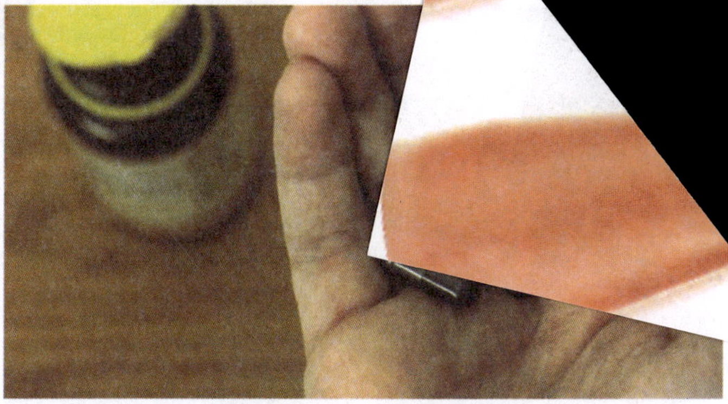

first aid kit, as they last a long time. Just store them in a cool, dry location. They can work to quickly rehydrate a person who is suffering from severe vomiting or diarrhea. They need to be administered as soon as possible when a person is sick since dehydration can come on quick and be very deadly. Use these as directed on the package.

Imodium: Imodium is an over-the-counter diarrhea medication. It can be helpful for those with severe diarrhea who are in danger of dehydration. However, sometimes diarrhea is the body's way of getting rid of something toxic. Diarrhea medications like this can be helpful to have in a first aid kit, but should be used mindfully in situations where they are actually needed (for very severe diarrhea that won't go away). Another option that also soothes the stomach is an over-the-counter medication like Pepto Bismol. Since this contains aspirin, take it mindfully and do not take it if you are taking other blood thinning medications.

Wound Care

If you find yourself in a situation where you have a wound, the first step is to clean the wound to prevent infection. Clean with soap and water and use hydrogen peroxide or rubbing alcohol as well. Dry the wound with a clean cloth and apply honey or triple antibiotic ointment to the wound. Cover it with gauze. Check the wound often, clean it often, and reapply ointment and gauze, especially if blood or other fluids soak into the gauze a lot. As it starts to heal, you can remove the gauze and let the wound get some air.

It may also be useful to add butterfly wound closures to your first aid kit in the event a wound needs stitches. Some people use super glue to close a wound in an emergency situation. In short, keep rubbing alcohol, hydrogen peroxide, gauze, tape for gauze, wound closures, honey, and triple antibiotic ointment in your first aid kit to treat a variety of wounds.

Poisoning or Drug Overdose

In the event you eat something that you shouldn't have, it pays to have activated charcoal capsules on hand. You can stock up on these and keep them in a cool, dry place to use when needed. They have a long shelf life as long as you keep them dry.

Activated charcoal may also be useful for drug overdoses. Activated charcoal can keep swallowed drugs and poisons from being absorbed from the gut into the bloodstream. This highly effective treatment needs to be administered as soon as possible for best results. Other useful properties of activated charcoal include the ability to help with gas and bloating, as well as lowering cholesterol.

INDISPENSABLE SURVIVAL ITEMS

Household Items You Need to Hoard Before It Is Too Late

Bugging in has many things going for it, but the biggest advantage is that you have access to an awesome survival resource: your home and everything in it. When you're bugging out, you'll have to grab what you can and go, but bugging in gives you access to everything. The key is to make sure your home contains everything you need to give you the best chance of survival.

Of course, you can't rely on stocking up on essentials when a crisis hits. The COVID pandemic showed us all what panic buying looks like and any future crisis could easily have the same results. When people start to panic, they'll strip the shelves of anything that might be useful, so if anxiety is already spreading, it could be too late to grab a few extra rolls of duct tape from the hardware store.

Survival is the ultimate come as you are party – and if you want to come as a well-stocked prepper, now is the time to build up your stocks of these useful household items.

Batteries

It's hard to have enough batteries. Many flashlights, portable radios, and other small devices run on AA or AAA cells; larger flashlights often use D cells. You can also use batteries in home-built projects; they're a very useful thing to have around and a large stockpile of them will make post-crisis life much easier and more comfortable.

One issue with batteries is that they can be expensive, but don't be tempted to save money by buying no-name Chinese brands from the dollar store. Yes, they're cheap, but they don't last long and they're also more likely to leak – and that can ruin vital equipment. Go for affordable but good quality brands instead.

Also look at rechargeable batteries. You can recharge these several hundred times and if you have a USB charger and a solar panel, it won't even cost you any energy to do it. Many modern flashlights also run on 18650 lithium-ion batteries and you'll need a charger for those anyway, so why not get rechargeable AA cells at the same time?

Candles

They might be old-fashioned, but candles are still a great light source. They don't need batteries or fuel, they can be stored for decades without losing effectiveness, and while they don't throw off a lot of light, they do give out some heat too. Candles will still work after being soaked and they can be used to help start a fire in wet weather. Boxes of either stick candles or tea lights deserve a place in your stores.

Vitamin Tablets

A simple daily multivitamin can keep you healthy even when your diet is poor. Don't risk crippling vitamin deficiencies; stock up on multivitamin tablets and make sure to rotate your stock.

Matches

Matches are old-fashioned too, but they're cheap, light, and simple. As long as you keep them dry, they last for years, so stock up whenever you get the chance.

Butane Lighters

Don't forget cheap, disposable cigarette lighters either. These are more fragile than matches, but also more resistant to damp. Fire is so important it's always good to have a few ways of starting one.

Solar Panels

Not long ago, solar panels were big things that went on the roof of your house and specialist portable ones were unaffordable for most people. Now there are a lot of small, cheaper models available – you can get a lightweight 30W one for less than $50 and use it with a USB cable to recharge your devices or a power bank.

You won't be running large appliances of one, but you can leave it to charge things while you get on with other tasks. Storing a few of them will let you keep rechargeable devices running when the power goes off. Look for bargains online or in local electronics stores and whenever you see a good deal, grab one.

If you can get hold of one, a solar generator is a great piece of equipment. Combining a high-capacity power bank with a large solar panel array, these have standard electrical outlets and can power small appliances.

Seeds

Properly stored seeds don't take up much space and can last for years. They're also essential if you want to establish a vegetable garden at your BIL. Many preppers go for the simple solution of buying a seed vault, which contains a variety of seeds already packed in a container designed for long-term storage, but that's an expensive option and not everyone can afford it. However, if you pick up a couple of packets every time you visit a store that sells them, you can build up an impressive collection surprisingly quickly.

Store them in a waterproof box and keep it somewhere cool, dry, and dark. If you have a vacuum sealer, you can also seal the seed envelopes into bags.

Unless you're really short of storage space, there's no need to rotate seeds; when you add new ones you might as well hang on to the old ones too. They're small and light, and while the germination rate will slowly drop as the seeds get older, it can take decades for it to fall to zero. If even a few seeds from an old packet germinate, that's still a few extra plants that could help keep you alive.

Salt

When times are good, we're always being told to eat less salt. That's because modern processed foods already contain enough of it. In a crisis, when we're foraging, hunting, and eating vegetables from our gardens, we'll need to add salt to our diets to stay alive. It's also an excellent food preservative that can help you stay alive through the winter. The problem is that unless you live on the coast and have a salt pan to evaporate seawater in, salt is very hard to obtain.

Stock up now; if you avoid fancy designer brands and stick with plain old table salt, it's cheap to buy in bulk.

Medications

In a crisis a simple aspirin can make a big difference. Hard physical work leads to aches and pains, and that can be demoralizing. Anything that takes the edge off it is worth having, so get as much over the counter pain relief as you can. Stock up on other things, too. Simple medications to treat diarrhea and constipation can make post-apocalypse life a lot less unpleasant.

Before the early 20th century an infected wound was often a death sentence. Now, it's easily treated. The difference? Antibiotics. If you can get your hands on antibiotics, do it. Mexican pharmacies will sell them over the counter without a prescription.

Failing that, tropical fish suppliers often stock antibiotics that are identical to human medicines. Just make sure you know exactly what you have, what the dosage is, and what kind of infections it's best against. And, once you start taking antibiotics, make sure you finish the full course. If you stop taking them when you feel better, you risk evolving antibiotic-resistant superbugs – and in a survival situation, that's really bad news.

Water Filters

You can make water filters yourself. There are many different options, from cut-down bottles packed with activated charcoal to large fixed filters using layered sand, gravel, and other materials to progressively remove particles from the water.

Commercial filters definitely have a place, though Survival straw-type filter cartridges can be used to drink directly from streams or pools; they can also be rigged up with a water bag and used to fill bottles. Even a regular filter jug is a useful tool when you need to purify your own water – as long as you have a good supply of cartridges for it. These are expensive in stores, but generic ones can be found online much cheaper.

Hand Tools

Modern power tools are great, but they have an obvious drawback – they need power. If society collapses, power is going to be in short supply and old-fashioned hand tools will be vital. A hand drill, crosscut saw, and wood saw will cover most jobs; check yard sales for cheap ones to add to your store.

Bleach

Simple bleach has many survival uses. The most important is purifying water; add a quarter teaspoon of bleach to a gallon of water, mix in well, then let it stand for 20 minutes to give the bleach time to kill any microorganisms in the water. It has many other uses too, though. A bleach solution will disinfect kitchen tools and food preparation surfaces. If you're treating sick people, dip rubber gloves in a mild bleach solution to prevent bacteria being transferred. A wash with diluted bleach, then a rinse in clean water, will sterilize baby toys, coolers, or bait boxes.

It's important to make sure you get chlorine-based bleach. If bleach is advertised as safe to use on colored clothes, it's probably made with peroxide, and won't be effective at killing germs. You also need to look for plain bleach that doesn't contain scents or other additives.

If you store bleach in a cool, dark place, it should last for around six months before it starts to chemically decompose. This means it isn't something you can store long term. Rotate your stockpile, using older bottles as you replace them with new ones, and if a crisis is developing, buy more to add to your supply. If you do have bleach that's past its sell by date, don't use it for purifying water – it can't be relied on. You can use it for general cleaning and disinfecting, though. Just increase the amount you use.

Faraday Cage

An ElectroMagnetic Pulse (EMP) attack is a very real danger. It's one way a rogue state like North Korea could cripple the US and, maybe, avoid a devastating nuclear retaliation. If you want to protect your electronic equipment from EMP, you need to store it in Faraday cages. Any prepper website will tell you how to build one of these, but it can be tricky to do. You need to be very careful about properly finishing seams and doors to make sure there's no way for EM radiation to leak inside.If you just want to protect small electronics though, small Faraday cages are now a consumer item. Many stores now sell neat, ready-made Faraday cages, built into a small box and designed to protect keyless car key fobs from being hacked by thieves. Many of these boxes are big enough to protect cell phones, GPS handsets, and even small handheld radios. There are even Faraday pouches that will slip in a pocket and can protect keys, credit cards, and other very small items.

BULLETS

As ammunition for your own weapons—but also as barter—these will be gold. Everyone will need ammo and will have trouble getting it. Even if they don't need any, they will recognize its value, making it a great barter item.

EMP Cloth

If you need to protect larger electronics, you might still have to build your own Faraday cage. As more people become aware of the threat, retailers are starting to stock the specialized material you need to make one with. This fabric, with a mesh of embedded wire, is a great addition to your survival gear.

Alcohol

No, this isn't essential for your survival. On the other hand, it's a great barter material. Once the first surge of post-crisis looting has passed, a bottle of cheap vodka could be worth its weight in gold as a trade good.

Soap

In a survival situation basic hygiene is vital. Disease can spread quickly; regular hand washing is the best way to keep it under control. Keeping yourself clean will also help prevent minor injuries, like cuts and scrapes, from becoming infected. We're all used to controlling minor infections with a quick visit to the doctor and a course of antibiotics. That might not always be an option, so it's best to have plenty of soap available and use it regularly.

Plain, old-fashioned lye soap is a good choice – but any soap is useful, so if you see a bargain, consider adding it to your stockpile.

Baking Soda

Baking soda is one of those common, slightly old-fashioned household chemicals that really comes into its own in a crisis. It can be used for first aid; a paste of baking soda and water will soothe poison ivy or insect bites. Added to a bath it will take the sting out of sunburn or diaper rash. Sprinkled on window ledges, it can deter bugs from coming into your house. It's good for cleaning and odor removal. Best of all, it has a long shelf life, it's easy to find, and it's cheap.

White Vinegar

Another miracle substance, vinegar can be used to clean wounds, disinfect surfaces, and preserve food. Many people swear by the health benefits of apple cider vinegar, but a few gallons of plain old white vinegar should definitely be in your stores.

Flashlights

Every prepper needs a good-quality flashlight (and, of course, enough batteries to keep it running). A stash of cheaper ones is also good to have, though. Flashlights do get lost or broken and a cheap replacement is better than no replacement at all. It's also a good idea to keep one in every room, in case the power goes off suddenly. That way, you'll always be able to get some light quickly so you can get to work on dealing with the situation.

Stick with flashlights that use common battery sizes – D, AA and AAA cells, or 18650 rechargeables. Keep fully charged batteries in EDC flashlights and the ones located around your home, but if you have a stock of spare ones in your stores, leave the batteries out to prevent power drain or leakage.

Fishing Gear

If there's a body of water near you, fish could become a valuable food source. Of course, to catch fish you need fishing gear – and in a survival situation, you can't spare the time to spend hours sitting beside the lake with a pole in your hands. You're going to want to set out lines and check them every day. That means you need heavy line for the mainline, lots of leader material, lots of sinkers, and lots of hooks.

Duct Tape

Duct tape is something no prepper can have enough of. It has an incredible range of uses, anything from patching tents, fletching arrows, or removing warts. A lot of the time, when something breaks, a quick duct tape repair will hold it together long enough for you to get your tools out and do a proper job.

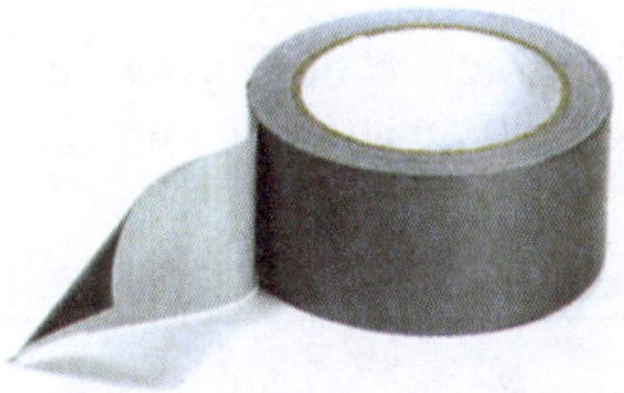

Like most other things, duct tape comes in different qualities. Expensive brand-name tape will usually be stronger, stickier, and more resistant to heat, sunlight, water, and chemicals than the cheap stuff; you should have a few rolls of high-grade 90mph tape among your supplies.

It's a good idea to buy up a load of discount store duct tape as well, though. After all, not every job needs the best tape. If you have a big supply of cheap tape, you can use that for all the quick and dirty repairs, and reserve the high-quality kind for when it's really needed.

Spare Clothes

Make sure you have plenty working clothes; you'll need them in a crisis. Look for comfort and durability – and don't forget to stockpile plenty of underwear and socks. Old jeans or shirts that won't do for going out anymore are still fine for working in, so add them to your stores.

Sewing Kit

Working outdoors is hard on clothes. You'll want to be able to carry out small alterations and repairs, so have a good supply of basic sewing gear. Lots of strong thread and needles are essential. A box of pins can make alterations much easier. Thimbles are worth having, too; if you're not an expert and keep puncturing your fingers with a needle, that risks infection.

Footwear

Most preppers already have good outdoor footwear, but do you have spares? Even the best boots can fall apart and, without specialist skills, they're hard to repair. A couple of pairs of army-surplus combat boots in your size are a valuable reserve.

Gloves

Protecting your hands is vital in an emergency. If they get injured, you'll struggle to get vital tasks done. Find a good brand of sturdy work glove that fits you comfortably and get several pairs.

Gasoline

When panic buying starts, gasoline is often one of the first things people want to stock up on. Gas stations can become snarled with long lines or short-tempered people desperate to fill their tanks. They can even become dangerous; early in the Covid pandemic some people were trying to fill garbage bags with gas. In a crisis, prices can also shoot up and of course supplies can dry up altogether.

Build up a gas reserve when times are good, then store it properly. Only use approved fuel containers and fill them right up to minimize the amount of air the gas is exposed to. Consider using fuel stabilizers to protect it. Store your fuel in a well-ventilated space and check it regularly for leaks. Gasoline needs care, because having large quantities of it around is dangerous, but it can be a life saver.

First Aid Kit

Every prepper should have a good first aid kit – a proper box, not just a pocket kit. Future-proof it by stockpiling more bandages, gauze, Band-Aids, and surgical tape.

Zip Ties

Cable ties aren't quite as versatile as duct tape, but they come close. They're quick and easy to fasten, strong, secure, and come in a huge range of sizes. You can use them to fasten insulation round a pipe, or fix cables to a frame.

You can even use them to hold down tarps, although it's better if you fasten them through eyelets rather than punching slits or holes in the tarp – that creates weak points that can tear.

Any size of cable tie can be useful, but if you need a small one you can always cut down a bigger one to fit, so focus

on six-inch ties or longer. Hardware stores often sell cheap packs of assorted ties, and these can be a good way to build up your supply.

Multitools

A quality multitool is a survival essential. Something like a Leatherman Super Tool or Wave fits easily in a pocket or on your belt, but gives you quick access to a whole range of tools. The only problem with Leatherman tools is that, at well over $100 for most models, they're expensive. Having one is great; having a couple of replacements on a shelf so you can replace a lost or broken one in an emergency just isn't affordable for most people.

On the other hand, most hardware stores sell cheap Leatherman clones for less than $20. Are they as good as the real thing? No, of course not – but 90% of the time they're good enough. They're also affordable enough that you can stash a couple away as spares.

Leatherman-style folders aren't the only multitool options, either. There's a whole range of one-piece steel multitools out there, too. Some are designed to fit in a credit card slot in your wallet; others come in novelty shapes, like snowflakes or trucks. What they all have in common is they include several useful tools, like screwdrivers and usually some kind of cutting edge. They only cost a few dollars and they're great for EDC, giving to the kids so they can have a survival tool of their own, or using in situations where you don't want to risk breaking or losing that expensive Leatherman.

Sharpening Stones

Knives and tools won't hold their edge forever, and when they get blunt, you need to be able to sharpen them again. A few honing stones in various grades will let you keep all your blades sharp.

Activated Charcoal

It's a simple substance, but activated charcoal has many uses. If you're suffering from diarrhea, a couple of spoonfuls of powdered activated charcoal will help absorb the harmful bacteria that are causing it, relieving the symptoms. If someone has swallowed poison, get them to chase it down with two to four ounces of activated charcoal as soon as possible. Mix some into a paste with water and use it to take the sting out of insect bites or poison ivy.

Perhaps the most important use of activated charcoal is as a water filter. Use it as the last stage in a filtration system; gravel and sand will remove debris and particles from the wa-

ter, then the charcoal layer will soak up toxins, bacteria and even microplastics and dissolved lead.

Regular charcoal is effective; activated charcoal is just regular charcoal that has had its surface area expanded for better adhesion to contaminants. If you are in a pinch, regular charcoal from non-toxic sources will work as well.

Lime

If you're relying on an outhouse in a crisis, you'll need a way to keep it fresh, and you can't beat lime for that.

Nails

Nails are essential for repairs and construction. You can build without them but it's much slower and more difficult. Make life easier by building up a supply of nails in various sizes. Three- and four-inch nails are good for general work, and you should aim to have as many of those as possible, but having some larger and smaller ones will give you more flexibility.

Toilet Paper

This doesn't need any explanation. A toilet paper shortage will make any crisis even more unpleasant than it already is, for the obvious reason – and toilet paper has other uses, too. You can blow your nose with it, stuff it into cracks in a shack wall to keep the wind out, or use it as emergency tinder. We all know what its main use is, though, and most people value it pretty highly. That's why, when the COVID pandemic hit in 2020, there was a global shortage of toilet paper. Desperate shoppers started fights over the last pack on the shelves; profiteers made money because people were willing to pay $10 a roll.

Folk memories are a fact of life and now there's a new one – the Great Toilet Paper Shortage of 2020. There's no particular reason why any future crisis should cause another shortage, but when things start going wrong again, plenty of people will decide to buy up a big supply "just in case." That pretty much guarantees that there will be another toilet paper shortage as soon as the smelly stuff starts approaching the fan. Don't be caught out; build up your supply now.

One downside of toilet paper is that it's bulky. If you're short of storage space, consider stockpiling toilet paper pills instead. These compressed wipes are incredibly compact, but just wet them with a few drops of water and they unfold into strong and absorbent sheets.

Paracord

String is a great thing to have. Garden twine, old-school parcel string; it doesn't matter – string has a million uses around the home and yard, and plenty more in a crisis. Most preppers have several balls of it in their supplies. 550 paracord is what string wants to be when it grows up. It's a lot more expensive than string, but it's also a lot stronger and more versatile. Any time you see a good deal on paracord, buy as much as you can.

Paper

It might not seem like it, but paper is very useful in a survival situation. You can use it to take notes about your vegetable garden, the best places to hunt and forage, or the state of your stockpiles. You can make lists of tasks that need to be done, or draw sketch maps to show other people where to find things. You can even give the kids a few sheets of paper and a pack of colored pencils to keep them amused when they get bored – and, with the TV, internet, and cell phones dead, they will get bored, a lot.

Any sort of paper can be useful, from Post-It notes to butcher paper. Stock up on cheap notebooks in various sizes. Reams of printer paper on sale at the supermarket? Buy a couple of those, too.

Pencils

Good old-fashioned pencils have a lot of advantages for preppers. They'll write on wet, greasy or dirty paper, unlike most pens. If they break, they're easily repaired – just sharpen them again. A few packs of pencils and some colored ones are a surprisingly useful addition to your supplies.

Don't forget to get some pencil sharpeners too. Again, these are cheap and it's a lot easier to sharpen a pencil with one than it is using a knife. When you sharpen your pencils, hang on to the shavings, too – they make great tinder. You can even use a pencil sharpener to shave down a dry twig and make more tinder that way.

There's a limit to how much most of us can stockpile; we need to fit inside our storage space and budget. Inside those limits, though, it's always a good idea to store as much as you can. If you find a useful item cheap, buy as many as you can. Even if you end up with more than you need yourself, they can always be used for barter.

Aluminum Foil

Aluminum foil has many uses in the kitchen. It has many more in a survival situation. As well as letting you cook fish, meat, and vegetables in the embers of a fire, it can also be used as

an emergency fishing lure, cut into strips to scare birds away from your garden or connected across the terminals of a battery as an emergency fire-starter. Aluminum foil is waterproof, electrically conductive, and reflects heat and light; these qualities make it a very versatile survival resource.

Bentonite Clay

Bentonite is a highly absorbent kind of clay with a lot of uses. It can be used to soak up oil or other spillages. Mixed into a paste with water, it can be spread on walls as a waterproofing layer. Many people also believe it has health benefits. Powdered bentonite can be added to food, which could remove toxins from the body. A bentonite paste can remove oil from the skin or take the sting out of poison ivy, similar to activated charcoal.

WaterBOB

Most preppers have an emergency water supply, but can you ever really have enough clean water? A WaterBOB is a great way to give your stockpile a last-minute boost when a crisis is approaching. This clever system is a large, transparent water bag that fits in an ordinary bathtub and holds up to 100 gallons of water. It's sealed, so the water stays clean, and has a handy built-in pump to transfer its contents to smaller containers with no risk of spillage.

Night Vision

Night vision systems aren't what most people think of as a household item, but they're actually becoming one. Wireless video doorbells and security cameras are increasingly common, and those have night vision capability. You can also get thermal imager attachments for smart phones, as well as military-style night vision goggles and thermal sights. Night vision will make a huge difference to knowing what's going on around your property – and to defending it, if you have to.

Space Blankets

Cold weather is demoralizing and can be a killer. Unfortunately, in a crisis there's a limit to how much fuel you can spare for heating. A simple, lightweight space blanket will let you conserve body heat. Laid between layers of bedding, tacked over windows at night or just wrapped around your shoulders, these can help you hold on to a lot of life-saving heat.

EMP Shield

Faraday cages will protect your small electronics, but what about all the other electrical and electronic stuff in your house? Give it a chance of survival by adding an EMP shield to your house's breaker box. This can protect your home's internal wiring against the power spike from EMP, or even a lighting strike.

Ham Radio

Survival is a lot easier when you can talk to other people, arrange to share resources, and get news about what's happening in the surrounding area. Unfortunately, in a serious crisis the modern communications we've all got used to will be among the first things that go down. An amateur radio set will let you stay in touch with the outside world – and with all the other preppers who're on the net.

SURVIVAL KNOWLEDGE

10 Things That Will Become Extremely Valuable After an EMP

Solar Panels

One thing that is bound to happen after an EMP hits is the lack of power. The affected area will most likely be cut out from the power grid, or the power grid gets fried.

Solar panels may be your only source of power after an EMP attack. Your ability to power up your home post EMP attack using solar energy makes it extremely valuable.

Cell Phones

Although the cell towers will be fried by an EMP, your cell phone will most likely survive an EMP attack so long as it wasn't connected for charging when the EMP went off.

While communicating will be impossible with the phone due to dead cell towers, you may find several apps useful.

Also, you can store vital information on it, which can be very helpful in survival situations.

However, this depends on you having solar panels to keep the phone charged as they won't be affected by an EMP.

Gasoline

Gasoline is easily the most important fuel in today's society. We use it to power our cars, generators, and other pieces of machinery. An EMP attack won't render most cars immobile, especially older vehicles with more simple motors. However, there will be a shortage of gas because gas pumps require electricity to run.

Pretty much any petroleum-based fuel will be scarce, implying that storing important fuels is a good idea.

Non-Electric Heater

Keeping warm after a blackout caused by an EMP attack is vital, especially during colder seasons. Living in an older home with a fireplace should combat this problem.

However, the design of most modern homes does not accommodate fireplaces as they do not have brick chimneys. This makes having a non-electric heater all the more valuable after an EMP hits. Non-electric heater options include kerosene, propane, and natural gas heaters.

Clean Water

Lack of power due to an EMP attack translates to a lack of clean water for most modern homes. If you have a well on your property, that solves half the problem. However, you will need to treat the water for kitchen use.

Transportation

As mentioned above, you will find that transportation wouldn't come easy anymore because there will be a gas scarcity. This will limit your movement drastically.

Also, any means of transport you find may be too expensive due to the demand. Keep in mind that this is a long-term effect of a continuous blackout.

Flashlights

The power grid will most likely be affected by an EMP, so flashlights and other portable lighting devices will be extremely valuable, especially if you do not have solar panels.

Although the LEDs producing the light can be affected by an EMP, flashlights do not have any external connections, implying that the effects of the EMP can't be transmitted to the flashlight. Also, flashlights with aluminum cases are better as they provide a Faraday Cage, protecting the LED inside.

First Aid Kit

A lot can happen within the first few moments of an EMP attack and could leave people injured. Unfortunately, you may not always have immediate access to a hospital in such situations.

The absence of quick health service makes a first aid kit a valuable survival item in the event of an EMP attack.

Batteries

You can't overemphasize the importance of batteries in a survival situation caused by an EMP, as several appliances use them. Contrary to popular belief, batteries will survive an EMP attack.

This is due to the fact that the chemicals inside the battery can't be affected by electromagnetic fields.

One this is certain – if we lose power as a result of an EMP attack, we will have to devise ways to survive it, and as you would know, it's all about being prepared.

Canned Food

One of the most effective methods of preserving food at home is by canning it. As a prepper, you know that freezing your food means relying on electricity.

But without preservation, food will go bad too often, leading to waste. This makes canned foods extremely valuable as they can last for many years.

It will be good to stockpile these canned foods because supermarkets will probably be closed after such emergencies.

Where To Take Shelter in Case Of A Nuclear Strike

The Actual Danger Caused by a Nuclear Explosion

In order to understand how to survive it, we need to understand just what it is that we're surviving.

There's a myth that nuclear bombs are all-powerful devices that will sweep life off the planet. While it may seem that way at ground zero, the reality is far from it.

Even the largest of nuclear explosives is limited in its power and the range at which it can cause damage.

This damage is caused by four things:

Fireball

This is the burning of the explosive contained I the bomb.

It would reach out several hundred meters, burning at a temperature to rival the sun and incinerating anything within it.

Blast

The explosive blast from the bomb will create an enormous pressure wave, causing winds of several hundred miles per hour. Within a two kilometer radius, all buildings would be flattened and the people inside them killed.

As the shockwave moves out from there, buildings would survive with various degrees of damage, based upon the distance and construction of those buildings.

Heat

While the fireball may be limited to a relatively small area, the heat from the explosion will be enough to ignite wood-frame buildings (homes) for several kilometers.

At 11 km, that heat will be enough to cause third-degree burns. Closer to the blast, clothing will ignite spontaneously from the heat.

Radiation

A nuclear explosion emits several different types of radiation, amongst the most dangerous of which is gamma radiation.

This is fast enough and strong enough to pass through almost any material and will continue moving in a straight line out beyond the horizon.

Radiation kills more slowly, through a breakdown of the body's organs, often referred to as radiation sickness.

It is clear that anyone who is within the fireball will be killed instantly. Going out from there, about half of the people between there and 11 km would be killed. Many of those people will die of radiation sickness over the week following the blast.

There is something else to be concerned about with the radiation; that's fallout.

The signature mushroom cloud from a nuclear explosion is caused by the wind from the blast, first moving out away from the epicenter of the explosion and then collapsing back on the low pressure area created by the blast wave.

Dust, created by the explosion is picked up in the air and carried up to the upper atmosphere.

Radioactive material from the bomb (little of which is actually lost in the explosion) becomes attached to that dust and is also carried up into the upper atmosphere, where it eventually falls back to earth.

Nuclear fallout can ultimately kill more people than the explosion of the warhead. Winds can blow that cloud of dust far downrange, where it can cover a much larger area.

As this dust is difficult to detect and most people don't have the capability to detect radiation, it becomes the silent killer, giving people radiation sickness over the next month to six weeks.

Surviving the Nuclear Explosion

To a large part, the number one defense against any nuclear explosion is distance.

The farther one is from ground zero, the less of a chance of being directly affected by any part of the explosion.

Of course, fallout can reach us anywhere, as the wind can carry that dust for hundreds of miles.

Before anything, take a good look at a nuclear targeting map.

This will show those places in the country which are considered to be targets for nuclear attack.

Those targets fall into just a few categories:

- Government installations that provide command and control
- Military bases and installations, including our missile fields
- Nuclear power plants (as an effort to blow up the plants, multiplying the effect of the warhead)
- Major population centers

If you don't live within 11 km of one of these targets, you're likely to be at least somewhat safe from the direct effects of a nuclear explosion.

To be sure, I'd double that and say 22 km. If I lived within that distance, I'd be looking for how to protect myself and my family.

So how do we do that?

The first option is to move farther away from any potential target. That fits in with most of our survival strategy anyway, so don't dismiss that option out of hand.

If you have the ability to move even a short distance out of town, it can make a big difference in your potential for survival.

I live in a small town, 34 miles from the nearest city. That's far enough to protect us, but still close enough that my wife drives to work in the city every day.

As an alternative to that, consider the possibility of whether or not you can get out of town quickly, in the event of a nuclear attack.

Keeping in mind that you'll have 30 minutes or less, is there someplace you could get to, which would put you far enough away to be out of the blast zone, keeping in mind that lots of other people will probably be trying to do the same thing?

Where to Hide

Since it's unlikely that you'll be able to get out of town fast enough to avoid the nuclear explosion, your time will probably be better spent getting to a place of safety to ride out the nuclear attack and the fallout period to follow.

So just what are these locations?

Bomb Shelter

To start with, the best possible place to go is an actual bunker or bomb shelter. Being below ground will protect you from the wind and heat, as well as doing a good job of blocking radiation.

If the shelter is properly stocked to hold out for weeks, it could keep your family safe through the fallout period as well.

During the Cold War, many people built bomb shelters under their homes or in their backyards. These were made of concrete, making them much more solid than most of the bunkers that preppers build.

Other than that, they were very similar, stocked to allow a family to survive a nuclear war.

Basement

If a bomb shelter isn't available, the next best thing is to get underground someplace. If your home has a basement, it will offer that possibility. The home above you might be blown away; but you'll still be protected.

It's actually fairly easy to build a bunker in the basement, constructing it out of solid cement blocks in a corner on the side closest to a potential nuclear explosion. The hard part is making the concrete roof.

To do that, you'd need to make a temporary support out of corrugated steel roofing or plywood, supported by 2"x 4"s. Be sure to put in sufficient rebar or remesh, then pour the concrete. The 2"x 4"s and plywood can be removed after the concrete sets.

Either way, stock your basement with everything your family will need to stay safe for six weeks or more. Add a chemical toilet, so that you don't have to go outside.

Make sure you have materials on hand to make a ceiling over your heads, if the existing structure blows away.

Concrete Building

While not as good as getting underground, any building made of precast concrete or concrete block will probably provide good protection if you are outside the immediate blast zone.

These buildings are made of materials that will withstand strong winds and the materials also withstand heat well.

The only problem might be if the building has windows in it, especially if they are facing the direction of the blast.

Retaining Wall

In a pinch, if the bomb is going off and you don' have anyplace to go, drop to the ground behind anything solid that will give you protection from the blast.

By something solid, I mean something like a concrete retaining wall; don't count on wood buildings or cars. It has to be strong enough to withstand the blast and heat, providing you with shelter from the direction of the blast.

Obviously, anything that would be ignited by the heat or blown down by the wind won't work.

If you take shelter from the blast in such a place, you will need to move once it is over and find something that can be used as fallout shelter.

Fallout will begin immediately, so you will need to move quickly to get to safety. Even so, if you don't have food and water, you'll probably need to take time to get them, exposing yourself for that time.

The Only 4 Knots You Need for Survival

Reef Knot

The reef knot is an old sailor's knot. It was originally used to tie the reef points on a sail – cords that are used to tie part of a sail against the spars, to make it smaller in high winds. This task needs a knot that won't slip, can be tied and untied in a hurry for fast adjustment of the sails, and that lies flat to avoid wearing holes in the canvas. The reef knot ticks all these boxes.

It's also a very simple knot to tie.

Simply take the ends of the two ropes and cross them, left over right.

Now double them back on themselves and cross them right over left. Pull the whole thing tight. There you go; you have a reef knot.

A reef knot has several advantages. Although it holds securely, it's also easy to untie. It's relatively flat, so it doesn't slide around as much as some other knots and also creates less wear on any surfaces in contact with it – which is important if you're lashing a tarp over something you don't want to get wet, because the reef knot won't wear holes in it. If you're using a rope as a belt, a reef knot will lie flat and minimize chafing.

Figure 8 Knot

Sometimes you need to tie a stopper knot in a rope or cord to make sure it doesn't slip out of where it's supposed to be. That could be the drawstring on your coat's hood, or the downhaul on a pulley, but either way the principle is the same – if there's a knot on the end, it will stop the cordage from escaping its task.

The simplest stopper knot, and the one everyone knows, is the pretzel-shaped overhand knot. Unfortunately it's also a terrible knot, with a nasty habit of binding so tightly against itself under tension that it can never be untied. A much better alternative is the figure 8 knot.

To tie a figure 8 knot, lay the end of the rope over itself to make a loop. Pass the end around the rope, then back through the loop, and pull it tight. You'll end up with a large and effective stopper knot that won't bind to itself, so it can be undone. Just don't tie it too close to the end of the rope – if you do that, occasionally it will undo itself.

Round Turn and Two Half Hitches

Ropes usually need to be attached to something, such as a branch, tie-down ring or bollard. A reliable way to do that is with a round turn and two half hitches. This is a strong knot that uses friction against both the support and the rope itself to resist slipping. It also has the advantage that the first part – the round turn – is very easy and quick to do, and will take a lot of the load while you finish it off. That makes it useful for tying up boats, or securing a load that's already starting to shift. To tie the knot, get one end of the rope round whatever you want to tie it to, leaving yourself with a good length to work with. If there's already a load on the rope that lets you snub it, helping to bring the load under control. Now pass the end round again, giving more friction and more control. If the load is very heavy you can add one or more additional turns.

Next, wrap the end round the standing (loaded) part of the rope and pass it through the loop you create. Repeat the process, wrapping it round again and through the new loop. Then just pull the end tight and you're done. The half hitches you formed by wrapping the end round the standing part will lock off the knot; if you have spare rope you can add more for extra security, but two is usually plenty.

Butterfly Knot

Need a secure loop in a rope? There are many ways of doing this, but the butterfly knot is one of the best. Often used by climbers, it's handy if you can get some slack in the rope and need a loop that won't slip under a heavy load.

Gather in some slack and form an 8-shaped loop in the rope. Fold the upper loop down, pass it round the rope then thread it through the lower loop and pull it tight. That's all it takes.

Are these all the knots you can use to help you survive? Nowhere near! There are hundreds of knots, some of them very specialized. The more you can learn, the better equipped you'll be to survive. These four will cover most things, though. Get some bits of rope and practice until you can tie them confidently, and you'll have a big advantage when modern fasteners aren't available anymore.

Things You Throw Away That You Should Add to Your Stockpile Instead

The Most Common Thing

There are obvious ways to repurpose plastic bottles and jugs for survival like keeping gallon jugs to transport drinking water or to store grains. However, there are lots of purposes you might not have considered. If you tape a flashlight or headlamp to a large bottle or jug filled with water so the light shines into it, you just made a lantern.

You can turn clear 2 Liter bottles into fish traps. You can use them as a float for fishing or cut out the plastic to make safety glasses. They work great for water filters. The list goes on and on.

Another Useful Item

Cans provide a unique opportunity in that you have reflective metal that can be easily cut or torn.

The can could be cut to use as a cooking vessel for water or food. You can use a can to fashion a small stove for heat. You can use the bottom of the can as a reflective surface to start a fire.

The tab can be fashioned into a fish hook. You can even drop a few stones in the bottom and attach it to a trip line for a perimeter warning system. Keep your cans!

Dryer Lint

Most people throw this in the trash at least once a week. Dryer lint makes a great fire starter. Just stuff a toilet paper roll with lint and throw it in your pack.

Egg Cartons

These are great because they give you a dozen uniform cups, but they are made of paper products or styrafoam. This makes them perfect for things like seed starters. Just add a little soil, plant your seeds, and water.

You can cut apart the cups and seal two of them together to make a bobber for fishing.

Make them into fire starters by stuffing each cup with tinder coated in wax. You can even use them as a candle mold. They work great as ice cube trays, or you can just use them to sort nuts and bolts.

Keep This for Your Survival Stockpile

Cotton by itself does not work great as a fire starter but add a little petroleum jelly and you are in business.

Dip all of your used cotton balls in petroleum jelly and put them in a container. They will take a spark and will stay lit for a minute or two even in the rain or wind.

Save Every Piece of That

As is with aluminum cans, foil gives you reflective metal that can be torn or formed easily. You can use foil with a battery and some tinder to start a fire.

Foil can be fashioned into a stove or can be formed into shapes that work as a bowl, cup, or plate. Because of its reflective qualities it can be used to signal for help, or you can make a solar oven in direct sunlight.

My mother in law grew up saving every piece of foil they used. It saved them money and gave them a valuable resource.

Pantyhose

When twisted and pulled tight, they can work well for a tourniquet. They are an excellent addition to your homemade water filter. You can even use them as a dust mask.

The Best Item to Keep

Bacon grease can be reused for cooking instead of using butter or oil and has better flavor in my opinion. You can also use it to lubricate metal parts or to preserve other foods. Just put a layer on anything you want to preserve, and it will seal the air out.

You can use it to season cast iron pan, make soap, or condition and waterproof your leather boots. It can be filtered and used as biodiesel to fuel a vehicle or generator. You can use it to make a candle or fire starter. Never throw away bacon grease.

Altoids Tins

The great thing about these tins is that they fit in your pocket and are waterproof. They work great to store a fishing kit or first aid kit. If you punch a small hole in the lid and fill it with small pieces of cotton cloth, you can throw it in the fire and make char cloth. I also use mine for a fire starting kit with char cloth, a ferro rod, a magnifying lens, and some waterproof tinder. You can use them to form candles or make an alcohol stove.

Soot

If you have a charcoal grill, a smoker, or a fireplace you probably dispose of a good amount of soot. You might think this is a nuisance, but it can be used again. Soot makes a great toothpaste in a pinch. It can be swallowed with some water to settle your stomach and even works if you accidently ate something poisonous.

It makes for good camouflage on your face and hands, especially at night. You can rub it on yourself or put it in your boots to help absorb odors.

INTELLIGENCE

Ingenious Ways to Outfox FEMA in the Next Crisis

When you face a crisis during which you need to "bug in" for an extended period, you will undoubtedly see a response from the Federal Emergency Management Agency (FEMA). While it seems on the surface that this agency is looking out for the population's best interests, there is cause for preppers to want to keep them at arm's length.

For the most part, FEMA will coordinate the response to the crisis, distributing aid and helping people apply for financial disaster relief. However, if the crisis was severe enough, they could also look to confiscate private property to redistribute to the less prepared in the community. The stockpiles that preppers and survivalists have accumulated are tempting targets for FEMA to raid.

There are ways that you can stay one step ahead of them.

Play the Victim

When FEMA knocks at your door, do not give the impression that you are a prepper. When they ask what you need, tell them you need everything they can provide you. This is where you should put your best acting skills to work. The goal is to make them think you are just as unprepared and desperate as your neighbours.

To do this effectively, here are a few things that you can do:

- Do not use devices that would require charging like smartphones and tablets.
- Do not run a generator unless you have a way to silence it.
- When talking to neighbors or FEMA employees, complain about how hungry and thirsty you are.
- When outside at like you have no energy and are suffering. Keep your head low, shuffle your feet, and pretend to be exhausted.
- Do not display any tactical gear or firearms.

If you look like a victim, FEMA will treat you like a victim and be unlikely to raid your home looking for supplies.

Practice Good OPSEC

The cornerstone to being a good prepper is strong Operational Security (OPSEC). No one outside your immediate family should know the extent of your preparedness, and as few people as possible should be aware that you are a prepper. Your neighbors may seem nice now, but when they are starving and desperate, they will be more likely to tell FEMA that you have a stockpile of preps that are ripe for the taking.

Some practical ways to practice good OPSEC are:

- Never post on social media about preparedness.
- Downplay the purpose of any gear you have as being for camping or hunting.
- Keep backup power out of sight.
- Any ham radio antennas should be low profile or portable.
- Do not tell friends or neighbors about prepping.
- Keep all stockpiles or food, water, and gear hidden from view.

OPSEC is challenging, especially when you have children. When it comes to your kids, make sure they know what not to talk about and keep them in the dark about the full scope of your preparedness.

Along with OPSEC is disinformation. You should make those around believe you are not a prepper and are just as unprepared as they are.

Hiding Your Preps

You need to hide your preps from prying eyes. Depending on the scope of your stockpile, this may be exceedingly difficult to accomplish. One way to do this is to create hidden spaces within your home that you can use to hide supplies. There are several ways to do this, but there are four that I will talk about here:

- Hiding preps inside of walls
- Creating a hidden room
- Building a hidden cache under your floors
- Burying drums in your backyard

Hiding Preps in Walls

This is good for items that you may need in an emergency but do not want government agencies to know about. Firearms and ammo, radio equipment, supplies for pandemics, or anything else you want to keep hidden specifically for future emergencies. One good thing about doing this is that you can use EMP cloth to create Faraday cages inside of your walls as well.

Doing this is simple and takes only a few steps:

1. Locate an interior wall to store items in. You can use walls inside of storage rooms or utility rooms and keep them as bare drywall so that you can remove them easily without having to destroy the drywall to get access to the stuff inside.
2. Remove the existing drywall and clean the areas between the studs to remove all dirt and debris.

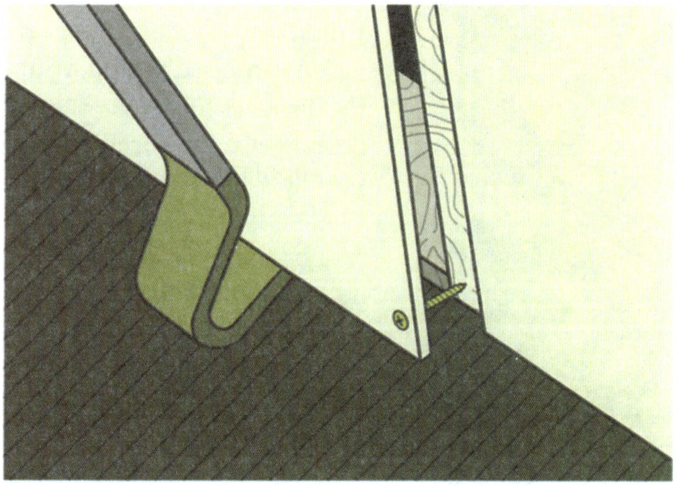

3. Pack the supplies for long term storage.
4. Place them in the spaces between the studs.
5. Secure the drywall by using drywall screws placed between 8 and 16 inches apart. Use a drywall screw bit so that you do not damage the paper when driving the screws.
    a. If you are going to paint the wall, tape, mud, and paint as you normally would. When you need to get access to the supplies inside the wall, you can use a magnet to find the screws to remove the drywall in one piece.
    b. If the wall is in an unfinished area of the home like a basement, garage, storage room, or utility room, you will see and be able to remove the screws easily.

If you do this in rooms that you will be using regularly and people can see, you will want to mud, tape, and paint it so it does not draw any suspicion.

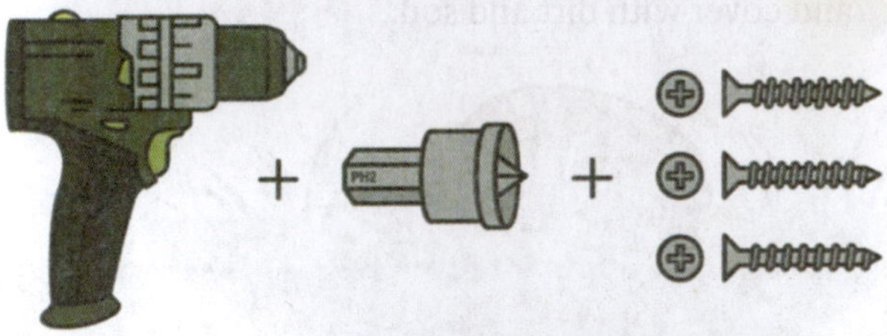

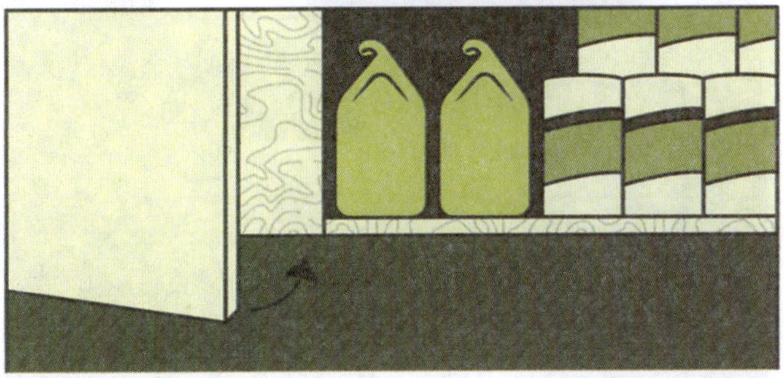

Creating a Hidden Room

This takes a lot more effort and work but can be worthwhile if you have the space and time.

To do this, you will have to follow these basic steps and adjust according to the space you have available.

1. Find a space that can be turned into a hidden room. This can be a closet, under stair space, or by reducing the size of an existing room.
2. Once you know where the room will be, draw up some plans and figure out what the hidden entrance will be. The entrance can be concealed by a mirror or picture, it can be a bookcase made into a door, or anything else you can imagine. Be creative with this.
3. Frame the room with lumber then drywall and paint over the exposed walls.
4. On the interior of the room, line the walls, floor, and ceiling with EMP cloth to create a Faraday cage.

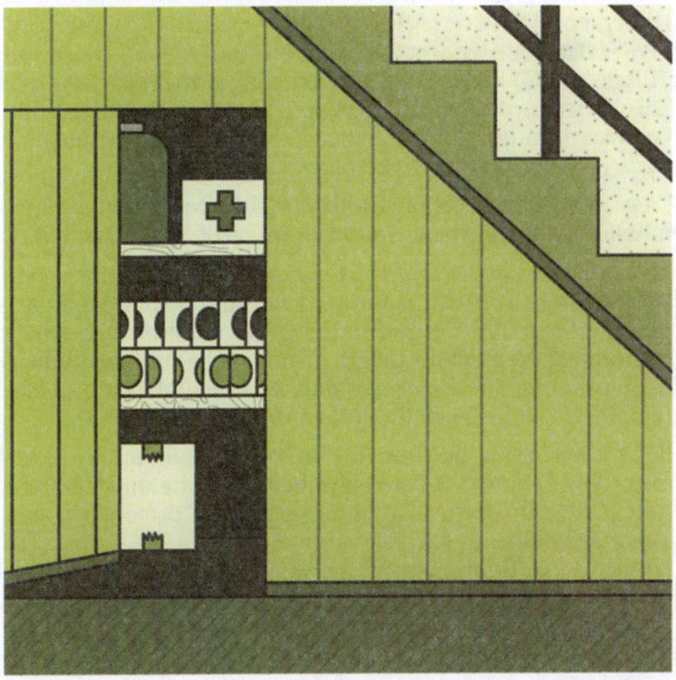

5. Build the doorway and make sure that it does not give away the existence of the room. Make sure that there is some type of hidden lock that keeps people from accidentally getting in.

Building a Hidden Cache Under Your Floors

This is a good option for areas of your home that have area rugs covering them, large furniture, or directly over a crawl space.

To do this follow these basic steps:

1. Remove all the existing rugs or furniture.
2. Layout and cut the opening for the hidden cache.

3. One method you can use is to leave the floorboards loose and have the subfloor be a hinged door. In this case you would have to carefully remove the floorboards, then cut a hole in the subfloor.
4. In the case of a crawlspace, you will have to create a framed area in the crawlspace with walls and a floor that

will be insulated from the cold and have a moisture barrier.

5. Construct a door that is easy to use but is also lockable.

Burying Drums in Your Backyard

This is a good option to consider but you will have to take great care to make sure that everything you place inside is protected from moisture. You can use any size or type of steel or plastic drum you would like. If you are using a steel drum, be mindful of the potential for it to rust.

To make these caches is simple:

1. Find an area where you can dig a hole deep enough to fit the drum.
2. Place the drum inside the hole and fill it with your supplies.
3. Seal the drum with a tight-fitting waterproof lid.

4. Place landscape fabric over the sealed top of the drum and cover with dirt and sod.

One option to consider is to bury the drums underneath the floor of a shed or other outbuilding. This way you do not have to worry about disturbed ground giving away their existence. You can also bury the drums in a garden so that disturbed soil will not look suspicious.

Ham Radio

All preppers need to be ham radio operators. As a ham radio operator, you can monitor the communications going on around you and keep an ear on what the local emergency ham radio groups are doing. Groups like Amateur Radio Emergency Service (ARES), Radio Amateur Civil Emergency Service (RACES) or Community Emergency Response Teams (CERT) will all be coordinating with FEMA and will also be transmitting in the clear without encryption. While you may not hear FEMA's radios, you will hear the amateur radio operators who are helping them.

Staying abreast of the local amateur radio community's transmissions will give you advanced warning of FEMA's activities.

Using LORA devices, you can set up encrypted mesh networks where you can send text messages between smartphones that FEMA cannot intercept or monitor. If you have a group of preppers in the area, you can coordinate a mesh network using these devices and keep each other up to date on FEMA's activities without fear of being discovered.

FEMA may seem like a savior for most people but for preppers they are at the least a nuisance and at the most a direct threat to your survival. While it may seem dishonest to actively deceive and stay one step ahead of FEMA, it is also critical to the protection of the supplies that you have taken so much care in stockpiling.

How to Stay Completely Off the Government's Radar

Governments are supposed to exist for the benefit of the governed. At least, that's the theory that our government was founded upon. I can't necessarily say the same for dictatorships or communist governments. But even the best-meaning governments can lose track of the people's needs and rights, as politicians and policy makers focus on the "bigger picture." In the wake of a disaster, that bigger picture just might be about making themselves, their departments or their political party look good, totally ignoring how their actions affect the people they are supposed to serve.

Considering the extraordinary power that has been granted to FEMA, for use in dealing with disasters, the only true protection any of us have against them, is to stay off their radar. If the government knows we are there, there's just too much of a chance that they're going to be coming around, causing us trouble, in the name of giving us unwanted help. After all, they think they know what we need, better than we know ourselves.

One thing that works in our favor, is that the government would have a lot of people to try and keep track of in such a situation. Government workers being who they are, they're not likely to go looking for people who don't show up on their radar. Going door to door is too much work, besides being a great way of getting yourself shot. So, if we can manage to stay off their radar, we should be okay.

Don't Break the Law

The first thing to do, in order to keep off the government's radar, might seem a bit obvious. It's to avoid breaking the law. Anything you do, which can be seen as breaking the law, may cause the police to look further into your life than you want. Even a minor infraction, in times of crisis, could lead to your home being searched. Should that happen, they'll surely find your prepping stockpile, increasing their curiosity.

All law-enforcement agencies are going to be on high alert during these times, perfectly willing to treat anyone with suspicion. They'll be ready to arrest you anyway, if they think you've broken the law. Adding a stockpile, a good supply of weapons and ammo and the other things we do as preppers set us apart from society, in a way that can seem highly suspicious.

The tricky part about this, is that there are things that we do, as part of prepping, which could be considered as breaking the law in some contexts. Rainwater harvesting is illegal in some states, as the state holds that all rain water belongs to the state. So, if you're going to harvest rainwater in those states, you have to make sure that your system is not visible; perhaps using underground storage tanks.

Avoid Government Functionaries

When FEMA arrives on the scene, it will be ostentatiously with the purpose of offering government aid. That mostly means money, which we are all going to be tempted to get our share of. But you can't get that government money, without filling out the paperwork. That's not only going to let the government know that you're there, but a whole lot more information about you than you probably want them to know.

This is a challenging one, as pretty much all of us are going to be in the position of needing that government aid. Hiding who you are or where you live will most likely end up with them denying you the aid. At the same time, if they catch on to what you are doing, it will pique their curiosity, leading them to investigate you further.

We need to go into this one with our eyes wide open and only after a lot of thought. While it is easy to say right now that we won't go ask the government for help, it's a whole other thing when our families are in need. What can we do to avoid finding ourselves in that position?

Don't Get People Mad

Part of avoiding government functionaries, especially the police, is avoiding making everyday ordinary people, like your neighbors, mad at you. That may be possible, especially with some neighbors; but it is worth investing some work into. People who are upset will call the police for the stupidest reasons, bringing those who have given rise to their ire a headache, as they are forced to deal with the police.

One of the things that might make those difficult neighbors mad is the realization that you're better off than they are. Jealousy causes people to do strange things, and when people are struggling through hard times, seeing others who have things that they don't is enough to cause many of them to fall on the side of calling the authorities, even if they wouldn't during normal times.

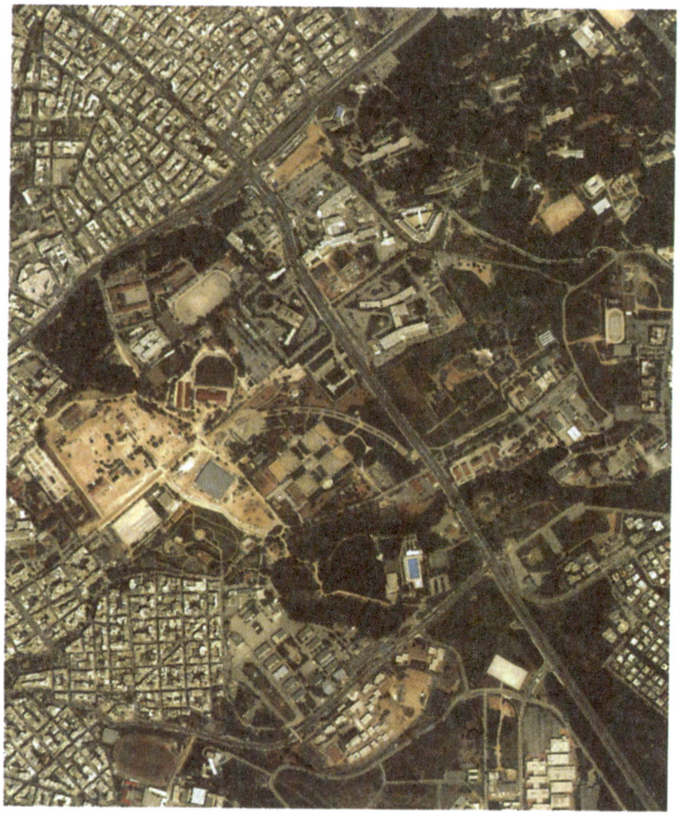

These calls to the police are nothing more than a hassle, during normal times; but we're not talking about normal times. We're talking about trying to stay off the government's radar, during times of crisis. The stakes are much higher than just a visit from the police; that call could lead to you losing everything. So, it's worth putting some effort into keeping a good relationship going with your neighbors, especially during those times of crisis.

Stay Inside

When I look at some people's bug in plans, I have to wonder. I see everything from scavenging from stores and businesses in their towns, to hunting in the countryside. While that can technically still be called bugging in, it's not really under the radar. People will see what those preppers are doing and make comment on it.

There's a reason it's called "bugging in" and part of that reason is that we really need to stay indoors as much as possible, where nosy neighbors aren't going to see what we're doing. While it might be necessary to do some tasks outdoors, like tending to our gardens and even cooking, the more we do outdoors, the more opportunity there is for people to see us and wonder what we are doing.

I'd not only recommend staying indoors, but also doing whatever you can to make it harder for people to see into your home. Full blackout curtains or covering the windows with plywood will keep nosy neighbors from seeing in; but they will also keep daylight out. You're better off with sheers that impede visibility, while still allowing light inside. I have shade screens on my home to cut down on the sunlight coming in and heating up my home. They also make it pretty much impossible to see inside.

Stay Off the Internet

Even if you have electricity, stay off the internet. One of the key ways that the government tracks us all is through the internet. Since about the 1960s, the NSA has been tracking every bit of electronic communications to go over the airwaves, through the phone lines and through the internet. If you say or do anything electronically, you can be sure that the government knows it. during a time when they're trying to keep track of everyone's activity or just find out who is in an area, you can be sure that the NSA will be tasked to find people's electronic footprint.

The only real solution to this is to keep of the internet altogether. It isn't just what you say on the internet that can be tracked, but everything you look at. Any time you visit a website or do a search, it is recorded. If the government wants to look for people who have done similar searches or have been on that website, your name will come up.

Don't Use Your Cellphone

In addition to our cellphones, the government can track us through our cellphones. Cellphones usually have a GPS chip in them, allowing them to accurately locate where they are. Don't assume that information is private, because it isn't. You can easily be tracked, just by following your phone.

But there's so much more to it than that. The modern smartphone is a portable computer, usually able to do just about anything that you can do from your home or laptop computer. That means the NSA is tracking every bit of information flowing into and out of your phone. They'll know what you're up to, even before you do.

If you have to use a phone, buy disposable "burner" phones. In other words, cheap prepaid phones that you can use, then throw away. Be sure to register them with a false name and address. That's about the only way that you can safely communicate, without them being able to use that phone to track you. They'll still be able to record your communications and see what you do on the internet; but once you throw the phone away, they'll lose the ability to track you; and the job of attaching those communications to you becomes a whole lot harder.

Putting It Another Way

An easy way to look at all this is to think of yourself living on a homestead, back in the early 1800s. You don't have any communications or electronics. You don't have contact with your neighbors, because they are too far away. It's just your family and your home.

As long as you live that way, you won't be attracting attention to yourself or doing anything that would interest the government.

Stop Your Phone from Tracking You

The smartphone has become one of the most ubiquitous pieces of technology to be part of the everyday lives of most Americans. According to ConsumerAffairs data, 92 percent of adults have a smartphone as of January 2023, and the average age at which a person gets their first smartphone is 11. For better or worse, this communication technology is here to stay.

An emergency like a power grid failure leading to a long-term blackout, a serious food or water shortage, or urban warfare can leave us all vulnerable to digital attacks while our environment is in a state of chaos. In that case, your top priority should be covering what you and your family need for survival and protection. Part of that preparation should be knowing what to do with your phone in such an emergency.

Communication with people you trust is important in an SHTF scenario, so you will need to keep your phone charged. Any good prepper has a generator at the ready, so that takes care of the phone battery issue. A more affordable alternative to a generator is a phone charger with a hand crank or a small solar panel. Many devices like these double as a flashlight and a radio, making them convenient to have alongside other emergency supplies.

Aside from keeping the battery topped off, many of the suggestions above are helpful in a worst-case scenario.

The more you're willing to sacrifice, the greater the reward when it comes to protecting your privacy. Small steps lead to small gains, and significant steps bring greater advantages. This is true in protecting your privacy in daily life and in dire emergency situations. The most important thing is to be conscious of how your cell phone tries to watch and track you. When you're aware of how big tech is trying to collect your data, it's easier to take steps to prevent it.

Use a Faraday Cage

There was no 5G network when Michael Faraday was experimenting with electromagnetism in the 19th century, but his discoveries are helpful for cell phone users in the 21st century. A Faraday cage is, traditionally, a literal cage that prevents electricity from coming in by being neutrally charged and grounded. The Faraday cage we're talking about isn't really a cage; it's more like a phone case.

Faraday cages (or Faraday bags) for electronic devices like cell phones, tablets, and laptops use materials like silicone-coated fiberglass and metallic fibers to block electromagnetic frequencies from coming inside. These include frequencies outside the visible light spectrum, like satellite signals, radio waves, and cell phone networks, including 5G. A cell phone encased in a good Faraday cage won't get any signal at all and would, theoretically, be untrackable via satellite. Faraday cages are excellent for people who travel a lot and want to protect their privacy.

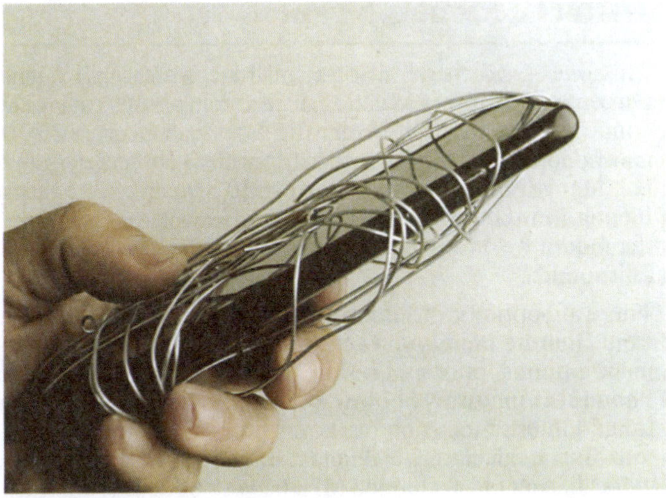

Just Turn It Off

One of the simplest and most effective ways to prevent your phone from tracking you is to simply turn it off when you're not using it. When the phone is turned off, no apps are running in the background, tracking your location or collecting your data.

Alternatively, you could put the phone in airplane mode while it's in your pocket and turn off airplane mode when you need to use it. Airplane mode turns off communications with Wi-Fi and mobile data networks while leaving the phone turned on. While in airplane mode, you can still use some functions like the camera and calculator and music apps like Spotify as long as you have music downloaded rather than streaming it.

Turn Off the GPS

Say you want the advantages of being connected to a 4G or 5G network but don't want your location tracked. In that case, you can simply turn off the GPS function. Your navigation apps won't work, but you can still stream music and videos and use social media via Wi-Fi or your mobile network. This isn't totally private since the apps you use can still collect data while your location is turned off, but it's a small, easy step toward privacy.

Change App Permissions

You may not realize what you permit apps to do when downloading them. There's a lot of fine print that we agree to when we download a new app if we want to use it normally. If you're a little more careful about the permissions you grant, it can give you a more private user experience.

With Android and iOS phones, you can turn permissions for different functions on and off for individual apps. If you go into "Privacy & Security" in the settings of your iPhone and tap "Tracking," you can see the apps that request tracking and turn them on or off. To maximize privacy, turn them all off. Android phones have a similar process, but you need to change them one app at a time. Apps request permission for things like your camera, microphone, calendar, contacts, and location. The fewer permissions you have turned on, the greater the privacy.

Ditch the Smartphone

This one is, admittedly, not a small step. Although a small percentage of the population had a cell phone that could connect to the internet before the iPhone came out in 2007, many people today think the smartphone is absolutely essential. Many users today think they need a smartphone just to function in their jobs or social lives. However, getting by in the modern world without a smartphone isn't as challenging as it sounds.

There are options for "dumb phones" beyond just flip phones from Chinese brands you've never heard of. There are minimalist phone options like the Light Phone II. The Light Phone II is innovative because of its user-friendly form factor and intense focus on privacy. It can call and text and has tools for a calculator, a calendar, an alarm clock, music (it works like an old-fashioned MP3 player), podcasts, and turn-by-turn navigation. There's no social media, web browser, email, camera, or games. It uses an e-ink display similar to an Amazon Kindle, so it's easy on the eyes and has excellent battery life. The Light Phone II also works with most major cell phone networks in the U.S.

A few similar modern cell phones that don't meet the traditional definition of a smartphone include the Techless Wisephone, the Punkt MP02, and the BoringPhone. Also, Nokia still offers a few feature phones that don't do a whole lot other than basic phone functions and come with the durability and reliability that Nokia is famous for.

What to Do if Your Phone Is Hacked

Hackers getting access to other people's phones is a growing problem. Since so much of our digital lives are centralized on our phones, it's an obvious target for hackers. Phone hacking often happens over public Wi-Fi networks, especially unsecured networks with no password protection. An easy way to prevent this is to avoid unsecured public Wi-Fi. If you follow some of our other advice, like turning off your phone or leaving it in airplane mode when you're not using it, you're already avoiding public Wi-Fi without taking any extra steps.

A few other small steps you can take to protect your phone from being hacked are keeping the phone locked with a passcode, using biometrics and two-factor authentication, and avoiding sketchy apps from suspicious developers.

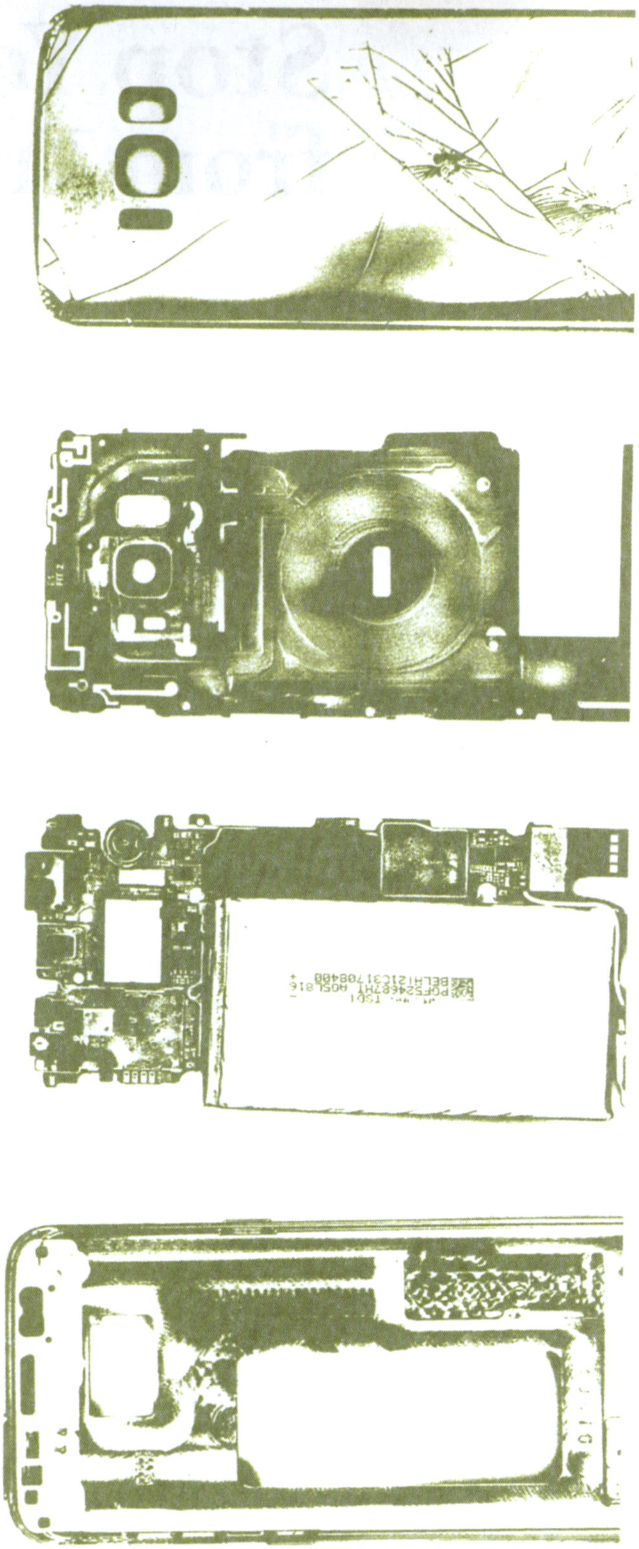

A Foolproof OPSEC Guide

How would you know if someone was invading your life and uncovering all your sensitive information? Thanks to social media, our life becomes a stage for the world to see, even if we do not participate in it. Even having forgone social media completely, you are surrounded by people who snap photos of everything, maybe even inside your home during a party or gathering.

The average person could really use a boost for their Operational Security or OPSEC. Whether we are talking about our daily lives or in a worst-case scenario where you have decided to bug in and protect your family from the dangers of the outside world, your OPSEC is paramount.

OPSEC is a Vietnam War era term. The concept has been around for 50 years. An American counterintelligence team known as The Purple Dragon was responsible for coining the term and defined it as follows: "The ability to keep knowledge of our strengths and weaknesses away from hostile forces is paramount".

OPSEC begins with categorization of information. You must understand the sensitivity of your information, both physical and digital, to protect it. For instance, your first name is information that you share with most of the world. Most people will divulge their first name when they meet someone. However, telling someone their home address at the first meeting is a little different. More sensitive still would be handing them a sheet of paper with their bank account information on it.

We hold onto a variety of information and to protect it, we must understand what needs protecting. Governments do this by categorizing the information under specific names. The most common designations are confidential, secret, and top secret.

Confidential information is the type that could be expected to cause damage to your personal security, finances, and wellbeing.

Secret information is the type that could cause serious damage to your personal security, finances, and wellbeing.

Top Secret information is the type that could cause exceptionally grave damage to your personal security, finances, and wellbeing.

We should all apply this type of categorization to the photos and videos that we share with the world, too. It's easy to understand how sharing your social security number can have serious implications but what about sharing a picture of your entertainment center or your new car? OPSEC is about restricting the kind of information we share with the world.

OPSEC with Covert Storage

Another area where we must be mindful of OPSEC is how we store things in our home. By this point you have come to realize that a bug in plan requires a certain number of resources in house. You need to store plenty of food, water, and other goods. Where and how you store these can either keep them out of sight visitors or inspire questions.

"Why Do You Have So Much Food?"

Avoid the rigors of answering questions like these by being more thoughtful about where things go. All your food does not have to be piled into your pantry. It can be spread throughout the home. In fact, this is arguably the better move because should your home be raided you don't want everything to be in one place. Make it hard on em'!

Covert storage can be a huge help when it comes to properly storing all of your bug in needs throughout the home. Traditional storage locations can work well but covert ones both hide your supplies and make them harder to find if someone goes snooping. There are many options and the more creative you are the longer the list gets.

- False Walls
- Under Furniture
- Concealed Safes
- Inside Furniture (like couches)
- Hollowed Out Books
- False Containers
- Under the Staircase

Denying access is another great technique for maintaining OPSEC. In the same way you keep sensitive digital data behind a password, you can keep all your physical storage behind a locked door in a room that is not being used. This denies access to anyone who might stumble upon the room by accident or with ill intent.

This room can become your "office" and that designation will almost instantly take the mystery out of what is hidden behind the door. Meanwhile, it can be stacked floor to ceiling with 5-gallon buckets filled with food and water storage.

Mind the Trash

OPSEC happens inside out your home. It even happens in your garbage. Shredding documentation and sensitive material packaging is a great way to keep your sensitive information safe.

If you have packages and boxes from buying preps or firearms, these boxes should also be burned or shredded. To sit on the curb with the rest of your trash is to give away far too much information about your intentions and what is inside your home.

Beware the Tiny Spies

It took me years to realize that my own son was one of the most devastating forces working against my OPSEC. My son would tell our neighbors, family, and some of his friends all about the things in our home. Even though we kept many of those things hidden from the eyes of visitors, our little guy knew about them and shared some confidential information.

Be careful what you let your kids know and see. They will devastate your OPSEC. You can also sit them down and explain the concept of top-secret information, allowing them to better understand what they should and should not share but also the reasons why.

Now you are ready to build an OPSEC plan. Your plan should answer three simple questions.

- What are you concealing?
- How could it be exposed?
- What can you do to prevent that?

Let's look at how you manage your OPSEC plan to make it effective in everyday life. Let's go back to food storage as an example.

1. **CONCEALING** – Your plan should identify what it is you are concealing. In this case, it's your food storage.
2. **EXPOSURE** – In your OSPEC plan understand how you can be exposed. In this instance, someone could find your 6 months' worth of food storage and ask questions.
3. **PREVENT** – Once you have identified the potential for exposure you need to take the proper action to avoid this. In the case of your food storage, you could hide it behind a locked door.

What else must you conceal for you're the sake of OPSEC?

Apply the conceal, exposure, and prevent process to all types of sensitive information and resources. Audit these processes with time as you might find that you need to upgrade where your store your guns to keep them concealed or how you prevent people from gaining access to sensitive data. We used to be able to shred all our mail. Now most of it is digital. Your OPSEC plan has to change with the times.

What's Your Cover?

No one is perfect. What happens if your OPSEC fails you? What if a neighbor stumbles upon a room filled with gas masks and #10 cans? Do you have a cover story prepared? Maybe that extra space turned into a free storage room for your church and their kitchen.

You can get as creative as you like. Just make sure that you have an out if someone finds your preps, your prepper library, or has questions about something your child told them. Also, be sure it makes sense!

I want to remind you that it's easy to get intimidated by military terms and tactics because we often feel like that stuff is above our pay grade. Most of the time these are just systems or processes that have been more thoroughly explored because the consequence of failure is much greater. If a hacker gets your bank account info that can be a big problem for you. If our enemy gains access to our nuclear launch codes and protocols that could potentially be an end of the world scenario.

Your personal OPSEC should be easier to manage than that of the US Military. With a little thought, planning, and storage considerations, you can have all the supplies you need to execute on your bug in plan without anyone ever knowing your intentions.

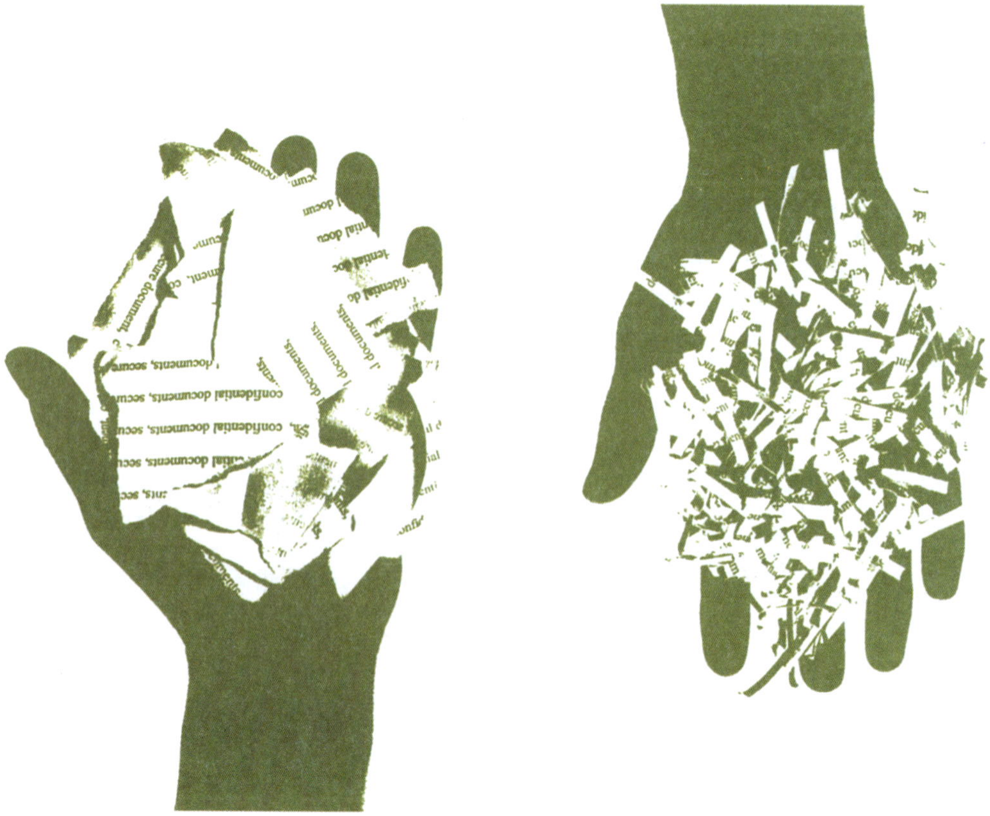

How to Hide from Thermal Vision

Thermal vision cannot see through walls. It can see through things like smoke, fog, and even densely wooded areas. However, our entire bug-in plan is not intent on us staying indoors 24/7. Duties like caring for chickens, tending gardens, and even some form of security will require that we leave the home for a moment. That is when we are susceptible to thermal vision.

If someone with resources is hunting you, they are using thermal vision. This passive infrared technology requires no light to be effective and merely depends on your body giving off its natural heat signature. There is a reason it dethroned night vision technology many years ago.

The good and also the bad part of thermal vision is its accessibility. A basic thermal scope for your weapon can run between $1-2,000 and a handheld thermal imager can be had for under $1000 dollars. So, it doesn't have to be a three-letter agency spying on you with thermal vision.

Drones can also be equipped with thermal imaging cameras, and these are around the same price point as a thermal scope. What's most unnerving is you may not hear or see a drone with thermal imaging while it is spying down on you.

Is there any chance of hiding from a group that is hunting you if they are using thermal vision? The answer is YES. There are many tactics for dealing with thermal vision and we are going to explore them all in this chapter.

Hiding Starts with Effective Cover

Your body is always radiating heat. Unless you're dead. To evade thermal vision, you need to put something between you and the thermals. There are several materials that perform well when it comes to blocking your heat signature.

Before we get into the various materials that can be used to hide from thermal vision, I think it is important to talk about the Columbia clothing company and their Omni Heat technology. While this line of clothing was not built for anti IR operations, the mylar lining will do that.

The Omni Heat line puts out coats, boots, shoes, pants, gloves and even hats. They were designing a line of clothing that can be used to retain more of your body heat. Columbia accomplished this and they inadvertently created tech that would simultaneously decrease the wearers heat signature.

Dirt

The cheapest and easiest material that you can use to thwart thermal vision is going to be dirt. A simple dirt mount shelter or even a trench that is covered using other IR reflective materials is more than enough to conceal your heat signature from thermal vision.

Dirt is usually overlooked as a tool for dealing with thermal vision. The earth is cool and if you can hide in it or under it, you will stay out of sight.

Glass

Glass completely conceals you from thermal vision if you have a large enough piece to get behind. Despite glass' efficacy it is very impractical to carry around. So, this is not a material that I would recommend for hiding from thermal vision.

The only instance where glass can be an extremely effective means of concealment is if you are growing food in a greenhouse. Managing the food growing in a greenhouse means that you are invisible while you work as the glass will diffuse your heat signal completely.

Mylar

The most affordable and easy to carry option for hiding from thermal vision is Mylar. Space blankets or mylar blankets are so effective because they are designed to hold onto your body heat and keep it close to your body. This makes them essential in your survival kit, first aid kit and winter car kits.

Mylar blankets can be purchased in a variety of forms. In most survival kits you find a small folded up Mylar blanket that is both compact and effective. However, you can buy heavy duty survival blankets that will not pack down as small but will have a fortified outer layer, usually green, and these also have grommets on the corners of the blanket. This makes it as much a tarp for shelter as it is a blanket.

Building a Mylar tarped shelter inside of a dirt trench would make you invisible to thermal vision as long as you did not add heat to the shelter like fire. This is as simple as staking down the corners of the mylar blanket over the trench and climbing in. It would also hold your heat really well!

Copper Mesh

After some research we found that copper mesh is another material that is easy to come by and has the ability to diffuse your body's natural heat. Clothing can be modified, sleeping bags can be modified and lined with copper mesh.

This method is more focused on the DIY crowd, but it is undoubtedly an effective way to hide your heat signature from thermal vision.

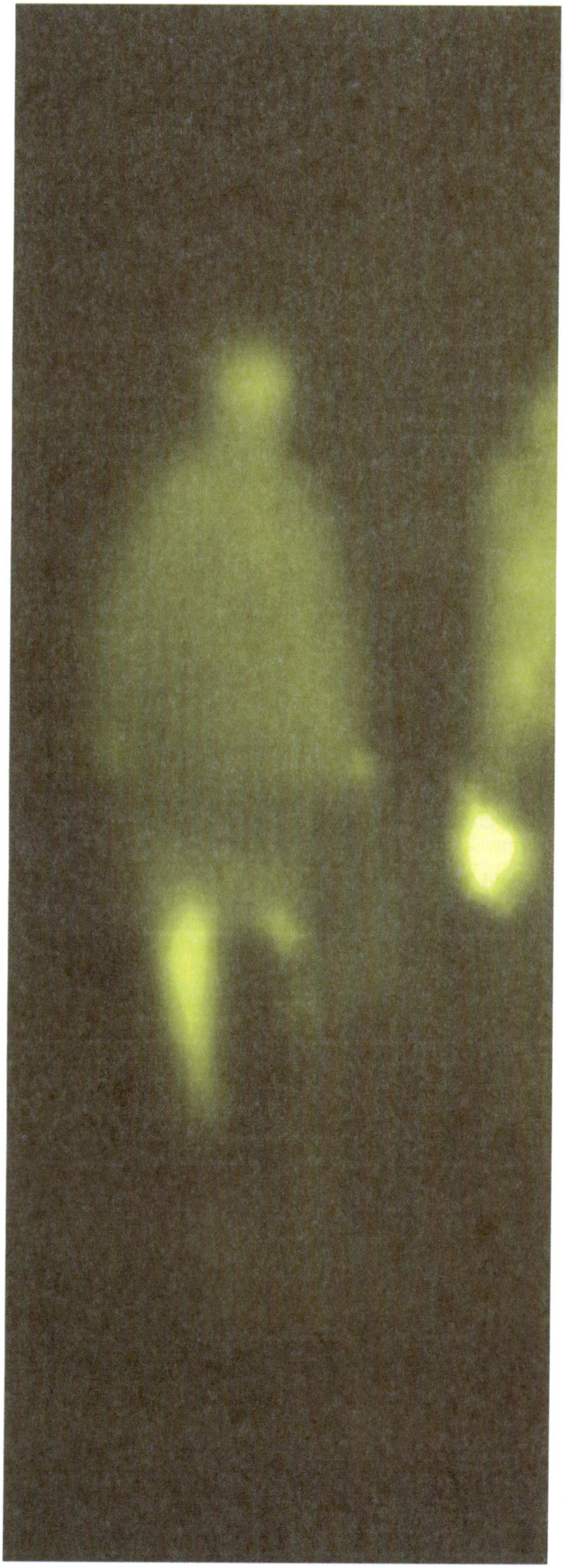

Thermal Vision Decoys

If you were being tracked in the daytime, you might run some tracks in one direction before turning them around in the other. You could hop a fence or jump on a road then step back onto the ground to put them off your track.

Trackers are looking for a certain sign. It might be footprints in the ground, it might be broken branches along a trail. When you are being tracked by someone using thermals, their primary sign is going to be heat signature.

Creating several decoy camps with small fires is a great way to throw a search party off. Five to ten fires spread throughout the woods might be a struggle to get started but it will create multiple heat signatures that will all require inspection. It could also distract from your own smaller heat signature if you are moving under cover.

By shielding your heat signature and creating a landscape of decoys you will have a better chance of going undetected.

Thermal Counter Tracking

As I mentioned, there are many ways that you can thwart thermally vision. Most people will think about using thermal blankets or hiding behind cover. However, you can also use your own thermal vision against those hunting you.

The weakness to exploit in those using thermals is the false sense of technological superiority. While this tech is accessible, it is also rare in the civilian armory. So, you might be dealing with people who think they own the darkness and are untouchable at night. Those tracking you may not be covering their own heat signature.

Since they must move to find you and you simply must stay put to stay hidden, if you have thermals, too, you have the upper hand. Then you go from the prey to the predator.

Thermal vision is a much different technology than night vision. Night vision is tech that is very effective at gathering light. It can also be overwhelmed by light. When you are using thermal vision there is no need for light of any kind. Remember, it is reading heat signatures.

Hiding from this tech is all about managing heat and you can do that in several ways. There are materials and methods you can use to confuse those trying to track you down. Also, don't forget about the possibility of using your own thermal vision to see them coming long before they see you.

Technology, both military and otherwise, is going to continue to improve. It is not up to us to be on the cutting edge of it all or to go broke trying to combat it. However, understanding how this tech works will keep you from becoming a victim of it. Thermal tech is no different.

How to Avoid CCTV Tracking You

CCTV cameras are everywhere.

While the 'official' reason for CCTV cameras is for public safety, many preppers may not have thought about the role CCTV cameras will play in a future disaster scenario.

Just because the power grid has gone down doesn't mean that CCTV cameras won't be up and running either. It's possible that many people, businesses, or government organizations will still keep their surveillance cameras running because of backup generators.

In any case, CCTV cameras may become more prominent in a disaster situation than they already are. The authorities would surely rely on them to help keep track of the population in the event of martial law, while people may set up surveillance cameras around their property and even use them to try and suspiciously spy on their neighbors.

Naturally, you won't want to be tracked by CCTV no matter who's doing it. Here's how to avoid CCTV cameras from tracking you in a disaster scenario where you're forced to bug-in.

Keep an Eye Out for Them

The first step to avoid CCTV cameras tracking you is to be aware of them. This way, you can try and avoid them, which is the easiest way to avoid being tracked.

Trying to tamper with CCTV cameras to disable them or attempting to hide your face could get you in serious trouble in a disaster. Tampering with government cameras either in everyday life or in a disaster martial law scenario will be a surefire way to get arrested, and doing the same to privately owned cameras could initiate a violent response from the owner(s) if you get caught.

That's why the safest and easiest way to avoid being tracked by CCTV cameras is to know where they are and to find alternate routes to get to where you need to go that don't have cameras to your knowledge.

If you can't find alternate routes to avoid walking by cameras, you can try other methods like sticking close to the wall to go 'behind' it or to watch the camera move and run right past it when it's looking away.

How to Avoid Being Recognized by CCTV Cameras

Let's say that it's impossible for you to avoid being caught by a CCTV camera. How can you avoid being recognized?

Cover Up Your Face

As simple as it sounds, the easiest way to avoid being recognized by most CCTV cameras is to cover up your face and head with a hoodie, scarf, hat, or sunglasses. The more you obscure your facial features the more difficult it will be for cameras to identify you.

There's a reason I say most cameras here. There have been tremendous advancements in facial recognition technology over the last several years that have made it possible for cameras to recognize people even when they are wearing coverings. The reason for this is because these cameras learn to recognize people by other factors (such as their shape or body movement) and are also interconnected with other surveillance systems to make it easier for the authorities to track people).

That being said, simply wearing a covering over your face should be enough to keep your identity hidden from most cameras. The best advice I would give here is to cover yourself up as best as you can without looking inconspicuous. If you're wearing a full mask, for example, you're likely going to get in trouble with the authorities. Instead, stick to sunglasses, scarves, or hats that are worn by people in everyday life and try to keep your head down.

Attempting to change your appearance, such as changing your hair color or wearing a wig or applying a significant amount of makeup, is a more drastic measure you could take but also one that could land you in trouble if you are caught.

Wear an IR LED

Another idea is to wear an IR LED on a hat over your head. An IR LED is an infrared light-emitted device that produces light in the infrared range of the electromagnetic radiation spectrum. That's a longer way of saying that they produce infrared light, which some surveillance cameras use as well in order to capture images in low light conditions.

So long as the security cameras in question do not operate using infrared light, you can hide your face by wearing an IR light on your hat or baseball cap. Otherwise, however, wearing an IR LED will only make your face easier to detect.

Take note that an IR LED light is a countermeasure to security cameras that is easily detectable. It might flag you to government agencies, which could only cause them to start tracking you. That's why I would only use IR LED lights around privately owned security cameras instead.

Disabling CCTV Cameras

Disabling or blinding CCTV cameras is actually not as easy as you may think, and like I mentioned above, it carries inherently more risk than attempting to merely avoid the cameras or keeping most of your face hidden.

Use a Flashlight

It's possible to use a flashlight to obscure a security camera. The problem is you have to keep the flashlight aimed directly at the camera lens directly, and if you move the flashlight at all you'll reveal your identity.

The only scenario where the flashlight technique could work is if you're trying to sneak other people past the cameras. You can hide your face, aim the flashlight at the camera, and then the other people you're trying to sneak past can quickly run past the camera.

Use a Red Laser

You've probably seen this in spy movies, where a secret agent infiltrates the mansion of the evil villain and uses a red laser to knock out the security cameras as he works his way down the hall. This is possible in real life, but it's also not as easy as it appears.

That's because you need to be extremely precise for this method to work. You need to shine the laser directly into the lens and hold it steady for the entire duration that you want to keep the camera obscured.

Cover the Camera

Perhaps the most basic method to 'disable' a camera is simply to cover up the lens, such as with a hat, shaving cream, paint, or anything that can obscure the lens. This is only a short-term solution, because eventually the owner of the camera will notice it, and you need to make sure you hide your face while in the process of blinding the camera.

Use a Camera Jammer

A camera jammer is a small device that emits a microwave pulse to interrupt the electrical signals used in the security cameras. This method only works, however, if you know the broadcast frequency of the camera.

Cut the Wires

This is another method you've likely seen in movies too, where the hero hugs the wall as he sneaks in behind the camera and then uses a knife or pliers to cut the wire. This can work, but some cameras rely on backup generators to stay running, so it may or may not work depending on the camera used. Cutting the wires may trigger an alarm on other cameras as well, so it can be risky.

This will also be regarded as intentful destruction of property, and will land you in serious trouble if you are caught.

It is possible to avoid being tracked by CCTV cameras in a duster scenario. The easiest way to know where the cameras are and avoid them. If you can't avoid the cameras, try to keep your face as covered as best as you can without looking too suspicious.

Attempting to disable or blind the cameras should only be done as an absolutely last resort method if absolutely necessary because of the severe consequences you can run into if you're caught and exposed.

DIY PROJECTS

An Affordable Rainwater Collection System for Your Roof Water

Constructing a rainwater collection system is very straightforward and requires easily obtained materials and basic hand tools. It also requires limited DIY and building skills, making this project accessible to everyone.

Tools and Materials

Everything you need to build this system can be found at your local hardware store or online.

Tools Required

- Small hand saw (like a drywall saw or hack saw blade) or sharp utility knife to cut the plastic lid. You can also use heavy duty hand shears.
- Cordless drill and drill bits. Drill bits need to be the same size as the outside diameter of the PVC pipe and the water spigots. For example, the outside diameter of the ¾" threaded end of the water spigots and ¾" PVC pipe is a little over 1" so if you use a 1" drill bit you can make a hole of the appropriate size for a tight fit.
- Tape Measure

Materials

- One or more trash cans (In my case I used 20 Gallon cans but you can use larger cans or sunsitute water barrels instead)
- One ¾" water spigot for each barrel with ¾" threaded nuts to secure to the wall of the can. You may also need a rubber washer or plubmers putty to prevent leaking. There are water spigots which are specifically designed for use on rain barrels which are available online.
- ¾" or 1" PVC pipe to connect the rain barrels and for overflow. 1 or 2 feet of pipe would be more than enough.
- One - 90-degree PVC elbow of the same diameter as the PVC pipe.
- Enough wire screen door screen material to cover the top of one of the cans.
- One tube of exterior silicone caulk for sealing around the PVC pipes.

Instructions

1. Locate an area for the rainwater collection system that is underneath a downspout and large enough to contain all the barrels you plan on using.
2. In this example, we are using garage cans for our rain barrels. First, we need to attach the spigots to each barrel. To do this, drill a hole about two inches up from the bottom of the can (Fig. 1) . The hole must be large enough to accommodate the male end of the spigot.
3. Install the spigot as per the manufacturer's instructions (Fig 2). In my case, I used two threaded nuts on either side of the wall of the trash can with a bit of plumbers putty to prevent leaks.

Fig. 1

Fig. 2

4. If you use multiple barrels in your system, you'll need to install a PVC pipe to connect the barrels. Drill holes to the outside diameter of the PVC pipe a few inches down from the top of the can (Fig. 3).
5. The last barrel in the system needs to have an overflow installed to ensure that the barrels do not overfill. To do this, drill a hole in the side of the can at the same level as the holes for the connections between the cans.
6. Use a small section of PVC pipe and a 90-degree elbow to make the overflow. Connect the short piece of PVC and the 90-degree elbow together and place it into the hole (Fig. 4). Secure it inside and out with caulk.

Fig. 3

Fig. 4

7. Cut a hole in the lid of one of the trash cans that will fit the downspout (Fig. 5). You'll need to ensure that the hole is positioned in such a way that when the rain barrel is in place, the downspout will run directly into the can. The best way to do this is to take the downspout and trace the profile onto the lid. Then cut it with a knife, saw, or shears.
8. Cut a section of screen large enough to fit over the top of the can. Place the screen over the top and use the lid to secure the screen in place (Fig. 6). Trim the excess around the can's lid. This screen is to keep debris out of the can from the gutter so you only need to have it on the first can in the system.

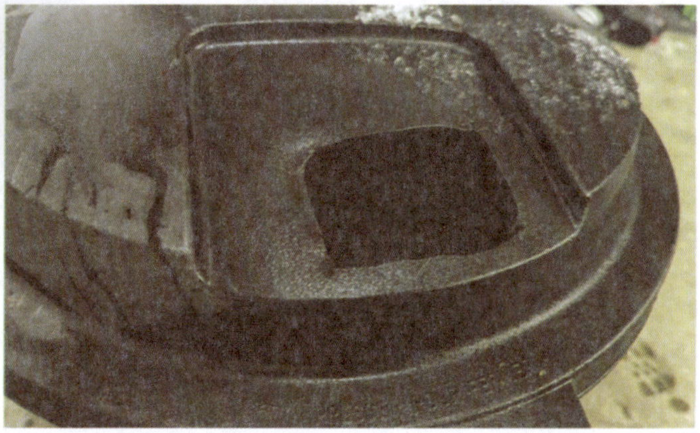

Fig. 5

9. Place the cans in their final location. You may need to elevate them to use the spigots effectively to drain the water. You can either build a platform for the barrels or use whatever you have on hand. In this case, I used milkcrates to hold the cans at a height that would be appropriate for the effective use of the spigot (Fig. 7).
10. Connect the cans with PVC pipe cut to size so that about an inch of pipe will stick into each can (Fig. 8). Secure these pipes with caulk inside and out.

Fig. 6

Fig. 7

Fig. 8

11. Trim and install the downspout.

Once the system is installed, you only need to wait until it rains and the barrels fill.

Considerations and Modifications

In the warmer months, you'll need to monitor your rainwater system to ensure mosquitos can not get inside to lay eggs. You can do this by sealing around the downspout. You will also need to check the screen from time to time to clear any debris that has accumulated.

You could install a filter to the spigot if you find one with a threaded end that can connect to the spigot. There are several water filters that are designed to be screwed onto disposable water bottles, and you could use one of them to screw onto the end of the spigot. If you do this, it is critical not to leave these filters on when the temperature gets below freezing. If water filters freeze, they can be damaged and not able to be used anymore.

The No-Electricity Coil Water Heater

In a survival situation, a warm water supply is a luxury we may not be able to afford. However, with a little grit, creativity, and determination, you can build your own Firewood-Powered coil water heater.

This chapter will walk you through how to use raw materials like firewood, soft copper tubes, and other easily accessible prepper materials, ensuring you have a dependable source of hot water for cooking, cleaning, and staying warm.

Choose a Simple yet Convenient Design

The first step will be choosing the most convenient design for survival. I decided to use a wood-heated water-heater system because all the required materials will be inexpensive, convenient, and easily accessible at home.

Materials and Tools

Start by assembling the following resources:

- soft copper tubing (approximately 10-25 feet)
- fire-resistant gloves
- firewood
- a metal frame or support structure
- two rubber hoses
- pipe cutter or hacksaw
- hose clamps
- a clean steel drum
- bricks or rocks
- a metal pot or plastic basin or an old water tank
- water source
- thermometer

Instructions

1. **Cut the Steel Drum**

Using a hacksaw, cut the ends of the steel drum to have a hollow design. Here, I used a 2-foot (60 cm) steel drum because I wanted to increase the number of loops around the tank.

2. **Coil the Copper Tube**

Take the copper tube and carefully coil it, ensuring the coils are tight and evenly spaced, resembling a spiral. In my case, I used a 25-foot (7.6-meter) long soft copper tube to increase the number of coils around the steel drum.

The copper tube allowed me to have 20 loops on the metal drum. These loops were enough to capture maximum heat transfer, via conduction, when the metal drum became hot.

3. **Set Up the Fire Pit and Water Basin Area**

Find a stable base using rocks for your metal drum. This

place will be used as the fire pit and should be sturdy enough to hold the steel drum. My base was large enough to accommodate the coil and support the weight of the metal drum.

Next, set up another spot that will hold your storage tank. My spot was approximately 4 feet (1.2 meters) away, to protect the tank from the firewood's heat.

4. **Prepare the Water Storage Plastic Basin**

Create two openings along the side of the heavy-duty water storage basin, just big enough for your copper tubing to fit through. I used a ½-inch copper tube. So, I made three ½-inch holes, two on the side and one for a ½-inch water tap. This tap will allow convenient use of the hot water.

Remember to seal off any gaps with heat-resistant putty or clay. I used clear caulk because it is a poor conductor of heat and will prevent heat from escaping, keeping the water hot for longer.

5. **Secure the Ends of the Copper Coil with Hose Clamps**

Carefully attach the hose clamps to both ends of the copper coil. Hose clamps are effective in keeping the coil in place and preventing any leaks.

6. **Position the Copper Coil Over the Fire**

Place the coiled copper tube on the firewood in the metal drum above the fire pit. However, you need to ensure the coil's ends are protruding from the metal drum, offering an inlet and outlet for the water. Also, you must adjust the height of the metal drum to control the intensity of the heat. Ensure the tubing is not in direct contact with flames but is close enough to absorb the radiant heat.

7. **Connecting the System**

Attach the two ends of the copper coil to the hose and the other ends to the heavy-duty plastic basin, making sure the connections are secure to avoid any leakages. I secured the connection with hose clamps and elevated the plastic basin to allow for natural water flow.

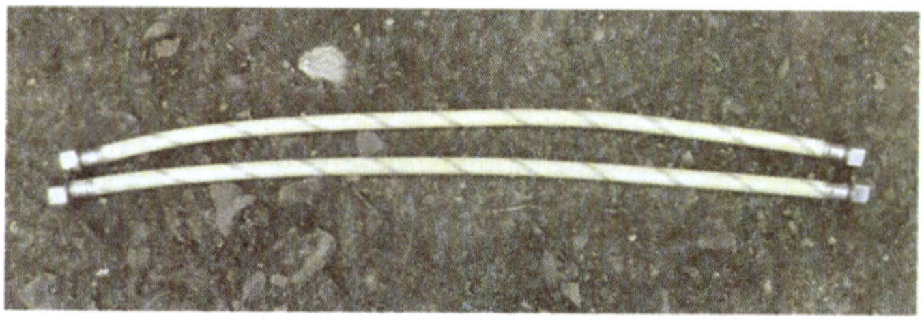

I used insulated ½-inch hose connectors to prevent any loss of heat during the exchange process.

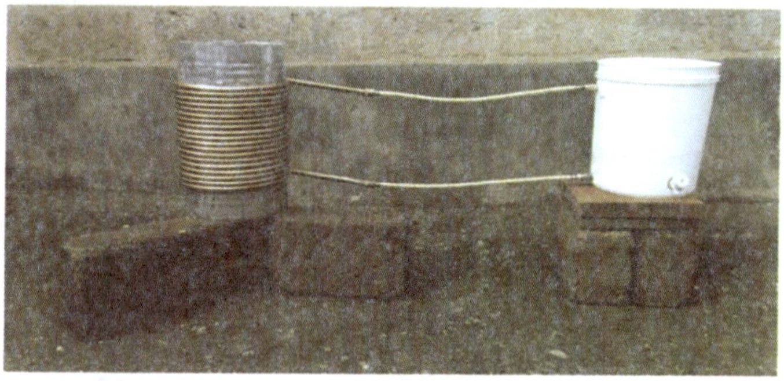

8. **Filling the Plastic Basin**

Using your hosepipe, fill up the plastic basin with water. But you should allow the water to flow through the coil to ensure the system is working properly. Ideally, this water should be above the outlet, ensuring the copper coil is filled with water.

9. **Building the Fire**

Build a fire inside the metal drum, making sure it is beneath it and heating the water (Fig. 1). However, this fire should not be so close to the water storage plastic basin that it poses a safety risk.

Keep feeding the fire with dry firewood to maintain a steady flame. As the fire heats up, it will transfer heat to the tubing and warm up the water inside the plastic basin.

10. **Monitoring the System**

Keep an eye on your system to ensure the fire keeps burning

Fig. 1

and the water keeps flowing. In about 20-30 minutes, you should begin to get hot water out of the other end of your coil.

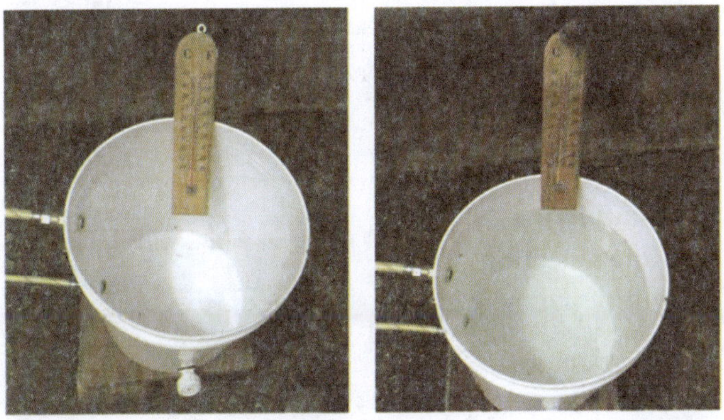

Always monitor the water temperature with a thermometer.

You now have hot water for cooking, cleaning, or even bathing.

11. Covering the System

Once you are certain that the system is functioning correctly, cover it with a heat-resistant tarpaulin or any other insulation material to conserve heat and protect it from the elements.

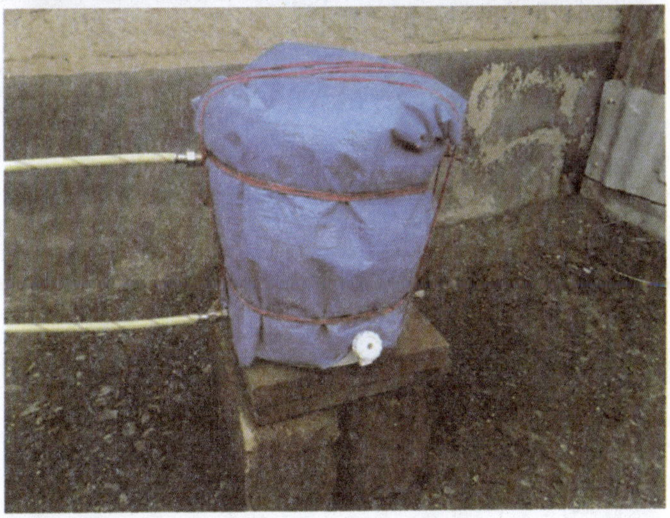

The Pressurized Backyard Well

This project aims to guide you through the construction of a system that not only guarantees a constant water supply, but does so with the autonomy necessary for any self-reliant lifestyle, providing you with an indispensable tool for any prepping scenario. With easily accessible materials such as PVC pipes, a well pump, and a few other common homestead tools, we're about to embark on a journey to create a self-sufficient water source.

Materials and Tools

Tools

- digging bar
- spade
- manual auger
- 2 pipe wrenches

Materials

- 15 to 20 feet 4-inch (10 cm) diameter PVC pipe
- 20-foot ¾-inch PPR Pipe or UPVC pipe, depending on the available one
- galvanized iron elbows for connecting the pump
- PVC pipe cutter
- a 1-horsepower electrical pump that pumps water up to 35 meters. I used one from Ingco manufacturers
- a long electrical wire for the pump

Instructions

1. Site Selection

The first and most important step is selecting an ideal spot for your well.

Remember that your location should be a well-drained area, away from potential contamination sources. This should include far-from-septic tanks and drain fields. Also, choose a site that is higher than the surrounding area to prevent surface water from entering the well.

2. Mark the Spot

Using a wooden stake, mark the exact location where you want to dig your well. This will guide you through the drilling process.

3. Dig the Well

Depending on the area's soil type, you can use a post-hole digger or a manual auger to dig the well. Continue drilling until you reach the water table.

Surprisingly, I only had to dig a 13-foot (4-meter) hole. This is because the water table at my location was higher. But in your case, you might have to go deeper or shallower.

The deeper you dig, the more likely you'll hit a sufficient underground water source.

The deeper you dig, the more likely you'll hit a sufficient underground water source.

Note that that the size of the hole should be slightly larger than the diameter of your well casing. I dug a 6-inch (15 cm) diameter hole for the convenience of installing the well casing.

4. Installing the Casing

Using a 4-inch (10 cm) diameter PVC pipe as the casing for my well will prevent the walls of my well from collapsing and also protect it from contamination.

Before I installed the casing into the hole, I attached a well screen to the bottom of the casing.

a. First, I drilled several ⅛-inch holes in the PVC pipe.

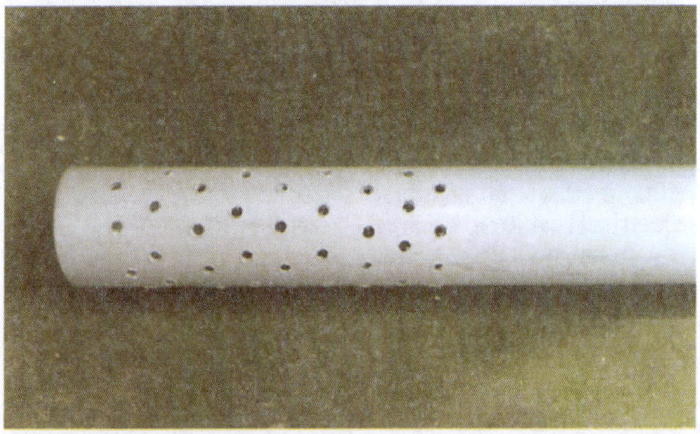

b. Next, I attached the well screen using heavy-duty goose wire mesh netting.

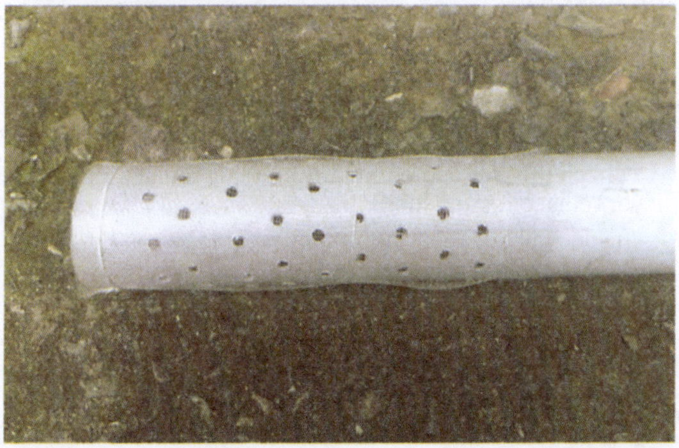

c. Once the well screen was secure, I placed the casing into the hole and secured it in place with gravel.

d. The well screen helps keep out debris and contaminants while allowing water to flow through easily.

5. Sealing the Well

Seal the upper few feet of the well with clay and concrete to prevent surface water from seeping into the well.

6. Set Up the Pump

In the next step, I gathered the necessary plumbing fittings. This included some PVC pipes and a pump.

Take the solar-powered water pump near the well, then secure it inside the well casing.

In my case, I used a ¾-inch high-quality water pipe to fix it to

the water pump to the casing's top, as shown below.

After that, I connected a ¾-inch pipe and ran it from the pump.

Here's how it turned out.

7. **Power Up the Pump**

In this step, I used a long (100 feet or 30 meters) electrical cable to power the pump and draw water from the well.

8. **Testing and Maintenance**

With everything in place, it's time to test your pressurized backyard well. Turn on the pump and check for water flow.

Note:

Regular maintenance is essential to keep your system functioning optimally:

- Check the well screen for any clogs or damage, and clean or replace it as needed.
- Inspect all connections and pipes for leaks, and make sure the pump is in good working condition.

How to Build an Electricity-Free Fridge

A refrigerator that keeps things cool without needing constant electricity is made possible through non-electric refrigeration, such as the Coolgardie safe.

These types of fridges work by using evaporative cooling, a simple yet effective concept. They show us a clever and eco-friendly way from the past that still makes sense today.

Materials and Tools

A modified Coolgardie Safe with Enhanced Convection Cooling can be made using the following materials:

Wooden Frame

- A 2-inch x 3-inch Standard Pine Construction Lumber, which is equivalent to 50mm x 75mm. You will need a total of 12 x 1m sections to complete the frame that is a 1m x 1m x1m cube. Most lumber yards sell lengths of around 3 metres or 10 feet. You will need 4 such lengths.

- A circular saw or handsaw to cut the lumber.

- Screws or nails at least 3" inches or 75mm long. It is recommended to use 4-inch nails or 100mm screws as they add strength to the frame. If you are using screws, it is recommended to do a pilot hole through the outer pieces of lumber. Hardware shops sell these screws or nails in packets or boxes containing quantities of around 40 to 80 pieces. Two packets will complete the project, with some to spare.

Insulated Panels (OSB and Wood Plane Shavings)

- Oriented Strand Board (OSB) sheets with a size of 8 feet x 4 feet or 2440mm x 1220mm. For double insulation, use at least 2 full sheets with a half-inch thickness (12mm thick).

- Wood plane shavings or other insulating materials such as peanut shells, ground polystyrene, or dried garden mulch for filling cavities in the double insulation frame.

- Adhesive or screws to attach the OSB panels to the frame. It is recommended to use screws as they make it easier to replace a panel if needed. Buy 30mm screws, you will need around 50 to complete the project. One 250ml bottle of cold wood glue will also suffice.

Evaporative Cooling Section

- Standard chicken coup wire with small enough holes to keep the charcoal in and allow easy airflow. You will need approximately 2 square meters for the project.

- For easy airflow, use an offcut piece of white shade net. It's a 20% shade net. You will need approximately 2 square meters for the project.

- For better results, use welded wire mesh in conjunction with the shade cloth. Use 1.2mm thick wire welded mesh with a hole size of around 25mm x 50mm. You will need approximately 2 square meters for the project.

- Charcoal chips to absorb moisture and as an essential part of the evaporative cooling system. I used 4 x 10-pound bags of charcoal.

- Use a bucket as a water tank to feed the cooling system. I used a 10-litre bucket. That's equivalent to about a 3-gallon bucket.

Chimney and Convection System

- Black paint for the chimney to ensure that it absorbs more heat, creating a better draft. 1 Lt of black paint will suffice.

- Galvanized pipes or 110mm PVC drain pipe to transfer heat. You will also need at least one bend and a cowl if your chimney is going outside. I used 5 metres worth of pipe, that's around 15 feet's worth.

Water Drip System

- A 15mm ball valve that can restrict and control the amount of flow.
- Steel pipe fittings to connect the valve to the bucket. Here I used a 15mm threaded steel socket that I threaded through the side of the bucket. I also put a locknut on the inside to help seal the connection from leakage.
- Plastic pipe fittings to connect the water distribution system to the valve. Here I used 15mm plastic fittings. This consisted of 3x T-pieces, 1x Threaded nipple and 4 end stops. I did not clamp the pipe onto the fittings as it's a low-pressure system and leakage won't occur easily.
- Thin spaghetti pipes as the final conduit through which water will drip onto the charcoal. I used 3mm spaghetti pipe with a 1mm hole size. These are sold in rolls of around 50 metres, but you will only need about 3 metres. I recommend buying a roll as these can come in handy for vegetable gardens etc.

Construction Tools

- Wire cutter to cut the chicken wire and the welded mesh.
- A staple gun and zip ties to fasten the chicken wire, shade net, and welded mesh onto the wooden frame. You will need around 40 Zip ties. Use thin zip ties, around 4mm wide and 1t least 300mm long. The zip ties will also help to stabilize the charcoal cavity, ensuring that all the charcoal doesn't accumulate at the bottom.
- A drill and bits of various sizes to install the chimney, and the valve, and to drive in screws. I would recommend having a 32mm spade bit in your arsenal. Other bits will include 2mm and 4mm wood drill-bits, and a 1,8mm steel but for drilling pilot holes in the galvanized chimney pipe
- A metal hack saw and a wooden panel saw to cut the required materials.

Construction Steps

1. Frame Construction

Cut the 2" x 4" wood to the desired lengths for the frame. Assemble the frame using screws or nails, ensuring it is sturdy (Fig. 1).

A 2-inch x 3-inch construction pine frame forms the base of your fridge. The thickness of the wood also creates cavities that can be filled with insulation where the charcoal will be placed (Fig. 2).

Fig. 1

Fig. 2

2. Panelling

Attach OSB sheets to the back, floor, door, and part of the roof using screws or adhesive. Apply wood plane shavings or insulation material to the interior side of the OSB panels.

Use some sections of OSB for cladding or pine ply. It is best to use something that can handle water (Fig. 3).

I keep bags of shavings for animal bedding or mulch, as it makes an excellent insulation filler (Fig. 4).

Close off the inside with a sheet of OSB and fill the space with shavings, then close it on the outside with OSB (Fig. 5). This provides excellent insulation.

Fig. 3

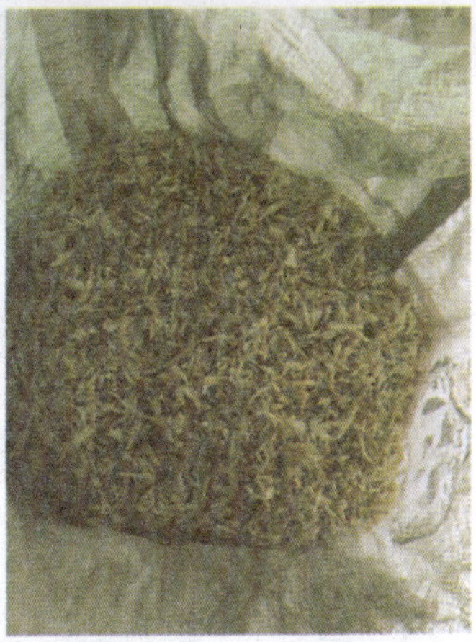

Fig. 4

Fig. 5

You need to cover the floor, the back, and the top in this manner. It would help if you also built a double insulated door using the same technique.

3. Evaporative Cooling Section

Use the chicken wire to create a framework on one side of the safe, leaving space for the panels (Fig. 6). Cover the chicken wire with shade cloth, securing it with a staple gun or zip ties. Place wire mesh inside the framework to contain the wet charcoal chips. Connect the water tank to the wire mesh to moisten the charcoal chips.

Fit the chicken wire as tightly as possible (Fig. 7). You can tighten the wire with long-nose pliers by pinching wires closer together.

Fig. 6

Fig. 7

Use OSB cleats to fasten the wire into place.

Make sure the chicken wire is secure. Once the chicken wire is in, you can fill the cavity with charcoal.

Cover the charcoal with a shade cloth, and then cover the shade cloth with the welded mesh. This lends the structure stability and prevents the charcoal from accumulating at the bottom.

Use 20% shade cloth and thin wire welded mesh to cover the charcoal on the outside.

4. Water Drip System

Use spaghetti pipe with a 1mm hole and a thick-walled container, as this facilitates the fitment of the valve.

You can drill the hole for the socket just a little smaller than the socket's diameter to ensure a tight fit.

Here, you can see the socket and valve fitted. The bucket has water in it, and there is no leakage. Thread a female socket onto the rear for a more water-tight fit. You can insert a seal here if you want to.

Cut the spaghetti pipe sharp in the front, allowing you to stick it through the hole easily (Fig. 8).

Use a scriber to press holes into the pipe. The hole must fit the spaghetti pipe snugly (Fig. 9).

Fig. 8

Fig. 9

Press the thin pipe into the larger one (Fig. 10).

Fill your bucket with water (Fig. 11). You can now fine-tune the amount of water that gets let through by regulating the valve.

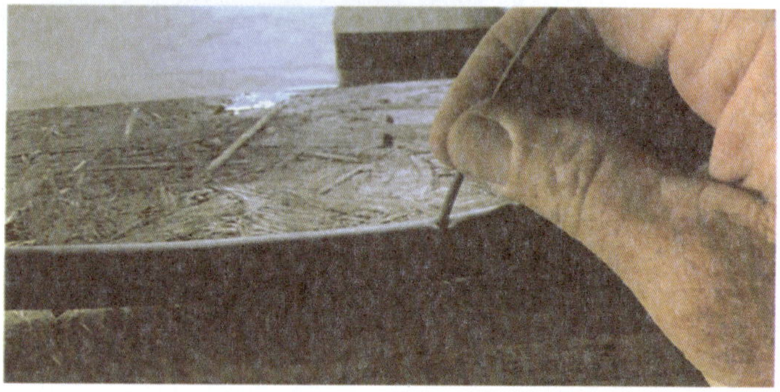

Fig. 10

Fig. 11

Fig. 12

Adjust until the required flow is achieved (Fig. 12).

Position the pipes evenly to wet all the charcoal.

5. Chimney and Convection System

Cut a slot into the pipe and drill three holes before bending the flanges (Fig. 13).

The flanges allow a secure fit to the OSB (Fig. 14).

Attach a chimney to the top of the safe (Fig. 15). Paint the chimney black to enhance heat absorption.

Fix the pipes into place.

Fig. 13

Fig. 14

Fig. 15

6. Assembly

Ensure a secure attachment of the chimney to the top of the safe. Confirm the door is well-sealed to optimize cooling efficiency (figures 16 and 17).

Fig. 16

Fig. 17

You'll need a placement strategy to ensure the chimney is exposed to sunlight, and additional ventilation holes or slots to facilitate air circulation.

7. Final Touches

Check for any gaps or areas that may compromise insulation. Test the cooling effect by wetting the charcoal chips and monitor the interior temperature.

The temperature inside the workshop is a toasty 38 degrees Celsius.

The temperature inside the fridge starts to drop as the charcoal wets.

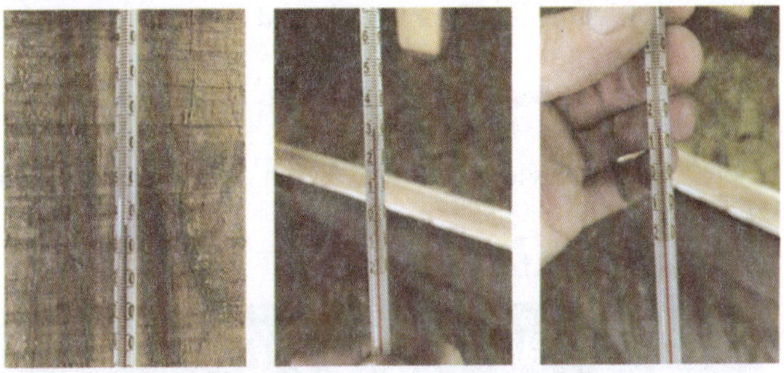

Monitoring the temperature

The final temperature was around 20 degrees Celsius (68 degrees Fahrenheit) below room temperature. All that remains is finding the ideal spot and installing semi-permanent.

Adjust the dimensions and materials based on your specific requirements and available resources.

An Underground Mini-Root Cellar

When it comes to prepping for any situation that might take you off the grid, an under-house mini root cellar can be a lifesaver. It provides a cool, dark, and moisture-controlled environment.

A root cellar is perfect for storing fruits and vegetables for extended periods.

Here's a step-by-step guide on how to create your own under-house mini root cellar.

Tools and Materials

Tools Required
• mattock
• a shovel or spade
• marker
• digging bar

Materials
• medium-size gravel
• sawdust
• wooden box or crate (preferably 2 by 4 feet, depending on the size you want), with a cover
• some root crops (onions, carrots, potatoes, sweet potatoes, and others of your choice)
• polythene and iron sheeting

Instructions

Here's a step-by-step guide on how to create your own under-house mini root cellar.

1. Choose Your Location

Start by identifying a suitable spot under your house. The location should be easily accessible, away from any heating sources, and preferably on the north side of your home to maintain a cool temperature.

2. Excavate the Area

Once you've located your spot, it's time to start digging. But note that this is the most challenging step in building the mini root cellar. Also, the size of your cellar will depend on your needs.

I started digging from the outside so that I could access underneath the house. Usually, houses in my location are built with concrete flooring. So, this was the main reason I had to

dig from the outside, progressing under the house.

You can see it in the photo below.

I dug a 2x4-foot hole because I did not intend to store a lot of vegetables this season. Also, I intended to install a small crate, allowing room for proper air circulation.

3. Preparing the Floor of the Cellar

In this step, I lay gravel to assist any additional water seepage into the ground. Also, the gravel will assist in controlling moisture levels underneath the root cellar.

I also added a thin layer of sawdust, just to control the environment inside the under-house root cellar.

The final result was like this.

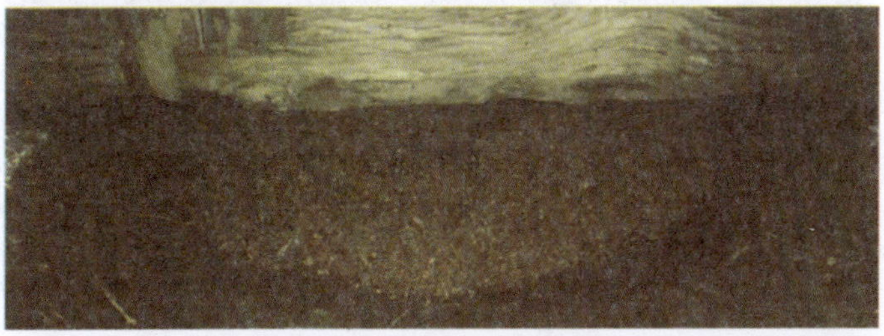

4. Preparing the Storage Box/Wooden Crate

Prepare a wooden box, as wood doesn't conduct heat and will help maintain a stable temperature.

Also, ensure you have enough space to store and easily access your goods.

I used a 1.5 by 3.5-foot box because my root cellar was 2 by 4 feet.

5. Adding Crops

Next, you can start adding your root crops, such as potatoes, carrots, onions, and other vegetables that thrive in cool temperatures.

Make sure to clean them before storage and keep them in a cool, dark place.

I also added some sawdust to help control the temperature and humidity inside the box.

6. Inserting the Crate

Once you have the root crops ready, insert them into your wooden crates and slide them into your cellar.

Make sure to include a wooden top to protect your crops.

7. Closing the Cellar

Before closing the cellar, double-check that everything is in its proper place and that there are no damages.

8. Covering the Entrance

Cover the entrance of your cellar with a layer of sawdust, soil, or grass to maintain an even temperature and camouflage the door.

I used sawdust because it was easily accessible.

I laid polythene on top of the sawdust to prevent water from sipping inside my cellar. Also, the polythene sheeting will protect against moisture and pests.

You can also use iron sheeting to further reinforce your cellar, providing extra protection against extreme weather conditions.

9. Maintaining Your Root Cellar

Periodically check your under-house root cellar for any signs of mold or rot. Make sure to rotate your crops as needed and keep an eye on humidity levels.

Note

Another alternative for creating a root cellar involves repurposing a trash can. Begin by digging the hole according to the size of the can.

Next, utilize an old paint drop sheet as a liner, creating a protective barrier for the can. Lower the can into the hole, ensuring it fits snugly within the sheet "tube" to prevent soil from entering.

Then, securely cover the top of the drum to maintain its integrity.

Finally, shield the trash can root cellar with corrugated sheeting and repurposed shade netting to deter water infiltration and minimize visibility.

DIY Greywater System for a World Without Electricity

A DIY greywater system is a practical and sustainable solution to manage water consumption.

By reusing greywater for non-drinking purposes, we reduce our overall water consumption and contribute towards sustainable living. You can use the recycled water for irrigation, flushing toilets, and other non-potable purposes.

This chapter will walk you through the creative and practical process of building your very own greywater system, designed specifically for a world without electricity. Also, the design we will use is simple, requires minimum maintenance, and is one of the most effective projects for preppers.

Materials and Tools

To get started, you'll need to gather the necessary materials and tools. Here's a list of what you'll need:

- one large barrel or container (at least 55 gallons, and preferably with a lid)
- 20-foot PVC pipe or longer
- PVC fittings (these include 8 pieces of 1-inch valve sockets, thread tape or plumber's tape, and 8 pieces of 1-inch galvanized iron back nuts to hold the PVC valve sockets securely in the barrel)
- a drill (optional) - to drill the holes in the two barrels
- pipe wrench or any other tightening tool to fix the valve sockets to the plastic barrels
- a spade
- a mattock and digging bar
- a hacksaw
- a mesh screen
- half a wheelbarrow of medium-sized gravel
- half a wheelbarrow of Sawdust
- a tape measure
- a marker

Instructions

1. Determine Your Water Needs

The first step in building a greywater system is to assess your daily water consumption. Consider how much water you use, and which activities generate the most greywater. This will help you determine the size and capacity of your DIY system.

2. Identify a Suitable Location

Before you start building your Greywater System, choose a suitable location for it. Start by identifying and separating greywater (from showers, baths, and washing machines) from blackwater (from toilets and kitchen sinks).

It should be close to the source of greywater and away from any food crops or edible plants. The ideal spot would be near your bathroom or laundry room.

Also, make sure the ground is level and that there's enough space for the barrel and pipes.

3. Create a Drainage Point for Greywater

After choosing your location, dig a hole deep enough to accommodate your plastic barrels and collection tank.

This will serve as the drainage point for your greywater system.

4. Preparing the Barrels

Cut a small section of the barrels using a hacksaw to allow efficient plumbing work. Also, this design will allow me to maintain the barrels and remove all the unwanted materials, before adding a new filtering system.

Using a drill, create an inlet on the side of your plastic barrel near the top. This will serve as the entry point for greywater into the barrel.

First, mark the exact spot, like this:

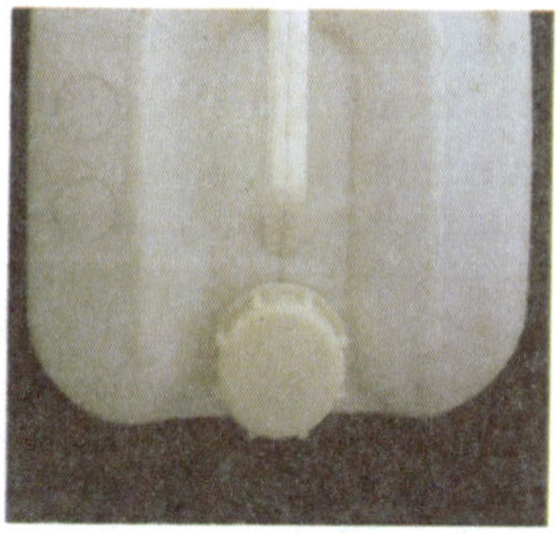

Then, using a hole saw, cut a hole near the bottom of the barrel for the outlet pipe.

5. Connect PVC Fittings

Connect the ends of the plastic barrels with the necessary PVC fittings.

I used plumbing valve sockets with a pipe wrench and thread tape to connect the fittings to the barrels.

I used 1-inch PVC fittings to connect the pipes, ensuring a secure fit.

6. Connect PVC Pipes to the Bathroom System

Next, connect PVC pipes from the bathroom outlets.

First, locate the drainage hole. The drainage hole is an ideal location because it is the central point of the greywater collection.

Open the lid like this:

The next step will be connecting your pipes to the drainage outlet. I used PVC glue to get a secure fit.

Here is how it turned out:

I closed the manhole cover to prevent dirt and debris from clogging my system.

These pipes should extend to the inlet on your plastic barrel. But make sure to slope the pipes downward towards the barrel for proper drainage.

Cover the drainage pipes to protect them from physical damage.

7. **Align the First Barrel on the Ground**

Position the first barrel in the trench and connect it to the inlet pipe from your house using PVC pipes and fittings.

8. **Adding Sawdust**

This first barrel will act as a biofilter.

Add a layer of sawdust or woodchips to the first barrel. This will help control any odor and promote the decomposition of organic matter in the greywater.

Note: Do not fill the barrel with sawdust to the brim. Allow enough space for the water to drain efficiently, and for impurities like grease, hair, and other household cleaning products to remain in the barrel.

9. Connect an Additional Barrel (2nd Stage of Filtration)

Simply repeat the same process you did in step 8 and connect another barrel using PVC pipes to create a continuous system.

Like this:

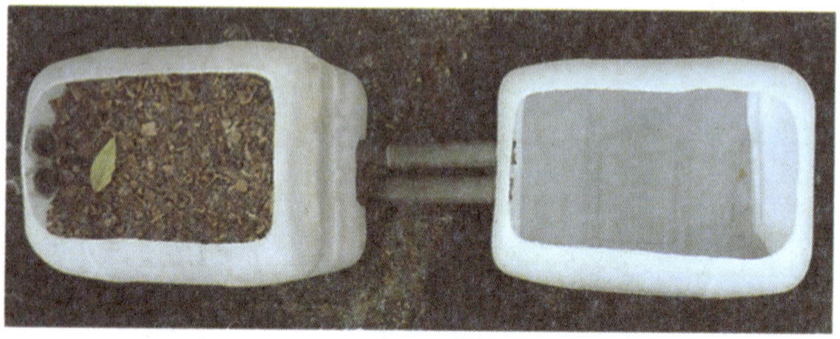

In this second barrel, I will filter the greywater more to reduce debris and other dirt using a coarse filtration system.

I used coarse and medium-size gravel.

Next, I put mesh screens at the tips of the PVC pipes to prevent gravel from draining into the collection tank from the second filtration barrel.

After preparing the PVC pipes, I connected them to the second barrel, making sure all connections were secure and watertight. You can use caulking or any other sealant.

After inserting the PVC pipes into the barrel and making sure it was secure, I put enough gravel into the barrel.

10. Preparing the Collection Tank

Install a collection barrel to gather the greywater, ensuring it is positioned correctly.

11. Test the System

Take a shower to check for any leaks in the system. If any, adjust and fix accordingly. If not, you can proceed to the next step.

Fortunately, my system worked perfectly. Everything turned out great (Fig. 1).

12. Cover the Trench with Soil

Cover the trench with soil. But before that, cover the barrels with the plastic you had previously cut.

It should look like this:

However, **do not cover the collection barrel** because you will regularly use a bucket to fetch water from it.

Now that your DIY Greywater System is complete, you can start using it.

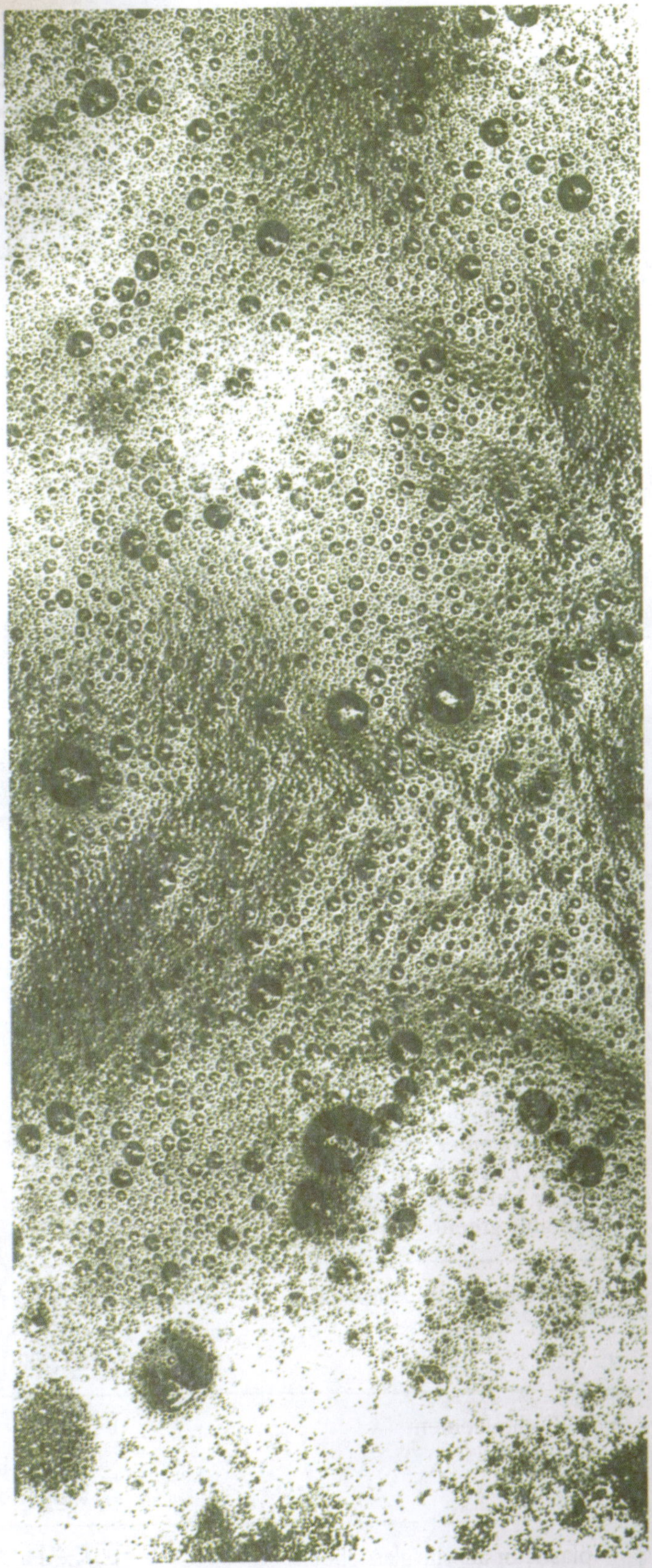

Tips for Using Greywater System

- If you are using greywater for irrigation, avoid using harsh chemicals or toxic products in your household, as this can harm the plants and soil when using greywater for irrigation. This includes using products with large concentrations of salt, chlorine, boron, and bleach.
- Make sure to regularly clean and maintain the system to prevent clogs and build-up of debris.
- Don't store greywater for more than 24 hours to prevent the nutrients from breaking down and creating bad odors.
- Educate yourself on any local regulations or restrictions regarding the use of greywater in your area.
- Continually monitor and adjust the system to ensure it is working efficiently and effectively. So, it can continue to provide a sustainable source of irrigation for your garden.

Fig. 1. Final result

The Perpetual Greenhouse

There are tons of benefits that come with building your own greenhouse. Compared to a traditional garden, a greenhouse allows for a much longer growing season, defense from pests and extreme weather, greater crop variety, and better water efficiency. If you build it yourself, you can customize it exactly to your needs and save money compared to buying a prefabricated unit.

Tools and Materials

Before we dive into how to build a greenhouse, let's look at the tools and materials you'll need. Materials will vary depending on the right greenhouse for you, but getting exactly what you need is one of the biggest advantages of building it yourself.

Materials Needed

- 4 wooden beams for the base. 6'x4' is a good starting point, and you can go bigger if you have the space.
- additional wooden beams for the door frame. Sizes will vary depending on your needs, but a height between 6'-7' is good for most uses.
- PVC pipes. Get enough to facilitate a height of at least about 7' at the top of the arch of the greenhouse. You'll also need cross members along the sides and the back. Thinner pipes are better for flexibility, but thicker pipes will create a more durable greenhouse.
- PVC elbows and couplings
- PVC glue/cement
- plastic or acrylic glass sheets. Calculate the total area of the exterior to determine how much you need.
- 4 staple nails for the base
- screws for the door frame and plastic covering
- 1 door handle (2 if you want a handle on both sides of the door)
- 3 hinges
- 1 latching device for the door
- desired plants

Tools Used

- tape measure
- hammer
- electric drill
- hole saw attachment for drill
- PVC cutting tool
- garden rake
- ladder

Instructions

Step 1

Build a rectangular wooden frame as the foundation for the greenhouse. Connect four wooden beams with screws, bolts, or by hammering a staple nail into each of the four corners.

Step 2

Drill four equidistant holes in the top of the long ends of the frame, with one at each corner and two in between. For best results, use a power drill with an appropriately sized hole saw attachment. **The holes should not go all the way through the beams.**

Step 3

Insert PVC pipes into the holes in the frame and arch them so the other end of the pipe reaches the opposite hole. If it is not flexible enough, cut the PVC with a PVC cutting tool and attach couplings to increase flexibility. Use PVC glue or cement in the couplings for added strength.

Step 4

Measure the PVC arches from the wooden frame to the top of the arch. Divide by three and mark the one-third points of each pipe, including at the top of the arch. Cut each pipe with a PVC cutting tool at the one-third marks and add an elbow attachment with the side openings facing each other. Reattach the arched PVC pipe to the top of each elbow using PVC glue or cement.

Step 5

Insert PVC pipes horizontally in the elbows you inserted in Step 4. Secure them with PVC glue or cement. These should be parallel with the long ends of the frame you made in *Step 1.*

Locate which side of the frame you'd like to be the back of the greenhouse. Measure and mark the halfway points of the arched pipes between the wooden frame and the first horizontal pipes along the sides of the greenhouse. Repeat between the lower and upper horizontal pipes. Only do this for the arched pipe that you want to form the back wall of the greenhouse.

Cut the arched pipe at the markings you made and insert PVC elbows. Create the back wall of the greenhouse by connecting PVC pipes in the elbows parallel to the short side of the wooden frame. Secure them with PVC glue or cement.

Step 6

Secure a wooden beam across the top of the front of the greenhouse where you'd like the top of the door to be.

Step 7

Build a door frame by securing vertical wooden beams between the frame you made in Step 1 and the cross member you placed in *Step 6*.

Step 8

Secure wooden beams diagonally between the corners at the top of the door frame and the corners of the frame you made in *Step 1*.

Step 9

Add three equidistant hinges to one of the vertical door frame beams and attach an identically-sized wooden beam. Ensure that the new beam swings **outside** the greenhouse.

Step 10

Complete the frame for the door of the greenhouse by adding three horizontal wooden beams perpendicular to the vertical beam you attached previously. When complete, attach another vertical beam perpendicular to the horizontal beams to complete the frame for the door. Ensure that the door fits and swings properly within the door frame.

Step 11

Place large sheets of plastic or acrylic glass over the arch of the greenhouse and drill them into the PVC and wooden frame with screws. Repeat on the two flat ends of the greenhouse. Trim coverings where needed.

Step 12

Attach a door handle and latching mechanism on the outside of the door.

Step 13

Thoroughly rake the inside of the greenhouse and remove any debris. Aerate the soil with a pitchfork, garden rake, or other aerating tool.

Step 14

Hang potted plants on the top beam of the greenhouse and plant your desired plants in the soil you aerated in *Step 15*. Make sure to leave a walking path in the middle between the door and the back of the greenhouse.

Step 15

Water and maintain plants accordingly.

Key Finder
Trip Wire Alarm

One of the best ways to secure your property is to place trip wires attached to alarm devices across areas intruders may use to access your property. The problem is that these trip wire alarms often rely on audible signals to let us know they have been triggered.

One way we can mitigate this is to use radio-controlled devices as a part of the trip wire system. This also allows the trip wire to be set longer distances from the home.

There are many ways to use radios as part of your trip wire alarm system, but I have devised a system that uses an inexpensive and widely available radio-controlled keyfinder to make this as beginner-friendly as possible.

How This Key Finder Trip Wire Alarm Works

The trip wire is strung across an area intruders may move through. As an alternative, this alarm can also be attached to a doorway. The trigger device will press a button on the remote, which will activate an audible alarm on the corresponding key tag inside the house. This system has a limited range, so it is vital that it be tested beforehand to ensure that when the trip wire alarm is activated, the signal will find its way to the key tag.

Building the Radio Trip Wire

I have designed this build to use only commonly available materials and require no special skills.

Tools

- Hot glue gun
- Drill with Bits

Materials

The materials for this build are easily obtained through many online retailers or local stores in your area.

- One radio-controlled key finder which is available on Amazon.
- Military trip wire, bankline, or fishing line. The only important thing here is that the line should be strong enough to trigger the alarm and thin enough to be virtually invisible.
- Metal Strapping

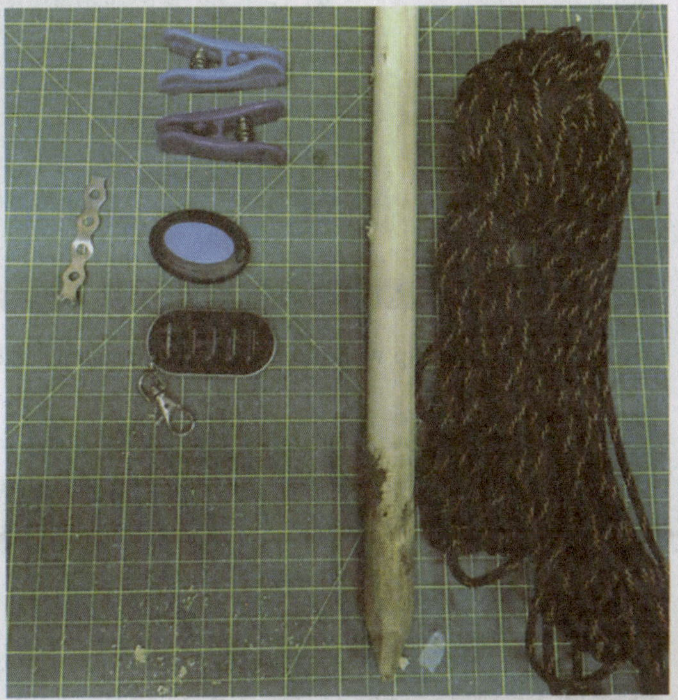

- Two plastic bag clips. These need to be of a style that is usually closed and only opens when the back end is squeezed. See the photo above for an example.
- Zip ties
- A stake or other object to attach the trip wire to

Instructions

There are two ways that I will describe for deployment of this trip wire alarm system. The first is a traditional trip wire, while the second is an alarm device that is attached to a door.

Traditional Trip Wire

1. Glue one of the plastic chip bag clips to the remote so that when the clip is closed, it presses one of the buttons.

2. Attach a second clip to the end of the trigger clip so that it holds the first clip open.

3. Secure the first clip with the remote to a wooden stake with a zip tie.

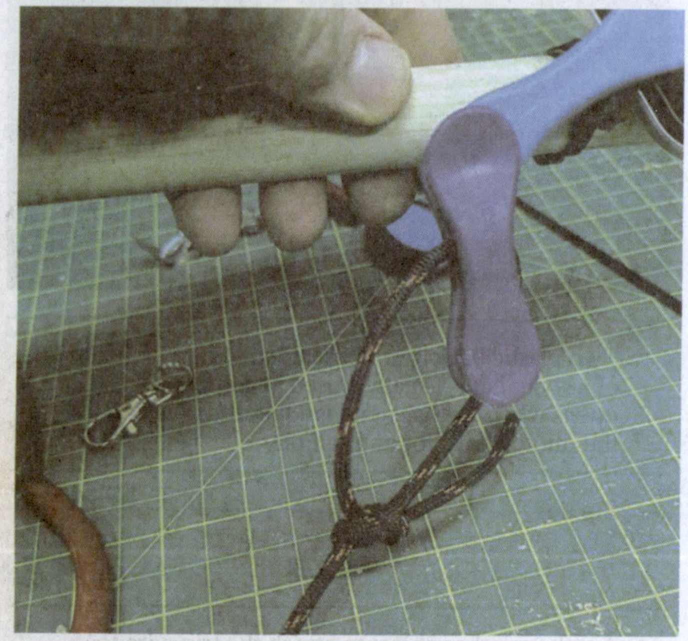

4. Tie one end of the tripwire to the clip holding the first clip open.

5. Place the stake at one end of the area you want to secure using this alarm.
6. Secure the other end of the trip wire.

7. Adjust until the wire is around shin height.

When the wire is pulled, the rear clip will disengage, causing the trigger clip to close on the remote button. This causes the keychain unit inside the home to beep loudly.

Door Alarm

1. Using a hot glue gun, glue the remote to a door.

2. Cut a small piece of metal strapping and bend the end to a 90-degree angle.

3. Screw the strapping to the door jamb so that the bent section of the strapping is directly over the appropriate button.

When the door opens, the strapping will press the button, which in turn activates the audible alarm on the keychain. The strapping will also move out of the way, allowing the door to open normally.

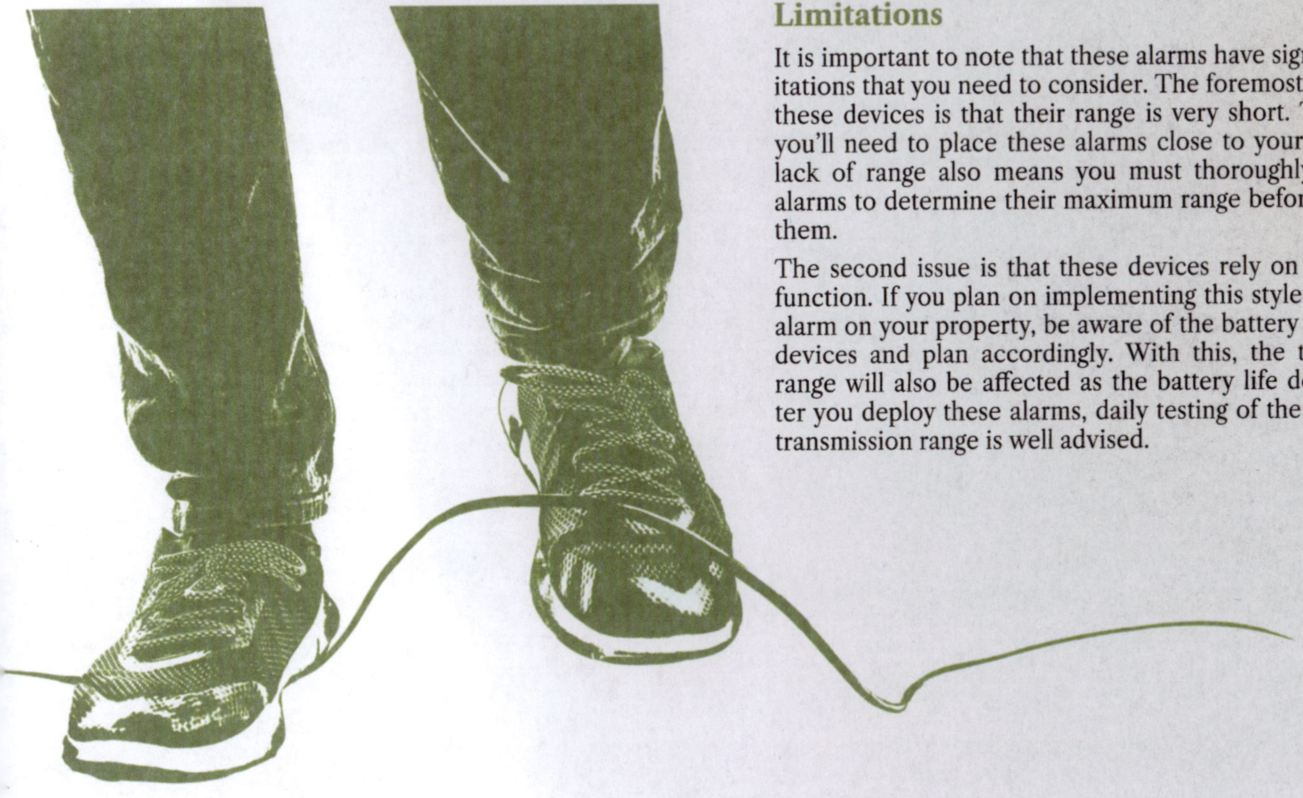

Limitations

It is important to note that these alarms have significant limitations that you need to consider. The foremost thing about these devices is that their range is very short. To this end, you'll need to place these alarms close to your home. The lack of range also means you must thoroughly test these alarms to determine their maximum range before deploying them.

The second issue is that these devices rely on batteries to function. If you plan on implementing this style of trip wire alarm on your property, be aware of the battery life of these devices and plan accordingly. With this, the transmission range will also be affected as the battery life degrades. After you deploy these alarms, daily testing of the battery and transmission range is well advised.